Istanbul

The Travellers' Companion series

General editor: Laurence Kelly

St Petersburg: a travellers' companion
Selected and introduced by Laurence Kelly (1981)

Moscow: a travellers' companion
Selected and introduced by Laurence Kelly (1983)

Naples: a travellers' companion
Selected and introduced by Desmond Seward (1984)

Edinburgh: a travellers' companion
Selected and introduced by David Daiches (1986)

Florence: a travellers' companion
Selected and introduced by Harold Acton and Edward Chaney (1986)

Delhi and Agra: a travellers' companion
Selected and introduced by Michael Alexander (1987)

View of the Seraglio Point, from Galata; from *Voyage Pittoresque de la Grèce*, 1782–1809 by M.G. Choiseul Gouffier (*overleaf*)

ISTANBUL

A Travellers' Companion

SELECTED AND INTRODUCED BY

Laurence Kelly

Atheneum · New York · 1987

Atheneum
Macmillan Publishing Company
866 Third Avenue, New York, N.Y. 10022

ISBN 0-689-70716-9

10 9 8 7 6 5 4 3 2 1
First American Edition

Printed in Great Britain

Contents

Illustrations

Acknowledgements

This book has been a labour of love for over four years – not surprisingly, considering the vast number of historians and travellers chronicling the city: three incarnations as a Roman, Byzantine and Ottoman capital of world empires. As with any major archaeological site, the spoil and detritus of rejected material would easily make second and third volumes to accompany this. Marvellous material has had to be set aside and deep surgical cuts incised into the existing selection. As with the previous books in this series, I have usually adhered to the spelling and punctuation of the original texts, so the same name may often appear in several guises.

I owe deep thanks to two enthusiasts who laboured alongside me during the four years, their love of the city never flagging – to Marina Berry, and to John Scott who showed me for the first time Sinan's masterpiece, the Sokollu Mehmet Pasha mosque, and knew his old Istanbul as well as any character in a Loti novel, from having walked it. Four years have taken their toll with the sad death of another great ally, Müharrem Nuri Birgi, in whose exquisite palace I was fortunate enough to stay whenever I visited the city: who could forget his myriad kindnesses and admirable judgement in all aesthetic questions, his wit and sense of fun, the life-enhancing qualities he brought to every expedition? Amongst those who were kind enough to suggest changes and improvements to my Introduction I must particularly thank the Hon. Sir Steven Runciman, Professor Godfrey Goodwin, and Mrs Nermin Streeter. And of the many Turks who took a kindly interest as the book progressed I must single out H.E. the Turkish Ambassador in London, Mr R. Gümrükçuoglu; the Director of Tourism in Istanbul, General Taner; and Mrs Nezihe Aygen, also from the Ministry of Tourism, a delightful companion during a week's tour of the city.

With the passage of time the dynamic efforts of the present Mayor of Istanbul, Mr Dalan, have begun the restoration of the Golden Horn to its former pollution-free glories and the liberation of both banks from their hideous festoon of factories; one day we hope to hear again the cheerful cry of Nedim, ''Let us go to Saadabâd.' Of other restorers of the city's past I must pay tribute to Çelik Gülersoy, whose Hotel Konak, under the minarets of Sultan Ahmet and Haghia Sophia, is the most charming of small hotels and whose every enterprise for the improvement of the city deserves support and applause.

For many of the translations I am indebted to the elegant and sensitive renderings of Marina Berry and my mother, Marie Noële Kelly (whose first book was on Turkey). Others who have provided me with invaluable material include Mr John Walsh, who translated for me the chronogram inscription on Sultan Ahmet III's fountain by the entrance to the Seraglio; Professor Karl Leyser of All Souls College, Oxford, who helped me find translations of some knotty Byzantine originals; Mr Jasper Ridley who drew my attention to the passage in Isabel Vesey's memoir, and Mrs Veronica Burnett who allowed me to quote from it. I am grateful, too, to the staffs of the London Library, the Royal Geographical Society, the Library of Trinity College, Cambridge and the Print Room at the Victoria & Albert Museum, and to Filis Çagman, curator of the Topkapi Library in Istanbul.

I should like to make acknowledgement to the following for extracts used from their writings, editions, or translations, or where copyright permission was needed: Metin And and Dost Publications, Istanbul, for *Turkish Shadow Theatre*; Princeton University Press for Franz Babinger's *Mehmed the Conqueror and his Time*, translated by Ralph Manheim and edited by William E. Hickman, and for *The History of Mehmet the Conqueror* by Kritovoulos, translated by Charles T. Riggs; A.D. Peters and Lesley Blanch for *Pavilions of the Heart*; Penguin Books for *The Alexiad of Anna Comnena* translated by E.R.A. Sewter, for *Chronicles of the Crusades* by Joinville and Villehardouin, translated by M.R.B. Shaw, and *The Secret History* by Procopius, translated by G.A. Williams; Alfred A. Knopf, Inc for Harold Bell and Theresa de Kerpely's translation of *Byzantine Empresses* by Charles Diehl; Jonathan Cape and Lord Kinross for *The Ottoman Centuries: the rise and fall of the Turkish Empire*; Oxford University Press for *Three Centuries: family chronicles of Turkey and Egypt* by Emine Foat Tugay, and for *The Complete Letters of Lady Mary Wortley Montagu*, Vol I, edited by Robert Halsband; Sir Steven Runciman for *Byzantine Civilisation*; Macmillan and Arthur Stratton for *Sinan*; A.P. Watt, Macmillan and Michael B. Yeats for 'Sailing to Byzantium' from the

Collected Poems of W.B. Yeats; John Murray and John Hearsey for *The City of Constantine*; Robert Mantran for *La Vie Quotidienne à Constantinople*; A. Pallis for *Days of the Janissaries*; Padraic Colum for *The Golden Fleece*; Halidé Edib for her *Memoirs*; R. Janin for *Constantinople Byzantine*; H. Sumner-Boyd for 'The Seven Hills of Istanbul' in the Bodleian, and H. Sumner-Boyd and J. Freely for *Strolling in Istanbul*; P.N. Ure for *Justinian and his Age*; the Nederlands Historich-Archaeologisch Institut te Istanbul and J.P.A. van der Vin for *Travellers to Greece and Constantinople*; Michael Joseph and I. and M. Orga for *Atatürk*; A.P. Watt for *Count Belisarius* by Robert Graves; and Mrs Linda Sewter for *Fourteen Byzantine Rulers* by Michael Psellus, translated by E.R.A. Sewter.

Finally, my thanks to Kim and Aydin Erkan for a host of valuable suggestions; to John Mitchell who drew the maps; to my wife Linda, as usual my first sub-editor; to the resident muse of my publishers, Prudence Fay, for her heroic work on the book when I was laid low by a stroke in its final stages, and to the devoted team at Constable. This book is longer than any of the others in the Travellers' Companion series as a tribute to the weight of history within.

L.K.
1987

Introduction

Ode to Istanbul

Stambul, peerless of cities, thou jewel beyond compare,
Seated astride upon two seas, with dazzling light aflare!
One single stone of thine, methinks, of greater worth by far
Than all the treasures of Iran!
Resplendent as the Sun whose rays the world in light enshrine,
Thy gardens, visions of delight, patterns of Joy Divine,
The shady nooks of rosebeds fair, of Love's enchantments full,
Challenge the Prophet's Paradise!

Ahmet Nedim[1]

In *St Petersburg, A Travellers' Companion*, and similarly in *Moscow* in this series, the Introduction gave the briefest of histories about each city, concentrating on the *genius loci*, and the vision, attitudes and prejudices which their denizens had of their own leviathan. In the case of Constantinople-Istanbul, the city's myths, prehistory, and recorded history span twenty-seven or twenty-eight centuries; ninety-seven Byzantine or Latin emperors and empresses as ruling sovereigns; thirty Sultans from AD 1453; countless major fires and earthquakes, disasters and acts of God and man. The sheer weight of history to be summarized would take up the whole Introduction, and in practice duplicate the competent summaries to be found in all guide-books, whether the *Blue Guide*, Çelik Gülersoy's *A Guide to Istanbul*, or Ernest Mamboury's classic *Tourist Guide*, written as long ago as 1925. In any event, this anthology's own extracts cover nearly all the major events in the city's history. So in this Introduction I have concentrated instead on certain themes, key-ideas if you will, to interpret the city's past.

In the beginning there were the myths. Zeus seduced Io, and, taking her revenge, his wife Hera spitefully turned Io into a heifer mercilessly pursued by a gadfly. To escape her tormentor, Io swam the straits and so gave them the name 'Bosphorus', or

[1] Ahmet Nedim (1681–1730) Turkish lyrical poet quoted in *In the Days of the Janissaries* by Alexander Pallis, London, 1951.

'ford of the ox'. The earliest Greek coins show a cow on a dolphin. But Keroessa, Io's daughter by Zeus, was herself mother of Byzas by Poseidon: and Byzas is the mythical founder of Byzantium.

The Argonauts rowed their way to the Land of the Golden Fleece (today Soviet Georgia) up the Bosphorus. Legend sites Pollux's epic boxing-match with the ferocious King Amycus at Beikos. (Travellers were shown a plane tree there whose leaves, if chewed, made any boxer with the *cestus* or leather gloves invincible.) The clashing rocks of the Symplegades at the entrance of the Bosphorus and the Black Sea (or Euxine) spelt doom to all sailors, until King Phineus told Argo and his fellow heroes how to set free a pigeon, whose flight through the awful foam would guide them:

> Jason shouted to each man to grip hard on the oars. The *Argo* dashed on as the rocks rushed toward each other again. Then there was such noise that no man's voice could be heard above it.
>
> As the rocks met, Euphemus loosed the pigeon. with his keen eyes he watched her fly through the spray. Would she, not finding an opening to fly through, turn back? He watched, and meanwhile the Argonauts gripped hard on the oars to save the ship from being dashed on the rocks. The pigeon fluttered as though she would sink down and let the spray drown her. And then Euphemus saw her raise herself and fly forward. Toward the place where she had flown he pointed. The rowers gave a loud cry, and Jason[1] called upon them to pull with might and main.
>
> The rocks were parting asunder, and to the right and left broad Pontus was seen by the heroes. Then suddenly a huge wave rose before them, and at the sight of it they all uttered a cry and bent their heads. It seemed to them that it would dash down on the whole ship's length and overwhelm them all. But Nauplius was quick to ease the ship, and the wave rolled away beneath the keel, and at the stern it raised the *Argo* and dashed her away from the rocks.
>
> They felt the sun as it streamed upon them through the

[1] Jason gave his name, Iasonion, to the settlement which today is the busy quarter of Beşiktaş.

> sundered rocks. They strained at the oars until the oars bent like bows in their hands. The ship sprang forward. Surely they were not in the wide Sea of Pontus.[1]

By the seventh century, men had replaced gods (at least according to the archaeologists), for a statue of Zeus Hippios and cyclopean walls have been found as evidence that there were Thracians and Megarians from Greece both in the valley of Chalcedon (today's Kadiköy) and along the Golden Horn. The Chalcedonians disregarded the obvious strategic merits of occupying today's Seraglio Point opposite them, probably because there was no fresh water there; nor did they choose the calm, protected waters of the Golden Horn, preferring the open seas of the Bosphorus. Seizing his opportunity, Byzas – allegedly inspired by the Delphic Oracle – installed a band of Megarians on the site of today's Topkapi – the new Acropolis – and thought (according to Tacitus) the community opposite quite blind to their opportunities.[2] Thus the *Byzantines* irrupted into history, circa 658 BC. As later conquerors decided, here was a prize worthy of the fight; Philip of Macedon, for example, sought to capture the city in a midnight raid in 340 BC, but Hecate, Goddess of the Moon, foiled him by denying him the necessary visibility. In gratitude the Byzantines adopted the horned crescent, which the Ottomans inherited in turn. Who today would know the antique origin of the most famous of all Islam's symbols?

As the heroic myths give way to recorded history, so economic advantage and military strategy combined to make the command of the Straits between the two seas of the Euxine (Black) and Marmara one of the keys to the ancient world.

Such a prize was as much a prey. 'No city', wrote the Russian historian of the Bosphorus, P. de Tchihatchef, 'has had to undergo so many and so disastrous a number of sieges and assaults as Constantinople, none saw under its walls or within its confines so many different races racing from all corners of Europe and Asia and of Africa to stake their thirst for loot, or love of conquest, or indulge their raving religious fanaticism.

[1] From *The Golden Fleece*, transl. by Padraic Colum, New York, 1965.
[2] *Constantinople Byzantine*, R. Janin, Paris, 1950.

Byzantium was twice besieged by the ancient Greeks (Alcibiades and Philip of Macedon); thrice by the Roman Emperors (Septimius Severus, Maximus, and Constantine the Great); once by the Franks, the Persians, the Avars, the Slavs, and by her own dethroned Emperor (Michael Paleologos); twice by the Bulgars; once by Byzantine rebels; seven times by the Arabs; thrice by the Ottomans. Of these twenty-two sieges, however, only six led to capture; by Alcibiades, Septimius Severus, Constantine, Doge Dandolo and the Crusaders, Michael Paleologos, and finally Mehmet II, the Conqueror.'[1]

Every traveller, every historian has had his say about the importance for the city of controlling the Bosphorus and its trade. One will serve for most others; in the words of the Imperial Envoy of the 1540s, Ghislain de Busbecq:

> as for the situation of the City itself, it seemed to me, to be naturally placed as fit to the Mistress of the World; it stands in Europe, and hath Asia in view, and on its right, hath Egypt and Africa, which though Countries not adjacent to it, yet by reason of frequent intercourse and naval commerce, they seem as it were, contiguous: on its left hand is the Euxin Sea, and the Palus Maeotis, whose banks are inhabited round about by many Nations, and so many navigable Rivers have influx into them, that there is no thing that grows in any of the Countries there about, fit for man's use, but there is a great conveniency of transporting it by sea to Constantinople.[2]

A Soviet strategist would hardly disagree today with this analysis.

Though the Bosphorus may be the same, its post-war story is one of incredible change. There is now the spectacular Bridge, the economic lifeline between Europe and Asia for all road freight, and plans for a second one. Hundred-thousand-tonne super-tankers, proudly flying the Turkish flag, glide smoothly under its soaring piers. Soviet cruisers, crammed with electronic

[1] From *Le Bosphore et Constantinople*, Paris, 1866. Michael Paleologos was in fact ruler of an Empire in exile at Nicea. It was, more accurately, the Empire that was dethroned, not the Emperor.

[2] *Travels into Turkey* A.G. Busbequius, London, 1744.

gadgetry emulating that of the American Fleet, monopolize the naval traffic overwhelmingly; their commercial traffic represents over fifty million tonnes of goods annually. The banks of each side have become disfigured by thousands of concrete matchboxes required to house Istanbul's population, which has exploded from one million after the war to six million today, and which is still expanding at some 6 per cent annually. Yet one constant remains, true not only between 1946 and today, but also under Ottoman and Byzantine rule: whoever controls the Bosphorus has a stranglehold over the traffic of the Black Sea. In the words of Peter Gilles, who described the Bosphorus in the 1550s, 'the Bosphorus is the one key which opens and closes two worlds'.

So the Bosphorus gave the city a strategic value no other capital city in the world enjoyed, and trading privileges no fairy godmother could have bettered (no one would ever go short of fish!); and it called forth water-borne pleasures that enhanced the lives of its lucky citizens beyond compare. Even Venice could not offer cool woods of cypresses and plane trees overhanging the water's edge, nor had Naples such variety within twenty square miles of the city. In that rather charmingly titled book *The Diary of an Idle Woman in Constantinople* (written in 1892), Frances Elliot reminds us that:

> The real beauty of Constantinople is in its water. Water everywhere, clear, blue and shimmering; away to the far south the serene face of the placid Sea of Marmora, the Archipelago leading into it, and beyond the Dardanelles forming the channel to the Grecian seas . . . This immensity of water is wonderful: coming from one knows not where, disappearing one knows not how, ever kissing the shores as it entwines itself in every view, and lending such a strange and marvellous grace to all it touches . . . A watery mystery mingling with every-day life, magical and strange! What scenes does it unfold! What memories does it awaken! Mythic, poetic, actual! Classic Greece hard by. The wild downs of Asia, the Kurdish Steppes, the Russian ice-ranges brought to hand, the whole history of the East lying veiled before one! . . .

If at all possible, one should arrive and leave by water. My own childhood memories are suffused with the beauties of the

Bosphorus. I first visited Istanbul as a schoolboy in 1946. My father had just been appointed Ambassador to Turkey, and the appointment carried with it two of the most magnificent perquisites an empire in decline could just afford; namely Sir Charles Barry's Italianate palace, still used as an Embassy in the summer months, built on land given by the Sultan to Queen Victoria on the heights of Pera facing the Golden Horn and Old Istanbul; and the *Makook III*, a seventy-ton motor yacht built in 1914 for use as a Nile boat by the Khedive Abbas Hilmi of Egypt.

Polished copper and teak fittings, immaculate canvas awnings, a captain and his crew of six in royal Navy-lookalike ducks, an enormous galley for my mother's chef to prepare elaborate picnics for the forty or fifty guests – it added up to a signal that a British *Büyük Elçi* (Ambassador) still counted for something on the world's greatest waterway.

A day on the *Makook* was obviously paradise for a thirteen-year-old schoolboy, whisked out for holidays from the austerity England of Attlee. Down would sweep the motorcade to the jetty of Kabataş; out stepped my father's *Kavas*, or bodyguard, Rustem, a fiercely mustachioed Albanian kitted out like a Guardsman, to hand my mother out of the Rolls, over the gangplank, on to the milk-white deck. The captain, after saluting the *Elçi*, ran up His Excellency's standard (which Turkish naval vessels always saluted); our Turkish guests arrived. Lord Stratford would not have been ashamed. Amidst much swirling of melon rinds and throbbing of diesels, we cast off, admiring the elegant mosques and fountains of Beşiktaş, the Corinthian ice-cream opulence of the Dolmabahçe Palace, and the tomb of the great Ottoman admiral, Hayrettin Pasha (Barbarossa).

No tourist should neglect a cruise up and down the Bosphorus, even if he has no *Makook* from which he can admire the fortresses of Rumeli or Anadolu Hisar, today bereft of their pepper-pot towers but as dominant as in the day of the Conqueror Mehmet II. In seeing the charming villages of the upper Bosphorus, such as Kandilli or Beykoz or Tarabya, he will appreciate the genius of the Turk in siting his kiosk or *yali* (wooden summer-house) in harmony with nature and water. Acacias, sycamores, judas trees, willows, plane trees, parasol pines and, above all, cypresses surround him. Magnolias, the thirty-petalled rose, violets and the scent of jasmine delight his senses. The *yali* is a peculiarly pleasing form of art. No more really than an elegant tent of wood, painted rusty red ('Ottoman Rose'), its main reception room overhangs the rippling waters of the Bosphorus, and its marble or stone quay has underneath it a caique house. Here, modestly, an awning or lattices would be let down to allow the pasha's ladies to have a bathe. Inside, mother-of-pearl decorations encrusted the wooden walls, often enlivened with paintings of carnations, tulips and lilies whose reds and golds contrasted with the deep blue of their painted vase. In the centre of the room there were bubbling fountains (the *fiskiyeh*), and in winter the comforting warmth of a charcoal brazier (*mangal*). In grander eighteenth-century *yalis* (such as those of the Ostrorogs at Kandilli) enormous mirrors reflected the sun-dappled waters, magnificent carpets and low bolsters awaited guests. Rising steeply behind the *yali* there were mysterious gardens beautified by marble fountains. Fortunately, enough still remain to recreate this paradise for us. No wonder the Sultans signed treaties in their *yalis*, and the Grand Viziers would receive negotiators, arriving waterborne for ices, coffee, sherbet, and a pipe.[1]

From such a vantage-point, the Ottoman delighted in contemplating nature – swift-flying shearwaters at dusk (who, it was said, reminded him of the souls of the damned flying to rejoin their corpses in Scutari's great cemetery); flights of exhausted quails from Russia falling into nets cunningly prepared to catch them; gambolling porpoise-schools; the sleek cormorant hunting for his lunch; the fisherman catching swordfish or bonito or turbot – or just listening to the squishy, lapping orchestra of the Bosphorus or to the song of the nightingale. Turkish ladies organized waterborne distractions. Here is Princess Zeynap at her *yali* at Bebek at the turn of the century:

> In summer there were moonlight parties on the Bosphorus. Veiled in white *yashmaks* and wrapped in silk *feraces* (cloaks), the ladies would be rowed in long *kayiks* manned by several pairs of oarsman. Attached to the stern of the *kayik*, squares of cloth or satin, embroidered in gold or silver and edged with little silver fishes, floated on the waves. Musicians, both

[1] Amongst the finest early *yalis* still on the Bosphorus today are those of the Köprülus at Amcazade, and Nuri Birgi Bey at Usküdar.

> players and singers, preceded them in a separate boat, and as the oars dipped rhythmically into the moonlit waters, strains of music were wafted towards the following *kayiks*. The windows of the *yalis* were crowded with onlookers. It was an accepted custom for many other boats and *kayiks* to accompany the party on the sea, forming a long procession, the bobbing lanterns attached to the craft shining dim and yellow under the brilliant moonlight.

Arbitrary privilege might have ruled Ottoman society, but the Bosphorus provided pleasures for all. Indeed, it was on the Bosphorus, and on the Sweet Waters of Europe (today an industrial slum above the heavily polluted Golden Horn), that Sultan Ahmet III and his son-in-law Damad Ibrahim provided the most spectacular of all free shows, their tulip festivals which were usually given in the spring. General Baron de Tott observed in 1790: 'Vases of every kind, filled with natural and artificial flowers, are brought for the occasion, and add to the splendour of an illumination caused by an infinite number of lanterns, coloured lamps, and wax candles, in glass tubes, reflected on every side by mirrors disposed for that purpose.' Candles were also placed on the backs of thousands of tortoises crawling along the tulip beds. Such was the Tulip Age (or *Lale Devri*) celebrated at the Çiragan Palace or at Saadabâd.

The tradition continued into the nineteenth century, using the eve of the Sultan's birthday as the time-honoured occasion for illuminated displays of the Bosphorus palaces. Thus was night turned officially into day. Thousands of lamps would be strung along trees, garden walls, and houses by expert Jewish workmen. Sherbet was offered by pashas to the gawking people entering their water-front parks. All the grand palaces along the Bosphorus, glittering as diamonds in the velvety night, were lit up. 'As the deepening darkness faced their outlines,' wrote Emine Foat Tugay, recalling her girlhood, 'the palaces of the Sultanas, the great *yalis*, and the rolling hillsides of the parks assumed an unearthly beauty.' For her, it was the most beautiful sight she had ever seen.

The tulip festivals; the befezzed Albanian *Kajikiçis* in their white shirts and frail skiffs; that departed symbol of our own power, the *Makook*, scrapped by stern Treasury economy: all these are past and gone forever. Yet the sparkling Bosphorus beyond remains, commanding two worlds and two seas. When I revisited Istanbul in the autumn of 1985, and awoke to the inescapable first call of the muezzin to prayer, the very next sounds I heard were the raw screeches of the seagulls wheeling around the buttresses and minarets of Haghia Sophia, the booming basses of the city's ferry steamers, and the rat-tat of the diesel engines belonging to the fishing-fleets chugging past the old Byzantine sea-walls. Frances Elliot's 'watery mystery mingling with everyday life, magical and strange' is still an essential part of Istanbul life.

Who would not feel sympathy for the tourist visiting the city itself for the first time? That is, the really curious tourist. Leaving the comfortable cocoons of a five-star coffee-shop or an air-conditioned bus, we enter the Great Church of the Holy Wisdom (Haghia Sophia), to contemplate, high above us, a serenely mysterious Mary and Christ Child in glittering mosaic, and two haloed Emperors who offer a city and a church to her; but as we admire their hieratic vestments, gold diadems, buskins, handsome black-haired heads and bold eyes, we realize – most of us, if we are honest – that we know almost nothing about Constantine and Justinian (when did we read Gibbon last?). On we move. Above the Imperial entrance we see a majestic Christ seated on a jewelled throne, towering above a prostrate suppliant Emperor Leo VI; in the galleries up the long ramp, another Christ, flanked by the bearded and glamorous Constantine IX Monomachus and the desirable Empress Zoë. Who were these departed captains and kings? Is this not a case of acute culture shock? The faces, clothes, inscriptions and ruling ideas remain coded mysteries, almost as remote as those of Egyptian gods and goddesses, or of the impassive Khmer rulers in relief on the walls of Angkor.

Another puzzle picture: on leaving the Great Church we find in the courtyard the tombs, or *turbés*, of Sultans and their families. We crane forward at, for instance, the dark-green catafalques in which lie the forty-eight children of Sultan Murad III. What catastrophe happened here? Upon it hangs the whole grisly tale of the Ottoman laws of succession.

By a religious ruling or *fetva*, the leading *Ulemas* of the Ottoman Empire had advised Sultan Mehmet II in the fifteenth century that he should safeguard the succession to the throne in favour of the eldest male in the Imperial family (*Ekberiyyet*) and not on a father-to-son principle. In practice this led to the barbarous custom of any newly acceded Sultan immediately killing any blood rivals, the most obvious being the children – male and sometimes female – of his predecessor (the 'law of fratricide'). From 1617 until the fall of the Ottoman dynasty in 1924, the practice of bowstringing young princes was relaxed; they were confined to a few miserable rooms in the Seraglio (the *Kafes*) and forbidden to have children, though some sterile concubines were provided. Twenty-two Sultans, in fact, came from such enervated and neurotic stock, pulled out of their cage *faute de mieux*. At most, eighty deaths are attributable to this principle, and in its defence it can be said it gave the House of Osman 650 years of unbroken rule and prevented the rise of an aristocracy of blood: no Bourbons, no Condés here. No visit to Topkapi makes any sense without a knowledge of the house rules of the Osmanli family: the children of Sultan Murad III had been executed in 1595 to ensure the unchallenged primacy of their brother, who became Sultan as Mehmet III.

Let us follow our crocodile of camera-festooned tourists into the fabled Seraglio, now called the Palace of Topkapi. Here another world of familiar, if contradictory, images crowds our imagination. A frowning and implacable Sultan, the 'Grim' or the 'Magnificent', sits on his throne, surrounded by kaftanned courtiers in turbans defying the laws of gravity; jugglers, buffoons and mutes cavort and cartwheel for his pleasure by softly murmuring fountains. Other images: the Janissaries break ranks, overturn their famous kettles, and mutiny: viziers are beheaded; the *padishah* (the original Ottoman word for Sultan) is himself strangled within his own palace. Yet another – understandably popular – image: the *padishah*, lord of two, three, even four hundred girls, indulges his every sexual whim in the total privacy of his domed, tiled, marble-lined harem, guarded by whip-wielding black and white eunuchs; he sets the girls to find jewels and sweets hidden in the flower beds or tossed into his fountains and pools, whilst he lolls voluptuously in the Erevan or Bagdad Kiosks where the 'winner' will later visit him. Such *images d'Epinal*, in their oriental version, are frivolous parodies of the organized and disciplined rituals that normally governed that extraordinary institution of Topkapi. Yet to understand them requires some knowledge in depth of the religion of Islam; of Byzantine or Persian court ceremonial, inherited gladly in many respects by the Ottomans; of their traditions of poetry, gardening, architecture, morality, and warfare. Acquisition of such knowledge can be fascinating, but it is hard work. The classic history of the Ottoman sovereigns, for example, written in the 1830s by Ritter J. von Hammer-Purgstall in seventeen volumes, is not yet translated from German into English.

Istanbul boasts not only an immensely rich and confusing history, but also an artistic heritage of unrivalled scope and variety. Consider a two- or three-hour visit that begins in the great Archaeological Museum of Topkapi with the finest of all sarcophagi to admire, namely that of Alexander the Great's lion-hunt from Sidon (fourth century BC). Opposite it, we admire the Ottoman Çinili Kiosk (AD 1472) whose *cuerda seca* tiles and Isnik ceramics dazzle the eye. A few minutes away, there stands the simple and early (*c.*AD 740) basilica of Haghia Eirene, a classic of Byzantine architecture. Within a further five minutes' walk the tourist is called upon to marvel at – and try to understand – the Sultan Ahmet Mosque and its associated complex (AD 1616); around the corner in the Hippodrome is the obelisk of Thutmoses (1500 BC) and the Serpentine Column, surviving even Apollo's Temple at Delphi (479 BC) juxtaposed with the restored splendour of an Ottoman palace (*c.*AD 1525) that belonged to the Grand Vizier Ibrahim under Süleyman the Law-giver. And around another corner is the most extraordinary of all the City's relics: the Column of Constantine (330 AD). Originally graced by a statue of Apollo, whose face was changed to represent Constantine's, this venerable, time-blackened stump (called *Çemberlitas* by the Turks) was burnt in 1779; its base allegedly contained the treasures of the Palladium (or image of Athens) brought from Troy, the axe with which Noah made the ark, the loaves from Cana and the alabaster box from which Mary Magdalene anointed Christ's feet.

Let us admit that the city is the world's record-holder of historic and cultural gear-changes, visual contrasts, and immediate demands on our historical and aesthetic knowledge. This indeed is the City of Cities, legatee of its three great empires, Roman, Byzantine and Ottoman, which fashioned our own civilization. Though Constantinople-Istanbul may have been dethroned as a capital city, she is now taking a quiet revenge on us, for she has become a city of mystery. Confronted by bare walls, archaic scripts, and religious faiths which we have jettisoned, we have become 'blind' men, latter-day Chalcedonians. How strangely, for example, the anguished lament of a Byzantine historian at the city's fall in 1453 sounds to our modern ears, how remote the Christian values that it mourns:

> O City, chief City of all Cities, City Centre of all parts of the World! O City! City, the glory of Christians, and confusion of barbarians! O City, City second Paradise planted in the West with every tree abundant in spiritual fruits! Paradise, where is your beauty; where is that copious outpouring of graces so salutary for body and soul?
>
> Where are the bodies of the Apostles of my Saviour, which were sown in this eternally green Paradise, amidst which there were the Purple Shroud, the Lance, the Sponge, which we could behold and see our very Saviour attached to the Cross? Where are those relics of the Saints and Martyrs? Where are the bodies of great Constantine and the other Emperors? The streets, the crossroads, the squares, the gardens are scattered with the noble relics of the Saints placed there by the impious; they are filled with the corpses of holy men and women. What a profanation![1]

Fashions in history change, but slowly. The denigration of the Byzantines began with Gibbons's famous judgement that 'the division of the Roman world between the sons of Theodosius marks the final establishment of the Empire of the East, which from the reign of Arcadius to the taking of Constantinople by the Turks, subsisted one thousand and fifty-eight years in a state of premature and perpetual decay.' Elsewhere he thundered inimitably against those 'subjects of the Byzantine Empire who assume and dishonour the names of both Greeks and Romans' and 'present a dead uniformity of abject vices which are neither softened by the weakness of humanity nor animated by the

[1] 'Lament of the Historian upon the Sack of Constantinople' from *The History of the Emperors John Manuel, John and Constantine Paleologus* by Michael Ducas, Bucharest, 1948.

vigour of memorable crimes'.[1] Lecky echoed this with his judgement that it is the 'universal verdict of history that the Empire constitutes the most base and despicable form that civilisation ever assumed'. Neither historian could stand the eclipse of the first Roman Empire by the second.

The Pope in Rome and his Church over the centuries did not mind the humbling of their Orthodox brethren. They had, as early as 1074, ex-communicated the Patriarch of Constantinople, leaving a Bull saying so on the high altar of Haghia Sophia!

The verdict of Odo de Deuil, a Crusader and chaplain to Louis VII of France, gives the popular western view of the Greeks as early as 1156: 'Constantinople is arrogant in her wealth, treacherous in her practices, corrupt in the faith; just as she fears everyone on account of her wealth, she is dreaded by everyone because of her treachery and faithlessness. If she did not have these vices, however, she would be preferable to all other places because of her temperate climate, rich fertility of soil, and location convenient for propagating the faith.'[2]

Nineteenth-century travellers, famous poets such as Byron and Chateaubriand, and the thousands of other Orientalists following them, knew their classical history, and threw off their learned allusions to the Symplegades, or Leander, or Hecate; but though they might be intent on rescuing virgins from the slave markets (as was Lamartine) or meeting pashas and the *padishah* himself, they had no room in their Ottomania for the Turkish Empire's precursor. When Lamartine rose at dawn to admire the sea view from his brig in May 1833, he exclaimed – gazing at the Seraglio point – that 'it was there that God and man, nature and art, had placed or created in harmony the most marvellous view that the human eye could contemplate on earth,'[3] without any credit to Justinian who had created part of that harmony with Haghia Sophia, or Theodosius II who had built the great land walls. Lamartine dismissed the Great Church: 'considering

[1] *The Decline and Fall of the Roman Empire* Vol. V, by Edward Gibbon, London, 1896.

[2] *De Profectione Ludovici VII in orientem* by Odo de Deuil, transl. V.G. Berry, New York, 1948.

[3] *Voyage en Orient*, Vol. III, A. de Lamartine, Paris, 1819.

the barbarity of art which presides over this mass of stone, it was a work born at a time of corruption and decadence . . . a confused and vulgar souvenir of departed fashion'.[1] Byron preferred the gothic Cathedral of Seville to Haghia Sophia.

The fact that the Byzantine Empire lasted for over a thousand years, preserved Roman law and orthodox Christianity, and saved the West itself by containing the Saracens, Arabs, Persians and other barbarian hordes, still counts for little against such a bad press.

Strange distortions result even today. Contrasts are emphasized (Christian–Muslim, the Cross–the Crescent) when what strikes the onlooker as forcefully, historically or topographically, are the links, and the fascinating continuities of Byzantine and Ottoman history. It could certainly be argued that the succeeding rulers of the city and their peoples have more in common than in contrast. Are there any real breaks between the Greeks and the 'new' Romans, between the latter and the Byzantine 'Greeks', or between the miserably few remaining Greeks of 1453 and the Ottomans? Constantine might worship the true Cross his mother Saint Helena had found, but he also enjoyed the sensuous forms of statues of Aphrodite of Cnidos by Praxiteles, Athena from Lindos and Zeus by Phidias which had been looted from other shrines to adorn his capital. The Muslim worshipped happily not only in the Great Church turned into a mosque, but in Kariye Camii (formerly St Saviour in Chora) in the Fethiye Camii (formerly the Theotokos Pammacaristos), in the mosque of Fenari Isa (formerly the monastery of Constantine Lips), in the (misnamed) Küçük Aya Sofya (formerly the Church of Saints Sergius and Bacchus), in Gül Camii (or St Theodosia). This list is not exhaustive. The ordinances of a Justinian set on beautifying his city would be echoed by Ottoman town-planners, who were just as ruthless in safeguarding their sovereigns' pleasure. Here is a sixth-century decree:

> In this our royal city one of the most pleasant amenities is the view of the sea; and to preserve it we enacted that no building should be erected within 100 feet of the sea front. This law has been circumvented by certain individuals. They first put up

[1] Lamartine, op. cit.

> buildings conforming with this law; then put up in front of them awnings which cut off the sea view without breaking the law; next put up a building inside the awning; and finally remove the awning. Anyone who offends in this way must be made to demolish the building he has put up and further pay a fine of ten pounds of gold.[1]

What is the debt of the great Ottoman architects to their Byzantine colleagues? The latter had improved on that simple Roman box, the basilica, with a rounded eastern end or apse. When Justinian's two architects of genius, Anthemius of Tralles and Isidore of Miletus, came in AD 532 to exploit the potential of the dome, symbol of heaven, they placed a super-dome of thirty-three metres in diameter upon two semidomes, supported by piers and pendentives. The traditional basilica had been superseded forever by the boldest of all churches, enclosing space whose only boundary was not a rectangle, but a soaring dome lifting body and soul to God. As Procopius said, 'the dome seemed not to rest upon the walls but to be suspended from without'; and the columns were arranged like 'the dancers in a chorus', combining vastness of space with an effortlessness achieved, as it were, by a miracle, and a sense of continual movement towards the Holy Spirit of Wisdom. The Conqueror in 1453 immediately re-dedicated this marvel to his God and to his Prophet, and its essential principles henceforth inspired Ottoman architecture, with some fascinating differences that may be classified as steps in evolution but not the break of a revolution.

The symbol of the Justinian dome, the idea of the circle representing God (supported on semidomes) was kept. The Ottoman architect Sinan and his school turned this Sophian dome of less than a hemisphere (or 162°) into proper hemispheres, and the semidomes, from being saucers, into full quarter-spheres. As a result, in all the great mosques we enjoy the amazing effect of dome cascading upon dome, so satisfying to the eye. They indeed have splendidly monumental, dominating, finished exteriors, in ways which Haghia Sophia, with her clumsy great buttresses, does not emulate: the Byzantines, after

[1] *Justinian and his Age*, P.N. Ure, London, 1951.

all, were not unduly concerned about the aesthetics of the exterior of the Great Church. She stood on her own by the Great Palace, the Baths of Zeuxippus, the Processional Way, and the Hippodrome, and thus had plenty of competition. In contrast, every great Imperial mosque is the centre of its own complex (the *Külliye*) of university lecture rooms, students' cells, kitchens, *imarets* or soup kitchens, fountains, tombs, and libraries. Caravans also needed somewhere to rest.

Without doubt, too, the unique audacity of Haghia Sophia, unrivalled by any later Byzantine church in scale, decoration, or spirituality, provoked Süleyman, and his architect Sinan to take up the challenge. Islam would have its own masterpiece of genius in the Süleymaniye Mosque. Süleyman and Justinian created empires of like immensity; and in their worship of God, their mosque and church share the honours.

Necessity, in a climate with very hot summers, laid on both Byzantine and Ottoman the need for a highly developed system of water supply. In providing it they shared the same creative genius. Never has a city boasted such a splendid network of reservoirs, cisterns, aqueducts, fountains and baths. The emperors themselves, legatees of the best in Roman civil engineering, took a great pride in these monuments; and Süleyman is recorded as saying that the building of waterworks was one of the three great tasks of his life (the other two being the Süleymaniye complex, and the siege of Vienna). Hadrian's and then Valens' aqueducts still dominate the Beyazit district today, after 1600 years. Byzantine hydraulics still ensure the reliable supply of clean pure water from the great reservoirs in the Forest of Belgrade on the European side of the Bosphorus. The names of Valens, Justinian and Andronicus Comnenus are not to be forgotten as creators of this asset of the city, emulated in their time by Süleyman (assisted naturally by Sinan as his architect) and Mahmoud I. With his need to wash before prayers, to relax in elaborate and luxurious baths or *hammans*, to drink water and not wine, and notably in his generous impulse to endow fountains of every conceivable shape and size, the Muslim had an even greater need for water than his Christian predecessors. Add to these motives the huge population explosion in the city in the sixteenth and seventeenth centuries, and the need to improve on the Byzantine systems became imperative – though even today some Byzantine sewers are still, I am told, in use.

A closer look at certain key customs and institutions in the Byzantine and Ottoman Empires reveals a fascinating continuity – if not in name, then certainly in idea. Roman emperors claimed descent from the gods. The Byzantine emperor – once the *Pontifex Maximus* – was the divinely appointed vice-regent of God on earth; he was head of the Church and took priority over the Patriarch, whose office was but a department of State. At the great ecumenical councils, it was the emperor who presided. As emperor, Leo the Isaurian wrote to the Pope: 'I am Emperor and priest, whom God has ordered to feed his flock like Peter, Prince of the Apostles.'[1] The *padishah* was also *caliph*, and appointed his *Seyh-ül-Islam* (or Chief Priest) and the other leading *muftis* and *imams*. Of course, holy men could thunder excommunications or, in the case of the senior Islamic priests, deliver a *fetva* sanctioning deposition of a *padishah*, but then martyrdom or exile awaited any imprudent ruler who had not counted the temporal odds against such *lèse-majesté*. In short, both empires came very close to sharing the same definition of theocracy, with a corresponding impact on the character of the city's religious buildings. As for theology, both Byzantine Orthodoxy and the Holy Koran rested, above all, on one tenet: conservatism.

The Great Palace of the Emperors was a sacred palace. One of the wonders of the world, its grandest dining-room (the Triclinos of the Nineteen) combined the idea of a Roman banquet with the Last Supper. Most state rooms were matched by a chapel or church. Pilgrims flocked from the four corners of the world to kneel in amazed worship before the portrait of Our Lady painted by St Luke, the Holy Wood of the Cross, the Holy Lance, the Cross of Thorns, the Holy Nails, even the Rod of Moses and the Mantle of Elijah (all treasures looted in 1204 or later by the avid bagmen of the Fourth Crusade). The identity of ruler with a semi-divine status had been created. The *padishah*, too, had his own monopoly of Holy Relics, jealously kept within the seraglio: the hair of the Prophet, his tooth, his Holy Mantle, above all the green sacred battle-standard used to proclaim Holy War against the infidel, or perhaps to quell rebellious mobs of Janissaries.

In both Imperial establishments there was a certain nomadic way of living. Faced by a glittering choice – whether of the

[1] *Byzantine Civilisation*, Steven Runciman, London, 1933.

earliest hall of the Chalce, the superb palaces of the Magnaura or the Mangana, or of the Chrysotriclinos – the Emperors had the habit of moving from one somewhat temporary 'home' to another, more altars of repose than bedrooms.[1] Likewise in the Seraglio, the *padishah* moved from kiosk to kiosk, and nothing seemed more natural to him, descendant of Turcomans accustomed to saddle and tent. The first ladies of each empire had their huge staffs, establishments, baths, prisons, and hospitals, as well as those rooms devoted to their priorities – ensnaring a ruler, breeding for him, and then keeping his affections. For the Imperial 'gynaeceum' read 'harem' – though of course a Byzantine empress (such as Irene) could and did rule as regent or sovereign, whereas the Sultan's chief ladies and mother exercised their power in private.

Both empires maintained a star-studded cast of mandarins and officials for every conceivable role. Ranks were classified, and people knew their station to the last shade of a buskin or number of horse-tails. The Byzantine Prefect of the City was a key appointment; the Grand Vizier was no less responsible for law and order. Tightly controlled guilds and corporations provided the commercial sinews in both empires. The emperor chose his counsellors from the senate, the *padishah* from his *diwan*.

Other examples spring to mind. The need for, and existence of, Praetorian Guards in autocracies is obvious. The Byzantines had their Varangian Guards (largely manned by Vikings and Anglo-Saxons, who were admittedly mercenaries); the Ottomans had their Schools of Pages brought up within the Seraglio walls, and Janissaries, drawn in the early years of the Empire from non-Muslim levies of twelve- to fourteen-year-olds, who in theory owed the Sultan total obedience as his slaves. Despite such differences, their roles were the same: sometimes the guards were saviours, but they could also be the most disloyal enemy of their sovereign, whether emperor or *padishah*. Both Courts relied heavily on eunuchs as a vital transmission belt (to use a Leninist phrase) of power from within the palace to the city and empire.

[1] The Byzantine Palaces did differ from Topkapi in that the many small rooms of the latter hardly existed; instead the various halls would be divided up by curtains when privacy was needed, a system very convenient for eavesdropping. I am grateful to Sir Steven Runciman for pointing this out to me.

They occupied the most important roles within the 'official' family and could also become successful generals, (e.g. Narses under Justinian). In the Ottoman Court, the white and black eunuchs also occupied the highest positions. In both empires, the Sacred Palace or the Seraglio, became such a closed and privilege-riddled institution that reformers and dissidents muttered that their high walls had cut off the rulers from the ruled, both physically and spiritually. In both empires the power of the Constantinopolitan mob was – if roused – the terrifying joker in the pack, and if not crushed could cost the ruler his throne. The Niké Riots under Justinian (AD 532) and Halil Patrona's takeover in 1730, are convincing examples of this. 'He who holds Constantinople holds the Empire,' was a maxim valid from Constantine to Ataturk.

To humour their good people, emperors and *padishahs* resorted to the Roman principle of bread and circuses. A triumphal procession of victory from the Golden Gate to the Hippodrome, with elephants, captive kings, games, and a few ceremonial executions, would greatly please the people. Let us hear Robert de Clari's thoughts on the subject:

> Elsewhere in the city there is another gate which is called the Golden Gate. On this gate there were two elephants made of copper which were so large that it was a fair marvel. This gate was never opened except when an emperor was returning from battle after conquering territory. Then the clergy of the city would come out in procession to meet him, and the gate would be opened, and they would bring out a chariot of gold, which was made like a cart with four wheels, such as we call a *curre*. Now in the middle of this chariot there was a high seat and on the seat there was a throne and around the throne there were four columns which bore a canopy to shade the throne, which seemed as if it were all of gold. Then the emperor, wearing his crown, would take his seat on the throne, and he would enter through this gate and be borne in this chariot, with great joy and rejoicing, to his palace.[1]

[1] *The Conquest of Constantinople*, Robert de Clari, transl. by E.H. McNeal, New York, 1936.

In the sixteenth century, an Ottoman triumph was as spectacular as, or even more than, a Byzantine one. It is recorded that groups of 120 prisoners, all tied to a chain in ranks of tens, were paraded, with each prisoner carrying four to five heads of their lamented comrades-in-arms.[1] Some Ottoman feasts, such as Ahmet III's for the circumcision of his sons, lasted a fortnight.[2] The Ottomans, with their *cjerid* or javelin practice, loved sport as much as the Byzantines, whose polo fields took up much space within the sacred enclaves.

The argument may be taken further. For both empires it was the demand from church or mosque, palace or seraglio, that set the pace (and usually paid) for not only architecture but decorative art in all its glittering forms – mosaics, tiles, calligraphy, miniatures, tapestry and textiles. The finest of these forms that one sees today reflect palace cultures.

In lesser matters, traditions seemed to have been handed down from one empire to the next. After the Conquest Constantinople became 'Konstantinye', and was proudly so called by the Ottomans; the name remained officially on coins and documents into this century and the time of the Republic. Ambassadors to both empires had to be impressed by elaborate ceremonial, and if possible, humiliated to reflect the grandeur of the emperor or *padishah* and the miserable rank of their own sovereign. They had to be clothed in robes or kaftans before admission to the Presence. Their swords had to be left behind. Prostration before the emperor was *de rigueur*, and the *padishah* expected almost as much. Only Christian visitors could enter the Imperial shrines in the Sacred Palace. Nor, as Grelot and Lady Mary Wortley Montagu discovered nearly at the cost of their lives, could a *giaour* or infidel visit a mosque without special dispensation.

In a more general manner, both empires excelled in one quality. They knew how to exploit their conquered and subject races whilst allowing them a degree of tolerant self-administration. In neither empire was there any unifying ideal except that of religion; certainly not race. One of the first acts of the Muslim

[1] *Histoire de l'Empire Ottoman*, Vol. III, J. von Hammer, trans. J.-J. Hellert, Paris, 1843.

[2] see page 266.

Conqueror was to appoint an Orthodox Patriarch. The city had a large Jewish community, under their own rabbis. Ottoman tolerance and understanding of minority problems might have had much to do with the fact that the mothers of the *padishahs* might be Circassian, Armenian, Greek, or from any other subject race; and so, naturally, were their own leading concubines. (Only five Sultans had Turkish mothers.) Different racial dynasties similarly ruled the Byzantine Empire – Bulgarian, Thracian or Anatolian. Every Janissary had begun his life as a Christian, or at least a non-Muslim, youth. Thus was an element, potentially of opposition, turned into the very backbone of a fighting empire. Considering the melting-pot of races jostling each other in the city, one can fairly say that – whether under Byzantine or Ottoman rule – the city was never a *national* capital (unlike Ankara today). It was always the forum, the meeting-place, of an empire.

Both empires, arrogant in their military pride, were to suffer from a crippling, and ultimately disastrous, practice. The Byzantines allowed the Venetians and Genoese, *primus inter pares*, to take over their foreign trade; and the Ottomans gave similar concessions to every major trading country of Europe (the French in 1535, the English in 1580, the Dutch in 1612). Both empires fell victim to the illusion that it was enough to be a kind of glorified customs officer, instead of profiting from their own imports and exports based on a huge imperial economy. A warrior caste, headed in each case by some kind of demi-god, might hold together the empire by conquest and war, but once success gave way to military or economic failures, shrinking territory, fewer slaves, less tribute, weak and self-indulgent rulers, these concessions fatally reduced their revenues.

There were, of course, radical changes in the city after 1453, as a Muslim theocracy sought (in Gilles' phrase) to give the Byzantine city its Muslim face. The importance in the city's life of the Hippodrome, where the people had solemnly acclaimed their emperors, had already declined by 1204 when the Crusaders despoiled it of its famous monuments, the Hercules of Lysippus, the Roman She-Wolf, the Eagle of Apollonius Tyanius. The sultans did not allow the Hippodrome to become the mob's rallying point; in fact, their architects raided one end of it, the Sphendone, for capitals, columns and building materials, and it became the sultans' zoo for lions, elephants and even giraffes.

The Conqueror had his own masterful ideas of town planning. He had taken into his own hand 'the stones and the land of the city'. It would become his capital, instead of Edirne or Bursa. The holy associations of Eyüp (where the body of the Prophet's companion, Abu Ansari, had been found) confirmed the city's sacred character. The Conqueror ordered the repair of walls, the building of the Yediküle fortress by the Golden Gate, and two palaces for himself (the Old and New Sarays). Most Byzantine churches, already much run down since the sack of the city by the Crusaders in 1204, were abandoned, and only those turned over to worship as mosques had much of a chance of survival, even if their once-glittering Christian mosaics were plastered over and whitewashed. He began to repopulate the shrunken and deserted city by ordering a *sürgün* or compulsory resettlement, of Muslims, Christians and Jews from Rumelia and Anatolia. His own great mosque, Fatih Camii, was completed by 1471 and took the place of the famous church of the Holy Apostles. It set the style for social and economic needs to develop under the shadow of the mosque. The idea of a religious charity, the *wakf*, gave security of tenure forever to mosques so endowed, and their associated buildings. Whole markets were grouped around one or other mosque: as examples one could quote Haghia Sophia and the Bedestan, or the Fatih complex with the Sultan Pazari and Saraçhane nearby. These 'foundation complexes' were called *mahalles* and their *imam* represented them, a *de facto* mayor of a whole district. The Conqueror's pashas were encouraged to copy his example by building a mosque and religious schools, a *khan* for merchants, a bath and a market. Within seventy years of the Conquest 219 *mahalles* were already thriving.[1]

Later, in the sixteenth century, the architect's department under Sinan, responsible directly to the *padishah*,, controlled this development and set the seal on the city's character with the great Süleymaniye complex (*c.* 1577). The last two such foundations were those of Ahmet I (1616) and of the Yeni Valide Camii (1663). By total theocratic power, direction of labour, and ownership of the land, the *padishahs* made this concept of holy Muslim city possible.

Until the end of the seventeenth century, the seventeen square

[1] 'Istanbul', Encyclopaedia of Islam, Leiden-London, 1960.

kilometres of the city within the walls were not fully built upon; nor had they been in Byzantine times. So the Turk could indulge his love of gardens, whether for pleasure or profit. (Evliya Celebi tells us the Sultans also had forty Imperial gardens, each tended by up to 300 gardeners, and racehorse stables 'ready day and night'.) The population explosion was to reduce such opportunities sharply. There may have been only some 30–40,000 Byzantine Greeks left to cower before the Conqueror when he rode into the city; it is estimated, nevertheless, that 800,000 Muslims, Jews and Christians cohabited in the city in the second half of the sixteenth century, making it the largest city in Europe. At least 400,000, up till this century, were living within the old Byzantine walls, in that 'old' Stamboul so beloved of Pierre Loti; thus excluding the Pera and Galata districts, and, of course, Scutari on the other side of the Bosphorus.

The city was always seriously at risk from fire, not surprisingly when nearly all two-storey houses, kiosks and even grand *Konaks* belonging to pashas and viziers, were built of wood, or of wooden frames filled up with sundried, unburnt brick, standing cheek by jowl in narrow streets and lanes. A few Greek merchants' houses in the Phanar were built of stone; otherwise only great public monuments, such as the mosques with their lead cupolas, the *turbés*, fountains, aqueducts, bazaars and city walls, were stone. Fish frying on a *mangal* could spark off a catastrophe; and disaffected Janissaries could turn to arson ('more particularly when they dislike the Grand Vizier'). To discourage carelessness and arson, it was the custom (according to Coryat in the 1630s) that 'when soever any fire riseth in the city to hang up him in whose house it beginneth'. But despite such deterrence, fires still started. The Sultan himself would come out to encourage his firefighters, the gardeners of the Seraglio (the *bostançis*), in their hopeless task. Fires crackled on for weeks. For example a fire which began in the port in early August 1633 was still climbing the hills towards the Mosque of the Conqueror, or of Sultan Selim I, even as far as the barracks of the Janissaries, at the end of the month and was only put out by 7 September. Its cost was reckoned at 20,000 buildings[1]. The great Bazaar had stone-built vaults for the protection of goods, but it too suffered from flames

[1] J. von Hammer, op. cit.

licking hungrily around it. In 1756 a fire began on 3 May which lasted until 6 July and consumed 200 mosques, 1,000 shops, 70 baths, and nearly 600 flour mills. Edicts (of 1696, 1703 and later) sought to encourage stone buildings.[1] But there were neither enough craftsmen nor rich customers to change the character of the city, from weathered wood for the most part, to stone.

There is no substitute, in making a selection of the wonders of the city so profusely on offer, for doing so on foot. (It is no accident that probably the best guidebook extant to Istanbul is that of Sumner-Boyd and Freely called *Strolling through Istanbul*, which offers twenty-three strolls admirably selected around the Seven Hills of old Stamboul, Pera and Galata.) To those on foot, the old sorceress yields some of her secrets. They become aware of the climate, of the weather, of the effects of light. Pierre Loti, today unfashionable and hardly read, was rightly obsessed by the seasons, with the bone-chilling winter winds, sweeping down from Russia, that howled through the denuded cemeteries of Eyüp or Scutari; with the copper clouds and livid skies of an October evening over the Sea of Marmara; the grey soot-laden mists wreathing the Golden Horn; or by that daily miracle, the flaming ball of the sun setting behind the city's minarets, cypresses and cupolas. Every change of season had its moment: the first swallows arriving in April heralding spring, the rippleless langour of a Bosphorus in high summer, and then its caique-capsizing ice-floes and frothing waves in winter. For me the most rewarding discoveries to be made on foot are, firstly, the city's countless fountains (called *çesmes* and *sebils*) elegantly cut in marble, sometimes richly tiled, whose chronograms, exquisitely lettered in fading gold, are dedicated to Allah and their founder; and secondly, those quiet paradises of scholarship, the eighteenth-century libraries tucked away here and there behind a busy street, their leather folios behind gilt baroque grilles, which were founded by one or other vizier, such as Mehmet Koprülü (1659) or Ragip (1762), who rest by a brace or two of wives under a cypress next to their pious foundation.

[1] *La Vie Quotidienne à Constantinople au temps de Suleiman le magnifique*, by R. Mantran, Paris, 1965.

These happen to be my own pleasures. For another visitor it could be the joy of a personal pilgrimage to Sinan's lesser-known mosques, such as that of Sokollu Mehmet Pasha; or to one of his marble-lined baths; or to the elegant charm of Admiral Piyale's mosque below the Field of the At Meydani. The Byzantine enthusiast could walk the length of the great walls which so often saved our very civilization. Whatever the choice, the city, sombre in her vanished glories, noble in her decayed stones and bricks, will repay more than any other city in West or East the effort to penetrate her mysteries. A city whose greatest church is dedicated to Holy Wisdom still has everything to teach us.

Rulers of the city

Emperors of Byzantium

		AD
Constantine dynasty	Constantine I	324–337
	Constantius II	337–361
	Julian	361–363
Non-dynastic emperors	Jovian	363–364
	Valens	364–378
Theodosian dynasty	Theodosius I	379–395
	Arcadius	395–408
	Theodosius II	408–450
	Pulcheria	450–453
	Marcian	450–457
Leonine dynasty	Leo I	457–474
	Zeno	474–491
	Leo II	474
	Anastasius I	491–518
Justinian dynasty	Justin I	518–527
	Justinian I	527–565
	Justin II	565–578
	Tiberius	578–582
	Maurice (married Tiberius's daughter)	582–602
Non-dynastic emperor	Phocas	602–610
Heraclian dynasty	Heraclius	610–641
	Constantine II	641
	Constantine III	641–668
	Constantine IV	668–685
	Justinian II	685–695 and 705–711
Usurpers during reign of Justinian II	Leontius	695–698
	Tiberius	698–705
Non-dynastic emperors	Philippicus Bardanes	711–713
	Anastasius II	713–716
	Theodosius II	716–717
Syrian dynasty	Leo III	717–741
	Constantine V	741–775

	Leo IV	775–780
	Constantine VI	780–797
	Irene (as Regent and then Empress)	780–802
Non-dynastic emperors	Nicephorus I	802–811
	Stauracius	811
	Michael I	811–813
	Leo V (the Armenian)	813–820
Phrygian dynasty	Michael II (the Stammerer)	820–829
	Theophilus (the Unfortunate)	829–842
	Michael III (the Drunkard)	842–867
Macedonian dynasty	Basil I	867–886
	Leo VI (the Wise)	886–912
	Alexander	886–913
	Constantine VII (Porphyrogenitus)	913–959
Usurpers during and after reign of Constantine VI	Romanus I	919–944
	Romanus II	959–963
	Nicephorus II	963–969
	John Tzimisces	969–976
Macedonian dynasty continued	Basil II (the Bulgar-slayer)	976–1025
	Constantine VIII	976–1028
	Zoë	1028–1050
	Romanus III	1028–1034
	Michael IV	1034–1041
	Michael V	1041–1042
	Zoë and Theodora (jointly)	1042
	Constantine IX Monomachus	1042–1055
	Theodora (as sole Empress)	1055–1056
Non-dynastic emperors	Michael VI Stratioticus	1056–1057
	Isaac I Komnenos	1057–1059
	Constantine X Dukas	1059–1067
	Romanus IV Diogenes	1067–1071
	Michael VII Parapinakes	1071–1078
	Nicephorus III Botaniates	1078–1081
Comnenus dynasty	Alexius I	1081–1118
	John II	1118–1143
	Manuel I	1143–1180
	Alexius II	1180–1183
	Andronicus I	1182–1185
Angeli dynasty	Isaac II Angelus	1185–1195 and 1203–1204

	Alexius III	1195–1203
	Alexius IV	1203–1204
Usurping emperor	Alexius V Dukas	1204
Latin emperors installed by the Crusaders	Baldwin of Flanders	1204–1205
	Henry of Flanders	1206–1216
	Peter de Courtnay (never ruled)	1217
	Yolande	1217–1219
	Robert II of Courtnay	1221–1228
	Baldwin II	1228–1261
	John de Brienne (Regent)	1229–1237
Byzantine emperors exiled at Nicaea during Latin occupation of the city	Theodore I Lascaris	1204–1222
	John III Dukas Vatatzes	1222–1254
	Theodore II	1254–1258
	John IV	1258–1261
Byzantine emperors restored: Paleologian dynasty	Michael VIII	1261–1282
	Andronicus II	1282–1328
	Michael IX	1295–1320
	Andronicus III	1328–1341
	John V	1341–1391
Usurping emperor	John VI Cantacuzenos	1341–1354
Paleologian dynasty continued	Andronicus IV	1376–1379
	John VII	1390
	Manuel II	1391–1425
	John VIII	1425–1448
	Constantine XI	1449–1453

Ottoman sultans

Mehmet II the Conqueror (Fatih)	1453–1481
Beyazet II	1481–1512
Selim I	1512–1520
Süleyman the Magnificent	1520–1566
Selim II	1566–1574
Murad III	1574–1595
Mehmet III	1595–1603
Ahmet I	1603–1617
Moustafa I	1617–1618
Osman II	1618–1622
Moustafa I (restored)	1622–1623

Murad IV	1623–1640
Ibrahim	1640–1649
Mehmet IV	1649–1687
Süleyman II	1687–1691
Ahmet II	1691–1695
Moustafa II	1695–1703
Ahmet III	1703–1730
Mahmoud I	1730–1754
Osman III	1754–1757
Moustafa III	1757–1774
Abdul Hamid I	1774–1788
Selim III	1788–1807
Moustafa IV	1807–1808
Mahmoud II, the Reformer	1808–1839
Abdul Mecit	1839–1861
Abdul Aziz	1861–1876
Murad V	1876
Abdul Hamid II	1876–1909
Mehmet V	1909–1918
Mehmet VI	1918–1922
Abdul Mecit (caliph)	1922
Declaration of the Turkish Republic (capital transferred to Ankara)	1923
Constantinople renamed Istanbul	1930.

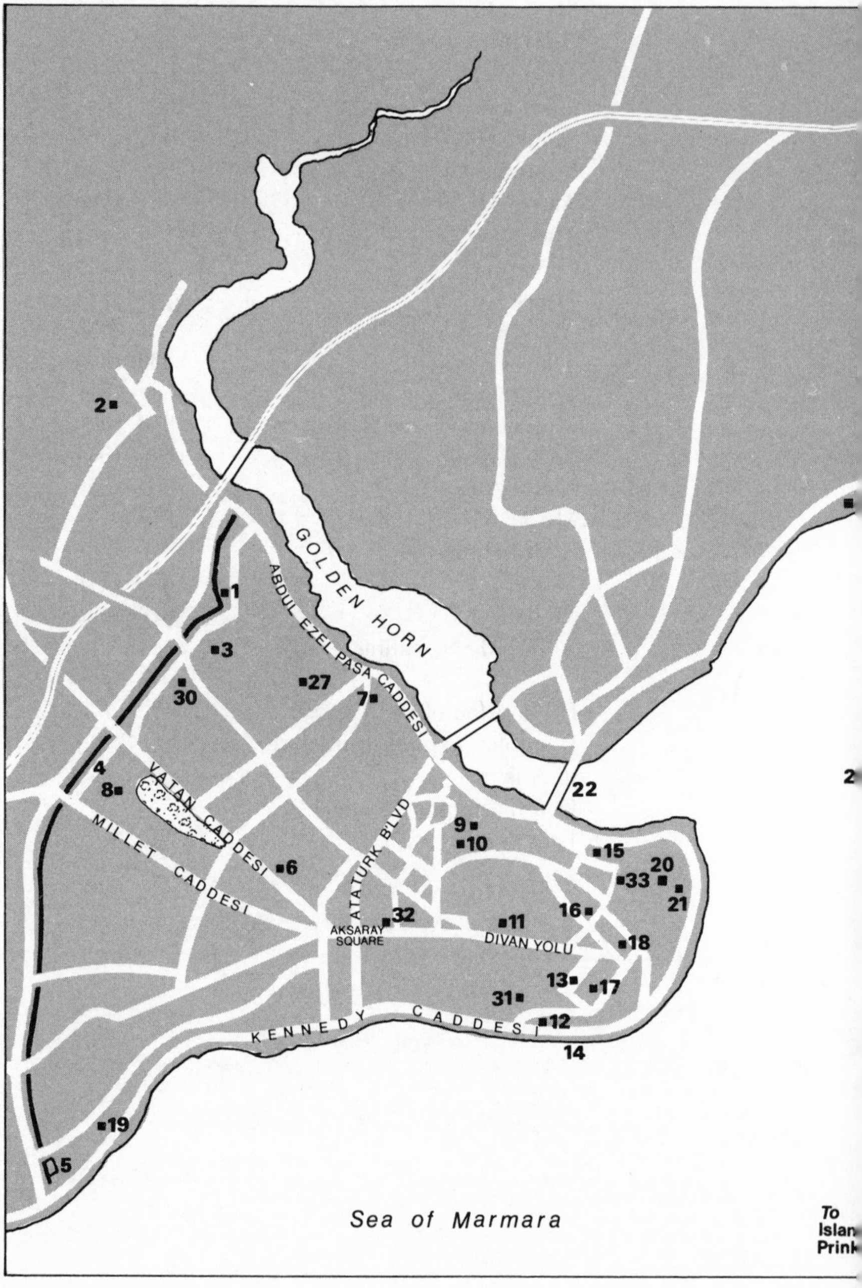

GOLDEN HORN
ABDUL EZEL PASA CADDESI
VATAN CADDESI
MILLET CADDESI
ATATURK B'LVD
AKSARAY SQUARE
DIVAN YOLU
KENNEDY CADDESI
Sea of Marmara
To
1
2
3
4
5
6
7
8
9
10
11
12
13
14
15
16
17
18
19
20
21
22
27
30
31
32
33

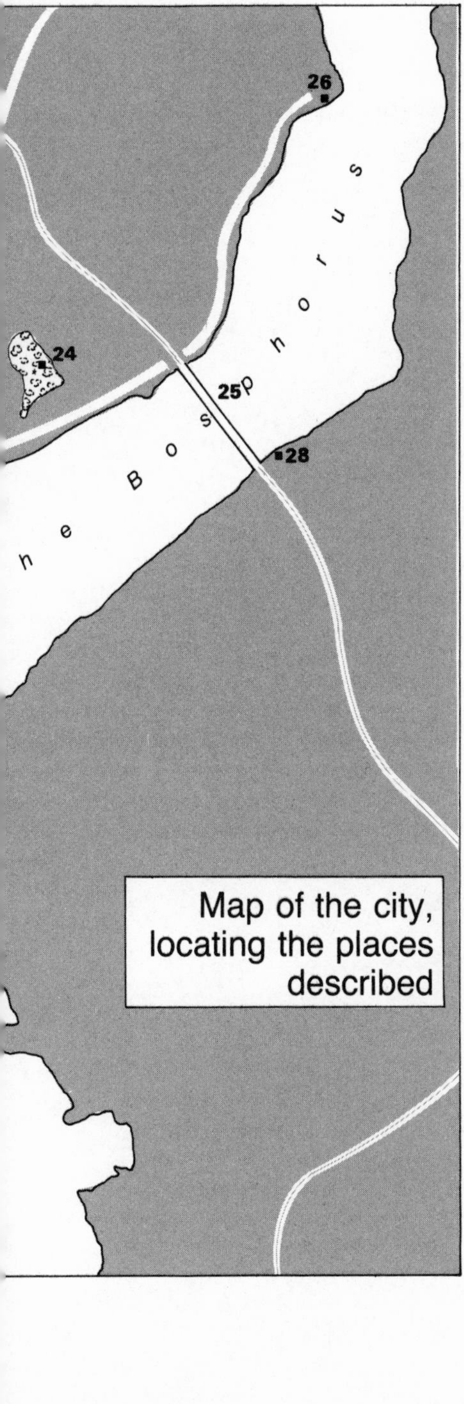

Map of the city, locating the places described

1 Tekfur Saray
2 Eyüp Mosque
3 St Saviour in Chora (Kariye Camii)
4 City Walls
5 Golden Gate (Yedikule)
6 Fatih Mosque
7 St Theodosia (Gul Camii)
8 Beyazet Aga Camii
9 Rüstem Pasha Mosque
10 Süleymaniye Mosque
11 Covered Bazaar
12 St Sergius and Bacchus (Küçük Aya Sofya)
13 Hippodrome (At Meydani)
14 Byzantine Sea Walls
15 Sirkeci Station
16 Cistern (Yerebatan Saray)
17 Sultan Ahmet Mosque (Blue Mosque)
18 Ayasofya (Haghia Sophia)
19 St John Studion (Imrahor Camii)
20 Haghia Eirene
21 Topkapi Palace (Seraglio)
22 Galata Bridge
23 Dolmabahçe Palace
24 Yildiz Palace
25 Bosphorus Bridge
26 Rumeli Hisari
27 Mosque of Selim I
28 Beylerbey Palace
29 Leander's Tower (Kiz Kulesi)
30 Mosque of Mihrimah Sultan
31 Mosque of Sokollu Mehmet Pasha
32 Laleli (Tulip) Mosque
33 Alay Kiosk

Byzantine Constantinople

Partons, la barque est prête, et Byzance m'appelle,
Salut, dieux de l'Euxin, Hellé, Sestos, Abyde
Et Nymphe du Bosphore et Nymphe propontide

André Chenier

Sailing to Byzantium

That is no country for old men. The young
In one another's arms, birds in the trees
– Those dying generations – at their song,
The salmon-falls, the mackerel-crowded seas,
Fish, flesh, or fowl, commend all summer long
Whatever is begotten, born, and dies.
Caught in that sensual music all neglect
Monuments of unageing intellect.

An agèd man is but a paltry thing,
A tattered coat upon a stick, unless
Soul clap its hands and sing, and louder sing
For every tatter in its mortal dress,
Nor is there singing school but studying
Monuments of its own magnificence;
And therefore I have sailed the seas and come
To the holy city of Byzantium.

O sages standing in God's holy fire
As in the gold mosaic of a wall,
Come from the holy fire, perne in a gyre,
And be the singing-masters of my soul.
Consume my heart away; sick with desire
And fastened to a dying animal
It knows not what it is; and gather me
Into the artifice of eternity.

Once out of nature I shall never take
My bodily form from any natural thing,
But such a form as Grecian goldsmiths make
Of hammered gold and gold enamelling
To keep a drowsy Emperor awake;
Or set upon a golden bough to sing
To lords and ladies of Byzantium
Of what is past, or passing, or to come.

William Butler Yeats

[1] The legend of the foundation of the city, as related by Bishop Arculf in *De Locis Sanctis*; from *Travellers to Greece and Constantinople* by J.P.A. van der Vin.

(Bishop Arculf, a Gallician bishop and pilgrim traveller whose account of the legend appears below, visited Constantinople about AD 675, and was one of the earliest Christian writers about the topography of the Near East after the rise of Islam. Driven off course after his great pilgrimage, he took shelter at Iona, where he narrated his experiences to Abbot Adamna, who in turn was the source for Bede on these topics in his famous *Ecclesiastical History*. Arculf's version of the martyrdom of St George, heard in Constantinople, may have been the first one presented to the British public.)

Concerning its foundation the following tradition is related by the citizens as proclaimed by their ancestors. The emperor Constantine (they say) collected a countless horde of men and unlimited money from every quarter, practically impoverishing all nations, and began to build a city under his own name on the Asiatic side, that is in Cilicia, beyond the sea which is the boundary in that area between Asia and Europe. Now one night, when throughout the whole camp the huge armies of workers were asleep in their tents, all kinds of tools which the artisans of the various trades were wont to use were suddenly removed in some unknown way. Early in the morning several worried and harried workers complained to the emperor Constantine himself about the sudden and unexplained disappearance, and the king then asked them saying: 'Have you heard whether anything else was taken from the camp?' 'Nothing', they say, 'except all the working tools.' Thereupon the king gave orders saying: 'Go quickly, traverse and search all the places bordering on the sea on the other side and on this. And if you find the tools in any quarter, guard them there meantime and do not bring them back here, but have some of your number come back to me so that I may know exactly about the discovery.' When they heard this the workmen obeyed the king's behest, and going forth as they were bidden, they searched the area bordering on the sea on both sides, and, lo, on the European side, beyond the sea, they found the heap of tools gathered into one place between two seas. Upon the discovery some were sent back to the king and they told him the tools had been found in that place. On learning this the king immediately ordered the trumpeters to sound their instruments throughout the whole circuit of the camp, and he ordered the army to move saying: 'Let us go forth from here to build a city in the place divinely indicated to us.' And simultaneously setting ships in readiness, he made the crossing with the whole army to the place where the tools had been found, realizing that by transporting the tools God was indicating the place prepared for him. Straightaway he founded a city there which is called Constantinople, a name formed by combining his own name with the word for city in Greek, in such wise that the name of the founder comprises the first part of the composition. Let this suffice as a description of the site and foundation of that royal city.

[2] The foundation of the city; from *The Decline and Fall of the Roman Empire* by Edward Gibbon.

After the defeat and abdication of Licinius, his victorious rival [Constantine] proceeded to lay the foundations of a city destined to reign in future times the mistress of the East, and to survive [his] empire and religion . . . [Constantine] had sufficient opportunity to contemplate, both as a soldier and as a statesman, the incomparable position of Byzantium; and to observe how strongly it was guarded by nature against an hostile attack, while it was accessible on every side to the benefits of commercial intercourse. Many ages before Constantine, one of the most judicious historians of antiquity had described the advantages of a situation, from whence a feeble colony of Greeks derived the command of the sea and the honours of a flourishing and independent republic[1].

If we survey Byzantium in the extent which it acquired with the august name of Constantinople, the figure of the Imperial city may be represented under that of an unequal triangle. The

[1] The navigator Byzas, who was styled the son of Neptune, founded the city 656 [*leg.* 657] years before the Christian aera. His followers were drawn from Argos and Megara. Byzantium was afterwards rebuilt and fortified by the Spartan general Pausanias.

Bust of Constantine the Great, Belgrade

obtuse point, which advances towards the east and the shores of Asia, meets and repels the waves of the Thracian Bosphorus. The northern side of the city is bounded by the harbour; and the southern is washed by the Propontis, or sea of Marmara. The basis of the triangle is opposed to the west, and terminates the continent of Europe. But the admirable form and division of the circumjacent land and water cannot, without a more ample explanation, be clearly or sufficiently understood.

The winding channel through which the waters of the Euxine flow with a rapid and incessant course towards the Mediterranean received the appellation of Bosphorus, a name not less celebrated in the history than in the fables of antiquity. A crowd of temples and of votive altars, profusely scattered along its steep and woody banks, attested the unskilfulness, the terrors, and the devotion of the Grecian navigators, who, after the example of the Argonauts, explored the dangers of the inhospitable Euxine. On these banks tradition long preserved the memory of the palace of Phineus, infested by the obscene harpies[1], and of the sylvan reign of Amycus, who defied the son of Leda to the combat of the Cestus. The straits of the Bosphorus are terminated by the Cyanean rocks, which, according to the description of the poets, had once floated on the face of the waters, and were destined by the gods to protect the entrance of the Euxine against the eye of profane curiosity[2]. From the Cyanean rocks to the point and harbour of Byzantium, the winding length of the Bosphorus extends about sixteen miles, and its most ordinary breadth may be computed at about one mile and a half. The *new* castles of Europe and Asia are constructed, on either continent, upon the foundations of two celebrated temples, of Serapis and of Jupiter Urius. The *old* castles, a work of the Greek emperors, command the narrowest part of the channel, in a place where the opposite banks advance within five hundred paces of each other. These

[1] There are very few conjectures so happy as that of Le Clerc, who supposes that the harpies were only locusts. The Syriac or Phoenician name of those insects, their noisy flight, the stench and devastation which they occasion, and the north wind which drives them into the sea, all contribute to form this striking resemblance.

[2] The deception was occasioned by several pointed rocks, alternately covered and abandoned by the waves. At present there are two small islands, one towards either shore: that of Europe is distinguished by the column of Pompey.

fortresses were restored and strengthened by Mahomet the Second, when he meditated the siege of Constantinople: but the Turkish conqueror was most probably ignorant that, near two thousand years before his reign, Darius had chosen the same situation to connect the two continents by a bridge of boats. At a small distance from the old castles we discover the little town of Chrysopolis, or Scutari, which may almost be considered as the Asiatic suburb of Constantinople. The Bosphorus, as it begins to open into the Propontis, passes between Byzantium and Chalcedon. The latter of those cities was built by the Greeks, a few years before the former; and the blindness of its founders, who overlooked the superior advantages of the opposite coast has been stigmatized by a proverbial expression of contempt.

The harbour of Constantinople, which may be considered as an arm of the Bosphorus, obtained, in a very remote period, the denomination of the *Golden Horn*. The curve which it describes might be compared to the horn of a stag, or, as it should seem, with more propriety, to that of an ox. The epithet of *golden* was expressive of the riches which every wind wafted from the most distant countries into the secure and capacious port of Constantinople. The river Lycus, formed by the conflux of two little streams, pours into the harbour a perpetual supply of fresh water, which serves to cleanse the bottom and to invite the periodical shoals of fish to seek their retreat in that convenient recess. As the vicissitudes of tides are scarcely felt in those seas, the constant depth of the harbour allows goods to be landed on the quays without the assistance of boats; and it has been observed that in many places the largest vessels may rest their prows against the houses, while their sterns are floating in the water. From the mouth of the Lycus to that of the harbour this arm of the Bosphorus is more than seven miles in length. The entrance is about five hundred yards broad, and a strong chain could be occasionally drawn across it, to guard the port and city from the attack of an hostile navy. . . .

Situated in the forty-first degree of latitude, the imperial city commanded, from her seven hills, the opposite shores of Europe and Asia; the climate was healthy and temperate, the soil fertile, the harbour secure and capacious; and the approach on the side of the continent was of small extent and easy defence. The Bosphorus and Hellespont may be considered as the two gates of Constantinople; and the prince who possessed those important passages could always shut them against a naval enemy and open them to the fleets of commerce. The preservation of the eastern provinces may, in some degree, be ascribed to the policy of Constantine, as the barbarians of the Euxine, who in the preceding age had poured their armaments into the heart of the Mediterranean, soon desisted from the exercise of piracy, and despaired of forcing this insurmountable barrier. When the gates of the Hellespont and Bosphorus were shut, the capital still enjoyed, within their spacious inclosure, every production which could supply the wants, or gratify the luxury, of its numerous inhabitants. The sea-coast of Thrace and Bithynia, which languish under the weight of Turkish oppression, still exhibits a rich prospect of vineyards, of gardens, and of plentiful harvests; and the Propontis has ever been renowned for an inexhaustible store of the most exquisite fish, that are taken in their stated seasons without skill and almost without labour. But, when the passages of the Straits were thrown open for trade, they alternately admitted the natural and artificial riches of the north and south, of the Euxine, and of the Mediterranean. Whatever rude commodities were collected in the forests of Germany and Scythia, as far as the sources of the Tanais and the Borysthenes; whatsoever was manufactured by the skill of Europe or Asia; the corn of Egypt, and the gems and spices of the farthest India, were brought by the varying winds into the port of Constantinople, which, for many ages, attracted the commerce of the ancient world.

The prospect of beauty, of safety, and of wealth, united in a single spot, was sufficient to justify the choice of Constantine. But, as some decent mixture of prodigy and fable has, in every age, been supposed to reflect a becoming majesty on the origin of great cities, the emperor was desirous of ascribing his resolution, not so much to the uncertain counsels of human policy, as to the infallible and eternal decrees of divine wisdom. In one of his laws he has been careful to instruct posterity that, in obedience to the commands of God, he laid the everlasting foundations of Constantinople: and, though he has not condescended to relate in what manner the celestial inspiration was communicated to his mind, the defect of his modest silence has been liberally supplied by the ingenuity of succeeding writers, who describe the nocturnal vision which appeared to the fancy of Constantine, as he slept within the walls of Byzantium. The tutelar genius of the city, a venerable matron sinking under the weight of years and infirmities, was suddenly transformed into a blooming maid, whom his own hands adorned with all the symbols of imperial greatness. The monarch awoke, interpreted the auspicious omen, and obeyed, without hesitation, the will of heaven. The day which gave birth to a city or colony was celebrated by the Romans with such ceremonies as had been ordained by a generous superstition; and, though Constantine might omit some rites which savoured too strongly of their Pagan origin, yet he was anxious to leave a deep impression of hope and respect on the minds of the spectators. On foot, with a lance in his hand, the emperor himself led the solemn procession; and directed the line which was traced as the boundary of the destined capital; till the growing circumference was observed with astonishment by the assistants, who, at length, ventured to observe that he had already exceeded the most ample measure of a great city. 'I shall still advance,' replied Constantine, 'till HE, the invisible guide who marches before me, thinks proper to stop.'

Haghia Sophia – the Church of the Holy Wisdom, or the Great Church – later the mosque of Ayasofya

A work as they report surpassing every edifice in the world.

William of Malmesbury

The fairest church in all the world.

Sir John Mandeville

A marvellous and costful temple, clept St Sophie.

Capgrave's Chronicle

[3] Haghia Sophia, rebuilt by Justinian in the sixth century, described by the historian Procopius; from *Sancta Sophia Constantinople: a Study of Byzantine Building* by W.R. Lethaby and Harold Swainson.

(Procopius was born in Caesarea, probably around AD 500, and modelled himself as a historian on Herodotus and Thucydides. He became private secretary and legal adviser to the triumphant General Belisarius in AD 527, and accompanied him on three major campaigns in North Africa, Italy and Persia which re-established the new Roman Empire in Justinian's name across the Mediterranean and the Near East. Granted the title of 'Illustris', Procopius may have been Prefect of Constantinople in AD 562.)

The emperor, thinking not of cost of any kind, pressed on the work, and collected together workmen (*technitai*), from every land. Anthemius of Tralles, the most skilled in the builder's art, not only of his own but of all former times, carried forward the king's zealous intentions, organized the labours of the workmen, and prepared models of the future construction. Associated with him was another architect (*mechanopoios*) named Isidorus, a

Milesian by birth, a man of intelligence, and worthy to carry out the plans of the Emperor Justinian. It is indeed a proof of the esteem with which God regarded the emperor, that he furnished him with men who would be so useful in effecting his designs, and we are compelled to admire the wisdom of the emperor, in being able to choose the most suitable of mankind to execute the noblest of his works. . . .

Now above these arches is raised a circular building of a curved form through which the light of day first shines; for the building, which I imagine overtops the whole country, has small openings left on purpose, so that the places where these intervals occur may serve for the light to come through. Thus far I imagine the building is not incapable of being described, even by a weak and feeble tongue. As the arches are arranged in a quadrangular figure, the stone-work between them takes the shape of a triangle, the lower angle of each triangle, being compressed where the arches unite, is slender, while the upper part becomes wider as it rises in the space between them, and ends against the circle which rests upon them, forming there its remaining angles. A spherical-shaped dome (*tholos*) standing upon this circle makes it exceedingly beautiful; from the lightness of the building, it does not appear to rest upon a solid foundation, but to cover the place beneath as though it were suspended from heaven by the fabled golden chain. All these parts surprisingly joined to one another in the air, suspended one from another, and resting only on that which is next to them, form the work into one admirably harmonious whole, which spectators do not dwell upon for long in the mass, as each individual part attracts the eye to itself. The sight causes men constantly to change their point of view, and the spectator can nowhere point to any part which he admires more than the rest. Seeing the art which appears everywhere, men contract their eyebrows as they look at each part, and are unable to comprehend such workmanship, but always depart thence, stupefied, through their incapacity. So much for this.

The Emperor Justinian and the architects Anthemius and Ididorus used many devices to construct so lofty a church with security. One of these I will now explain, by which a man may form some opinion of the strength of the whole work; as for the others I am not able to discover them all, and find it impossible to describe them in words. It is as follows: The piers, of which I just now spoke, are not constructed in the same manner as the rest of the building; but in this fashion; they consist of quadrangular courses of stone, rough by nature, and made smooth by art; of these stones, those which make the projecting angles of the pier are cut angularly (*engonios*), while those which go in the middle parts of the sides are cut square (*tetragonos*).

They are fastened together not with lime (*titanos*), called 'unslaked' (*asbestos*), not with asphaltum, the boast of Semiramis at Babylon, nor anything of the kind, but with lead, which, poured into the interstices, has sunk into the joints of the stones, and binds them together; this is how they are built.

Let us now proceed to describe the remaining parts of the church. The entire ceiling is covered with pure gold, which adds to its glory, though the reflections of the gold upon the marble surpass it in beauty. There are two aisles one above another on each side, which do not in any way lessen the size of the church, but add to its width. In length they reach quite to the ends of the building, but in height they fall short of it; these also have domed ceilings adorned with gold. Of these two porticoes one [ground floor] is set apart for male and the other [upper floor] for female worshippers; there is no variety in them, nor do they differ in any respect from one another, but their very equality and similarity add to the beauty of the church. Who could describe these gynaeceum galleries, or the numerous porticoes (*stoai*) and cloistered courts (*peristuloi aulai*) with which the church is surrounded? Who could tell of the beauty of the columns and marbles with which the church is adorned? One would think that one had come upon a meadow full of flowers in bloom! Who would not admire the purple tints of some, and the green of others, the glowing red and the glittering white, and those too, which nature, painter-like, has marked with the strongest contrasts of colour? Whoever enters there to worship perceives at once that it is not by any human strength or skill, but by the favour of God, that this work has been perfected; the mind rises sublime to commune with God, feeling that He cannot be far off, but must especially love to dwell in the place which He has chosen; and this is felt not only when a man sees it for the first time, but it always makes the same impression upon him, as though he had never beheld it before. No one ever became weary of this spectacle, but those who are in the church delight in what they see, and, when they leave, magnify it in their talk. Moreover it is impossible accurately to describe the gold, and silver, and gems, presented by the Emperor Justinian; but by the description of one part, I leave the rest to be inferred. – That part of the church which is especially sacred, and where the priests alone are allowed to enter, which is called the Sanctuary (*thusiasterion*), contains forty thousand pounds' weight of silver.

The above is an account, written in the most abridged and cursory manner, describing in the fewest possible words the most admirable structure of the church at Constantinople, which is called the Great Church, built by the Emperor Justinian, who did not merely supply the funds for it, but assisted at its building by the labour and powers of his mind.

[4] The poetic description of Haghia Sophia by Paul the Silentiary; from *Sancta Sophia Constantinople: a Study of Byzantine Building* by W.R. Lethaby and Harold Swainson.

(The Silentiaries, of whom Paul was one, were court officials. Their office was an exalted one, as they ranked with the senators, and were employed on all kinds of service, not infrequently becoming the historians of the emperor. Paul belonged to the cultivated and literary circle, who during Justinian's reign interested themselves in literature. The description or rather explanation of Haghia Sophia, in long Homeric hexameters, was most probably written and recited as an Opening Ode at the *Encaenia* of 24 December 563.)

At last the holy morn had come, and the great door of the new-built temple groaned on its opening hinges, inviting emperor and people to enter; and when the inner part was seen sorrow fled from the hearts of all, as the sun lit the glories of the temple. 'Twas for the emperor to lead the way for his people, and on the morrow to celebrate the birth of Christ. And when the first gleam of light rosy-armed driving away the dark shadows, leapt from arch to arch, then all the princes and people with one voice hymned their songs of prayer and praise; and as they came to the sacred courts, it seemed to them as if the mighty arches were set in heaven.

Towards the East unfold triple spaces of semicircular form; and above, on an upright band of wall, soars aloft the fourth part of a sphere. Even so, high over its back and triple crest, shimmer the tail feathers of a peacock, with their countless eyes. These crowning parts men learned in the builder's art call conchs; and certain it is they call them so from a shell of the sea, or 'tis a craftsman's name. . . .

Exedras. – And westwards again are two conchs on columns, one on either side; projecting as if stretching out bent arms to embrace the people singing in the church. They are borne by columns of porphyry, bright of bloom ranged in semicircular line, and with capitals (*karenoi*) of gold, carrying the weight of the arches (*kukloi*) above. These columns were once brought from the cliffs of Thebes, which stand, like greaved warriors, by the banks of Nile. Thus, on two columns, on either side, rise the lower parts of either exedra (*apsis*). And for the support of each, the skilled workman has bent from below three small semicircular arches (*apsides*); and, beneath their springing, the tops (*kareata*) of the columns are bound with well-wrought bronze, overlaid with gold, which drives away all fear. Now above the prophyry columns stand others from Thessaly, splendid flowers of fresh green. Here are the fair upper galleries for the women. These too have arches, as may be seen from below, though they show six Thessalian columns and not two. And one wonders at the power of him, who bravely set six columns over two, and has not trembled to fix their bases over empty air. [Column does not stand directly over column.] . . .

Narthex. – And outside of the doors (*pulai*) there stretches a long porch (*aulon*), receiving beneath wide portals (*thuretroi*) those that enter; and it is as long as the wondrous church is broad. In the Greek speech this part is called the narthex. Here through the night swells the melodious sound, pleasing to the ears of Him who giveth life to all; when the psalms of David are sung in antiphonal strains – that sweet-voiced David, whom the divine voice of the Almighty praised, and whose glorious posterity conceived the sinless Son of God, who was in Virgin's pangs brought forth, and subjected to a Mother's care. Now into this porch open seven wide holy gates (*puleones*), inviting the people to enter. One of them is on the south of the narrow porch, and another opens to Boreas, but the others are opened on creaking hinges by the doorkeeper (*neokoros*) in the west wall. This wall is the end of the church. . . .

The Dome. – And above all rises into the immeasurable air the great helmet [of the dome], which, bending over, like the radiant heavens, embraces the church. And at the highest part, at the crown, was depicted the cross, the protector of the city. And wondrous it is to see how the dome gradually rises, wide below, and growing less as it reaches higher. It does not however spring upwards to a sharp point, but is like the firmament which rests on air, though the dome is fixed on the strong backs of the arches.

With dauntless pen I will describe what plan the emperor devised for the broad church, and how, with builder's skill, both the curves of the arches and the vault of the wide-extended house were formed with thin bricks (*plinthoi*), and raised on firm foundations. Thus the skilful master-man, well versed in every craft, formed a ceiling to the lofty nave. Yet he did not send to the hills of Phœnician Lebanon, nor to search the dark woods of the Alpine crags, nor where some Assyrian or Celtic woodman goads on the oxen in dense forests, nor did he think to use fir (*peuke*) or pine (*elate*) to roof the house. From neither the glades of Daphne by Orontes, nor from the wooded crags of Patara came cypress wood, to form a covering for the mighty temple. For our noble king, since nature could produce no timber great enough, had it covered with stones (*lithoi*) laid in a round form. Thus on the four arches (*apsides*) rose, like a beauteous helmet, the deep-bosomed swelling roof (*kaluptra*): and it seems that the eye, as it wanders round, gazes on the circling heavens. And beneath the two great arches (*apsides*), to the east and to the west, you must know that it is all open, and extended in the air. . . .

The Marbles. – Yet who, even in the measures of Homer, shall sing the marble pastures gathered on the lofty walls and spreading pavement of the mighty church? These the iron with its metal tooth has gnawed – the fresh green from Carystus, and many-coloured marble from the Phrygian range, in which a rosy blush mingles with white, or it shines bright with flowers of deep red and silver. There is a wealth of porphyry too, powdered with bright stars that has once laden the river boat on the broad Nile. You would see an emerald green from Sparta, and the glittering marble with wavy veins, which the tool has worked in the deep bosom of the Iassian hills, showing slanting streaks blood-red and livid white. From the Lydian creek came the bright stone mingled with streaks of red. Stone too there is that the Lybian sun, warming with his golden light, has nurtured in the deep-bosomed clefts of the hills of the Moors, of crocus colour glittering like gold; and the product of the Celtic crags, a wealth of crystals, like milk poured here and there on a flesh of glittering black. There is the precious onyx, as if gold were shining through it: and the marble that the land of Atrax yields, not from some upland glen, but from the level plains; in parts fresh green as the sea or emerald stone, or again like blue cornflowers in grass, with here and there a drift of fallen snow, – a sweet mingled contrast on the dark shining surface. . . .

The Mosaic. – Now the vaulting is formed of many a little square (*psephos*) of gold cemented together. And the golden stream of glittering rays pours down and strikes the eyes of men, so that they can scarcely bear to look. One might say that one gazed upon the midday sun in spring, what time he gilds each mountain height.

Iconostasis. – Our emperor has levied from the whole earth, and brought together the wealth of the barbarians of the west; for as he did not deem stone a fitting adornment for the divine, eternal temple, on which [New] Rome has centred the expectancy of joy; he has not spared enrichments of silver, and so the ridge of Pangaeus and the height of Sunium have opened all their silver veins, and many treasure-houses of our subject kings have yielded their stores.

For as much of the great church by the eastern arch as was set apart for the bloodless sacrifices, no ivory, no stone, nor bronze distinguishes, but it is all fenced with the silver metal. Not only upon the walls, which separate the holy priests from the crowd of singers, has he placed mere plates of silver, but he has covered all the columns themselves with the silver metal, even six sets of twain; and the rays of light glitter far and wide. Upon them the tool has formed dazzling circles, beautifully wrought in skilled symmetry by the craftsman's hand, in the centre of which is carved the symbol of the Immaculate God, who took upon Himself the form of man. In parts stand up an army of winged angels in pairs, with bent necks and downcast mien (for they could not gaze upon the glory of the Godhead, though hidden in the form of man to clear man's flesh from sin). And elsewhere the tool has fashioned the heralds of the way of God, even those by whose words were noised abroad, before He took flesh upon Him, the divine tidings of the Anointed One. Nor had the craftsman forgotten the forms of those others, whose childhood was with the fishing-basket and the net; but who left the mean labours of life and unholy cares to bear witness at the bidding of a heavenly king, fishing even for men, and forsaking the skill of casting nets to weave the beauteous seine of eternal life. In other parts art has limned (*kategraphe*) the Mother of Christ, the vessel of eternal light, whose womb brought Him forth in holy travail. . . .

The Lighting. – No words can describe the light at night-time; one might say in truth that some midnight sun illumined the glories of the temple. For the wise forethought of our king has had stretched from the projecting rim (*antux*) of stone, on whose back is firmly planted the temple's air-borne dome, long twisted chains (*seirai*) of beaten brass, linked in alternating curves with many windings. And these chains, bending down from every part in a long course, come together as they fall towards the ground. But before they reach the pavement, their path from above is checked, and they finish in unison on a circle.

And beneath each chain he has caused to be fitted silver discs, hanging circle-wise in the air, round the space in the centre of the church. Thus these discs, pendent from their lofty courses, form a coronet above the heads of men. They have been pierced too by the weapon of the skilful workman, in order that they may receive shafts of fire-wrought glass, and hold light on high for men at night.

And not from discs alone does the light shine at night, but in the circles close by a disc you would see the symbol of the mighty cross, pierced with many holes, and in its pierced back shines a vessel of light. Thus hangs the circling chorus of bright lights. Verily you might say that you gazed on the bright constellation of the Heavenly Crown by the Great Bear, and the neighbouring Dragon.

Thus through the temple wanders the evening light, brightly shining. In the middle of the larger circle you would find a crown with lightbearing rim; and above in the centre another noble disc spread its light in the air, so that night is compelled to flee.

Near the aisles too, alongside the columns, they have hung in order single lamps (*lampter*) apart one from another; and through the whole length of the far-stretching nave is their path. Beneath each they have placed a silver vessel, like a balance pan, and in the centre of this rests a cup of well-burning oil.

There is not however one equal level for all the lamps, for you may see some high, some low, in comely curves of light; and from twisted chains they sweetly flash in their aerial courses, even as shines twin-pointed Hyas fixed in the forehead of Taurus.

One might also see ships of silver, bearing a flashing freight of flame, and plying their lofty courses in the liquid air instead of the sea, fearing no gale from south-west, nor from Boötes, sinking late to rest. And above the wide floor you would see shapely beams (with lamps), running between two-horned supports of iron, by whose light the orders of priests, bound by the rubrics, perform their duties. . . .

A thousand others within the temple show their gleaming light, hanging aloft by chains of many windings. Some are placed in the aisles, others in the centre or to east and west, or on the crowning walls, shedding the brightness of flame. Thus the night seems to flout the light of day, and be itself as rosy as the dawn. And whoever gazes on the lighted trees, with their crown of circles, feels his heart warmed with joy; and looking on a boat swathed with fire, or some single lamp, or the symbol of the Divine Christ, all care vanishes from the mind. So with wayfarers through a cloudless night, as they see the stars rising from point to point; one watches sweet Hesperus, another's attention is fixed on Taurus, and a third contemplates Boötes, or Orion and the cold Charles' Wain; the whole heaven, scattered with glittering stars, opens before them, while the night seems to smile on their way.

Thus through the spaces of the great church come rays of light, expelling clouds of care, and filling the mind with joy. The sacred light cheers all: even the sailor guiding his bark on the waves, leaving behind him the unfriendly billows of the raging Pontus, and winding a sinuous course amidst creeks and rocks, with heart fearful at the dangers of his nightly wanderings – perchance he has left the Ægean and guides his ship against adverse currents in the Hellespont, awaiting with taut forestay the onslaught of a storm from Africa – does not guide his laden vessel by the light of Cynosure, or the circling Bear, but by the divine light of the church itself. Yet not only does it guide the merchant at night, like the rays from the Pharos on the coast of Africa, but it also shows the way to the living God.

[5] The coronation of a Byzantine emperor, described by Cantacuzenus (Paleologus); from *Sancta Sophia Constantinople: a Study of Byzantine Building* by W.R. Lethaby and Harold Swainson.

And about the second hour of the same day the prince who is to be anointed is set upon a shield; the reigning emperor, who may be his father, and the patriarch take hold of the front part of the shield, which is also held by the officials of rank and the nobility. They then raise it, and show the new emperor to the assembled populace. After he has been greeted with acclamation, they attend him into the church, where the rest of the ceremony must be completed. Now a little edifice of wood has previously been prepared for this very purpose, into which they lead the new emperor, and put on him the purple and the diadem, which have been blest by the bishops. And round his head it is customary to put only a chaplet. After this the service of the Mass (*mustagogia*) proceeds. And near the erection just mentioned a set of movable steps, also of wood, are prepared, and these they cover with purple silk. And upon it are placed golden thrones, according to the number of the princes, not like other thrones, but raised on four or five steps; here the princes take their seats. The princesses also ascend with them, and sit on the thrones, wearing their crowns, but she that is about to be crowned wears a chaplet. Now before the hymn *Trisagion* is sung, the patriarch comes out of the bema and ascends the ambo, and with him are the rulers of the church, all wearing their sacred robes. He then dismisses them, and summons the princes, and they immediately arise from their thrones and come to the ambo, while profound silence is kept by the whole congregation. Then the patriarch goes through the prayers appointed for the anointing, some silently by himself, others out loud, praying for the blessing of God on him who is about to be anointed. After this the new emperor removes from his head whatever he is wearing, and then it is right for all, as many as are present, to stand with bared heads. Then the patriarch with the holy oil anoints the head of the emperor with the form of the cross, saying with a loud voice 'Holy'; and as soon as they hear it those standing on the ambo pronounce it three times, and after them all the people. After this the crown is brought by deacons from the bema where they keep it (now it is not above the Holy Table as some say), and taken to the ambo. If any previously crowned emperor be there, he and the patriarch take the crown together, and place it on the head of the prince, the patriarch saying 'Holy' in a loud voice. Those in the ambo repeat it three times, and the people, as after the anointing. Then the patriarch repeats some more prayers, and the prince descends from the ambo, not on the side by which he ascended, but on the side which is turned towards the solea. If he is unmarried he then ascends the steps and reseats himself upon his throne, but if he has a wife then she also must be crowned. She is then led, as she rises from the throne, by two kinswomen one on either side, or if she has no relatives, eunuchs lead her down from the steps, and stand with her before the solea. Then the emperor descends from the ambo, and takes the crown held ready by the kinswomen or eunuchs, and places it upon the head of his wife, and she kneels before her husband, swearing fealty to him. And the patriarch, standing by the solea, offers up a prayer for the emperor and empress, and all their people. Thus the emperor crowns his own wife. And then both ascend the steps, and sit upon their thrones, and the rest of the mysteries are proceeded with. But at the singing of the *Trisagion*, or at the reading from the apostolic writings, or the Gospels, they stand up. . . . And after the elevation, if he is not prepared for the communion he remains seated till the end of the service. But if he is prepared the deacons again come and summon him. And with them he enters into the bema and, having been given a censer, he censes the Holy Table, looking first of all to the east, then north, west, and south, and having again censed towards the east, he censes the patriarch also. The patriarch bows to him and takes the censer, and censes the emperor in return. After this the emperor removes the crown, and gives it into the hands of the deacons. Then the patriarch puts into his hand a portion of our Lord's body, and after that he drinks of the life-giving blood, not from a spoon like the rest of the people, but from the cup itself like the priests. Then the emperor replaces the crown, and comes out of the bema, and after the congregation has shared in the Communion, and he has been blessed by the patriarch, and the priests, and has kissed their right hands, they lead him to the part called catechumena to receive the acclamations of the people. When this is finished, he comes down again, and he and the empress mount on horseback, and ride back to the palace to partake of a banquet.

[6] The desecration of Haghia Sophia by the Latin Crusaders in 1204; from *The Decline and Fall of the Roman Empire* by Edward Gibbon.

(The Fourth Crusade, ostensibly to recapture Jerusalem from Saladin, never achieved its holy purpose. The Emperor Alexius had made some kind of promise to the Pope that he would bring the Greek Church under Roman authority; and the Pope, with hesitation and some doubt, had let it be known that the expedition could dally at Constantinople if this would lead to a reunion of the two Churches. The plunder of Christendom's greatest city was a stronger motive in the minds of the crusading barons than any Christian one.)

Pope Innocent the Third accuses the pilgrims of respecting, in their lust, neither age nor sex nor religious profession; and bitterly laments that the deeds of darkness, fornication, adultery, and incest were perpetrated in open day; and that noble matrons and holy nuns were polluted by the grooms and peasants of the Catholic camp. It is indeed probable that the licence of victory prompted and covered a multitude of sins; but it is certain that the capital of the East contained a stock of venal or willing beauty, sufficient to satiate the desires of twenty thousand pilgrims; and female prisoners were no longer subject to the right or abuse of domestic slavery. The marquis of Montferrat was the patron of discipline and decency; the count of Flanders was the mirror of chastity: they had forbidden, under pain of death, the rape of married women, or virgins, or nuns; and the proclamation was sometimes invoked by the vanquished and respected by the victors. Their cruelty and lust were moderated by the authority of the chiefs and feelings of the soldiers; for we are no longer describing an irruption of the northern savages; and, however ferocious they might still appear, time, policy, and religion had civilised the manners of the French, and still more of the Italians. But a free scope was allowed to their avarice, which was glutted, even in the holy week, by the pillage of Constantinople. . . .

In the cathedral of St Sophia the ample veil of the sanctuary was rent asunder for the sake of the golden fringe; and the altar, a monument of art and riches, was broken in pieces and shared among the captors. Their mules and horses were laden with the wrought silver and gilt carvings, which they tore down from the doors and pulpit; and, if the beasts stumbled under the burden, they were stabbed by their impatient drivers, and the holy pavement streamed with their impure blood. A prostitute was seated on the throne of the patriarch; and that daughter of Belial, as she is styled, sung and danced in the church, to ridicule the hymns and processions of the Orientals. Nor were the repositories of the royal dead secure from violation; in the church of the Apostles the tombs of the emperors were rifled; and it is said that after six centuries the corpse of Justinian was found without any signs of decay or putrefaction. In the streets the French and Flemings clothed themselves and their horses in painted robes and flowing head-dresses of linen; and the coarse intemperance of their feasts insulted the splendid sobriety of the East. To expose the arms of a people of scribes and scholars, they affected to display a pen, an ink-horn, and a sheet of paper, without discerning that the instruments of science and valour were *alike* feeble and useless in the hands of the modern Greeks.

[7] The coronation of the Crusader, Baldwin of Flanders, as Emperor of Byzantium in 1204; from *The Conquest of Constantinople* by Robert de Clari, translated by E.H. McNeal.

(Robert de Clary, or Clari, described himself as a 'knight' and witness of the conquest of Constantinople in the Fourth Crusade. Naive, provincial in tone, amazed at the sacred marvels of the city, de Clari was nevertheless a truthful chronicler and his account supplements in rich detail the better known ones of Geoffrey de Villehardouin, Nicetas, or William of Tyre. He disappears from history after 1216.)

When the mass was chanted, the electors assembled and took counsel together, and they talked of one and of another, until the Venetians and the bishops and abbots, all twenty electors, agreed all together that it should be the count of Flanders, nor was there one of them who was against it. When they were agreed together and their council was about to break up, they gave the bishop of Soissons the charge of saying the word. When they had separated, all those of the host assembled to hear and to learn whom they would name emperor. When they were thus assembled, they were all very quiet, and most of them were afraid and fearful that they would name the marquis, but those who held to the marquis were greatly afraid that they would name someone other than the marquis. And as they were waiting there all quiet, the bishop of Soissons rose to his feet and said to them: 'Lords,' said the bishop, 'by the common consent of all of you we have been delegated to make this election. We have chosen one whom we ourselves knew to be a good man for it, one in whom rule is well placed and who is right well able to maintain the law, a man of gentle birth and a high man. We will name him to you. He is Baldwin, count of Flanders.' When the word was heard, all the French were right glad of it, but there were some others, like those who held for the marquis, who were greatly displeased.

When the emperor was elected, the bishops and all the high barons and the French, who were very happy over it, took him and led him to the palace of Boukoleon, joyfully and with great rejoicing. When the high men were all together there, they chose a day for crowning the emperor. And when it was come to that day, the bishops and abbots and all the high barons, both Venetians and French, mounted their horses and went to the palace of Boukoleon. Then they led the emperor to the church of Saint Sophia, and when they were come to the church, they took the emperor to a place apart in the church into a chamber. There they divested him of his outer garments and took off his *chausses* and put on him *chausses* of vermilion samite and shoes all covered with rich stones. Then they put on him a very rich coat all fastened with gold buttons in front and behind from the shoulders clear to the girdle. And then they put on him the *palle*, a kind of cloak which fell to the top of the shoes in front and was so long behind that he wound it about his middle and then brought it back over his left arm like the maniple of a priest. And this *palle* was very rich and noble and all covered with precious stones. Then over this they put a very rich mantle, which was all covered with precious stones, and the eagles on it were made of precious stones and shone so that it seemed as if the whole mantle were aflame. When he was vested in this manner, they led him in front of the altar, and as they led him there, Count Louis bore his imperial standard and the count of St Pol bore his sword and the marquis bore his crown, and two bishops held up the arms of the marquis who bore the crown and two other bishops stood at the sides of the emperor. And all the barons were very richly clothed and there was no Frenchman or Venetian who did not have a robe either of samite or of cloth of silk. When the emperor was come before the altar, he knelt down and they took off first the mantle and then the *palle*, so that he was left in his coat, and then they unfastened the coat by the gold buttons in front and behind, so that he was all bare from the girdle up, and then they anointed him. When he was anointed, they put on again the coat with its gold buttons, and then they vested him again with the *palle* and then they fastened the mantle over his shoulder. When he was thus vested and the two bishops were holding the crown on the altar, then all the bishops went and took hold of the crown all together and blessed it and made the sign of the cross on it and put it on his head. And then to serve as a clasp they hung about his neck a very rich jewel which the emperor Manuel had once bought for sixty-two thousand marks.[1]

When they had crowned him, they seated him on a high throne, and he was there while the mass was sung, and he held in one hand his scepter and in the other hand a golden globe with a cross on it. And the jewels which he was wearing were worth more than the treasure of a rich king would make. When the mass was heard, they brought him a white horse on which he mounted. Then the barons took him back to his palace of Boukoleon and seated him on the throne of Constantine. Then when he was seated on the throne of Constantine, they all did homage to him as emperor and all the Greeks who were there bowed down before him as the sacred emperor. Then the tables were placed and the emperor ate and all the barons with him in the palace. When they had eaten, the barons all departed and went to their houses and the emperor remained in his palace.

[1] Chalandon cites from Kinnamos a description of the robes worn by Manuel I at the reception of Kilidj-Arslan in 1161 – a great purple robe encrusted with carbuncles and pearls, and on his breast an enormous ruby the size of an apple.

[8] The sacred relics in the Great Church; from *Sancta Sophia Constantinople: a Study of Byzantine Building*, by W.R. Lethaby and Harold Swainson.

The True Cross. – There would seem to be little doubt that a discovery was made about 326 of what was supposed to be the true Cross. S. Cyril of Jerusalem, writing some twenty-five years later, says that portions of the Cross were spread all over the world. We have seen that early historians relate that a portion of this precious relic was sent to Constantinople by Helena. The principal part however remained at Jerusalem until it was taken by Chosroes. It is described by some of the pilgrims to the holy city as being encased in silver. Brought back from Persia by Heraclius in 628 together with the spear and sponge, it rested for a brief interval in S. Sophia, where it was 'uplifted'; but it was again returned to Jerusalem until 636, when under the fear of the coming troubles the larger portion at least was removed. Rohault de Fleury, who devoted a folio volume to the Instruments of the Passion, quotes a letter from Anseau, a priest of the Holy Sepulchre in the twelfth century, which was sent to Paris with a portion of the Cross. According to this account the Holy Wood was divided into nineteen small Crosses, of which Constantinople possessed three besides the 'Cross of the Emperor,' and Jerusalem retained four. We have positive evidence that in the century before Heraclius Constantinople was a centre where portions of the Cross were to be obtained: thus Radegunde, wife of Clothaire, received a fragment from Justin II and Sophia in 569. At this time, according to John of Ephesus, there was 'a day of the adoration of the Holy Cross of our Saviour; on this festival the Cross is brought out and set up in the Great Church, and the senate and all the people of the city assemble to worship it.' Probably the Exaltation was celebrated concurrently at Jerusalem and at Constantinople.

When we more definitely hear of the True Cross at S. Sophia, it is evident, from the frequent occasions in which it is transported to different parts of the church, and to the palace, that it was quite small, a relic in fact.

Arculf (*circa* 680), as we have seen, describes it as kept in a chest, on a golden altar, which was only two cubits long by one broad. He says: 'it should be specially noticed that there are not two but three short pieces of wood in the cross; that is, the cross beam, and the long one divided into two equal parts.'

Fig. 14 [*left*] represents the Poitiers reliquary . . . We cannot doubt that the Cross at Constantinople was of this form. Was it the result of the conjunction of three pieces as mentioned by Arculph, or did the upper arm from the first represent the label?

With the Cross were associated the other instruments of the Passion – the Crown of Thorns, the Sponge and Spear, and slabs from the Tomb.

The catalogue of relics by Nicholas Thingeyrensis (1200) says, 'In S. Sophia is the Cross of the Lord which Helena the Queen brought;' but at that time the greater part of the Cross and other relics of the Passion seem to have been transferred to the chapel in the palace of Boucoleon, where they were seen by Robert de Clari (1200). The anniversary of the day on which they were moved from S. Sophia, August 14th, was kept as a holiday. According to Paspates all the relics of the Passion were removed in 1234. Baldwin II took the Crown of Thorns which was acquired by S. Louis. It is evident, however, from the later Pilgrims quoted below, and from Mandeville, that a part of the Passion relics remained or that others were acquired.

Other Treasure and Relics. – A description of the relics and the treasure of Constantinople is given in the letter supposed to have been written in 1095 by Alexius Comnenus to Robert, Count of Flanders, in which he craves the assistance of the West against the Turks. After enumerating the relics scattered throughout the city, he continues, 'If you do not care to fight for these, and gold will tempt you more, you will find more of it at Constantinople than in the whole world, for the treasures of its basilicas alone would be sufficient to furnish all the churches of Christendom, and all their treasures cannot together amount to those of S. Sophia, whose riches have never been equalled even in the temple of Solomon.'

The dispersion of the relics and treasures of S. Sophia and the other churches at Constantinople has been exhaustively treated by Count Riant. The description by Anthony, Archbishop of

Novgorod, who visited S. Sophia in 1200, three years before the capture by the Crusaders, furnishes the best account of the accumulated riches of the great church. We give this in full from the French version contained in *Itinéraires Russes en Orient*.

'I, Antonius, Archbishop of Novgorod, an unworthy and humble sinner, by the grace of God and by the help of S. Sophia, who is the Wisdom and the Eternal Word, reached in safety the imperial city, and entered the great Catholic and Apostolic Church. We first worshipped S. Sophia, kissing the two slabs of the Lord's sepulchre. Furthermore we saw the seals, and the figure of the Mother of God, nursing Christ. This image a Jew at Jerusalem pierced in the neck with a knife, and blood flowed forth. The blood of the image, all dried up, we saw in the smaller sanctuary.

'In the sanctuary of S. Sophia is the blood of the holy martyr Pantaleon with milk, placed in a reliquary like a little branch or bough, yet without their having mixed. Besides that there is his head, and the head of the Apostle Quadratus, and many relics of other saints: the heads of Hermolaus and Stratonicus; the arm of Germanus, which is laid on those who are to be ordained patriarchs; the image of the Virgin which Germanus sent in a boat to Rome by sea; and the small marble table on which Christ celebrated His Supper with the disciples, as well as His swaddling clothes and the golden vessels, which the Magi brought with their offerings. . . .

'Outside the smaller sanctuary is erected the "Crux Mensuralis," which shows the height of Christ when on earth; and behind that cross is buried Anna, who gave her house to S. Sophia, where now is the smaller sanctuary, and she is buried near. And near this same smaller sanctuary are the figures of the holy women and of the Virgin Mother holding Christ, and shedding tears which fall on the eyes of Christ. They give of the water of the sanctuary for the blessing of the world.

'In the same part is the chapel of S. Peter the Apostle, where S. Theophania is buried. She was the guardian of the keys of S. Sophia, which people used to kiss. There is also suspended the carpet of S. Nicholas. The iron chains of S. Peter are kept there in a gold chest; during the feast of "S. Peter's Chains" the emperor, the patriarch, and all the congregation kiss them. Near by, in another chapel, is also shown the crystal of the ancient ambo, destroyed when the dome fell. . . .

'When one turns towards the gate one sees at the side the column of S. Gregory the Miracle-Worker, all covered with bronze plates. S. Gregory appeared near this column, and the people kiss it, and rub their breasts and shoulders against it to be cured of their pains; there is also the image of S. Gregory. On his feast day the patriarch brings his relics to this column. And there placed above a platform is a great figure of the Saviour in mosaic; it lacks the little finger of the right hand. When it was finished, the artist looked at it and said, "Lord, I have made thee as if alive." Then a voice coming from the picture said, "When hast thou seen me?" The artist was struck dumb and died, and the finger was not finished, but was made in silver-gilt. . . .

'Above the great altar in the middle is hung the crown of the Emperor Constantine, set with precious stones and pearls. Below it is a golden cross, which overhangs a golden dove.'

[9] The fate of many treasures from the great Church; from *Sancta Sophia Constantinople: a Study of Byzantine Building by* W.R. Lethaby and Harold Swainson.

Frankish Occupation and After. – Three years after the visit of Anthony [*of Novgorod*], Constantinople was taken by the Latins. One of the Crusaders, Villehardouin, writes, 'Of holy relics I need only say it contained more than all Christendom combined; there is no estimating the quantity of gold, silver, precious vessels, jewels, rich stuffs, silks, robes of vair, gris, and ermine, and other valuable things – the production of all the climates in the world. It is the belief of me, Geoffrey Villehardouin, maréchal of Champagne, that the plunder of this city exceeded all that has been witnessed since the creation of the world.'

Much of the accumulated wealth of six centuries – the gifts from emperors and private individuals of 'sacred vessels of gold and pearls and precious stones' – was removed by the Venetians and Franks. Many of these precious objects are lost beyond hope of recovery; such are the candlesticks and crosses. In the treasury of S. Mark's at Venice there is however a rich hoard of vessels, lamps, and other objects, which were taken from the churches of Constantinople; and many of these crystal lamps, agate cups, and enamelled book-covers doubtless belonged to S. Sophia.

[10] The Great Church becomes Catholic after a reconciliation with Rome in 1452, but the Patriarch Gennadius and the Grand Admiral Notaras are bitterly opposed to it; from *Histoire de l'Empire Ottoman* by Ritter J. von Hammer-Purgstall. Translated by Laurence Kelly.

(Freiherr Joseph von Hammer (he added the Purgstall to his name to qualify for an inheritance) was born in Graz, Austria in 1774 and died, covered in academic honours, in 1856. His reputation rested on a prodigious output of books on Oriental languages, and he also served as a Court interpreter and diplomat in Constantinople. *The History of the Ottoman Empire* published in 1835, was his *magnum opus*.)

At the same time as Mohammed's troops were threatening the very gates of Constantinople with their sorties, its denizens were torn asunder in mad quarrels about whether or not to reunite the Orthodox and Latin Churches. In the Great Church on 12 December 1452 there had been a semblance of reconciliation between the two factions, but this 'reconciliation' was born only of the hope of persuading the Great Powers of Europe to come to their aid. The fires of schism still burnt, and every day witnessed another outbreak of scandalous disputes . . . The reciprocal hatred of the dissidents was at its peak; the Court clergy, chaplains and deacons took part in the Latin Mass celebrated by Cardinal Isidore, at which the Emperor was present, but the abbots, archimandrites and monks abstained in horror, and clustered about the cloister of the Church of the Pantocrator where the Patriarch Gennadius was under house arrest. From his cell this fanatic thundered anathema against the Azymites and considered the *henoticon*, or decree ordering the reunion of the Churches, an impious agreement; St Thomas Acquinas, he proclaimed, was capable of heresy. The Patriarch's speeches – heard as Gospel truth – excited a large public blindly ready to abet discord; its attitudes were already poisoned by the unyielding hatred of the Grand Duke Lucas Notaras, who was the most powerful enemy of the Catholics at Court. One day he went so far as to say that he would prefer to see in Constantinople not the hat of a cardinal but rather the turban of a Turk. The public, less fanatical than that, was prepared to accept the Latin yoke if a choice had to be made – since they did believe in Christ

Haghia Sophia; by G. Fossati in *Aya Sofiya Constantinople as recently restored*, 1852

and Our Lady – rather than that of Turks who were the sworn enemies of the Christian faith.

[11] The Fall of Constantinople, 1453 – Sultan Mehmet II enters Haghia Sophia and turns it into a mosque; from *The Decline and Fall of the Roman Empire* by Edward Gibbon.

The celestial image of the Virgin had been exposed in solemn procession; but their divine patroness was deaf to their entreaties: they accused the obstinacy of the emperor for refusing a timely surrender; anticipated the horrors of their fate, and sighed for the repose and security of Turkish servitude. The noblest of the Greeks, and the bravest of the allies, were summoned to the palace, to prepare them, on the evening of the twenty-eighth, for the duties and dangers of the general assault. The last speech of [Constantine] Palaeologus was the funeral oration of the Roman Empire: he promised, he conjured, and he vainly attempted to infuse the hope which was extinguished in his own mind. In this work all was comfortless and gloomy; and neither the gospel nor the church have proposed any conspicuous recompense to the heroes who fall in the service of their country. But the example of their prince and the confinement of a siege had armed these warriors with the courage of despair; and the pathetic scene is described by the feelings of the historian Phranza, who was himself present at this mournful assembly. They wept, they embraced; regardless of their families and fortunes, they devoted their lives; and each commander, departing to his station, maintained all night a vigilant and anxious watch on the rampart. The emperor, and some faithful companions, entered the dome of St Sophia, which in a few hours was to be converted into a mosque; and devoutly received, with tears and prayers, the sacrament of the holy communion. He reposed some moments in the palace, which resounded with cries and lamentations; solicited the pardon of all whom he might have injured; and mounted on horseback to visit the guards and explore the motions of the enemy. The distress and fall of the last Constantine are more glorious than the long prosperity of the Byzantine Cæsars. . . .

From the first hour of the memorable twenty-ninth of May, disorder and rapine prevailed in Constantinople till the eighth hour of the same day; when the sultan himself passed in triumph through the gate of St Romanus. He was attended by his vizirs, bashaws, and guards, each of whom (says a Byzantine historian) was robust as Hercules, dexterous as Apollo, and equal in battle to any ten of the race of ordinary mortals. The conqueror gazed with satisfaction and wonder on the strange though splendid appearance of the domes and palaces, so dissimilar from the style of Oriental architecture. In the hippodrome, or *atmeidan*, his eye was attracted by the twisted column of the three serpents; and, as a trial of his strength, he shattered with his iron mace or battle-axe the under-jaw of one of these monsters, which in the eye of the Turks were the idols or talismans of the city. At the principal door of St Sophia, he alighted from his horse and entered the dome; and such was his jealous regard for that monument of his glory that, on observing a zealous Musulman in the act of breaking the marble pavement, he admonished him with his scymetar that, if the spoil and captives were granted to the soldiers, the public and private buildings had been reserved for the prince. By his command the metropolis of the Eastern church was transformed into a mosque: the rich and portable instruments of superstition had been removed; the crosses were thrown down; and the walls, which were covered with images and mosaics, were washed and purified and restored to a state of naked simplicity. On the same day, or on the ensuing Friday, the *muezin* or crier ascended the most lofty turret, and proclaimed the *ezan* or public invitation, in the name of God and his prophet; the imam preached; and Mahomet the Second performed the *namaz* of prayer and thanksgiving on the great altar, where the Christian mysteries had so lately been celebrated before the last of the Caesars. From St Sophia he proceeded to the august but desolate mansion of an hundred successors of the great Constantine; but which, in a few hours, had been stripped of the pomp of royalty. A melancholy reflection of the vicissitudes of human greatness forced itself on his mind; and he repeated an elegant distich of Persian poetry, 'The spider has wove his web in the imperial palace; and the owl hath sung her watch-song on the towers of Afrasiab'.

[12] Sultan Mehmet's first service in the mosque of Ayasofya – an Ottoman description; from *Narrative of Travels in Europe, Asia, and Africa in the Seventeenth Century* by Evliya Efendi, translated by Ritter J. von Hammer Purgstall.

(Evliya Celebi Efendi (1611–1684) was the author of the *Seyahatname* (Travels); 'Evliya' was his pen-name, adopted in veneration of his teacher, the Court Imam. His father was chief jeweller to the Court and consequently a very rich man; his mother a Causasian odalisque from the Imperial harem. He was brilliantly trained as a Koran reciter, calligraphist, musician and Arabist. Sultan Murad IV greatly appreciated his talents as a storyteller, and his lively character. He travelled widely through the Ottoman Empire and spent eight or nine years in Egypt. The Encyclopaedia of Islam says that he 'prefers legend to bare fact'; but his travels are an invaluable source-book for the life of contemporary Istanbul.)

Sultan Mohammed Khan, Father of Victory (*i.e.* the Conqueror), a Sultan son of a Sultan of the Islamitic sovereigns of the House of Osman, entered Islambol victoriously on Wednesday the 20th day of Jumaziu-l-akhir, in the year of the Prophet's flight 867 [1st July, AD 1453], as was expressed by the prophetic and descriptive letters of the text *beldetun toyyibetun* (a good city), and in the day, hour, and minute, which had been foretold to the Sultan by Ak-Shemsu-d-din. Several poets and men of learning have made other lines and technical words containing the date of this victory of victories; but the date found in the exalted Koran is complete, if the last letters are counted as they are pronounced. Sultan Mohammed II on surveying more closely the church of Aya Sofiyah, was astonished at the solidity of its construction, the strength of its foundations, the height of its cupola, and the skill of its builder, Aghnadus. He caused this ancient place of worship to be cleared of its idolatrous impurities and purified from the blood of the slain, and having refreshed the brain of the victorious Moslems by fumigating it with amber and lign-aloes, converted it in that very hour into a jami (a cathedral), by erecting a contracted mihrab, minber, mahfil, and menareh, in that place which might rival Paradise. On the following Friday, the faithful were summoned to prayer by the muezzins, who proclaimed with a loud voice this text (Kor. xxxiii. 56): 'Verily, God and his angels bless the Prophet.' Ak-Shemsu-d-din and Karah Shemsu-d-din then arose, and placing themselves on each side of the Sultan, supported him under his arms; the former placed his own turban on the head of the conqueror, fixing in it a black and white feather of a crane, and putting into his hand a naked sword. Thus conducted to the minber he ascended it, and cried out with a voice as loud as David's, 'Praise be to God the Lord of all worlds,' (Kor. i. 1.) on which all the victorious Moslems lifted up their hands and uttered a shout of joy. The Sultan then officiating as khatib pronounced the khutbeh, and descending from the minber, called upon Ak-Shemsu-d-din to perform the rest of the service as Imam. On that Friday the patriarch and no less than three thousand priests who had been concealed underneath the floor of the church, were honoured by being received into Islam. One of them, who was three hundred years old, they named Baba Mohammed. This man pointed out a hidden treasure on the right side of the mihrab, saying it was placed there by Suleiman (Solomon), the first builder of this ancient place of worship. The Sultan having first offered up prayer there for the prosperity and perpetuity of the place, caused the ground to be dug up beneath it, and during a whole week many thousand camel-loads of treasure in coins of Tekiyanus and Okiyunus, were carried away and deposited in the royal treasury and in the garden of the arsenal.

[13] The Mausoleum of Sultan Murad III and his children at Ayasofya; from *Narrative of Travels in Europe, Asia, and Africa in the Seventeenth Century* by Evliya Efendi, translated by Ritter J. von Hammer-Purgstall.

Murad was born in 953 (1546), and ascended the throne in the year 962 (1554) on Wednesday the eighth of Ramazan. When his father Selim waged war with his brother Bayazid at Konia, Murad witnessed it from the walls of that town, and was sent with the news of its issue to Sultan Suleiman, his grandfather, who rewarded him, although he was then only two years of age, with the government of Magnesia. Murad III never himself took the field, but the conquests of the empire were multiplied every year by his generals. He was buried beneath a separate cupola with his children, in the harem (court-yard) of Aya Soifiyah. He was the first Ottoman sovereign who lived and died at Constantinople without having once left it. Being much given to women and pleasure he had an immense number of male and female children, altogether three hundred and twenty-six. It is stated that in one single night fifty five of his women were lying in. At his death nineteen princes were killed according to the bloody code of the Ottoman empire. One of them, a very young boy, was eating chesnuts at the moment the executioner came in, to whom he said, 'Let me eat my chesnuts, and strangle me afterwards.' A request with which the executioner did not comply. Another was torn from his mother's breast and put to death, emitting at the same time his mother's milk by the nose, and his soul by his mouth. Twenty six daughters, some of them married to vezírs, survived their father. They all now lie buried in his sepulchre. God's mercy upon them!

[14] A Christian Frenchman visits the mosque of Ayasofya in the 1670s, and is nearly caught; from *A Late Voyage to Constantinople (1680)* by G.J. Grelot, translated by J. Philips.

(Guillaume Joseph Grelot, traveller and painter, was born in 1630. He accompanied John Chardin on his famous journey to the Crimea, Persia and India between 1671 and 1676. His visit to Constantinople took place before 1680, in which year he published his account of it. Grelot also illustrated Chardin's *Travels*, his work being highly praised for its accuracy and admirable detail.)

[In Constantinople Grelot meets two men who have a commission from a Christian king to draw the interior of Haghia Sophia: since they are too nervous to attempt it, he decides to hazard it instead. He bribes a Greek goldsmith to introduce him to some of the Candilasti – *Turks who look after the 2,000 lamps in the mosque – and asks their chief to help him, an infidel, enter the mosque in secret for this purpose.]*

I understood by his canting what he drove at, and that there was a necessity of some other than the usual key to open the Gallery doors. To this end I made use of a neat Watch that I had bought by chance for three *Venetian Sequins*, though it were worth above six, and which I carry'd with me out of a design to present him if he accomplish'd my purpose. This Watch I drew out, lookt what was a Clock, and then wound it up before his face. The baite took, the *Muchtar* fail'd not to ask me to let him see it, and finding it pleas'd his fancy, demanded of me if I would sell it. I answer'd the Watch Was worth ten *Sequins*, but since it pleas'd him, I would present it to him *jaba* or gratis, if by his permission I might see the inside of *Sancta Sophia*, and stay there three or four days at several times, that I would go in before *Salem-namasi*, or before day break Prayer, and that I would not stir out till after *Accham-namas* or Evening Prayer: which since he had the Keyes himself, might be done without any hazard to himself or me, so he let no body in besides my self.

The covetous fox, having his eyes dazl'd with the sight of my

Watch, cry'd out, *bré guidi kiafer choc istersen bir sahat ichun. Ah Devil of an Infidell you ask too much for your Watch.* However he added, that seeing the earnest desire I had, he willingly granted for his part what I demanded; but that not being the only person that kept the Keyes of the Galleries, therefore to make sure work, it behov'd me to speak to two Officers of the Mosquee, who as well as himself had all the Keyes of the same places; however he did not question but that for some small matter he should prevail with them to my satisfaction, and that he would give notice to the Goldsmith of his success.

The *Greek* either out of affection or interest seem'd to be most passionately concern'd in my behalf, not giving himself any rest for solliciting the *Candilasti* or Lamp-lighter to perform his promise, so that in few days he came to me like one overjoy'd, and told me that my business was effected, that I had nothing to do but to go the next Morning, being *Monday*, and wait at the private door of the *Mosquee*, which would not fail to fly open to me, by vertue of the charmes of my Watch and four *Sequins* more, which I was to give to the two other Officers mention'd by the *Muctar*: who being satisfy'd, I might have liberty to draw, take measures, and do what else I pleas'd, but dig up the Foundations of the Mosquee.

I that had never pay'd less than five and twenty *per cent* for my Bills of Exchange, that I might not fail of my time, and thought my Watch a sufficient price for the satisfaction of my curiosity, was very loath to part with my four *Sequins*, to the value of Ten Crowns; considering withal, that it was not a Mile to the bottom of my purse. Nevertheless after many contests in vain, feeing those *Adorers* of Silver would not bate me a doit, alleadging still the great danger and hazard which they ran for my sake, I was perswaded to cross the Cudgells, that I might see some thing in *Constantinople*, which was a raritie, and which I was assur'd that no person but my self was ever before Master of: Thereupon I went to the place appointed, and foreseeing that there would be some want of a little refreshment in regard I was not going to keep the *Turkish* Ramazan or Lent, but only to draw the Draught of the Church, I carry'd with me a *Bologna Sawsage*, a Bottle of Wine, and a Loaf. Which had been sufficient to have cost me my dear life, had they found me eating Bacon and drinking Wine, the two abominations chiefly forbidden by their Law, and polluting with them the holyest of all their Mosquees. Thus I

Interior of the mosque of Ayasofya; by G. Fossati in *Aya Sofiya Constantinople as recently restored*, 1852

spent the first day well enough without any interruption in the Gallery. But the next day was not so calm. For whilst the *Turks* were at their Devotions, I fell to my Sawsage and Wine, and by that time they had done Praying, I had done eating; and was fallen very serious again to my business. When lo, athwart the Pillars at the other end of the Church in the Galleries, I perceiv'd a tall long fellow stalking toward that part where I was, who I found had let himself in at another door than that at which my Introductor had let me in.

I was firmly of belief, seeing a white Turbant, and a person whom I knew not, that my business was done, should it prove to be any other, than one of those whom the Muctar had made of the conspiracy. I was in a strange *Quandary*; sometimes I thought, because I was at my repast while the *Turks* were at Prayers, that some person had spy'd me from below, as having perhaps had the ill luck while the people in the Mosquee were prostrated with their heads to the earth, and kissing the Ground and crying out *Alla hecher*, to have too much exalted mine out of my zeal to drink their healths, and to play upon my soft Instrument to their lowd Musick. I was in a peck of troubles, and knew not what to do in the condition wherein I was: besides that I knew not where to bestow my papers, pencills and Bottle, for which I could find no excuse in the world. It was a crime that neither stake nor fire could hardly have expiated, to find a *Giaur* making figures, eating Pork, and drinking Wine, in the *Turks Holy of Holyes*. I must confess I was never in such a Pannic dread in all my life, and that I never saw the shape and likeness of death so exactly drawn before my eyes in all my days.

However though I firmly believ'd my self to be a person no longer of this world, yet that I might not be surpriz'd with my Bottle and Sawsage, I hid them together with my papers under a Carpet in a dark corner, with all the speed I could, and so drawing forth my Rosary, and a certain book which I had about me, written by *Peter Gilius*, I return'd to my seat, and put my self into a posture of one that had but newly said his Prayers. Every step the *Turk* made toward the upper *Portico*, from whence I had been drawing the bottom of the Church, my deadly fears augmented. But in regard he came but slowly on, I had time to recollect my Spirits, to put on a good face, and confirm my self in those resolutions I had always taken, which were rather to lose my Life a thousand times, than my *Praeputium* once.

Thus feigning my self to be at my Prayers, held my book, which I had no great maw to look in at that time, in my left hand, and my Rosary in my right hand, with the Beads whereof I was fumbling, when the *Turk* approach'd me; and instead of a

Salamalek, or *How d'ye do*, cry'd, *Brè guida giaur ne uhlersen bonda; Villain of an Infidel! what mak'st thou here?* I answer'd him, after I had look'd very seriously in my Book, and turn'd over two or three of my Beads according to the Musselmen's manner: *Sir, I am at my Prayers, stay a little while I beseech ye.* – After which, having made a Genuflexion, together with the sign of the Cross, I rose up to speak to him. *Salamalekum Aga*, said I, or *Good day t'ye, Sir*; then going on, *You need not wonder, Sir*, quoth I, *to find a Christian alone in the Galleries of* Sancta Sophia; adding, *he knew it was a Church formerly built by the Christians, who had still a great Veneration for it, and being one of those, that I had obtain'd permission to be let in, to the end I might spend some few hours in Devotion and Prayer, and that I expected him who had let me in, to come suddenly and let me out again.*

The *Turk*, who was one of those who had shar'd my four *Sequins*, having heard me, presently seren'd his tempestuous Countenance, not being able to forbear laughing, to see in what a cold sweat he had put me (for he might easily read my distemper in my looks), and to hear what a fine lye I had got already chew'd for him. Thereupon he bid me be of good comfort, and cry'd, *Courcmas Adam, Fear nothing*; *I knew*, said he, *you were here*; and so having shew'd him some of my Draughts which he desir'd to see, he left me to take off the rest of my Bottle to recruit my Spirits.

[15] The Friday prayers, or *Namaz*, in Ayasofya; from *Turkey in Europe* by Sir Charles Eliot KCMG.

(Sir Charles Eliot (1862–1931) served at Constantinople from 1893 to 1898 as Third Secretary. He was a Privy Councillor, as well as an excellent linguist, and a scholar in Sanskrit and Syrian. He became an honorary Fellow of Trinity College, and had a second life as an academic, being Vice Chancellor of Sheffield University in 1905 and running the University of Hong Kong, before becoming a distinguished Ambassador to Japan.)

A little before the time for prayer an official called Muezzin mounts the minaret and calls out a formula known as the Ezan, which is as follows: 'God is most great (*four times*). I testify that there is no God but God (*twice*). I testify that Mohammed is the Prophet of God (*twice*). Come to prayer (*twice*). Come to salvation (*twice*). God is most great (*twice*). There is no God but God.' Inside the mosque the Mollahs sitting on the elevated platform repeat the same call, adding at the end, 'Prayers are now ready.' Meanwhile worshippers have been dropping in and take their places in long lines across the mosque. As they enter they put off their shoes and leave them at the door. This usage is not really ceremonial, but intended to keep clean the floor, which is covered with matting. Those who have not performed their ablutions at home wash their hands, feet, and faces in the mosque, and take water into their mouths. Before beginning his prayers each person repeats to himself a formula called Niyet: 'I propose to offer up this day to God alone, with a sincere heart and my face turned towards Mecca, prayers of' so many *rikats*. The Imam stands alone in front of the congregation, facing the Mihrab. The first part of the Namaz is not said in unison, but by each person for himself, kneeling and rising independently of his fellows. This is because the *rikats* in question are *sunnet*, and not *farz*. As soon as the *farz rikats* begin the whole congregation perform the prescribed gestures simultaneously with the regularity of soldiers at drill. The movements of the Imam are the same as those of the congregation, and, as already explained, all the *rikats* are similar. The worshipper raises his hands to the side of his head, and, touching his ears with his thumb, says, 'God is most great.' Then, with his hands folded below his waist and looking at the ground, he says, 'I extol Thee, O God, and praise be to Thee: blessed be Thy name and Thy greatness be magnified and Thy praise be glorified, for there is no God save Thee.' Then he says, 'I seek refuge in God from Satan, the accursed,' and then recites the Fatiha, or first chapter of the Koran: 'In the name of God, the Merciful, the Compassionate, Praise be to God, the Lord of the Worlds, the Merciful, the compassionate, the Ruler of the Day of Judgment. Thee do we serve, and of Thee we ask aid: lead us in the straight way, the way of those to whom Thou art gracious, not of those against whom Thou art wroth, nor of those that err.' After this he repeats as many verses of the Koran as he thinks proper. As a rule the Ikhlas (LXII.) is used, 'Say, He is God alone: God the eternal: He begetteth not, and is not begotten: And there is none like unto Him.' Then he bows down, placing his hands on his knees, but still standing, and says, 'God is most great. I praise God' (Subhana 'llah), the latter thrice. Then, still erect, but with his hands at the side of his body, 'God hears him who praises Him. O Lord Thou art praised.' Then he falls on his knees and again says, 'God is most great;' and then prostrating himself, with his forehead on the ground, repeats thrice 'Subhana 'llah.' Then raising his body and sitting on his heels, he says, 'God is most great;' and then prostrating himself again, again repeats, 'God is most great – I praise God.' This ends one *rikat*. The second *rikat* of a series omits the introductory formulae and commences with the *fatiha*. After every two *rikats* the worshipper sits down with his left foot under him, and spreading his hands on his knees says the following prayers: 'Homage is due to God, and prayers and good works. Peace be upon thee, O Prophet, and the mercy of God and His blessing. Peace be upon us and on the righteous servants of God.' Then holding up the first finger of the right hand, 'I testify that there is no God but God, and I testify that Mohammed is His slave and prophet.' Every two *rikats* end with this formula, which is called Teshahhud. At the end of the whole set of *rikats* which make up any set of prayers, the following is recited in the same sitting posture:—

'O God, have mercy on our Lord Mohammed and the family of Mohammed, as Thou didst have mercy on Abraham and the family of Abraham; for Thou art worthy to be praised, and Thou art glorious.'

'O God, bless our Lord Mohammed and the family of Mohammed, as Thou didst bless Abraham and the family of Abraham; for Thou art worthy to be praised, and Thou art glorious.'

'O Lord God, give us the blessings of this life and the blessings of life everlasting; save us from the torments of hell.'

Then turning the head first to the left and then to the right, he says twice, 'The peace and mercy of God be with you.'

The full mid-day prayer on ordinary days consists of ten *rikats*, four *sunnet*, four *farz*, and two more *sunnet* after the *farz*. On Friday two extra *sunnet rikats* are recited, and there is also a sort of sermon. A Mollah ascends the pulpit and pronounces an oration called *khutbe*. In St Sophia, and other mosques which were once churches, he leans on a sword when preaching, and it is said that in time of war he holds a drawn sword in his hand. The *khutbe* is perhaps hardly a sermon in our sense of the word, for it is largely addressed to the Deity, and contains prayers for the protection and triumph of Islam. It also contains a commemoration of the early Caliphs and companions of the Prophet (after each of whose names the congregation respond, 'May God be pleased with him'), and a prayer for the present Caliph. In Afghanistan and other independent Moslim kingdoms I believe the sovereign of the country is prayed for. In Russia and India prayers are sometimes offered for the long life of the Czar or Queen, but this is a very different matter to mentioning their name in the *khutbe*. 'God bless the King, God bless the faith's defender, God bless (no harm in blessing) the Pretender,' as the old Scotch song has it. On solemn occasions it is usual for the Imam to offer up extra prayers, selected or composed as he thinks best, which are called Munajat. I believe they are always recited when the Sultan is present.

Ruins of the Hippodrome as they appeared in AD 1450; after Onophrius Panvinius of Verona

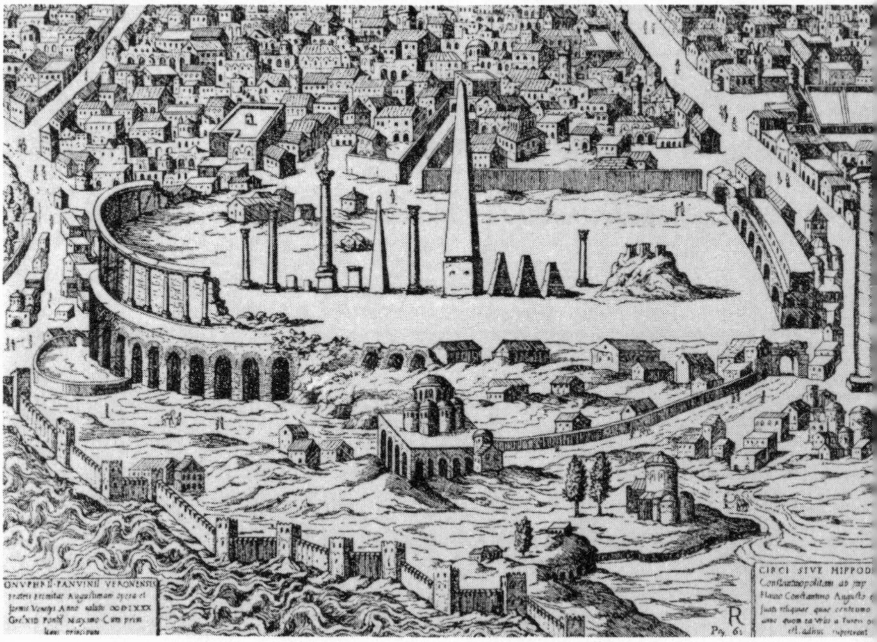

The Hippodrome (now the At Meydani)

[16] The ancient treasures of the Hippodrome; from *The Decline and Fall of the Roman Empire* by Edward Gibbon.

1. The victorious charioteers were cast in bronze, at their own or the public charge, and fitly placed in the hippodrome; they stood aloft in their chariots, wheeling round the goal; the spectators could admire their attitude, and judge of the resemblance; and of these figures the most perfect might have been transported from the Olympic stadium. 2. The sphynx, river-horse, and crocodile denote the climate and manufacture of Egypt and the spoils of that ancient province. 3. The she-wolf suckling Romulus and Remus: a subject alike pleasing to the *old* and the *new* Romans, but which could rarely be treated before the decline of the Greek sculpture. 4. An eagle holding and tearing a serpent in his talons: a domestic monument of the Byzantines, which they ascribed, not to a human artist, but to the magic power of the philosopher Apollonius, who, by his talisman, delivered the city from such venomous reptiles. 5. An ass and his driver, which were erected by Augustus in his colony of Nicopolis, to commemorate a verbal omen of the victory of Actium. 6. An equestrian statue, which passed, in the vulgar opinion, for Joshua, the Jewish conqueror, stretching out his hand to stop the course of the descending sun. A more classical tradition recognized the figures of Bellerophon and Pegasus; and the free attitude of the steed seemed to mark that he trode on air rather than on earth. 7. A square and lofty obelisk of brass: the sides were embossed with a variety of picturesque and rural scenes: birds singing; rustics labouring or playing on their pipes; sheep bleating; lambs skipping; the sea, and a scene of fish and fishing; little naked Cupids laughing, playing, and pelting each other with apples; and, on the summit, a female figure turning with the slightest breath, and thence denominted *the wind's attendant*. 8. The Phrygian shepherd presenting to Venus the prize of beauty, the apple of discord. 9. The incomparable statue of Helen, which is delineated by Nicetas in the words of admiration and love: her well-turned feet, snowy arms, rosy lips, bewitching smiles, swimming eyes,

arched eye-brows, the harmony of her shape, the lightness of her drapery, and her flowing locks that waved in the wind: a beauty that might have moved her barbarian destroyers to pity and remorse. 10. The manly or divine form of Hercules, as he was restored to life by the master-hand of Lysippus, of such magnitude that his thumb was equal to the waist, his leg to the stature, of a common man; his chest ample, his shoulders broad, his limbs strong and muscular, his hair curled, his aspect commanding. Without his bow, or quiver, or club, his lion's skin thrown carelessly over him, he was seated on an osier basket, his right leg and arm stretched to the utmost, his left knee bent, and supporting his elbow, his head reclining on his left hand, his countenance indignant and pensive. 11. A colossal statue of Juno, which had once adorned her temple of Samos; the enormous head by four yoke of oxen was laboriously drawn to the palace. 12. Another colossus, of Pallas or Minerva, thirty feet in height, and representing, with admirable spirit, the attributes and character of the martial maid. Before we accuse the Latins, it is just to remark that this Pallas was destroyed after the first siege by the fear and superstition of the Greeks themselves. The other statues of brass which I have enumerated were broken and melted by the unfeeling avarice of the crusaders; the cost and labour were consumed in a moment; the soul of genius evaporated in smoke; and the remnant of base metal was coined into money for the payment of the troops.

[17] The sixth-century Niké Riots; from *Count Belisarius* by Robert Graves.

(Constantinople at this period was divided into two municipal bodies, the Blues and the Greens: fierce rivalry existed between them, and this centred on the Hippodrome where all the Circus events became competitions between the two factions. Their rivalry even spilled over into theological disputes, the Greens supporting Monophytism against the Orthodoxy of the Blues. In 532, however, they combined against the Emperor Justinian because of heavy taxation.)

It was not until the fifth day of the riots, which was the eighteenth of January, that Theodora managed to persuade Justinian to

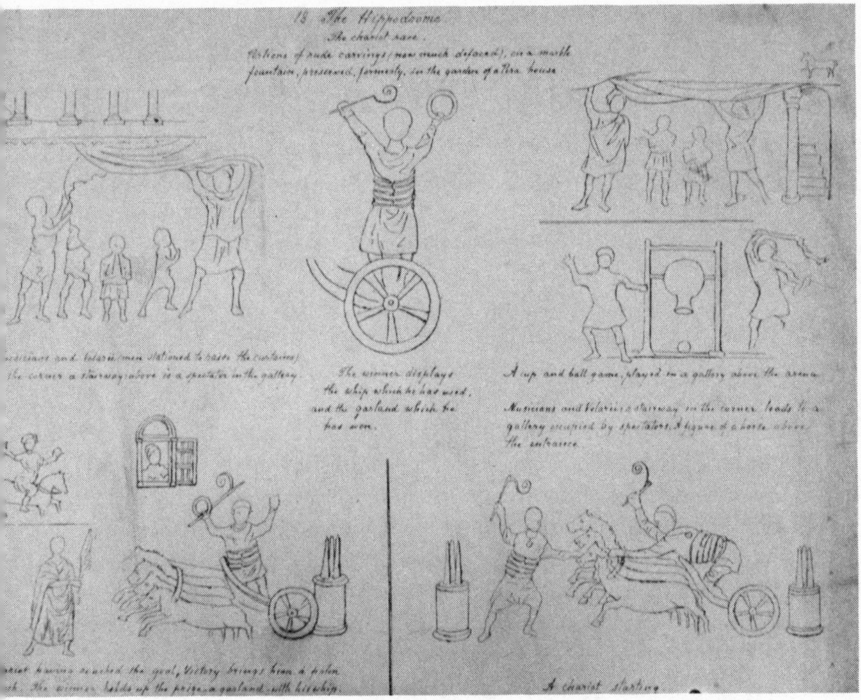

Chariot racing and other games in the Hippodrome; drawings from Broken Bits of Byzantium, 1887–91 by the Revd C.G. Curtis

enter the Hippodrome and make a public appeal for peace. The Hippodrome runs parallel with the Palace, on the slope leading down to the Sea of Marmora. At the northern end are two towers, and stables, chariot-sheds, and offices for the entertainers, and, high up to one side, at the point commanding the best view of the start, the Royal Box surmounted by the gilded horses from Chios. This Box was reached by a private colonnade from the Daphne Palace, skirting St Stephen's Church, so Justinian did not need to risk driving through the public streets. Holding a copy of the Gospels, he appeared in the Royal Box before the packed Hippodrome and began one of those vague paternal exhortations to peace and harmony, combined with vague promises, which are usually effective, after a riot, when popular heat is beginning to cool somewhat and the graver sort of people have begun to reckon up the damages. But it proved perfectly useless, because not backed up by any show of force. Half-hearted cheers came from the Blue benches, interspersed with hisses – but yells of execration from the Greens, who were now in the ascendant again, many deserters having returned to their old allegiance. Stones and other missiles were thrown at the Royal box, as once in Anastasius's time, and Justinian retired precipitately, the mob streaming out of the Hippodrome in pursuit of him. Thereupon the Thracian-Gothic Guards withdrew from the Palace and joined their fellows in the Brazen House. The mob plundered and burned down the extensive block of Palace buildings, adjacent to St Stephen's Church, which was the residence of the eunuchs of the Civil Service.

Now, the least worthless perhaps of Anastasius's worthless nephews, of whom one or other had been expected to succeed to the Throne before Justin seized it, was Hypatius. He had served under Belisarius at Daras, somewhat ingloriously indeed – it was his squadron that had been forced from the trenches on the right wing when the Immortals charged; but it could at least be held of him that his ambitions did not exceed his capacities. As soon as the riots broke out he came modestly to Justinian, with his brother Pompey, and said that the Greens had made approaches to him, offering him the Throne; that he had indignantly refused to countenance any movement on his behalf, and that to show his loyalty he now put himself at Justinian's disposal. Justinian praised and thanked Hypatius, though unable to understand his frankness in admitting that he had been offered the Throne – unless possibly as an attempt to disarm suspicion and seize the supreme power as soon as a favourable opportunity offered. But after this attack on the Palace, Justinian sent word to him and Pompey that they must leave at once if they did not wish to be executed as traitors. As soon as dark came, they slipped away, very unwillingly, and managed to enter their houses unnoticed. Unfortunately the news somehow reached the Greens that Hypatius was at large. They surrounded his house, forced it open, and carried him off in triumph to the Square of Constantine. There, at the centre of a tightly packed, screaming crowd, he was duly proclaimed Emperor, and crowned with a golden collar for want of a diadem, though the remainder of the insignia was available, having been plundered from the Palace. Hypatius was genuinely unwilling to accept the Throne; and his wife Mary, a pious Christian, wrung her hands and wailed that he was being taken from her along the road to death. But the

Greens were not to be gainsaid. . . .

Theodora entered the Council Chamber uninvited. She was so terrible in her scorn and rage that not only Justinian himself but everyone else present would sooner have died a hundred times than oppose those blazing eyes. She said: 'This is all talk, talk, talk, and as a woman of sense I protest against it, and demand that strong action be taken at once. This is already the sixth day of the disturbances, and each day I have been assured that "the matter is well in hand", and that "God will provide", and that "all possible steps are being taken", and so on and so forth. But nothing has been done yet – only talk, talk, talk, Bishops sent out with frivolous relics. The Gospels flourished in the faces of a great rabble of impious pigs – and then we run away when they grunt and squeal! You seem almost to have decided on flight, Justinian the Great. Very well, then, go! But at once, while you still possess a private harbour and boats and sailors and money! If, however, you do go, remember: you will never be able to return to this Palace, and they will hunt you down in the end and put you to a miserable and deserved death. . . . No, gird up your robes and run, for Heaven hates you! I shall remain here and face whatever doom my dignities enjoin upon me.'

Then Mundus and Belisarius put themselves under Theodora's orders – for nobody else seemed inclined to give them any. Justinian was wearing a monk's habit, as if for humility, but rather for a disguise should the Palace be attacked again. He was hard at prayer in the Royal chapel, his face covered with the coarse brown cowl. At this juncture an unexpected message came from Hypatius to Theodora: 'Noblest of women, since the Emperor suspects me and will do nothing for me, I beg you to trust my loyalty and send soldiers to release me from this predicament.' Theodora thereupon told Belisarius to place himself at the head of the Guards, rescue Hypatius, and bring him back to the Palace. Belisarius summoned the men of his Household who were encamped in the Palace grounds, and Mundus summoned his escort of Herulian Huns. The two forces together did not amount to more than 400 men, for the greater part of Belisarius's people had been lent to the Imperial Forces and were away in Thrace, under the command of Armenian John, enforcing the collection of taxes. Belisarius desired Mundus to take his Huns round by the winding alley called 'The Snail' to the Gate of Death, at the south-east of the Hippodrome, through which the dead bodies of gladiators had formerly been dragged. He was to wait there for orders. Then Belisarius himself rode with his people through the Palace grounds to the end of the High Street, where the Senate House is, and turned left to the gates of the Brazen House. Finding no sentry outside and the gates still shut, he rapped with the pommel of his sword and shouted: 'I am Belisarius, Commander of the Armies in the East. Open in the name of his Sacred Majesty, the Emperor Justinian!' But no answer came. The soldiers preferred, like the Senate, to wait on events. The gates were of massive brass and not easily forced, so after a second summons he went back to the Palace and reported to Theodora that the Guards were not available. She told him that he must do what he could with the few men at his disposal.

He decided to go past St Stephen's Church, now also burned, and straight up to the Royal Box. To do so he must pass through the ruins of the Eunuchs' Residence, which were still smouldering. Every now and then a wall would collapse or a sudden fire blaze up again. The horses were terrified by the smoke, and would not face it, so he gave the order to dismount and sent them back. Wetting their cloaks and wrapping them about their faces, his people rushed across in twos and threes and reached the Blue Colonnade of the Hippodrome (it is ornamented with sheer lapis-lazuli) which mounts gradually to the Royal Box. But they found the door at the end barred and guarded. It was dangerous to force it: that would mean fighting a way in darkness up a narrow staircase, while perhaps a crowd of Greens was sent round to attack them in the rear. Belisarius gave the order to turn about. This time he led his people along to the main entrance of the Hippodrome, on the northern side, between the towers.

I cannot say what the Greens were doing in the Hippodrome all this time, but I know that the Demarch and Democrat of the Greens both made boastful speeches, while the Blues present sat in glum silence. It was now plain that the Greens had succeeded in appointing an Emperor of their own colour; and the Blue Demarch bitterly repented having made that truce with them. Then suddenly a cry arose and Belisarius was seen marching into the Hippodrome, with his sword drawn, at the head of his mail-clad soldiers. He turned and called out to Hypatius as he sat in the Box above him: 'Illustrious Hypatius, it is the Emperor's seat that you have taken; and you have no right to occupy it. His orders are that you return at once to the Palace and place yourself at his disposal.'

To the general surprise (for only the leading factionists were aware how unwilling a monarch he was), Hypatius rose obediently and moved towards the door of the Box; but the Demarch of the Greens, who was seated near him, roughly forced him back into his chair. Then a crowd of Greens began to threaten Belisarius's men. He charged along the benches at them. They yelled and scrambled back in disorder. They were only a mob of City loafers, and their weapons were adapted for murder, not for fighting; moreover, they wore no armour. So Belisarius's 200 men, fully armoured, were fully a match for their thousands. Meanwhile Mundus, waiting outside the Gate of Death, heard the roar of alarm from within, and realized that Belisarius's people were engaged. He charged in with his Huns against the Greens, who were leaping over the barriers into the arena, and slaughtered them in droves. Some of them tried to take refuge on the pedestals of the statues ranged along the central barrier – that of the Emperor Theodosius with the napkin in his hand, and the three great twisted serpents, brought from Delphi, which once supported the priestess's tripod there, and the statues of famous charioteers, including one of my former master Damocles which Theodora had recently erected there – but these fugitives were soon pulled down and killed. Then the Blues, who were all seated together as usual, joined in the fight. Led by two of Justinian's own nephews, they made a rush for the Royal Box and, after a severe struggle, killed the Green Demarch and his men, secured Hypatius and Pompey and handed them over to Rufinus, who was assisting Belisarius. Rufinus conducted them to the Palace by way of the narrow staircase and the Blue Colonnade.

The Greens had now recovered from their surprise and began to fight desperately. Belisarius and Mundus were forced to go on killing methodically until once more the silk-clad simpletons with their billowing sleeves and their long, pomaded hair retreated in panic. At last Belisarius was able to withdraw some of his men peaceably to the North Gate and send others to guard the remaining gates; and Mundus also called off his Huns. But there was no holding back the Blues, who would now be satisfied only with a total extermination of the Greens. Belisarius and Mundus did not think it wise to interfere: they stood and grimly watched the fratricidal slaughter, as one might watch a battle between cranes and pygmies – with sympathies somewhat perhaps inclined to the side of the pygmies, who were almost as inhuman as the cranes, though not less grotesque in appearance. When it was clear that the Blues had won a handsome victory (in the names of the double-natured Son of his Vice-regent, the double-dealing Emperor), Belisarius returned to the Palace for further orders, and Mundus with him. Soon my mistress was embracing her dear husband, all bespattered with blood as he was. But a whole horde of Blues from the suburbs, where the Colour was very strong, now came running up with all sorts of weapons and burst into the Hippodrome to assist in the massacre. They had been armed at the Arsenal by Narses, who had bribed the Democrat of the Blues to call for volunteers against the usurping Hypatius. They were followed by the Guards from the Brazen House, equally eager now to show their loyalty to Justinian by a butchery of the Greens.

Thirty-five thousand Greens and a few hundred Blues were killed outright before the day ended, and a great many more were severely wounded. The crowd had also attacked the Green stables – killing grooms, and hamstringing the horses and burning chariots. Then began a furious hunt for unrepentant Greens throughout the City, and by the next morning there was not a man or woman left who was still wearing the hated favour. . . . Thus ended the so-called Victory Riots, and with them, for a time at least, the feud between Greens and Blues. The Greens were utterly broken, and Justinian stabilized this happy state of affairs by putting an end by edict to all chariot-racing in the City. However, it was revived again a few years later; so the Green faction was bound to be revived too. The Blues could not, after all, compete against themselves. In a few years' time the Greens had become as rowdy as ever, gathering together under the protection of their Colour all elements in the City hostile to the Emperor and to the Orthodox Faith; and once more there were murder-gangs abroad at dusk.

[18] The burning of the Bulgarian heretic Basil the Bogomil in the Hippodrome in 1116; from *The Alexiad of Anna Comnena*, translated by E.R.A. Sewter.

(The Princess Anna Comnena was born in 1083, first child of the Emperor Alexius and the Empress Irene. By 1097 she was married off to the Caesar, Nicephorus Bryannius, to whom she bore four children. Gibbon sums up her general theme: 'the life of the Emperor has been delineated by a favourite daughter, who was inspired by a tender regard for his person and a laudable zeal to perpetuate his virtues'. But in a characteristic side-swipe he then found fault with her affected rhetoric which betrayed 'in every page the vanity of the female author'. *The Alexiad* is a prime source of outstanding originality, and her English translator, after due thought, suggests that Anna's major sins are those of omission only; though her geography is a little vague, many questions are not answered to the satisfaction of academics, and she is perhaps lacking in a sense of humour.)

As for Basil, since he was their leader and showed no sign whatever of remorse, the members of the Holy Synod, the chief monks, as well as the patriarch of that time (Nicolas) unanimously decided that he must be burnt. The emperor, who had interviewed the man at length on many occasions, cast his vote for the same verdict. He had recognized Basil's perversity and knew that his attachment to the heresy [*he and his fellows held that all things of the flesh, including labour, obedience to authority, and the procreation of children, were wicked*] was permanent. So a huge fire was kindled in the Hippodrome. An enormous trench had been dug and a mass of logs, every one a tall tree, had piled up to a mountainous height. Then the pyre was lit and a great multitude of people quietly collected on the floor of the arena and on the steps; everybody waited impatiently to see what would happen. On the other side a cross had been set up and the godless fellow was given an opportunity to recant: if by some chance through dread of the fire he changed his mind and walked over to the cross, he could still escape the burning. I must add that the Bogomils were there in force, watching their leader Basil. Far from giving way, it was obvious that he despised all punishment and threats, and while he was still some distance from the flames he laughed at them and boasted that angels would rescue him from the midst of the fire. He quoted David, softly chanting, 'It shall not come nigh thee; only with thine eyes shalt thou behold.' But when the crowd stood aside and let him see clearly that awe-inspiring sight (for even afar off he could feel the fire and saw the flames rising and shooting out fiery sparks with a noise like thunder, sparks which leapt high in the air to the top of the stone obelisk which stands in the centre of the Hippodrome), then for all his boldness he seemed to flinch before the pyre. He was plainly troubled. Like a man at his wits' end he darted his eyes now here, now there, struck his hands together and beat his thighs. And yet, affected though he was at the mere sight of it, he was still hard as steel; his iron will was not softened by the fire, nor did the messages sent by the emperor break his resolve. Maybe in his hour of supreme need and misfortune a great madness possessed him, so that he lost his mind and was utterly unable to decide what was best for him; or perhaps – and this was more likely – the devil that possessed his soul had shed about him a profound darkness. There he stood, despicable, helpless before every threat, every terror, gaping now at the pyre, now at the spectators. Everyone thought he was quite mad, for he neither rushed to the flames, nor did he altogether turn back, but stayed rooted to one spot where he had first entered the arena, motionless. Now there was much talk going on, as everyone repeated the marvellous prophecies he had made, and the public executioners were afraid lest somehow the demons that protected Basil might perform some extraordinary miracle (with the permission of God) – the scoundrel might be seen in some public place, where many people met, coming unscathed from the midst of this tremendous fire; thus the last error might be worse than the first. So they decided to put him to the test. While he was talking marvels and boasting that he would be seen unharmed in the midst of the flames, they took his woollen cloak and said, 'Let's see if the fire will catch your clothes!' And straightway they hurled it into the centre of the pyre. So confident was Basil in the demon that was deluding him that he cried, 'Look! My cloak flies up to the sky!' They saw that this was the decisive moment, lifted him up and thrust him, clothes, shoes and all, into the fire. The flames, as if in rage against him, so thoroughly devoured the wretch that there was no odour and nothing unusual in the smoke except one thin smoky line in the centre of the flame. For even the elements are stirred against the wicked, but they truly spare those who are dear to God, just as once they yielded to those young men in Babylon [*Shadrach, Mesach and Abednego*] and submitted to them because they were loved of God; and the fire enveloped them like some golden shrine. But on this occasion the executioners who lifted Basil up in their arms were barely poised for the throw when the flame seemed to leap forward and snatch him. The crowd standing by was excited, struggling to throw on the fire all the rest of Basil's pernicious sect, but the emperor would not allow them. On his orders the Bogomils were kept in custody in the porticoes and colonnades of the Great Palace. The spectators then dispersed.

[19] A sixteenth-century description of the long-vanished pillar and statue of Justinian near the Hippodrome – written within 200 years of its disappearance; from *The Antiquities of Constantinople* . . . by Petrus Gyllius (Peter Gilles).

(Peter Gilles (or Petrus Gyllius, as he appears on the title-page of his book) was born at Albi in 1490. A classicist by education, and a naturalist by study and observation, he enlisted as a mercenary under Süleyman II, then at war with the Shah of Persia. Friends rescued him by 'buying him out' in 1550, and he remained in Constantinople in the French Ambassador's suite. He died in 1555. His three-volume description of the Bosphorus appeared in 1561 at Lyons; his book about Constantinople at Leyden (not before 1632).)

The Augusteum was a large Pillar of Brass, erected by *Justinian*, as *Cedrinus* relates, who tells us, that in the fifteenth Year of the Reign of *Justinian*, was finished the great brazen Pillar, which is called the *Augusteum*. Upon it was placed the Statue of *Justinian* on Horseback, holding in his Right Hand an Apple, in Imitation of a Globe, to signify that the whole World was subject to his Government. He sat with his Right Hand stretched out, pointing to the *Persians* to stand off, and not to approach his Dominions. All the Coverings of the Passage of Entrance into the Imperial Palace, were made of gilded Brass. This is still called the Brazen Passage, as the Pillar is call'd the *Augusteum*. *Procopius* speaks largely of it in the Oration *de Ædis. Justin.* where he writes, that

The brass statue of the Emperor Justinian on his horse

not the Pillar, but the Place where the Pillar stood, was called the *Augusteum*, as it was also the *Macellum*. The principal Pillar, says he, is to be admired for its Size, yet is it no regular and uniform Structure, but made of Stones of a vast Compass. The Pedestal and Top of it is covered with the most refined Brass, which by cramping its Stones together, does at the same time both strengthen and adorn it. The Brass, as to its Lustre, is not much inferior to pure Gold, and at least of equal Worth and Beauty with the finest Silver. At the Top of this Pillar was placed a very large Horse cast in Brass, facing the East, wonderful in his Kind, in a walking Posture, with his Head bending downwards, lifting up his near Fore-Foot, as though he would paw the Ground. His Off-Foot is fixed to the Pedestal, on which he stands; and his Hind-Feet are so closely contracted, as if he was rising upon his Speed. Upon him sits the Statue of the Emperor in Brass, whom they call *Achilles*, because he is somewhat like him. He has no Boots, but his Feet are bound round with a kind of Sandals. He is armed with a radiant Breast-plate and Head-piece, and looks, you would fancy, as if he were marching, in a warlike Posture, against the *Persians*. In his left Hand he bears a Globe, by which 'tis signified, that the Earth and the Sea is subject to his Power. He is not equipped either with Sword nor Spear. There's a Cross fixed upon the Globe, intimating, that under its auspicious Influence, he arrived to the Imperial Dignity; and that all Success in War is to be attributed to the Omnipotency of the Saviour of Mankind. His Right Hand, which is open, is stretched Eastward, and seems to forbid the barbarous Nations to approach his Territories.

(For the At Meydani, *see also extracts 74 and 75.*)

The Imperial Cistern (Yerebatan Saray)

[20] The discovery of the Cistern by a Frenchman in the sixteenth century; from *The Antiquities of Constantinople* . . . by Petrus Gyllius (Peter Gilles).

. . . the Imperial *Portico*, and the Imperial *Cistern*, stood in the same Place. The Imperial *Portico* is not to be seen, though the *Cistern* is still remaining. Through the Carelesness and Contempt of every thing that is curious in the Inhabitants, it was never discover'd, but by me, who was a Stranger among them, after a long and diligent Search after it. The whole Ground was built upon, which made it less suspected there was a *Cistern* there. The People had not at least Suspicion of it, although they daily drew their Water out of the Wells which were sunk into it. I went by Chance into a House, where there was a Descent into it, and went aboard a little Skiff. The Master of the House, after having lighted some Torches, rowing me here and there a-cross, through the Pillars, which lay very deep in Water, I made a Discovery of it. He was very intent upon catching his Fish, with which the *Cistern* abounds, and spear'd some of them by the Light of the Torches. There is also a small Light which descends from the Mouth of the Well, and reflects upon the Water, where the fish usually come for Air. This *Cistern* is three hundred and thirty six Foot long, a hundred and eighty two Foot broad, and two hundred and twenty four *Roman* Paces in Compass. The Roof, and Arches, and Sides, are all Brickwork, and cover'd with Terrass, which is not the least impair'd by Time. The Roof is supported with three hundred and thirty six Marble Pillars. The Space of *Intercolumniation* is twelve Foot. Each Pillar is above forty Foot nine Inches high. They stand lengthways in twelve Ranges, broadways in twenty eight. The *Capitals* of them are partly finish'd after the *Corinthian* Model, and part of them not finish'd. Over the *Abacus* of every Pillar is placed a large Stone, which seems to be another *Abacus*, and supports four Arches. There are abundance of Wells which fall into the *Cistern*. I have seen, when it was filling in the Winter-time, a large Stream of Water falling from a great Pipe with a mighty Noise, till the Pillars, up to the

The Imperial Cistern – Yerebatan Saray; drawing by William H. Bartlett from Julia Pardoe's *The Beauties of the Bosphorous*, 1861

Middle of the *Capitals*, have been cover'd with Water. This *Cistern* stands Westward of the Church of St *Sophia*, at the distance of eighty *Roman* Paces from it.

The Great Palace of the Emperors
(now vanished)

[21] An Italian bishop visits first the Emperor Nicephorus, and then the Emperor Constantine, as Ambassador in the tenth century; from *The Works of Liutprand of Cremona*, translated by F.A. Wright.

(Bishop Liutprand (920–972) was born at Pavia into a wealthy and learned family: his father was Ambassador to Constantinople before him. As Bishop of Cremona, Liutprand went twice to Constantinople, once as envoy on behalf of the then Longobardian king (949), and then for the German Emperor, Otto I (969). Not all was to his satisfaction during these missions, as the texts comically prove. Three of his books are extant.)

[The Emperor's] nobles . . . were dressed in tunics that were too large for them and were also because of their extreme age full of holes. They would have looked better if they had worn their ordinary clothes. There was not a man among them whose grandfather had owned his tunic when it was new. No one except Nicephorus wore any jewels or golden ornaments, and the emperor looked more disgusting than ever in the regalia that had been designed to suit the persons of his ancestors. By your life, sires, dearer to me than my own, one of your nobles' costly robes is worth a hundred or more of these. . . .

As Nicephorus, like some crawling monster, walked along, the singers began to cry out in adulation: 'Behold the morning star approaches: the day star rises: in his eyes the sun's rays are reflected: Nicephorus our prince, the pale death of the Saracens'. And then they cried again: 'Long life, long life to our prince Nicephorus. Adore him, ye nations, worship him, bow the neck to his greatness'. How much more truly might they have sung:—'Come, you miserable burnt-out coal; old woman in your walk, wood-devil in your look; clodhopper, haunter of byres, goat-footed, horned, double-limbed; bristly, wild, rough, barbarian, harsh, hairy, a rebel, a Cappadocian!' So, puffed up by these lying ditties, he entered St Sophia. . . .

On this same day he ordered me to be his guest. But as he did not think me worthy to be placed above any of his nobles, I sat fifteenth from him and without a table cloth. Not only did no one of my suite sit at table with me; they did not even set eyes upon the house where I was entertained. At the dinner, which was fairly foul and disgusting, washed down with oil after the fashion of drunkards and moistened also with an exceedingly bad fish liquor, the emperor asked me many questions concerning your power, your dominions and your army. My answers were sober and truthful; but he shouted out:— 'You lie. Your master's soldiers cannot ride and they do not know how to fight on foot. The size of their shields, the weight of their cuirasses, the length of their swords, and the heaviness of their helmets, does not allow them to fight either way'. Then with a smile he added: 'Their gluttony also prevents them. Their God is their belly, their courage but wind, their bravery drunkenness. Fasting for them means dissolution, sobriety, panic. Nor has your master any force of ships on the seas. I alone have really stout sailors, and I will attack him with my fleets, destroy his maritime cities and reduce to ashes those which have a river near them. Tell me, how with his small forces will he be able to resist me even on land? . . .'

I wanted to answer and make such a speech in our defence as his boasting deserved; but he would not let me and added this final insult: 'You are not Romans but Lombards'. He even then was anxious to say more and waved his hand to secure my silence, but I was worked up and cried: 'History tells us that Romulus, from whom the Romans get their name, was a fratricide born in adultery. He made a place of refuge for himself and received into it insolvent debtors, runaway slaves, murderers and men who deserved death for their crimes. This was the sort of crowd whom he enrolled as citizens and gave them the name of Romans. From this nobility are descended those men whom you style "rulers of the world". But we Lombards, Saxons, Franks, Lotharingians, Bavarians, Swabians and Burgundians, so despise these fellows that when we are angry with an enemy we can find nothing more insulting to say than – 'You Roman!' For us in the word Roman is comprehended every form of lowness, timidity, avarice, luxury, falsehood and vice. You say that we are unwarlike and know nothing of horsemanship. Well, if the sins of the Christians merit that you keep this stiff neck, the next war will prove what manner of men you are, and how warlike we'.

Nicephorus, exasperated by these words, commanded the long narrow table to be removed and then calling for silence with his hand ordered me to return to my hateful abode, or, to speak more truly, to my prison. . . .

Next to the imperial residence at Constantinople there is a palace of remarkable size and beauty which the Greeks call Magnavra, the letter v taking the place of the digamma, and the name being equivalent to 'Fresh breeze'. In order to receive some Spanish envoys, who had recently arrived, as well as myself and Liutefred, Constantine gave orders that this palace should be got ready and the following preparations made.

Before the emperor's seat stood a tree, made of bronze gilded over, whose branches were filled with birds, also made of gilded bronze, which uttered different cries, each according to its varying species. The throne itself was so marvellously fashioned that at one moment it seemed a low structure, and at another it rose high into the air. It was of immense size and was guarded by lions, made either of bronze or of wood covered over with gold, who beat the ground with their tails and gave a dreadful roar with open mouth and quivering tongue. Leaning upon the shoulders of two eunuchs I was brought into the emperor's presence. At my approach the lions began to roar and the birds to cry out, each according to its kind; but I was neither terrified nor surprised, for I had previously made enquiry about all these things from people who were well acquainted with them. So after I had three times made obeisance to the emperor with my face upon the ground, I lifted my head, and behold! the man whom just before I had seen sitting on a moderately elevated seat had now changed his raiment and was sitting on the level of the ceiling. How it was done I could not imagine, unless perhaps he was lifted up by some such sort of device as we use for raising the timbers of a wine press. On that occasion he did not address me personally, since even if he had wished to do so the wide distance between us would have rendered conversation unseemly, but by the intermediary of a secretary he enquired about Berengar's doings and asked after his health. I made a fitting reply and then, at a nod from the interpreter, left his presence and retired to my lodging.

[22] The murder of the Emperor Nicephorus in 969 by his nephew John Tzimisces; from *Byzantine Empresses* by Charles Diehl, translated by Harold Bell and Theresa de Kerpely.

Nicephorus had a nephew, John Tzimisces. He was forty-five years of age, short, but well built and very elegant. He was white of skin, with blue eyes, a halo of light-golden hair, a reddish beard, a delicate and beautiful nose, and a bold look – a man who feared nothing and nobody. Being likewise strong, clever, agile, open-handed, and magnificent, and a bit of a rake into the bargain, he was very fascinating. Theophano [the Empress] in her boredom naturally found him pleasant; and it was now that passion led her on to crime. Tzimisces was ambitious; he was vastly irritated, moreover, at the disgrace which had befallen him: as the result of an incident of war, the Emperor had degraded him from his post of Domestic of the Oriental Scholae and had invited him to retire to his estates, and his one thought was to revenge himself for an outrage that he deemed unmerited. Theophano, for her part, was utterly weary of Nicephorus; their former understanding had been succeeded by dislike and suspicion, and the Empress even affected to fear that her husband intended to make some attempt upon the lives of her sons. She was still more impatient at being separated from her lover, for Tzimisces seemed to have been the great and probably the only real love of her life. In these circumstances, she surrendered herself gradually to the contemplation of a most revolting crime.

Nicephorus, since his return from Syria, at the beginning of 969, had been a prey to dark forebodings. He had a feeling that plots were being hatched against him in the dark. The death of his aged father, the Caesar Bardas Phocas, had increased his melancholy. However, he still loved Theophano. The latter perfidiously used her influence to have Tzimisces recalled to court. She pointed out to the Emperor how annoying it was to have to forego the services of such a man; and very cleverly, in order to prevent Nicephorus from becoming suspicious at too open an espousal of John's cause, talked of marrying him to one of her relatives. The Basileus, as usual, gave way to his wife's wishes. John returned to Constantinople; and, owing to channels of information skilfully contrived by Theophano in concert with

One of the Imperial residences of early Byzantium; drawing by William H. Bartlett from Julia Pardoe's *The Beauties of the Bosphorous*, 1861

some of her household, the two lovers met in the Palace itself, unknown to Nicephorus, and prepared their plot. No less was planned than the assassination of the Basileus. Among the discontented generals John readily found accomplices; many conferences were held between the conspirators and between Tzimisces and the Empress; at last, thanks to the many ramifications of the Gynaeceum, armed men were smuggled into the Palace and hidden in the Augusta's apartments.

Leo Diaconus, who has left us a very striking account of the drama, says that it was now early December. The murder had been set for the night between the 10th and the 11th. The day before, several of the conspirators, dressed as women, had, with Theophano's aid, entered the Sacred Palace. This time the Emperor was mysteriously warned, and he gave orders to one of his officers to search the women's quarters; but, whether the search was carelessly carried out, or whether by deliberate intention, no one was discovered. Meanwhile, night had fallen; they awaited only the coming of Tzimisces to strike the blow. The conspirators became apprehensive; if the Emperor were to lock himself in his room, if they had to break open the door and he were to awake, would it not ruin everything? Theophano, with revolting composure, took upon herself to overcome this obstacle. At a late hour she went to see Nicephorus in his apartments and chatted pleasantly with him; then, on pretext of having to visit some young Bulgarian women staying in the Palace, she went out, saying that she would be back presently and asking him to leave the door open: she would close it on her return. Nicephorus agreed, and when he was left alone, said his prayers and fell asleep.

It was about eleven o'clock at night. Outside, snow was falling, and on the Bosphorus the wind was blowing a hurricane. In a little boat John Tzimisces reached the deserted strip of shore under the walls of the imperial castle of the Bucoleon. By means of a basket fastened to a rope, he was hoisted up to the Gynaeceum, and at the head of the conspirators went to the sovereign's bedchamber. They had a moment of fright, for the bed was empty. But a eunuch of the Gynaeceum, who was acquainted with Nicephorus's habits, pointed out the Basileus lying asleep in a corner on his panther-skin. They rushed furiously at him, whereupon he awoke and jumped up. One of the conspirators with his sword split open the Emperor's head to the eyebrows. The wretched man, drenched in blood, cried out: 'Mother of God, help me!' The murderers, paying no heed, dragged him to the feet of Tzimisces, who abused him indecently and tore out his beard. At this they all fell upon the poor creature, who was now in the last throes. Finally John, with a kick, turned him over and, drawing his sword, struck him a great blow on the head; another of the assassins finished him off. The Emperor fell dead, bathed in his blood.

At the noise of the struggle, the soldiers of the guard hurried to the scene, but arrived too late. They were shown by torchlight at a window the severed, bleeding head of their master. This tragic sight stifled at once all thought of resistance. The people followed the Empress's example and proclaimed Tzimisces Emperor.

[23] The ancient 'Gothic Games' still performed in the Bucoleon Palace (part of the Great Palace) in the tenth century; from *The City of Constantine* by John Hearsey.

Without doubt the oddest ritual described by Constantine Porphyrogenitus is 'What shall be observed at the Banquet of the Nineteen Couches, during the Gothic Games'. These games, more a stylized dance, were performed once a year in the banqueting chamber of the Boucleon Palace. Even then, in the tenth century, their origins were already obscure and the meaning of the gibberish the performers had to declaim lost to the world. Presumably their origins go back to the time of the Gothic invasions at the end of the fourth century.

'On the left side . . . stands the maistor [spokesman] of the Blue Faction with a small number of demotes and lute players with their instruments and behind them, the Goths wearing skins turned inside out and different types of masks, holding a shield in the left hand and rods in the right.'

The same order was observed on the right side for the Greens. When the Emperor gave the signal for the evolutions to begin, they were accompanied with declaimed phrases, for the most part completely incomprehensible.

'Striking the shields with the rods as they run forward the Goths exclaim: "Toul, Toul", saying it without stopping, they ascend close to the Imperial table [of gold], and a little distance from it . . . they position themselves in a circular movement like an army. When they have taken up their places: those of the Blues to the left, those of the Greens to the right . . . all together they sing the Gothic songs, the lutes playing the appropriate melodies: "Deumonobuggubele, Gubilous, Gubelares", declaimed the performers, together with phrases like "Ezechias having taken in war the arms of the Assyrians, putting his sole hope in God who loves mankind, has subjugated all the races and the tyranny of the atheists. That the Saviour, good Sovereign, reduces all your enemies to slavery beneath your feet."'

Off they go again: '*Iber, Iberiem, Tou Iggerous, Gergerethro*.' Then the maistores, together with the demotes, say the alphabet, declaiming a statement in praise of the Emperor at each letter. This extraordinary alphabetical game is punctuated throughout with the evolutions of the Goths.

'When the alphabet has been completed, they say "God grant long days to your Holy Empire!" And the Goths striking their shields with their rods, saying without ceasing: "Toul, Toul", leave at a run.'

The Mad Hatter would surely have been in his element at such a party.

[24] Life in the Palace in the eleventh century – the Empress Zoë chooses a lover, and the Emperor Romanus, her husband, is murdered in his bath in 1034; from *Fourteen Byzantine Rulers, the chronographia* of Michael Psellus, translated by E.R.A. Sewter.

(Michael Psellus (the Younger, 1018–1078) was born in Constantinople of a noble family, and made his name teaching Platonic philosophy at the newly founded Academy (or University) of the city. He also pursued a successful career at Court, as the *Chronographia* show, serving Regents and Emperors as Grand Chamberlain and Chief Minister for many years. This wit and leading intellectual of the Empire has been accused of every Byzantine failing: lack of scruple, weakness, intrigue, servility and vanity; but his vivid prose in fact places him in the top rank of eye-witness recorders of any Empire, and can scarcely be surpassed for its immediacy, raciness and interest.)

This eunuch had a brother, a mere youth before Romanus became emperor, but now in his early manhood. He was a finely-proportioned young man, with the fair bloom of youth in his face, as fresh as a flower, clear-eyed, and in very truth 'red-cheeked'. This youth was led by his brother into the emperor's presence when he was seated with Zoe that they might see him, at the express command of Romanus. When the two men came in, the emperor, casting him one glance and asking a few questions, brief enough, bade him retire but stay on in the court. The effect of the interview on Zoe was quite different. Her eyes burned with a fire as dazzling as the young man's beauty and she at once fell victim to his charm. From some mystic union between them she conceived a love for him. But most people knew nothing of that at the time.

Zoe could neither regard the young man with philosophic

detachment, nor control her desires. Consequently, though in the past she had more than once shown her dislike for the eunuch, she now approached him frequently. Her conversations would begin with reference to some extraneous matter, and then, as if by way of digression, she would end with some remark about his brother. Let him be bold, she said, and visit her whenever he wished. The young man, so far knowing nothing of the empress's secret, supposed the invitation was due to her kindness of heart, and he accepted it, although in a modest and timorous fashion. This bashful reserve, however, only made him the more dazzling. His face, suffused with blushes, shone with a glorious colour. She eased his fear, smiling on him gently and forgetting her usual grim arrogance. She hinted at love, tried to encourage him, and when she proceeded to give her beloved manifest opportunities to make love on his part, he set himself to answer her desire, not with any real confidence at first, but later his advances became more brazen and he acted as lovers will. Suddenly he threw his arms about her, kissing her and touching her hand and neck, as his brother had taught him he should do. She clung to him all the closer. Her kisses became more passionate, she truly loving him, he in no way desiring her (for she was past the age of love), but thinking in his heart of the glory that power would bring him. For this he was prepared to dare anything, and bear it with patience. As for those who lived in the palace, they at first only suspected or conjectured what was going on, but afterwards, when the affair broke all bounds of modesty, everyone knew of it. There was nobody who did not perceive how it was going, for their embraces had already ended in carnal union, and they were discovered by several people sleeping together on the same couch. He blushed with shame and was filled with apprehension for the outcome of this, but she did not conceal it. In the eyes of all she clung to him and offered her kisses, boasting that she had more than once had her joy of him.

That she should adorn him, as if he were some statue, cover him with gold, make him resplendent with rings and garments of woven gold cloth, I do not regard as anything remarkable, for what would an empress not provide for her beloved? But she, unknown to the world, sometimes went so far as to seat him, turn by turn with herself, on the imperial throne, to put in his hand a sceptre; and on one occasion even deemed him worthy of a crown. . . .

Although nobody else had failed to notice this, it did not come to the knowledge of the emperor. Romanus was so completely blind. However, when the flash of the lightning and the roar of the thunder did eventually play round his eyes and deafen his ears, when he himself saw some things going on and heard of others, even then, as if he preferred to be blind and deaf, he closed his eyes again and refused to listen. Worse than that, many a time when he was sleeping with the empress and she, clothed in some garments of purple, was waiting for him to lie down on their couch, he would call for Michael, bidding him come alone, and order him to touch and massage his feet. In fact, he made him servant of the bed-chamber, and, in order that the young man might do this office, deliberately abandoned his wife to him. When his sister Pulcheria and some of the chamberlains discovered a plot against his life and told him of it and warned him to be on his guard, still he did not destroy the secret adulterer and cut short the whole drama, as he could have done. He could have suggested any reason but the real one and still have had his way, but he refused. He made no effort to combat the intrigue. Once he did send for the lover – or the beloved – and questioned him about the affair; however, as Michael pretended to know nothing about it, Romanus made him give his word of honour and swear by the Holy Relics, and after the other had completely perjured himself, the emperor looked upon the stories of the rest as mere calumny, listening only to Michael and calling him 'his most faithful servant'. . . .

Whether the loving couple themselves, and their accomplices, committed a very horrible crime against him, I would not say with any certainty, because it is no easy thing for me to bring accusations in matters that I still do not thoroughly understand. However, it was universally accepted among the rest that they first bewitched him with drugs, and later had recourse to a mixture of hellebore as well. I am not disputing that for the moment – it may or may not be true – but I do maintain that Zoe and Michael were the cause of his death. His state of health being what it was, the emperor made his preparations for the Resurrection that awaits all of us alike. At the same time, he was making himself ready for the public services on the morrow (Good Friday). Before dawn he set out to bathe in one of the baths situated near the imperial quarters. There was no one to assist him, and he was certainly not at death's door then. He got up in a perfectly normal way to anoint and bathe himself and take his aperitives. So he entered the bath. First he washed his head, then drenched his body as well, and as he was breathing strongly, he proceeded to the swimming pool, which had been deepened in the middle. To begin with, he enjoyed himself swimming on the surface and floating lightly, blowing out and refreshing himself with the greatest of pleasure. Later on some of his retinue came in to support him and give him a rest, according to his own orders. Whether they made an attempt on the emperor's life after they entered the bath I cannot say with any conviction. At any rate, those who see some connexion between these events and the rest of their version say that when Romanus plunged his head under the water – his usual custom – they all pressed his neck and held him down for some considerable time, after which they let him go and went away. The air inside him, however, caused his body to rise and it brought him to the surface, almost breathless. There he floated about in a haphazard way, like a cork. When he had recovered a little and saw in what an evil plight he was, he stretched out his hand and begged someone to take hold of it and help him to his feet. In pity for him, and because of his sad condition, one man did indeed go to his aid. Putting his arms round him, he drew him out of the water and carried him to a couch, where he laid him, just as he was, in a pitiable state. At this an uproar ensued. Several persons came into the room, among them the empress herself, without any bodyguard and apparently stricken with grief. After one look at him, however, she went off, having satisfied herself with her own eyes that he was a dying man. Romanus gave one strong deep moan, and then kept looking round, this way and that, without being able to speak, but showing by signs and nods what he wanted. Then, as still nobody could understand him, he shut his eyes and began to breathe more fast again. Suddenly his mouth gaped open and there flowed gently from it some dark-coloured, coagulated matter, and, with two or three gasps, he died.

[25] The Crusaders find treasures in the Palace of the Bucoleon during the Latin occupation of the thirteenth century; from *The Conquest of Constantinople* by Robert de Clari, translated by E.H. McNeal.

When the city was captured and the pilgrims were quartered, as I have told you, and the palaces were taken over, then they found in the palaces riches more than a great deal. And the palace of Boukoleon was very rich and was made in such a way as I shall tell you. Within this palace, which was held by the marquis, there were fully five hundred halls, all connected with one another and all made with gold mosaic.[1] And in it there were fully thirty chapels, great and small, and there was one of them which was called the Holy Chapel, which was so rich and noble that there was not a hinge nor a band nor any other part such as is usually made of iron that was not all of silver, and there was no column that was not of jasper or porphyry or some other rich precious stone. And the pavement of this chapel was of a white marble so smooth and clear that it seemed to be of crystal, and this chapel was so rich and so noble that no one could ever tell you its great beauty and nobility. Within this chapel were found many rich relics. One found there two pieces of the True Cross as large as the leg of a man and as long as half a *toise*, and one found there also the iron of the lance with which Our Lord had His side pierced and two of the nails which were driven through His hands and feet, and one found there in a crystal phial quite a little of His blood, and one found there the tunic which He wore and which was taken from Him when they led Him to the Mount of Calvary, and one found there the blessed crown with which He was crowned, which was made of reeds with thorns as sharp as the points of daggers. And one found there a part of the robe of Our Lady and the head of my lord St John the Baptist and so many other rich relics that I could not recount them to you or tell you all the truth.

[1] In these terms Robert attempts to describe the great complex of buildings lying between the Hippodrome and the sea walls, which was known as the Great Palace. Begun by Constantine, it was added to by later emperors, until the time of the Comneni, who abandoned it for the palace of Blachernae at the other end of the city . . . The Great Palace was occupied again by Andronicus and by Alexius III, as also later by the Latin emperors.

Other Byzantine palaces

[26] Bertha of Sulzbach, a foreigner who became the Empress Irene, settles into the Palace of Blachernae (where the Ivaz Efendi Camii now stands) in 1146; from *Byzantine Empress* by Charles Diehl, translated by Harold Bell and Theresa de Kerpely.

What could have been this foreigner's impressions, at the time of her arrival in Constantinople, of the new world to which she was banished? An attempt to find out may prove rewarding, and, to help us, we have at our disposal a number of rather curious descriptions of the Byzantine capital as it was in the middle of the twelfth century. One of them is particularly worthy of our attention, since it is the work of a Westerner, Eudes de Deuil, who visited the city of the Basileis in 1147, just after the marriage of Irene and Manuel [Emperor Manuel Comnena].

The imperial city had great prestige in the West, a prestige that seems to have been justified. On account of its delightful climate, its fertile soil, and its enormous wealth, Constantinople appeared to the Latins as a city beyond compare. 'It is the glory of the Greeks,' says Eudes de Deuil, 'rich in repute, and even richer in reality.' (*Graecorum gloria, fama dives et rebus ditior.*) The chronicler never tires of praising the splendor of the palaces, the magnificence of the churches, and the host of precious relics preserved in them. He is equally impressed by the picturesque view from the city walls, at whose base large gardens extend far out into the countryside, and by the viaducts that provide the capital with a full and constant supply of fresh water. But besides the public buildings, Eudes de Deuil – and herein lies the great interest of his description – has managed to see the city itself, and it strikes him as peculiarly dirty, malodorous, and dark. . . . By night . . . the unlighted streets become the roving ground of thieves, and of the stray dogs that pullulate in Constantinople to this day. Respectable citizens shut themselves up in their houses. . . .

But an Empress had little opportunity to see these 'sights unfitting for a sovereign' (*ἀβασίλευτον*). The Constantinople she knew was that of the imperial residences, and in particular the Palace of Blachernae, which became in the twelfth century the usual home of the Basileis. It was situated at the point of the Golden Horn, and its triple façade commanded views of the sea, the city, and the countryside. The exterior was magnificent, and the interior even more so. On the walls of the great colonnaded galleries glittered mosaics set in gold and executed with 'admirable artistry.' They represented in blazing colors the exploits of the Emperor Manuel, his wars against the barbarians, all that he had done for the good of the Empire. The floors were richly paved with mosaics. 'I do not know,' writes a contemporary, 'what contributes most to its beauty and its worth, the cleverness of the art or the value of the materials used.' Everywhere was the same luxury, which it delighted the Emperors of the Comnenian dynasty to increase, and which made of the Palace of Blachernae one of the marvels of Constantinople. Foreigners who were permitted to visit it have left us dazzling descriptions: 'Its exterior beauty,' writes Eudes de Deuil, 'is almost beyond compare, and that of the interior far surpasses anything that I can say about it. On every side one sees gilding and paintings in variegated colors; the court is paved in marble with exquisite skill.'

Benjamin de Tudele, who visited Constantinople some years later, expresses the same admiration. 'In addition to the Palace inherited by Manuel from his ancestors, he has had built, beside the sea, another, called Blachernae, whose walls, and whose pillars too, are covered with gold and silver on which he has had depicted his own wars as well as those of his forefathers. In this Palace he has had made a throne of gold embellished with precious stones and ornamented with a crown of gold suspended by chains that are likewise of gold. The rim of this crown is studded with pearls and with priceless diamonds whose glittering fires almost suffice to illumine the dark without the help of any other light. An infinite number of other things are to be found there that would seem incredible if one were to describe them. To this Palace are brought the annual tributes, both in gold and in garments of purple and scarlet, with which the towers are filled to bursting. So for beauty of structure and abundance of riches, this Palace surpasses all the other palaces of the world.'

An Empress also knew the exquisite residences to which the Basileis went to spend a cool summer. At the foot of the Palace of Blachernae was the beautiful park of Philopation, a vast, walled enclosure, where the air was kept perpetually cool by running waters, and where the great woods stocked with game provided the pleasures of the hunt. Here the Emperor had constructed a charming country seat, and the whole formed what Eudes de Deuil describes as 'the Greeks' paradise.' Elsewhere, by the sea of Marmora, there were splendid villas, where the Emperors had revived the oriental luxury 'of Susa and Ecbatana,' and where Manuel, weary from his wars, sought rest and relaxation in the refinements of the table and in the pleasures of music.

[27] The Palace of Constantine Porphyrogenitus (the Tekfur Saray) on the Sixth Hill; from 'The Seven Hills of Istanbul', the unpublished manuscript of H. Sumner-Boyd in the Bodleian.

Whatever the facts about its date and history in the Byzantine period, the palace has undergone many vicissitudes in Ottoman times. In the sixteenth and seventeenth centuries it was used as one of several imperial menageries, particularly for the housing of larger and tamer animals such as elephants and giraffes. The latter animal caused stupefaction and incredulity among the European travellers, for they had never seen one before. In 1597 Fynes Moryson, a guest of the English Ambassador Edward Barton, describes it:

> a beast newly brought out of Affricke, (the Mother of Monsters) which beaste is altogether unknowne in our parts, and is called *Surnapa* by the people of *Asia*, *Aslanapa* by others, and *Giraffa* by the *Italians*, the picture whereof I remember to have seene in the Mappes of *Mercator*; because the beast is very rare, I will describe his forme as well as I can. His haire is red coloured, with many blacke and white spots; I could scarce reach with the points of my fingers to the hinder parte of his backe, which grew higher and higher toward his foreshoulder, and his necke was thinne and some three els long, so as he easily turned his head in a moment to any part or corner of the roome wherein he stood . . . by reason whereof he many times put his nose in my necke, when I thought my selfe furthest distant from him, which familiarity of his I liked not; and

howsoever the Keepers assured me he would not hurt me, yet I avoided those his familiar kisses as much as I could.

Two somewhat earlier travellers could have reassured Moryson about the 'familiar kisses'. Thus Pierre Belon, the French naturalist, visiting the Levant about 1551, also gives an enthusiastic description and a charming woodcut, and concludes, 'C'est une beste moult belle, la plus doulce qui soit, cōme une brebis, et autãt amiable que nulle autre beste sauvage.' A little later (1567) a nobleman from Vicenza, Marc'Antonio Pigafetta, in the suite of the Ambassador of the Emperor Maximillian II, confirms this – 'è di mansueta natura et piacevole' – and tells us that the Ambassador dearly wanted the beast for his imperial master; the Grand Vezir Sokullu Mehmet Pasa at first promissed it to him but later had to retract because it was the only giraffe in the country and 'era molto cara al Gran Signore.' Pigafetta goes on to say that giraffes had only twice been imported into Italy, the first by Julius Caesar; the second, 'in the time of our grandfathers, was sent by the Sultan of Egypt as a gift to Lorenzo de' Medici.'

Before the end of the seventeenth century the beasts had died or been moved away and the palace was being used for what Schneider modestly describes as 'weniger ehrbaren Zwecken,' quoting in a footnote another Italian traveller, B.G. de Burgo: 'nelle rovine del palazzo fanno prostibuli le donne turche.' But it was soon redeemed from use as a brothel: in 1719 there was set up here the famous Tekfur Saray pottery which produced a new kind of Turkish tiles, inferior indeed to those of Iznik and beginning to show European influence, but nevertheless quite charming. The project, however, was shortlived and by the second half of the eighteenth century the building was in full decline and finally lost its roof. Texier in an unpublished drawing of 1833 marks the middle floor as 'partie occupée par des habitations juives' and the top floor as 'grande salle sans toit.' And a few years later Julia Pardoe paints a lugubrious picture: 'The building has been given up to the Jews as a pauper hospital. . . . It is almost unapproachable, being the headquarters of filth, and the hotbed of pestilence, where every sense is painted by scents and sights calculated to inspire dread and disgust. . . . On one side the visitor is jostled by disease, and on the other persecuted by importunity.' The roof being gone, it was not long before the floors went also; nevertheless, about 1860, the American missionary Cyrus Hamlin, searching for a site for the future Robert College, seriously considered purchasing the palace and restoring it for use as an educational establishment; perhaps fortunately, the idea was abandoned in favour of the present site of the College on the Bosphorus. The building is now a mere shell; in recent years a small amount of first-aid has been given to it, but the whole area cries out for scientific excavation and judicious maintenance.

Byzantine churches

[28] Haghia Eirene – the Church of the Divine Peace – is the centre of violent disputes between the Arians and the Orthodox party, the upholders of the Nicene Creed, during the reign of Constantius in the fourth century; from *Byzantine Churches in Constantinople* by Alexander van Millingen.

Upon the death of Alexander in 343, at the age of ninety-eight, the two parties came into collision in regard to the question of his successor. The deceased prelate had recommended two persons as suitable to fill his place: the presbyter Paul, because of his abilities; the deacon Macedonius, on account of his age and venerable appearance. The Arians favoured Macedonius, as more in sympathy with their opinions; the orthodox, however, carried the election and installed Paul in S. Irene. The defeated party seems to have submitted, but the Emperor Constantius, a violent Arian, quashed the election, and appointed Eusebius of Nicomedia, a prominent upholder of the view of Arius, bishop of the capital. Upon the death of Eusebius in 346 the theological combatants again seized the opportunity to try their strength. The orthodox recalled Paul; the Arians consecrated Macedonius. Incensed by these proceedings, Constantius, then at Antioch, ordered Hermogenes, the magister militum in Thrace, to proceed to Constantinople and drive Paul from the city. But no sooner did Hermogenes attempt to execute his instructions than the populace rose, burnt his house to the ground, and after dragging him along the streets, killed him. The emperor was furious. He hurried back to Constantinople, banished Paul, and reduced by one-half the amount of free bread daily distributed among the citizens. Nor did he fully recognize Macedonius as bishop. Under these circumstances Paul made his way to Rome, and, having secured the support of the Pope, reappeared in Constantinople as the rightful bishop of the see. But the emperor, again in Syria, was not to be baffled. More angry than ever, he sent peremptory orders to Philip, the prefect of Constantinople, to expel Paul and to recognize Macedonius. By skilful arrangements Paul was quietly removed from the scene. But to install Macedonius was a more difficult undertaking. The prefect, however, ordered his chariot, and with Macedonius seated by his side made for S. Irene, under an escort of troops carrying drawn swords. The sharp, naked weapons alarmed the crowds in the streets, and without distinction of sect or class men rushed for the church, everybody trying to outstrip his neighbour in the race to get there first. Soon all the approaches to the building were packed to suffocation; no one stirred backwards or forwards, and the prefect's chariot was unable to advance. What seemed a hostile barricade of human beings welded together obstructed his path. In vain did the soldiers brandish their swords in the hope of frightening the crowd to disperse. The crowd stood stock still, not because it would not, but because it could not move. The soldiers grew angry, resorted to their weapons, and cut a way to the church through that compact mass of humanity at the cost of 3150 lives; some of the victims being crushed to death, others killed at the point of the sword. So was Macedonius conducted to his throne in the temple of Peace. But the conflict between the opposite parties continued, and after six years spent in efforts to recover his position, Paul was restored to office through the intervention of the Pope of Rome, of the Emperor Constans, and of the Synod of Sardica. It was a brief triumph. In 350 Paul was exiled for life to Cucusus, and Macedonius ruled once more in his stead. For the next thirty years S. Irene with the other churches of the capital remained in the hands of the Arians.

[29] Theological schisms of the sixth century: Justinian's policemen try to arrest Pope Vigilius in the church of Sts Sergius and Bacchus (the Küçük Aya Sofya Camii); from *Byzantine Churches in Constantinople* by Alexander van Millingen.

A remarkable scene was witnessed in the church in the course of the controversy which raged around the writings known in ecclesiastical history as 'The Three Chapters,' the work of three theologians tainted, it was alleged, with the heretical opinions of Nestorius. Justinian associated himself with the party which condemned those writings, and prevailed upon the majority of the bishops in the East to subscribe the imperial decree to that effect. But Vigilius, the Pope of the day, and the bishops in the

West, dissented from that judgment, because the authors of the writings in question had been acquitted from the charge of heresy by the Council of Chalcedon. To condemn them after that acquittal was to censure the Council and reflect upon its authority. Under these circumstances Justinian summoned Vigilius to Constantinople in the hope of winning him over by the blandishments or the terrors of the court of New Rome. Vigilius reached the city on the 25th of January 547, and was detained in the East for seven years in connection with the settlement of the dispute. He found to his cost that to decide an intricate theological question, and above all to assert 'the authority of S. Peter vested in him' against an imperious sovereign and the jealousy of Eastern Christendom, was no slight undertaking. Pope and Emperor soon came into violent collision, and fearing the consequences Vigilius sought sanctuary in the church of S. Peter as he styles it, but which Byzantine writers who record the scene name S. Sergius.

Justinian was not the man to stand the affront. He ordered the praetor of the city to arrest the Pope and conduct him to prison. But when that officer appeared, Vigilius grasped the pillars of the altar and refused to surrender. Thereupon the praetor ordered his men to drag the Pope out by main force. Seizing Vigilius by his feet, holding him by his beard and the hair of his head, the men pulled with all their might, but they had to deal with a powerful man, and he clung fast to the altar with an iron grip. In this tug-of-war the altar at length came crashing to the ground, the Pope's strong hands still holding it tight. At this point, however, the indignation and sympathy of the spectators could not be restrained; the assailants of the prostrate prelate were put to flight, and he was left master of the situation. Next day a deputation, including Belisarius and Justin, the heir-apparent, waited upon Vigilius, and in the emperor's name assured him that resistance to the imperial will was useless, while compliance with it would save him from further ill-treatment. Yielding to the counsels of prudence, the Pope returned to the palace of Placidia, the residence assigned to him during his stay in the capital.

[30] The rule for monks at St John Studion (Imrahor Camii, now in ruins); from *Byzantine Churches in Constantinople* by Alexander van Millingen.

The monks of the Studion, like most Greek monks, lived under the rules prescribed by S. Basil for the discipline of men who aspired to reach 'the angelic life.' Theodore, however, quickened the spirit which found expression in those rules, and while inculcating asceticism in its extremest form, showed greater consideration for the weakness of human nature. The penalties he assigned for transgressions were on the whole less Draconian than those inflicted before his time.

According to the moral ideal cherished in the monastery, the true life of man was to regard oneself but dust and ashes, and, like the angels, to be ever giving God thanks. If a monk repined at such a lot, he was to castigate himself by eating only dry bread for a week and performing 500 acts of penance. The prospect of death was always to be held in view. Often did the corridors of the monastery resound with the cry, 'We shall die, we shall die!' The valley of the shadow of death was considered the road to life eternal. A monk could not call even a needle his own. Nor were the clothes he wore his personal property. They were from time to time thrown into a heap with the clothes of the other members of the House, and every monk then took from the pile the garment most convenient to his hand. Female animals were forbidden the monastery. A monk was not allowed to kiss his mother, not even at Easter, under penalty of excommunication for fifty days. Daily he attended seven services, and had often to keep vigil all night long. There was only one set meal a day; anything more in the way of food consisted of the fragments which a monk laid aside from that meal. No meat was eaten unless by special permission for reasons of health.

If a brother ate meat without permission he went without fish, eggs, and cheese for forty days. The ordinary food consisted of vegetables cooked in oil. Fish, cheese, and eggs were luxuries. Two, sometimes three, cups of wine were permitted. If a brother was so unfortunate as to break a dish, he had to stand before the assembled monks at dinner time with covered head, and hold the broken article in view of all in the refectory. It was forbidden to a monk to feel sad. Melancholy was a sin, and was to be overcome by prayer, one hundred and fifty genuflexions, and five hundred

The ruins of the church of St John Studion, now the Imrahor Camii; from *Voyage Pittoresque de la Grèce*, 1782–1809 by M.G. Choiseul Gouffier

Kyrie Eleisons a day. The monks were required to read regularly in the monastery library. The task of copying manuscripts occupied a place of honour, and was under strict regulations. Fifty genuflexions were the penalty prescribed for not keeping one's copy clean; one hundred and fifty such acts of penance for omitting an accent or mark of punctuation; thirty, for losing one's temper and breaking his pen; fasting on dry bread was the fate of the copyist guilty of leaving out any part of the original, and three days' seclusion for daring to trust his memory instead of following closely the text before him.

Ignatius of Smolensk found Russian monks in the monastery employed in transcribing books for circulation in Russia. Stephen of Novgorod met two old friends from his town busy copying the Scriptures. A good monastic scriptorium rendered an immense service; it did the work of the printing-press.

Yet, notwithstanding all restrictions, men could be happy at the Studion. One of its inmates for instance congratulates himself thus on his lot there, 'No barbarian looks upon my face; no woman hears my voice. For a thousand years no useless (ἄπρακτος) man has entered the monastery of Studius; none of the female sex has trodden its court. I dwell in a cell that is like a palace; a garden, an oliveyard, and a vineyard surround me.

Before me are graceful and luxuriant cypress trees. On one hand is the city with its marketplace; on the other, the mother of churches and the empire of the world.'

[31] The flight of Emperor Michael V and his uncle to St John Studion, and their blinding, after a palace revolution in 1042; from *Fourteen Byzantine Rulers, the Chronographia* of Michael Psellus, translated by E.R.A. Sewter.

When news of this reached Michael, fearing that the rebels would suddenly come upon him and lay violent hands on him there in the palace, he embarked on one of the imperial ships and landed with his uncle at the holy Studite monastery. There he laid aside his emperor's garments and put on the clothes of a suppliant and refugee. As soon as their flight became known in the city, the hearts of all men, hitherto filled with fear and grim forebodings, were now relieved of anxiety. Some made thank-offerings to God for their deliverance, others acclaimed the new empress, while the common folk and the loungers in the market joined in dancing. The revolution was dramatized and they composed choral songs inspired by the events that had taken place before their eyes. More numerous still was the crowd that rushed in one wild swoop upon the tyrant himself, intent on cutting him down, on slitting his throat.

So much for them. Theodora's companions meanwhile sent a guard for him. The guard commander was one of the nobles and I myself accompanied him (I was a personal friend of the man). Actually, he had invited me to advise him and help in the carrying out of his orders. On our arrival at the doors of the church, we saw another guard, composed of volunteers, a company of citizens who had completely surrounded the sacred building. They were ready to do everything but tear it down. So it was not without difficulty that we made our way into the church. Along with us a great multitude of folk poured in, roaring abuse at the accursed fellow. All manner of indecent epithets were hurled at him.

Up till then I too had gone along with the mob, having no particularly moderate feelings about him. I was not indifferent to his treatment of the empress, and a certain mild resentment against the man stirred me on my own account. But when I reached the sacred altar where he was, and saw both the refugees, one, who had been emperor, clinging to the Holy Table of the Word, the other, the Nobilissimus, standing on the right of the altar, both with their clothes changed, their spirit gone and utterly put to shame, then there was no trace whatever of anger left in my heart. I stood there dumbfounded, mute with astonishment, as if I had been struck by a hurricane. I was transformed at the strangeness of the thing. Then, recovering my spirits, I began to curse this life of ours, in which these strange and terrible things so often come to pass, and as if some spring had welled up within me, a flood of tears beyond control poured from my eyes. This outburst finally gave way to groans. . . .

Day was already drawing to a close when suddenly there arrived one of the newly-appointed officials, saying that he had received an order from Theodora to remove the refugees to some other place. He was accompanied by a crowd of citizens and soldiers. Approaching the altar at which they had sought sanctuary, he invited them, in a somewhat peremptory manner, to leave the church. Despite this, when they saw the mob talking of public execution and when with their own eyes they perceived the mob leader signalling that the moment was at hand, and when they observed the change in the man – he was more insolent than usual – they refused to come forth and clung even more resolutely to the pillars that support the altar. . . .

[*The mob finally forces the fugitives out of the church*] A shameful reception awaited them outside, where the rabble made fun of them, naturally enough under the circumstances. Sometimes the insults were tempered with laughter, but malice inspired others. Anyhow, they brought them out, intending to drive them through the centre of the city, but they had not gone far on the journey when they were encountered by the man who had been commanded to blind the two criminals. His party showed their instructions to the mob and they began preparing for the execution; the iron was sharpened for the branding. Meanwhile the victims heard what wretched fate was in store for them. There was no longer any hope of escape, for while some applauded the sentence, the others did nothing to oppose it, and the two were instantly struck dumb with fright. In fact, they would have nearly died, had not one of the senators stood by them to help. He offered consolation in their misery and little by little restored some courage in their hearts.

In spite of this encouragement the emperor, overwhelmed by the situation and his dreadful misfortunes, showed the same weakness of character throughout the whole time of his tribulation. He moaned and wailed aloud, and whenever anyone approached him, he begged for help. He humbly called on God, raised hands in supplication to heaven, to the Church, to anything he could think of. His uncle, on the other hand, although at first he followed his companion's example, once he was convinced that safety really was out of the question, braced himself for the trial and, having armed himself, as it were, against the shock of catastrophe, faced suffering bravely. The fact is, he was a man of more dignified and steadfast character than his nephew, a man who would not willingly surrender to adversity. Seeing the executioners all ready for their work, he at once offered himself as the first victim and calmly approached them. They waited with hands athirst for his blood. As there was no clear space between himself and the mob – for everyone there present wished to be the first witness of their punishment – the Nobilissimus quietly looked round for the man to whom the miserable job had been entrusted. 'You there,' he said, 'please make the people stand back. Then you will see how bravely I bear my calamity!'

When the executioner tried to tie him down, to prevent movement at the time of blinding, he said, 'Look here. If you see me budge, *nail* me down!' With these words he lay flat on his back on the ground. There was no change of colour in his face, no crying out, no groaning. It was hard to believe that the man was still alive. His eyes were then gouged, one after the other. Meanwhile the emperor, seeing in the other's torment the fate that was about to overtake him, too, lived through Constantine's anguish in himself, beating his hands together, smiting his face, and bellowing in agony.

The Nobilissimus, his eyes gouged out, stood up from the ground and leaned for support on one of his most intimate friends. He addressed those who came up to him with great courage – a man who rose superior to the trials that beset him, to whom death was as nothing. With Michael it was different, for when the executioner saw him flinch away and lower himself to base entreaty, he bound him securely. He held him down with considerable force, to stop the violent twitching when he was undergoing his punishment. After his eyes, too, had been blinded, the insolence of the mob, so marked before, died away, and with it their fury against these men. They left them to rest there, while they themselves hurried back to Theodora. One of the two empresses was in fact in the palace, the other in the great cathedral of St Sophia.

The Senate was unable to decide between them. Zoe, who was in the palace, they respected because she was the elder; Theodora, who was in the church, because it was through her that the revolt had been brought to an end and to her they owed their preservation. Each, therefore, had a claim on the Empire. However, the problem was settled for them by Zoe. For the first time, she greeted her sister and embraced her with affection. What is more, she shared with her the Empire they both inherited. The question of the government was thus resolved by agreement between them.

[32] The cult of St Theodosia at her church (now the Gül Camii) which was famous for its miracle-working relics; from *Byzantine Churches in Constantinople* by Alexander van Millingen.

There can be no doubt that the mosque Gul Jamissi (mosque of the Rose), that stands within the Gate Aya Kapou, near the Golden Horn, was the Byzantine church of S. Theodosia. . . . The saint is celebrated in ecclesiastical history for her opposition to the iconoclastic policy of Leo the Isaurian. For when that emperor commanded the eikon of Christ over the Bronze Gate of the Great Palace to be removed, Theodosia, at the head of a band of women, rushed to the spot and overthrew the ladder up which the officer, charged with the execution of the imperial order, was climbing to reach the image. In the fall the officer was killed. Whereupon a rough soldier seized Theodosia, and dragging her to the forum of the Bous (Ak Serai), struck her dead by driving a ram's horn through her neck. Naturally, when the cause for which she sacrificed her life triumphed, she was honoured as a martyr, and men said, 'The ram's horn, in killing thee, O Theodosia, appeared to thee a new Horn of Amalthea.' . . .

The shrine of S. Theodosia was famed for miraculous cures. Her horn of plenty was filled with gifts of healing. Twice a week, on Wednesdays and Fridays, according to Stephen of Novgorod, or on Mondays and Fridays, according to another pilgrim, the relics of the saint were carried in procession and laid upon sick and impotent folk. Those were days of high festival. All the approaches to the church were packed with men and women eager to witness the wonders performed. Patients representing almost every complaint to which human flesh is heir filled the court. Gifts of oil and money poured into the treasury; the church was a blaze of lighted tapers; the prayers were long; the chanting was loud. Meanwhile the suffererers were borne one after another to the sacred relics, 'and whoever was sick,' says the devout Stephen, 'was healed.' So profound was the impression caused by one of these cures in 1306, that Pachymeres considered it his duty, as the historian of his day, to record the wonder; and his example may be followed to furnish an illustration of the beliefs and usages which bulked large of the religious life witnessed in the churches of Byzantine Constantinople . . .

The last scene witnessed in this church as a Christian sanctuary was pathetic in the extreme. It was the vigil of the day sacred to the memory of the saint, May 29, 1453. The siege of the city by the Turks had reached its crisis. The morning light would see the Queen of Cities saved or lost. All hearts were torn with anxiety, and the religious fervour of the population rose to the highest pitch. Already, in the course of the previous day, a great procession had gone through the streets of the city, invoking the aid of God and of all His saints. The emperor and the leading personages of his court were in S. Sophia, praying, weeping, embracing one another, forgiving one another, all feeling oppressed by a sense of doom. In the terrible darkness the church of S. Theodosia, ablaze with lighted tapers, gleamed like a beacon of hope. An immense congregation, including many women, filled the building, and prayers ascended to Heaven with unwonted earnestness – when suddenly the tramp of soldiers and strange shouts were heard. Had the city indeed fallen? The entrance of Turkish troops into the church removed all doubt, and the men and women who had gathered to pray for deliverance were carried off as prisoners of war. According to the *Belgic Chronicle*, the body of the saint and other relics were thrown into the mire and cast to the dogs.

[33] The restoration and redecoration of the church of St Saviour in Chora (the Kariye Camii) by Theodore Metochites in the early 1300s; from *Byzantine Churches in Constantinople* by Alexander van Millingen.

But the decay into which the establishment had fallen could not be long ignored, and a wealthy, talented, and influential citizen who resided in the neighbourhood, Theodore Metochites, decided to restore the edifice as a monument of the artistic revival of his own day.

Theodore Metochites was one of the most remarkable men of his day. His tall, large, well-proportioned figure, his bright countenance, commanded attention wherever he appeared. He was, moreover, a great student of ancient Greek literature and of the literature of later times, and although never a master of style, became an author and attempted verse. . . . In fact, he belonged to the class of brilliant Greek scholars who might have regenerated the East had not the unfortunate political situation of their country driven them to Italy to herald and promote the Renaissance in Western Europe. Theodore Metochites was, moreover, a politician. He took an active part in the administration of affairs during the reign of Andronicus II., holding the office of Grand Logothetes of the Treasury; and such was his devotion to politics, that when acting as a statesman it might be forgotten that he was a scholar. The unhappy strife between Andronicus II. and Andronicus III. caused Theodore Metochites the profoundest anxiety, and it was not his fault if the feud between the grandfather and the grandson refused to be healed. His efforts to bring that disgraceful and disastrous quarrel to an end involved great self-sacrifice and wrecked his career. For the counsels he addressed to Andronicus III. gave mortal offence, and when the young emperor entered the capital and took up his quarters in the palace of the Porphyrogenitus (Tekfour Serai), his troops sacked and demolished Theodore's mansion in that vicinity. The beautiful marbles which adorned the residence were sent as an imperial present to a Scythian prince, while the fallen statesman was banished to Didymotica for two years. Upon his return from exile Theodore found a shelter in the monastery which he had restored in his prosperous days. But there also, for some two years longer, the cup of sorrow was pressed to his lips. A malady from which he suffered caused him excruciating pain; his sons were implicated in a political plot and thrown into prison; Andronicus II., between whom and himself all communication had been forbidden, died; and so the wornout man assumed the habit of a monk, and lay down to die on the 13th of March 1331, a month after his imperial friend. His one consolation was the beautiful church he bequeathed to succeeding generations for the worship of God.

To the renovation of the church Theodore Metochites devoted himself heart and soul, and spent money for that object on a lavish scale. As the central portion of the building was comparatively well preserved, it was to the outer part of the edifice that he directed his chief attention – the two narthexes and the parecclesion. These were to a large extent rebuilt and decorated with the marbles and mosaics, which after six centuries, and notwithstanding the neglect and injuries they have suffered during the greater part of that period, still excite the admiration they awakened when fresh from the artist's hand.

The connection of Theodore Metochites with his splendid work is immortalised not only by historians of his day and by himself, but also by the mosaic which surmounts the main entrance to the church from the inner narthex. There the restorer of the building, arrayed in his official robes, and on bended knees, holds a model of the church in his hands and offers it to the saviour seated on a throne. Beside the kneeling figure is the legend, *ὁ κτήτωρ λογοθέτε̂ης τοῦ γεννικοῦ Θεόδωρος ό Μετοχίτης*, 'The builder, Logothetes of the Treasury, Theodore the Metochites'.

The restoration of the church must have been completed before the year 1321, for in that year Nicephorus Gregoras describes it as then recently (*ἄαρτι*) renovated, and in use for the celebration of divine service. How long before 1321 the work of repair precisely commenced cannot be determined, but it was in process as early as 1303, for that date is inscribed in Arabic numerals on the mosaic depicting the miracle at Cana, which stands to the right of the figure of Christ over the door leading from the outer to the inner narthex. But to have reached the stage at which mosaics could be applied the work of restoration must have been commenced sometime before 1303.

The Great Walls of Constantinople

[34] The construction, maintenance and importance of the walls of Constantinople, and the Golden Gate (now part of the Yedikule); from *Byzantine Constantinople* by Alexander van Millingen.

The erection and repair of the fortifications of a city was an undertaking which all citizens were required to assist, in one form or another. On that point the laws were very stringent, and no rank or privilege exempted any one from the obligation to promote the work. One-third of the annual land-tax of the city could be drawn upon to defray the outlay, all expenses above that amount being met by requisitions laid upon the inhabitants. The work of construction was entrusted to the Factions, as several inscriptions on the walls testify. In 447, when the Theodosian fortifications were repaired and extended, the Blues and the Greens furnished, between them, sixteen thousand labourers for the undertaking.

The stone employed upon the fortifications is tertiary limestone, brought from the neighbourhood of Makrikeui, where the hollows and mounds formed in quarrying are still visible. The bricks used are from 1 foot 1 inch to 1 foot 2 inches square, and 2 inches thick. They are sometimes stamped with the name of their manufacturer or donor, and occasionally bear the name of the contemporary emperor, and the indiction in which they were made. Mortar, mixed with powdered brick, was employed in large quantities, lest it should dry without taking hold, and bound the masonry into a solid mass, hard as rock.

The wall of Anthemius was erected in 413, the fifth year of Theodosius II, then about twelve years of age, and is now represented by the inner wall in the fortifications that extend along the west of the city, from the Sea of Marmora to the ruins of the Byzantine Palace, known as Tekfour Serai. The new city limits were thus placed at a distance of one mile to one mile and a half west of the Wall of Constantine.

This change in the position of the landward line of defence involved the extension likewise of the walls along the two shores of the city; but though that portion of the work must have been included in the plan of Anthemius, it was not executed till after his day. As we shall find, the new seaboard of the capital was fortified a quarter of a century later, in 439, under the direction of the Prefect Cyrus, while Theodosius II was still upon the throne.

The bulwarks of Anthemius saved the city from attack by Attila. They were too formidable for him to venture to assail them. But they suffered at the hands of the power which was to inflict more injury upon the fortifications of Constantinople than any other foe. In 447, only thirty-four years after their construction, the greater portion of the new walls, with fifty-seven towers, was overthrown by a series of violent earthquakes. . . .

As the Porta Triumphalis of Constantinople, the Golden Gate was the scene of many historical events and imposing ceremonies.

So long as the inauguration of an emperor upon his accession to the throne was celebrated at the Hebdomon (Makrikeui), it was through the Golden Gate that a new sovereign entered his capital on the way to the Imperial Palace beside St Sophia. Marcian (450), Leo I (457), Basiliscus (476), Phocas (602), Leo the Armenian (813), and Nicephorus Phocas (963), were welcomed as emperors by the city authorities at this portal.

Distinguished visitors to the Byzantine Court, also, were sometimes allowed to enter the city by this gate, as a mark of special honour. The Legates of Pope Hormisdas were met here upon their arrival on a mission to Justin I: here, in 708, Pope Constantine was received with great ceremony, when he came to confer with Justinian II: and here, in the reign of Basil II, the Legates of Pope Hadrian II were admitted. Under Romanus Lecapenus, the procession which bore through the city to St Sophia the Icon of Christ, brought from Edessa, entered at the Porta Aurea.

It was, however, on the return of an emperor to the city after a victorious campaign that the Porta Aurea fulfilled its highest purpose, and presented a brilliant spectacle of life and splendour.

Through this triumphal arch came Theodosius the Great, after his defeat of Maximus; by it Heraclius entered the capital to celebrate the success of his Persian expeditions; through it passed Constantine Copronymus, after the defeat of the Bulgarians; Theophilus, on two occasions, after the repulse of the Saracens; Basil I, after his successes at Tephrice and Germanicia; Zimisces, after his victories over the Russians under Swaitoslaf; Basil II, after the slaughter of the Bulgarians; and, for the last time, Michael Palæologus, upon the restoration of the Greek Empire in 1261.

It would seem that, in accordance with Old Roman custom, victorious generals, below Imperial rank, were not allowed to enter the city in triumph through this gate. Belisarius, Maurice, Nicephorus Phocas, before he became emperor, and Leo his brother, celebrated their respective triumphs over the Vandals, Persians and Saracens, in the Hippodrome and the great street of the city.

An Imperial triumphal procession was marshalled on the plain in front of the Golden Gate, and awaited there the arrival of the emperor, either from Hebdomon or from the Palace of Blachernæ. The principal captives, divided into several companies, and guarded by bands of soldiers, led the march. Next followed the standards and weapons and other spoils of war. Then, seated on a magnificent white charger, came the emperor himself, arrayed in robes embroidered with gold and pearls, his crown on his head, his sceptre in his right hand, his victorious sword by his side. Close to him rode his son, or the Cæsar of the day, another resplendent figure of light, also on a white horse. Upon reaching the gate the victor might, like Theophilus, dismount for a few moments, and falling thrice upon his face, humbly acknowledge the Divine aid to which he owed the triumph of his arms. At length the Imperial *cortège* passed through the great archway. The civic authorities came forward and did homage, offering the conqueror a crown of gold and a laurel wreath, and accepting from him a rich largess in return; the Factions rent the air with shouts – 'Glory to God, who restores our sovereigns to us, crowned with victory! Glory to God, who has magnified you, Emperors of the Romans! Glory to Thee, All-Holy Trinity, for we behold our Emperors victorious! Welcome, Victors, most valiant sovereigns!' And then the glittering procession wended its way to the Great Palace, through the dense crowds that packed the Mesè and the principal Fora of the city, all gay with banners, flowers, and evergreens.

Sometimes the emperor, as in the case of Heraclius, rode in a chariot instead of on horseback; or the occupant of the triumphal car might be, as on the occasion of the triumph of Zimisces, the

Icon of the Virgin. Michael Palæologus entered the city on foot, walking as far as the Church of St John Studius before he mounted his horse. On the occasion of the second triumph of Theophilus, the beautiful custom was introduced of making children take part in the ceremonial with wreaths of flowers. . . .

One cannot bring this account of the Walls of Constantinople to a close without calling to mind, again, the splendid part they played in the history of the world. To them the Queen of Cities, as her sons loved to call her, owed her long life, and her noble opportunity to advance the higher welfare of mankind. How great her services in that respect have been, we are coming to recognize more clearly, through a better acquaintance with her achievements, and a fairer judgment upon her faults. The city which preserved Greek learning, maintained Roman justice, sounded the depths of religious thought, and gave to Art new forms of beauty, was no mean city, and had reason to be proud of her record.

But never was she so grand as in her attitude towards the barbarous tribes and Oriental peoples which threatened her existence, and sought to render European civilization impossible. Some of her foes – the Goths and the great Slavic race – she not only fought, but also gathered within the pale of civilized Christendom. With others, like the Huns, Persians, Saracens, Turks, she waged a relentless warfare, often achieving signal triumphs, sometimes worsted in the struggle, always contesting every inch of her ground, retarding for a thousand years the day of her fall, perishing sword in hand, and giving Western Europe, meantime, scope to become worthy to take from her dying hands the banner of the world's hope. This is service similar to that which has earned for Ancient Greece men's eternal gratitude, and has made Marathon, Thermopylæ, Salamis, Platæa, names which will never die.

[35] The invading Crusaders breach the city walls in 1204; from *Chronicles of the Crusades* by Joinville and Villehardouin, translated by M.R.B. Shaw.

(Geoffroy de Villehardouin, son of a French nobleman from the Champagne country, was appointed Marshal of Champagne in 1185 – Chief of Staff, as it were, to Thibaut, the Count of

Champagne, an appointment he shared with the Sieur de Joinville. As such, he joined the loot-hungry band of Western warriors who enrolled in the Fourth Crusade and 'took the cross'. His account is a kind of official history, not a daily record or campaign journal, and he writes with authority and experience. His book, famous as one of the main sources about the Crusade, is also a tribute to the noble, often chivalrous, virtues of the Marshal himself, despite the horrors perpetrated by his allies and troops upon the finest city in Christendom. He probably died around 1218, in Rumania, whose Marshal he had by then become. He never went home.)

On the Friday morning the warships, galleys, and other vessels approached the city in due order, and began to deliver a fierce and determined assault. In many places the Crusaders landed and advanced right up to the walls; in many others the scaling ladders on the ships came so close to the battlements that those on the walls and the towers crossed lances hand to hand with their assailants. The assault continued, fast and fierce and furious, in more than a hundred places, till round about three o'clock in the afternoon.

But, for our sins, our troops were repulsed in that attack, and those that had landed from the galleys and transports were forcibly driven back aboard. I must admit that on that day our army lost more men than the Greeks, and the latter were greatly delighted. Some of our people withdrew from the assault, taking their ships right out of the battle; others let their vessels ride at anchor so near the walls of the city that each side was able to launch stones from petraries and mangonels at the other.

That evening, towards six o'clock, the barons and the Doge of Venice assembled for a conference in a church on the further side of the harbour, close to where they had been encamped. Many different points of view were exchanged at that meeting; the French, in particular, were greatly distressed by the reverse they had suffered that day. Many of those present advised an attack on the city from another side, at a place where the defences were weaker. The Venetians, who had more experience of the sea, pointed out that if they went to that side, the current would carry them down the straits, and they would be unable to stop their ships. There were, I might say, certain people in the company who would have been only too pleased if the current had borne them down the straits, or the wind had done so; they did not care where they went, so long as they left that land behind and went on their way. Nor was that to be wondered at, for we were in very grave danger at the time.

After much discussion, it was finally decided to spend the next day, which was a Saturday, and the whole of Sunday, repairing the damage done to the ships and the equipment, and to renew the assault on the Monday. This time they would have the ships that carried the scaling ladders bound together, two by two, so that each pair could make a combined attack on one tower. This plan was adopted because, in that day's engagement, they had noticed that when only one ship had attacked each tower, the greater number of men on a tower than on a ladder had made it too heavy a task for a ship to undertake alone. It was therefore reasonable to assume that two ships together would do more effective damage than one. This plan of binding the ships in pairs was carried out while the troops were standing by on the Saturday and the Sunday.

Meanwhile the Emperor Murzuphlus had come to encamp with all his forces on an open space directly opposite our lines, and had pitched his scarlet tents there. Thus matters remained till the Monday morning, when all the men on the various ships got their arms and equipment ready. The citizens of Constantinople were now much less afraid of our troops than at the time of our first assault. They were, in fact, in such a confident mood that all along the walls and towers there was nothing to be seen but people. Then began a fierce and magnificent assault, as each ship steered a straight course forward. The shouts that rose from the battle created such a din that it seemed as if the whole earth were crumbling to pieces.

The assault had been going on for a considerable time when our Lord raised for us a wind called Boreas, which drove the ships still further on to the shore. Two of the ships which were bound together – one called the *Pilgrim* and the other the *Paradise* – approached so close to a tower, one of them on one side and one on the other, as God and the wind drove them onwards, that the ladder of the *Pilgrim* made contact with it. Immediately a Venetian, in company with the French knight named André Durboise, forced their way in. Other men began to follow them, and in the end the defenders were routed and driven out.

The moment the knights aboard the transports saw this

happen, they landed, and raising their ladders against the wall, climbed to the top, and took four more towers. Then all the rest of the troops started to leap out of warships, galleys, and transports, helter-skelter, each as fast as he could. They broke down about three of the gates and entered the city. The horses were then taken out of the transports; the knights mounted and rode straight towards the place where the Emperor Murzuphlus had his camp. He had his battalions drawn up in front of the tents; but as soon as his men saw the knights charging towards them on horseback, they retreated in disorder. The Emperor himself fled through the streets of the city to the castle of Bucoleon.

Then followed a scene of massacre and pillage: on every hand the Greeks were cut down, their horses, palfreys, mules, and other possessions snatched as booty. So great was the number of killed and wounded that no man could count them. A great part of the Greek nobles had fled towards the gate of Blachernae; but by this time it was past six o'clock, and our men had grown weary of fighting and slaughtering. The troops began to assemble in a great square inside Constantinople. Then, convinced that it would take them at least a month to subdue the whole city, with its great churches and palaces, and the people inside it, they decided to settle down near the walls and towers they had already captured. . . .

Our troops, all utterly worn out and weary, rested quietly that night. But the Emperor Murzuphlus did not rest; instead, he assembled his forces and said he was going to attack the Franks. However he did not do as he had announced, but rode along certain streets as far away as possible from those occupied by our army, till he came to a gate called the Golden Gate through which he escaped, and so left the city. . . .

The Marquis de Montferrat rode straight along the shore to the palace of Bucoleon. As soon as he arrived there the place was surrendered to him, on condition that the lives of all the people in it should be spared. . . . In the same way that the palace of Bucoleon was surrendered to the Marquis de Montferrat, so the palace of Blachernae was yielded to the Comte de Flandre's brother Henri, and on the same conditions. There too was found a great store of treasure, not less than there had been in the palace of Bucoleon. . . . The rest of the army, scattered throughout the city, also gained much booty; so much, indeed,

The Castle of the Seven Towers on the Great Walls, and a view of Constantinople from the Propontide; from *Voyage Pittoresque de la Grèce*, 1782–1809 by M.G. Choiseul Gouffier

that no one could estimate its amount or its value. It included gold and silver, table-services and precious stones, satin and silk, mantles of squirrel fur, ermine and miniver, and every choicest thing to be found on this earth. Geoffroy de Villehardouin here declares that, to his knowledge, so much booty had never been gained in any city since the creation of the world.

[36] The Egyptian mummy at the Castle of Seven Towers (Yedikule) on the walls; from *Christianity and Islam under the Sultans* by F.W. Hasluck.

A more extraordinary story is related by Lady Mary Montagu in 1717 of an Egyptian mummy sent by way of Constantinople as a present to Charles XII of Sweden, then at Bender. 'The Turks', she says, 'fancied it the body of God knows who; and that the state of their empire mystically depended on the conservation of it. Some old prophecies were remembered upon this occasion, and the mummy was committed prisoner to the Seven Towers.' This might be disregarded as the empty gossip of contemporary Constantinople, were it not corroborated nearly a hundred years later. Pouqueville says that the story of the mummy was told in a Turkish history, of which part was translated for him by M. Ruffin; the mummy, which was sent ninety-four years before as a present from the King of France to the King of Sweden, 'was about to be forwarded to its destination when it was stopped by the Janissaries upon guard at the gate of Adrianople. Being sealed with the signet of the kaimakam, it was supposed to be the relic of some saint, and was deposited at the Seven Towers.' The reason of Pouqueville's interest in the mummy was that he had himself happened to re-discover it, during his captivity in that fortress, in a chamber of the northern tower of the Golden Gate. He 'never heard it said, as Lady Mary Wortley Montagu affirms, that the Turks attached to it the idea of a palladium on which hung the preservation of the empire', a statement which he regarded as 'one of the pleasing fictions of her work'. But in the light of the prophecies which have circulated for so long among Greeks and Turks alike of the saviour-king who should arise from the dead to deliver the city from the Moslem yoke, it is probable that Lady Mary Montagu's story is substantially correct, and that in the occurrences she relates is to be found one source of the modern tradition locating the tomb of Constantine Palaiologos at the Golden Gate. For our present question it is interesting to remark that the Turkish guardians are said to light to him a lamp every night and to cover him with a shawl which they renew once a year.

[37] Byron's description of the walls in the early nineteenth century; from *Letters and Journals of Lord Byron* by Thomas Moore.

The walls of the Seraglio are like the walls of Newstead gardens, only higher, and much in the same order; but the ride by the walls of the city, on the land side, is beautiful. Imagine four miles of immense, triple battlements, covered with ivy, surmounted with 218 towers, and, on the other side of the road, Turkish burying-grounds (the loveliest spots on earth), full of enormous cypresses. I have seen the ruins of Athens, of Ephesus, and Delphi. I have traversed great part of Turkey, and many other parts of Europe, and some of Asia; but I never beheld a work of nature or art which yielded an impression like the prospect on each side from the Seven Towers to the end of the Golden Horn.

[38] A lovers' walk beside the walls in the 1890s; from *Aziyadé* by Pierre Loti, translated by Marjorie Lawrie.

(Pierre Loti (*a nom de plume* – he was born Julien Viand in 1850) died in 1923, world-famous. His career in the French Navy, as a member of the French Academy, as the semi-canonized friend of Turkey, and as a lover and writer, has provided the glittering, exotic material for half-a-dozen biographies. Politically he pleaded Turkey's cause before a Europe sceptical of 'the sick man of Europe'; as a novelist he was a creator of legends and a master fantasist. His novels today are largely unread, but in his elegant, often romantic, sometimes intoxicated prose he recorded forever a private Stamboul almost totally lost to us today.)

It was over there in Stamboul. We were engaged on one of our rashest ventures, one of our days of reckless truancy. But

Stamboul was so big, we argued, nobody knew us, and old Abeddin was away in Adrianople.

It was a bright winter afternoon and we were out wandering together, she and I, rejoicing like a couple of children to be out in the sun for once, and roaming the countryside. But we had chosen a cheerless region for our walk. We were strolling along by the great wall of Stamboul, the most solitary spot in the world, where nothing seems to have stirred, since the days of the last Byzantine Emperors. This great city's means of communications are all by sea. The ancient ramparts are steeped in a silence, such as broods over the approach to a necropolis. Here and there a gate has been built in the thickness of these walls, but to no purpose, for never a soul goes in or out. These queer, little, low doors have an air of mystery, and above the lintels are gilded inscriptions and curious decorations. Between the inhabited quarters of the town and the fortifications, lie great tracts of waste land, dotted with suspicious-looking hovels, and with crumbling ruins, dating from every epoch of history. There is nothing from without to break the eternal monotony of these walls, save here and there the white shaft of a minaret, rising in the distance. Always the same battlements, the same turrets, the same dark hues, laid on by the hand of time, the same regular lines, running straight and dreary, till they are lost on the far horizon.

We were walking all alone at the base of these great walls. The surrounding country was studded with clumps of lowering cypresses, as tall as cathedrals, beneath whose shade thousands of Osman sepulchres lay crowded together. In no other country have I seen so many cemeteries, so many tombs, so many dead.

'This,' said Aziyadé, 'is a favourite haunt of Azrael. He alights here at night, folds his great wings, and wanders in human shape beneath these fearsome shades.'

It was very still in this realm of the dead, in those solemn, awe-inspiring groves. But we two were enjoying the adventure, glad to be young, and, for once, roaming together in the open air, under the clear blue sky, like ordinary mortals.

The Fall of Constantinople, 1453

[39] The long siege of Constantinople by Sultan Mehmet II the Conqueror in 1453; from *Histoire de l'Empire Ottoman* by Ritter J. von Hammer-Purgstall. Translated by Marie Noële Kelly.

On the Friday after Easter, 6 April 1453, Mohammed appeared in front of the city, and put his tent behind a hill facing the gate Charsis (or Caligaria). The line of his troops extended from the wooden Gate of the Palace to the Golden Gate. The great cannon was placed in front of this Caligaria gate which the Emperor had recently fortified. Knowing the gate was impregnable, the Sultan moved the cannon to face St Romanus' Gate (which to this day carries this name); on each side of it there were two smaller cannons of a minor calibre whose balls nevertheless weighed 150 pounds. These were as a prelude for the 'monster' cannon. Loading the latter took two hours and therefore it could only fire eight times a day. At dawn the first shot signalled the attack, but it burst immediately, blowing up the chief gunner, Orban. Once more it was tried, but failed.

Meanwhile, Hunyade's envoy arrived at Mohammed's camp to tell the Sultan that the year-old truce arranged between him and Hunyade, though it had not yet expired, was cancelled, as his master had handed over the Kingdom's business to his sovereign, Vladislas. . . . One day watching the firing of the monster cannon and pitying the ineptitude of the gunner, he showed him how, by first hitting the furthest point of the wall, he could create a breach more quickly. This advice was followed with complete success. So it was a Hungarian who had cast the cannon, and it was a Hungarian who taught the Turks to use it efficiently.

As well as this monster and its two satellites, other less powerful guns lined the walls from the Golden Gate to the Wooden Gate; fourteen batteries and many missile-throwers (*balistae*) thundered at Constantinople's walls, whilst the archers rained arrows on the besieged. Sappers (from hilly Novoberda) mined into the city's moat; they dug many openings into the exterior walls whereby the Turks greatly harmed the Greeks and were at no risk themselves. Mohammed had also built four towers mounted on wheels, and a huge siege machine called by the Greeks 'Epesolin' ('Taker of Towns'). The walls of this machine were worked by many wheels which were sheathed by a triple leather cover, always kept wet. Its top was finished with turrets and parapets to protect the soldiers: below, three gates opened towards the city. The machine carried wood and bundles to fill the ditch and drawbridges which, when lowered, allowed hand-to-hand fighting with the Greeks defending the ramparts.

The Turkish army facing Constantinople numbered a quarter of a million men, 100,000 cavalry were in reserve, 100,000 infantry composed the right wing backing on to the Golden Gate, and the left wing, consisting of 50,000 infantry, reached down to the Blachernae Palace. The Sultan chose the centre with 15,000 Janissaries. Saganos Pasha had been posted with a few troops on the heights dominating Galata, facing Constantinople itself, on the other side of the port. As to the fleet, there were eighteen triremes, twenty-five transport vessels and more than 300 smaller ships; in all, 420 vessels. Under the orders of Baltaoghli, this fleet had been equipped during the winter in a bay (still called Baltaoghli to *this day*) in the Bosphorus.

Therefore the Turks were twenty times stronger than the Greeks, and their will to attack was far stronger than the courage of the besieged. Defending the Greeks under arms there were only 5,000 men, according to a list compiled during the siege by Phranzes at the Emperor's order. Added to this were 2,000 mercenaries and between 300 and 500 Genoese brought by two galleys under the command of John Longus, a member of the aristocratic Giustiniani family. The Emperor showed his gratitude for this 'last-ditch' help by promoting the brave Longus to be captain of a body of 300 men with a Golden Charter (*bulla*) investing him with the property of the Isle of Lemnos in case Mohammed II, through unexpected circumstances, gave up the siege (as had his father Murad). The Greeks, backed by the Genoese in Galata, were still full of this hope. The latter were giving the besieged all manner of help, whilst at the same time assuring Mohammed they would observe the ancient treaties and keep a strict neutrality. The Sultan, aware of these manoeuvres, swore he would smite the serpent as soon as he had killed the dragon.

As for the Greek fleet, it was composed of three Venetian merchantmen (called *galliasses*) with three Genoese, one Spanish, and two from Cydon: altogether fourteen sails. The same inferiority existed with regard to the artillery. In fact, the Greeks did not regret not having a monster cannon similar to that of the Turks, as their 150-pound balls shook the walls more fatally from the inside than those of the Turks from the outside. The Greeks, to punish the gunner who had allowed one of their large guns to explode, were going to kill him, accusing him of being a traitor – but as there was not sufficient proof, he was released. At dusk the Greeks filled barrels with stones and earth to repair the breaches, while their workmen neutralized the Turkish mines.

John Grant, a German, taught the besieged how to exploit Greek fire; with it they balanced the advantage the Turks gained from their familiarity with artillery. The fire reduced to ashes the great machine which had, in a night, toppled the Tower of St Romanus. Seeing the destroyed machine, Mohammed praised the Greeks: he had just never thought they would be capable of such a great triumph in one night.

On 15 April 1453, the Turkish fleet, in its pride of 450 sails, left the Bay of Philidia and dropped anchor opposite the Two Columns [today Beşiktaş].

A few days later five vessels appeared in the Propontide, one belonging to the Emperor and four to the Genoese. During the whole of March, they had been unable to leave Chios; but, a south wind rising, they arrived opposite Constantinople, all sails up. A squadron of the Turkish fleet, 150 strong, advanced to cut off the Christians and guard the harbour; there was a cerulean sky, the sea was calm, and spectators were looking out over the walls. The Sultan himself was on the shore to enjoy the battle, certain that the numerical strength of his fleet would bring about victory. But the eighteen galleys leading the squadron were manned by inexperienced soldiers; they were low in the water and in an instant were deluged with missiles, a shower of stones and canisters of Greek fire. They were twice repulsed.

The Greeks and the Genoese rivalled each other in valour. Flectanella, captain of the Imperial Galley, fought like a lion; Cataneo, Norarra, and Bala Neri, captains of the Genoese, followed his example. The Turkish ships could not use their oars as the sea was covered with arrows: they collided with each other and two caught fire.

Mohammed, at this sight, lost any self control, and, foaming with rage, he forced his horse into the sea as if he were going to snatch victory from the Greeks. His officers did the same to reach

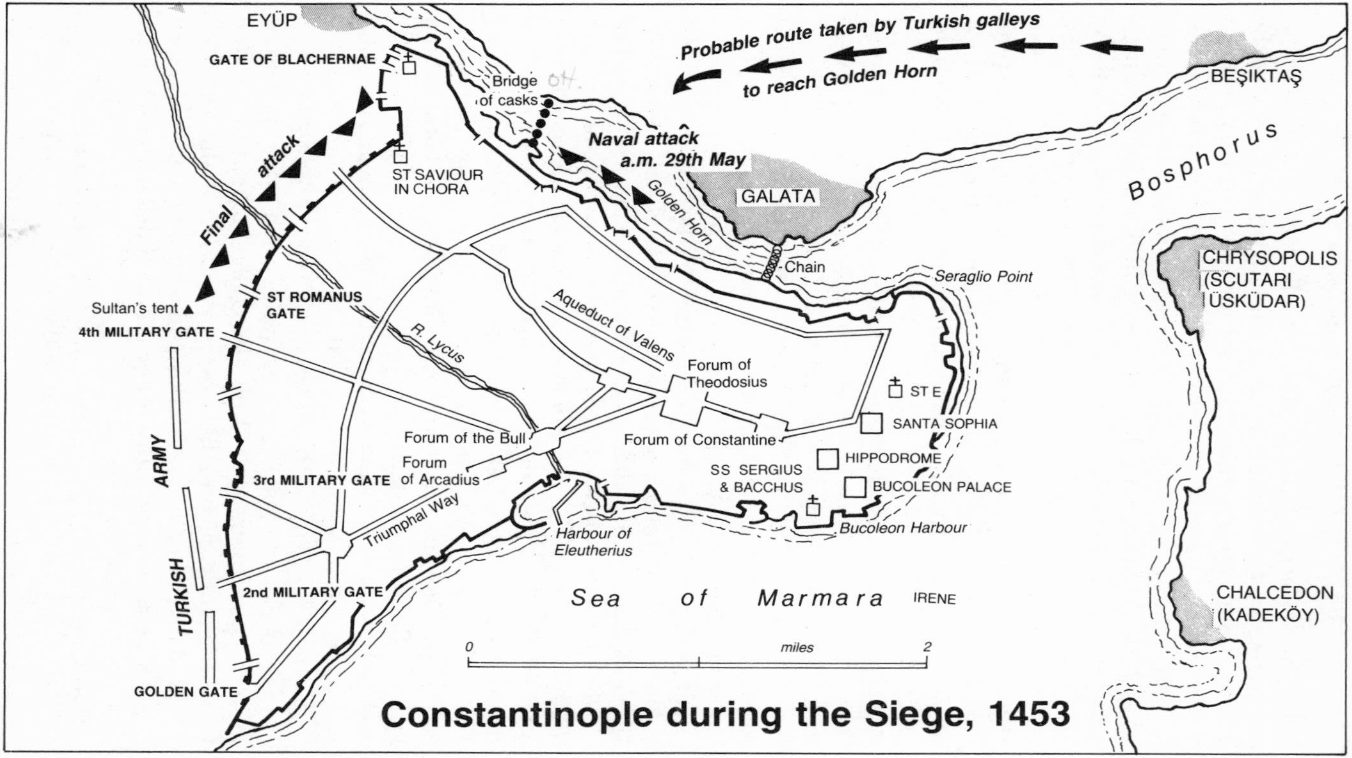

Constantinople during the Siege, 1453

the ships, which were fighting only a stone's throw away. The soldiers, excited by shame or fear, renewed the attack but failed. Profiting from a fresh breeze five vessels glided through the Turkish fleet and entered the port. The iron chain linking the fish market in Galata with its counterpart in Constantinople was lowered to let them through, and then immediately raised again. The Turks' loss was immense and their confusion even greater. At this humiliation, Mohammed flew into such a fury against his admiral Baltaoghli that it was only at the prayers of the Janissaries that he relented from impaling him, to punish him for treachery. He allowed him to live instead, but was determined to punish him with his own hand: four slaves threw the admiral on to the ground and the Sultan gave him a hundred blows with his heavy mace . . . which inflicted as many wounds. One stone thrown at him tore his eye and his cheek.

The failure of Baltaoghli, the High Admiral of the Ottoman Empire, gave some credence to the opinion (since adopted by them) that God meant the Turks to own the earth and that the dominion of the seas was reserved to the Infidels. A *divan* was called after this naval battle. Khalil Pasha thought it would be wise to take the opportunity to spare Constantinople, and suggested the Sultan made peace with the Emperor. In vain he argued that reinforcements might get through to the enemy. Against him were the Vizier, Saganos Pasha, brother-in-law and favourite of the Sultan, the *molla* (priest) Kourami who had brought up the Sultan, and Sheikh Aksehemzeddin, whose preaching excited the troops. But when Mohammed consulted them about the best way to cut the chain barring the port, or about how to attack the city simultaneously from the left and the right, they were silent. An original idea resolved the debate. Muslim historians all attribute it to Mohammed; it might have been so, since only his bold and audacious spirit could have thought it out, but examples of this kind from ancient history might also have occurred to him. It meant dragging the fleet overland to reach the port. Though very difficult, this operation was not unique. Justin recounts that the inhabitants of Colchis, pursuing the Argonauts, sailed up the Danube and, putting their boats on their shoulders, carried them across the mountains to the Adriatic shore.

The distance was only two leagues – but the ground was very bumpy. Mohammed ordered them to make a 'road' of planks covered with the grease of oxen and rams to ease the passage, and seventy biremes, and some triremes or quinqueremes, were dragged over the valleys and hillocks from the shores of the Bosphorus to the Gulf of the Golden Horn in a single night. On each ship the captain was at the prow, the helmsman at the rear. Sails were unfurled, trumpets sounded, drums beat dawn. The besieged saw with as much surprise as horror more than seventy Turkish men-o'-war anchor before their walls. Giustiniani decided at once to burn the flotilla, but the Turks were informed by the Galata Genoese, who throughout the siege were traitors to both camps. At night they secretly forwarded help to the Greeks, and during the day gave the Turks unlimited oil to wash down the great cannon after each discharge. At midnight Giustiniani approached the enemy vessels, but the watchful Turks, observing him, blew up his ship with one enormous shot. It went down with 150 young Italians. Giustiniani escaped with difficulty, but most of his loyal aides were drowned.

The Turks answered their cries of distress with a shout of victory, which re-echoed from the shores and the seven hills of the city. At dawn again, to ensure the efficiency of their artillery, the Turks aimed one of their great cannons at a richly appointed Genoese vessel anchored in front of Galata. It blew up with all its treasures. Crossly, the Genoese deputies complained to the Sultan at this treatment by way of thanks for their services, without which the Turks would never have entered the harbour. The Sultan replied that it had been thought the vessel belonged to the enemy, and that the Genoese would be compensated after the war. The Ottomans murdered the prisoners they had taken during the night under the city walls. Now master of the harbour, Mohammed decided to build a bridge from shore to shore. Barrels forming a chain and fixed to each other by iron clamps, extended across the harbour carrying wooden planks: as it was very firm, this allowed the army to cross it in ranks of five men. It could also carry a cannon to protect their passage. The Turkish fleet had dropped anchor under the very walls of the city. In this extreme danger, the Greeks conceived the idea of burning both bridge and vessels, and the Venetian Jack Kok, undertook this perilous task. He chose three small vessels with athletic oarsmen; carrying Greek fire and other inflammable material, he rowed out with his forty determined sailors. As soon as the Greeks saw the ships ignited, two sailors (placed by Kok near the bridge) were to set the bridge on fire. But the Turks were on their guard, and a hail of stones sank Kok's ships. Only one of the Turkish galleys caught fire and the flames, starting on the bridge, were put out. The crews of the three vessels were murdered under the very eyes of the Greeks, who, in revenge, fixed the heads of 260 Turkish prisoners on their crenellated towers. This ill-fated enterprise caused despair among the besieged. It might have had even worse consequences than the disaster itself, since the Genoese of Giustiniani accused Kok of inefficiency. This enraged the Venetians and had not the Emperor intervened, the row might have been bloody.

Seven weeks the siege had already lasted on land: four towers had been demolished and a breach opened at St Romanus' Gate. The army occupied the ditch which was half filled with the debris of the ruined fortifications. Mohammed now wished to send a last message to the Emperor, either to fulfil the law which required a peace offer to be made before exterminating him, or to find out if the city could still hold out. Isfendiaroghli, a son-in-law of the Sultan, found his way into Constantinople, not as the Sultan's envoy but as if moved by pity at the fate of the Greeks. He was received by the Emperor, surrounded by all his Court, and he pleaded with the sovereign to submit promptly so as to avoid slavery for the city's inhabitants and their women and children.

In the council which the Emperor immediately held, the dictates of honour, abetted only by those of despair, were heeded. The Emperor replied to the Turkish envoy that he thanked God if the Sultan offered him peace; that he would pay a tribute to Mohammed; but that he had sworn never to yield the city. Hearing this, the Sultan proclaimed that a general assault would take place on 29 May, from both the harbour and land sides.

At nightfall a trumpet-call proclaimed a general illumination (a Dowanma). On the shores of the Bosphorus and on the heights of Galata all the tents were lit up. The lower harbour and all the lines resounded with hymns and with the cry, a thousand times repeated, '*There is no other God but God and Mohammed is his prophet: God is one and none is like to him.*' This resounded from the Blachernae palace to the Golden Gate. The beleagured, surrounded by a luminous half-circle, might have believed that a vast fire had taken hold of the camp and the Turkish fleet. But soon the dervishes, chanting and dancing, warned them that the enemy were celebrating their victory in advance. The city then became a pitiful spectacle as in pitch darkness the inhabitants milled about in disarray and despair. A lugubrious lament rose from their midst '*Kyrie eleison! Kyrie eleison! Spare us, O Lord, your well-founded menaces and deliver us from our enemies.*' All knelt before the image of the Virgin and declaimed their sins, as if on their deathbeds.

Now certain that the Ottomans were ready to attack, Constantine, to fortify the courage of his soldiers, himself inspected all the defence posts. Gathering together the Greek nobility and the elite of his European allies, he exhorted them to do their duty and follow his example.

Up to now the Byzantines had persuaded themselves that the Turks would only bombard the city but would not dare assault it. Feeling secure, a great number of the inhabitants had abandoned the fortifications and gone home. Armed with hooks, the Turks seized the opportunity to remove the gabions with which the Greeks had filled in the breaches as they were made. Hearing this, the Emperor violently reproached the deserters and warned them of dire punishments. Some of them gave as an excuse the lack of food for themselves, their wives and children, so the Emperor ordered nourishment for all the defence lines and sent food to their homes.

During this night Giovanni Giustiniani made the most urgent repairs to Constantinople's walls, and facing St Romanus' Gate (which was completely broken up by the Turkish artillery) the Genoese dug a deep trench, behind which they erected a new rampart with brushwood fillings. Giustiniani asked Lucas Notaras for a few guns, but he replied that they were not needed. Giustiniani retorted that they were needed even less in the harbour. At these bitter words, worse insults followed, and the Emperor once more had to impose upon them both an apparent reconciliation, for the common good. The jealousy of the Greeks often interfered with Giustiniani's plans, and he found help only with seven other foreign captains who, like him, were devoted to Constantinople's cause; the Genoese Careto, Bochiardi, Fornari, Selvatico, Gatelusio, Cataneo and John the Illyrian.

The Sultan, who honoured talent and courage in an enemy, more than once exclaimed, observing the wise dispositions of Giustiniani: 'What wouldn't I give to attach this man to me.' He tried in vain to seduce him, but was repulsed with disdain. The pitiful state of the defences and the cowardice of the Greeks brought his heroic and generous endeavours to naught.

When money had been plentiful, before the Turkish siege, two monks, Manuel Giagari and Neophytus of Rhodes, had been ordered to repair the walls, but instead they buried the treasure, to the tune of 70,000 gold pieces, which had been given by the Emperor for the reconstruction of Constantinople's fortifications. It was found when the city was pillaged.

[40] The address of Sultan Mehmet to his troops on the eve of the assault; from *The History of Mehmet the Conqueror* by Kritovoulos, translated by Charles T. Riggs.

(Critobulus of Imbros was a Byzantine historian, witness of the death-agony of the Empire, and much inclined to model himself on Herodotus and the grandest historians of antiquity. Hence the fine phrases which he attributes to the Sultan were perhaps not exactly those used; but Critobulus did, in the modern term, collaborate with the conquerors after 1453 and become a friend of Admiral Hamza, who was present at the Sultan's address and would have given him the key points of it.)

My friends and my comrades in the present struggle! I have called you together here, not because I would accuse you of any laziness or carelessness in this business, nor try to make you more eager in the present struggle. For a long time past I have noted some of you showing such zeal and earnestness for the work that you would willingly undergo everything necessary rather than leave here without accomplishing it, and others of you not only zealous themselves but even inciting the rest with all their might to redouble their efforts.

So it is not for this that I have called you together, but simply in order to remind you, first of all, that whatever you have at present you have attained, not by sloth and carelessness, but by hard work and with great struggles and dangers together with us, and these things are yours as the rewards of your own valor and manliness rather than as gifts of fortune. And secondly, as to the rewards now put before you here, I wish to show you how many and how great they are and what great glory and honor accompany the winning. And I also wish that you may know well how to carry on the struggle for the very highest rewards.

First, then, there is great wealth of all sorts in this city, some in the royal palaces and some in the houses of the mighty, some in the homes of the common people and still other, finer and more abundant, laid up in the churches as votive offerings and treasures of all sorts, constructed of gold and silver and precious stones and costly pearls. Also there is countless wealth of magnificent furniture, without reckoning all the other articles and furnishings of the houses. Of all these, you will be the masters!

Then too, there are very many noble and distinguished men, some of whom will be your slaves, and the rest will be put up for sale; also very many and very beautiful women, young and good-looking, and virgins lovely for marriage, noble, and of noble families, and even till now unseen by masculine eyes, some of them, evidently intended for the weddings of great men. Of these, some will be wives for you, while others will do for servants, and others you can sell. So you will gain in many ways, in enjoyment, and service, and wealth.

And you will have boys, too, very many and very beautiful and of noble families.

Further, you will enjoy the beauty of the churches and public buildings and splendid houses and gardens, and many such things, suited to look at and enjoy and take pleasure in and profit by. But I must not waste time listing all these. A great and populous city, the capital of the ancient Romans, which has attained the very pinnacle of good fortune and luck and glory, being indeed the head of the whole inhabited globe – I give it now to you for spoil and plunder – unlimited wealth, men, women, children, all the other adornments and arrangements. All these you will enjoy as if at a brilliant banquet, and will be happy with them yourselves and will leave very great wealth to your children.

And the greatest of all is this, that you will capture a city whose renown has gone out to all parts of the world. It is evident that to whatever extent the leadership and glory of this city has spread, to a like extent the renown of your valor and bravery will spread for having captured by assault a city such as this. But think: what deed more brilliant, what greater enjoyment, or what inheritance of wealth better than that presented to you, along with honor and glory!

Sultan Mehmet II; by G. Bellini, 1480

And, best of all, we shall demolish a city that has been hostile to us from the beginning and is constantly growing at our expense and in every way plotting against our rule. So for the future we shall be sure of guarding our present belongings and shall live in complete and assured peace, after getting rid of our neighbouring enemies. We shall also open the way to further conquest.

You must never imagine that, although this is all true, the city is impregnable or its wall hard to approach and difficult to pierce, or that very great danger awaits those who attack it, as if it were not easily to be taken. Lo, as you can see, the moat has all been filled up and the land-wall at three points has been so broken down that not only heavy and light infantry like yourselves, but even the horses and heavily armed cavalry can easily penetrate it. Thus I do not offer you an impregnable wall, but a wide plain fit for cavalry for you to cross with your weapons.

And what should I say about our opponents? There are very few of them, and most of these are unarmed and inexperienced in war. For, as I have learned from deserters, they say that there are but two or three men defending a tower, and as many more in the space between towers. Thus it happens that a single man has to fight and defend three or four battlements, and he, too, either altogether unarmed or badly armed.

How then can they do anything against such a multitude as we are? And especially since we are fighting by relays, and new troops are constantly coming into the fray, so that our men have time to indulge in sleep and food and to rest themselves, while they on the other hand fight continuously, without intermission, and desperately, and have no time to snatch sleep or food or drink or rest, since we are attacking in battle and forcing the fighting. Now we shall no longer merely use skirmishes and sallies, or simple attacks and feints, as we did at first – and as they anticipate – but once we have begun to fight, the battle will be continuous and uninterrupted, night and day, without any rest or armistice until all is up with them. Therefore I think these men, under the constraint of continuous fighting and of distress and starvation and sleeplessness, will easily yield to us. . . .

Then be brave yourselves and urge all the men under you to follow you bravely, and to use all zeal and diligence in the task, in the belief that there are three elements in good fighting: the will to fight, a realization of what is and is not honourable, and obedience to authority. Know that this obedience involves each keeping his own position and going to the attack quietly and in good order so that one can quickly hear the commands given and pass them on to the rest: when they must advance silently, to be silent, when they must shout and yell, to do so with fearsome yells. For while many of these things are wise in every sort of fighting, they are not the least so in battles at the walls. As for the rest, order them all to do everything well and in good order and discipline.

So then, fight bravely and worthily of yourselves and of those who have fought before you; and do not weaken, for you see how much hangs on this struggle, and do not allow any of your men to do so either. I myself will be in the van of the attack [applause by all the gathering]. Yes, I myself will lead the attack, and will be fighting by your side and will watch to see what each one of you does. . . .

Having said this much, he dismissed the assembly. Each man went to his own troops and tents, and the Sultan himself, after his evening meal, went to rest.

[41] The sack of the city by the Sultan Mehmet, the death of Constantine XI, and the end of the Byzantine Empire; from *Histoire de l'Empire Ottoman* by Ritter J. von Hammer-Purgstall. Translated by Marie Noële Kelly.

On the eve of the day when the assault was to start, Constantine had, by a fatal imprudence, had the Cercoporta gate opened to make a sortie on Mohammed's camp, and by another imprudence it had not been closed. Fifty Turks forced a passage with hardly an obstacle, and fell upon the Greeks from behind. This fearful news flew from the harbour to St Romanus' Gate, and dismayed the few – already well informed – still fighting beside the Emperor: Theophilus Paleologos, Francesco of Toledo and John the Dalmatian. Despite their prodigious efforts, Constantine, seeing their uselessness and the hordes advancing into the city itself, threw himself on to the Turks, seeking death. Abandoned by his men, he shouted: 'Is there not one Christian to kill me?' At the same moment he was laid low by two sabre blows, one on the face, the other from behind. He fell amongst a crowd of victims. At the same time the Turks were entering by the Eghri Capou gate, over a heap of dead that filled the ditch, and massacring all whom they met, thinking these were part of a garrison of 50,000 men. Then, realizing the weakness of the Greeks, they stopped the butchery, preferring to take prisoners, such a capture appealing both to their cupidity and lust. The inhabitants had rushed off towards the harbour which the enemy had not yet conquered, since the Turks had not forced the underground door of Eghri Capou; only a very few were able to find a refuge there, as the mobs were too much for the narrow gate. The soldiers who had the keys, only thinking of their own safety, closed the gates and threw the keys into the sea. Following an ancient prophecy they believed that the Turks, once arrived at the Square of the Bull, would be stopped in their turn by the besieged.

Unable to use the port, the mob in flight reached Sancta Sophia – men, women, children, monks, nuns. There they awaited, according to another prophecy, the vision of an angel who was to descend from Heaven at the very moment when the Turks would reach the column of Constantine the Great. It was said that this angel would put a sword in the hands of a man of common birth sitting at the foot of this column and order him to avenge God's people. The Turks, in a panic, would flee and would not only be thrown out of the city and the lands of Asia Minor and Greece, but would be driven as far as the frontiers of Persia. If, at this ultimate hour, an angel had appeared to the Byzantines and had told them: 'Admit the union of the two Churches and I will scatter your enemies,' the Greeks would not have listened and would have preferred the yoke of the Ottomans; such deep traces had the schism left.

No miracle was to save the Empire. The gates were hacked down by axes; the Turks flooded the streets; looting started, a looting which nothing was to stop, neither weeping women and girls, nor cries of the children nor the oaths of the wounded. No restraint could curb soldiers intoxicated with victory. The only criteria that affected the fate of the trembling creatures were those of youth, beauty and fortune. Without any distinction of rank or sex, prisoners were tied two by two with their belts or veils. Next it was the turn of the churches: pictures of saints were torn from their walls and cut up; sacred vessels were destroyed; vestments were turned into coverings; the crucifix, capped by a Janissary's bonnet, was carried around streets; altars were profaned and used as dining-tables, or as beds to violate girls and boys, or as stalls for horses. 'Aya Sophia,' says Phranzes, 'God's santuary, the throne of His glory, the marvel of the earth, was transformed into a place of horrors and abominations.'

Thus antique Byzantium fell, 1125 years after having been

built by Constantine. The siege, which had lasted fifty-three days, ended on 29 May 1453; it was the 29th it had undergone since its foundation. The city had been besieged three times by the Greeks under Pausanias, Alcibiades and Leo, a general under Philip of Macedon; three times by the Roman Emperors Severus, Maximus and Constantine; twice by rebels Thomas and Tornicius; twice by Byzantine Emperors, Alexis Comnenus and Michael Paleologus; twice by Paganus and Simeon, Bulgarian *krals*; once by Khosroes; once by the Chakhan of the Avars; once by Krumus, despot of the Slavs; once by the Russians under the orders of Dir and Askold; once by the Latins, under Doge Dandolo; seven times by the generals of the Arab Caliphs; five times by the Turks – twice running by Bayezid, then by Mousa, Murad II and Mohammed II. Only seven of these actually took the town: Pausanias, Alcibiades, Septimus Severus, Constantine, Alexis Comnenus, Dandolo, and Michael Paleologos; Mohammed was the eighth. But this last occupation decided the fate of Byzantium and forever incorporated it in the Ottoman Empire. The Paleologues lost their crown which they had so often compromised before through imprudence or cowardice; the Greeks bowed their heads forever beneath a foreign yoke.

By midday, Mohammed heard that the city was his, and he rode in through St Romanus' Gate, surrounded by his viziers, his pashas and his guards. His march was a triumph. When he arrived in front of the Basilica of Aya Sofia, he dismounted to take possession of this splendid metropolis of the East. He was overwhelmed by admiration at the sight of its riches: the 107 columns which upheld it, dressed with the rarest marbles, serpentine, pink lace from Synada, green from Laconia, blue from Libya, Bosphorus white, starry granite of Thessalia, Epirus and Egypt; the eight porphyric columns brought from Aurelian's sun temple at Balbek and from the temples of Ephesus, Cyzicus, Alexandria Troas, Athens and the Cyclades; and the pictures of the Evangelists and of the Apostles, of the Virgin, and Crucifix, all in glass mosaics of different colours, which he particularly noticed. He visited the upper galleries and the Church's vaults. Coming down from the dome, he saw a soldier looting a marble slab from the entrance; proudly possessive, the Sultan hit him violently with his scimitar saying: 'I have only given you the loot; I reserve the buildings for myself.'

The looter was carried away half-dead. His visit over, he ordered one of the muezzins who accompanied him to call the faithful to prayer. Giving the example himself, he ascended the altar and prayed. So was initiated the Prophet's cult in the Christian church of Santa Sophia and the unresolved controversy between the Greeks and the Latins was thus followed by the dogma of the Muslims: 'There is only one God!'

If one is to believe the Greek historians, an angel had been Santa Sophia's architect and Heaven had provided the gold for its construction. Founded under Constantine the Great, burnt twice in a riot, shaken by an earthquake, rebuilt by Theodosius and Justinian, this basilica served only for great State and Church occasions, coronations, triumphs, weddings of the Emperor, and the Synods; it was the masterpiece of sacred architecture in all the Christian world. The Turks respected Aya Sofia, but other buildings were not so lucky. The convent of St John the Baptist (at Petra) by the harbour was devastated, as was that of the Virgin Hodegetria crowning the Acropolis, where the conquerors broke into pieces a miraculous and venerated statue. The Greek Emperors had carried this statue before the troops when they started a campaign, and when they triumphantly returned. This very statue, too, had been carried around the ramparts to frighten the enemy when the Saracens besieged the city under Leo the Isaurian.

After converting the Great Church into a mosque, Mohammed called Lucas Notaras to him and said: 'Look at your work: this crowd of prisoners, these piles of corpses are the result of your refusal to give up the town when there was still time for it.'

Notaras answered that neither the Emperor nor he could decide this, especially as the former had received many letters encouraging him to resist. This knowledge gave the Sultan fresh doubts as to Khalil Pasha's fidelity; still, he waited. He asked Notaras if Constantine had embarked on one of the five Genoese ships that had escaped to the high seas. Notaras explained that, being at the palace door when the Turks forced the Charis gate, he could not know. At the same moment a few officers told Mohammed that two Janissaries were boasting aloud that they had killed Constantine. The Emperor ordered he should be found amongst the corpses, and his head brought to him.

As to Notaras, the Emperor graciously gave him 1,000 aspers and the same to his sons. He further promised him the restitution of his goods and of his dignities. The traitor, thus indulged, gave Mohammed a list of the principal officers of state and dignitaries; the Emperor promised 1,000 aspers to each soldier who would bring him the heads of these. Constantine's body was found, and identified by his purple shoes embroidered with golden eagles. His head, as well as that of Ourkhan, Suleyman's grandson, were laid at Mohammed's feet . . . The Emperor Theodosius had elevated on the Augusteon a lead column surmounted by his statue in silver, weighing 700 lbs; Justinian had substituted for the lead column one of porphyry, and Theodosius's statue had been melted down and replaced by one bronze, representing Justinian on horseback. In his left hand he held an orb surrounded by a cross; the other pointed to the Orient, as if subjecting it to his power. The head of Constantine, the last Greek Emperor, was placed on the top of this column under the horse's feet – a cruel irony, if one remembers that the Oriental prays for victory in the following terms: 'Let your enemy's heads be crushed under your horse's hooves.' This bloody trophy was then shown in Asiatic towns, as the head of Vladislas had been after the battle of Warna. Only then were the Greeks allowed to perform the last rites for the Emperor's remains.

Galata made its own submission after the fall of Constantinople. It was protected by a strong wall and lived in by the Genoese whose squadrons covered the sea. To it the Turks brought the Greeks who had not yet been reduced to slavery. The Genoese deputies sent to Saganos Pasha [vizier, and the Sultan's son-in-law] and asked, and obtained, that Galata should be spared the pillage.

The next day, 30 May, Mohammed rode to the palace of the Grand-Duke Notaras, who, after the Emperor, had been the second person in the Empire. He put his treasures and monies at the feet of the Sultan, saying he had kept them for him. 'Who,' said the Sultan 'has put the city and its treasures into my hands?' Trembling, Notaras answered, 'God.' 'Well,' said the Sultan, 'it is therefore to God I owe them, and not to you.' Still, he went to offer condolences to the Princess, spouse of the Duke, who was ill in bed, and asked to meet their sons. Later, he rode through the deserted streets, seeing Turkish soldiers still trying to rob the vanquished of whatever they had not lost the previous day. At the Imperial Palace, he went through the empty apartments, and cited a Persian poem on the vicissitudes of this world: the allusion was only too apposite. A splendid repast was prepared for him nearby. Mohammed drank his fill of wine, and, half-drunk, ordered his chief eunuch to bring to him Notaras's youngest son, aged fourteen. The father opposed this, telling the messenger that his son would never serve the infamous lusts of the Sultan. He would prefer to see him hacked to death.

Mohammed, hearing of this refusal, sent for Notaras, his sons and Cantacuzeno. He took the youngest child and condemned the others to death. Notaras then recovered all his dignity and, without showing any weakness, exhorted his sons to die as Christians, exclaiming, 'You are just, my God.' After the beheading of his sons, he asked to say his prayers in an adjacent chapel, then was executed in his turn. The bodies of the martyrs were thrown into the street and their heads placed on Mohammed's table. His natural ferocity was further stimulated by a fierce passion he conceived for the daughter of a stranger and to please this man he killed all the Greeks whom he had promised to spare the previous day. Among them were the Bayle of Venice, the Spanish Consul, and their sons, who were despatched at the foot of Arcadius' column in the slave market for women. Cantareno and other Venetian nobles would have died too, had they not given 70,000 ducats to Saganos Pasha to save themselves. Cardinal Isidore had been sold as a slave, but was able to throw himself into a vessel leaving Galata. His touching threnody has survived to reach us. Phranzes and all his family were sold to Mohammed, the Master of the Horse: he escaped with his wife to the Peloponnesus, but his son and daughters remained in the harems of the Sultan.

'Three days later,' writes Ducas, 'Mohammed ordered his fleet to retire. It left laden with gold and silver chalices, precious clothes and prisoners. But the camp was still full of loot. Here a soldier was dressed in religious ornaments, there another led dogs with a golden chain, a third drank wine out of a chalice or profaned holy vessels by eating out of them. Countless books filled chariots and were dispersed to all the provinces: ten volumes of Plato, Aristotle, and theological works were sold at a penny a piece. All the gold ornaments had been torn off the richly bound Gospels, and the pictures thrown in the fire.'

At last these scenes of desolation and destruction ended. Mohammed concentrated on repopulating the city, repairing its monuments and building it anew. The first part of the history of the Turks, a belligerent and triumphant one, was by then over; it had lasted 150 years. The authority of the Sultans had been consolidated and extended, according to Othman's own wishes, through war. The annihilation of Byzantium after a thousand years, and the conquest of its capital by the sovereign of the Ottoman dynasty, would now usher in a long series of calamities and struggles for the peoples of Europe.

Ottoman Istanbul

The City

There is no place where knowledge and learning
Find so ready a welcome as Istanbul.

No city has eaten the fruits of the garden of art
So richly as the city of Istanbul.

May God cause Istanbul to flourish
For it is the home of all great affairs.

Birthplace and school of famous men,
The nursery of many nations,

Whatever men of merit there may be
All win their renown in Istanbul.

There every perfection finds its measure,
There every talent attains its value.

There are the ranks of glory and honour
Anywhere else life is frittered away.

The heavens may turn about the earth as they will
They will find no city like Istanbul.

Drawing and painting, writing and gilding
Achieve beauty and grace in Istanbul.

However many different arts there may be
All find brilliance and lustre in Istanbul.

Because its beauty is so rare a sight
The sea has clasped it in an embrace.

All the arts and all the crafts
Find honor and glory in Istanbul.

To ascend the throne like Suleyman
And lord it over sea and air,

Leaning on a cushion,
Looking in the silver mirror,

Where in faultless order are combined
The sounds of music, the lyre of joy.

We have not seen its peer in any land
It has none, save perhaps in Paradise.

The threshold of the Ottoman Sultanate
The delight of the imperial realm.

In this life giving place
Whatever you wish is forthcoming.

Whatever thing may come into your mind
The finest and best of it is here.

Bey, Pasha, Efendi, Chelebi,
Here are the choicest of them all.

Soldiers and scholars and knights
Here are the kings of them all.

Here every problem of the world finds solution
Here every effort achieves its goal.

Were it not for all kinds of diseases
Were it not for the accursed plague

Who would ever leave this place like paradise
This grief-dispelling city?

If its weather were only more equable
Who would ever look at any other place?

There is no land or city that is like it
No place to live that can compare with it.

Nâbî (1642–1712)

The mosques

[42] The transition from Byzantine to Ottoman art – the Mosque of the Conqueror (Fatih Camii); from *Mehemed the Conqueror and his Time* by Franz Babinger, translated by Ralph Manheim.

The sultan [Fatih Mehmet II] spent almost the whole of 1471 in his capital. In all likelihood it was chiefly his physical condition that deprived him of his freedom of movement. Presumably in the summer, the large 'new mosque' that bears his name was completed. As we have seen, construction was begun in the spring of 1463 after Mehmed had taken the collapsing Church of the Holy Apostles away from the patriarch and torn it down, along with the neighbouring church of Constantine Lips. Over a period of roughly eight years the mosque was built a short distance to the north of the ruins of the two churches by an architect of Christian origin, allegedly named Christodoulos, later in any case known as the 'freedman' (*atik*) Sinan.[1] In response to his employer's ambitious desires, the architect succeeded, thanks to his own talent and the sultan's money, in building an edifice magnificent for those times. The structure reflects the transition from Byzantine to Ottoman art or, one might say, the posthumous renaissance of Byzantine architecture. In this mosque, which probably more than any other was to serve as a shining example to all subsequent Turkish builders, we find reminiscences of Christian architecture at a time when Hagia Sophia had already been remodeled in accordance with the requirements of the Islamic cult.

The Mosque of the Conqueror (Fatih Camii) with its numerous dependencies forms an enormous rectangle. It is situated in the center of a large park, today traversed by several streets. In front of it lies a rectangular courtyard, which seems to have preserved its original form. The eighteen columns of granite and marble, of varying thickness but all without exception antique, support twenty-two cupolas. Above the

[1] Not to be confused with the great Sinan, the Royal Chief Architect (see page 184). He died, or was executed, on 3 September 1471.

barred, marble-trimmed windows of the courtyard is a frieze, in which is gracefully engraved the first *sura* of the Koran, regarded as a symbol of the power of Islam. In the interior, to the right of the main entrance, there is a marble tablet, framed in lapis lazuli, which in golden letters traced by a master of Islamic calligraphy bears the words (of doubtful authenticity) of the Prophet: 'They will conquer Kostantiniya. Hail to the prince and the army to whom this is given.' The interior of the mosque is of almost overpowering puritanical simplicity. The unobscured light enters through numerous windows ordered in six superimposed rows. The imitation of Hagia Sophia is obvious. But in the magnificence of its plan, in the deliberate execution of the underlying idea, and in its simplification on a scale a third smaller, the Conqueror's mosque, in the opinion of connoisseurs, is superior even to the most famous of Istanbul mosques. Around it lie numerous benevolent institutions established by the sultan. The whole occupies a large area: the two courtyards, eight colleges (*medreses*) with dormitories for students, the garden of the tombs with its octagonal mausoleum and the catafalque of the Conqueror, the *türbe* of his wife Gülbahar, the hospital and almshouse, the kitchens, and a bath give the edifice an impressive, almost unique stamp. . . .

> How the columns were then brought from distant lands and what sums were spent in transporting them, God alone knows. Who can indicate the sums expended in Istanbul for the new mosque, especially in view of the fact that all the columns and stones were ready and prepared. Merely to transport them from one place to another so much money was spent that God alone knows how much. . . . In those days [referring to former times] building was not done by means of coercion. All work was paid for. If today we wished to erect a building, we would collect money from all the provinces and cities and we would transplant architects and artisans by force from all the provinces. And none of those who have been transplanted, whether architect or artisan, ever returns to his home. . . .

Three centuries later, on the evening of May 22, 1766, the third day of the Moslem sacrificial feast (*kurban bayramî*), the Conqueror's mosque was in large part destroyed by a terrible earthquake which shook all Istanbul. Sultan Mustafa III (1757–

1773), it has been maintained, caused the ruins of the mosque to be razed and entrusted an architect by the name of Haci Ahmed Dayezade with the task of rebuilding, which went on from 1767 to 1771. The vestiges of fifteenth-century architecture still discernible in the courtyard and also in the ground plan of the mosque lead us to doubt this contention. Be that as it may, a large part of the edifice was rebuilt. Older descriptions and drawings by sixteenth-century travelers, especially Melchior Lorichs of Holstein and Wilhelm Dillich (1606, 1609), show that the mosque possessed a central cupola and two rows of four smaller cupolas on either side of the central axis. On the east the mosque was prolonged by a prayer niche (*mihrap*) covered by a half-cupola.

[43] A Frenchman smokes his pipe by the Mosque of the Conqueror (Fatih Camii); from *Les Désenchantées* by Pierre Loti. Translated by Marina Berry.

As he felt deeply Turkish on this warm, clear evening, when the full moon would soon shine blue on the Sea of Marmara, he returned to Stamboul at nightfall, and climbed up to the heart of the Muslim quarter, to go and sit on the familiar esplanade in front of Sultan-Fatih's mosque. He wanted to dream there, in the pure cool of the evening, and in sweet Oriental peace, smoking hookahs while surrounded by dying splendour, decay, religious silence and prayer.

When he arrived at the square, all the little cafés had lit their modest lamps; lanterns hanging in the trees – old oil lanterns – also cast a discreet light; and everywhere, on benches, on stools, turbanned dreamers smoked, talking little and in low voices; hundreds of hookahs made a curious whispering sound – water bubbling in the flask as the smoker takes a long, deep breath. They brought him one, with small, live embers on leaves of Persian tobacco, and soon like all around him, he felt a gentle semi-intoxication, harmless and thought-inducing. He sat under the trees, where the hanging lanterns cast barely any light, facing the mosque on the far side of the esplanade. The square was empty and full of shadows, with uneven paving stones, dirt and holes; the wall of the mosque filled the entire far side, tall, huge, imposing, severe, like a rampart with only one opening: the thirty-foot-high archway leading to the holy court. On the right and the left, in the distance, the night was blurred; there was some deep black – trees, perhaps, vaguely outlined cypresses, marking a spot for the dead. The darkness was more mysterious than anywhere on earth; it was the peace and mystery of Islam. The moon, which had risen one or two hours earlier from behind the mountains of Asia, began to appear above the façade of Sultan-Fatih; it emerged slowly, and began to rise, perfectly round and silvery-blue, so free and so light above this massive earth-bound object that its infinite distance and isolation in space were wonderfully emphasized! . . . The blue light spread more and more; gradually it bathed the wise, devout smokers; but the deserted square remained in the shadow of the massive sacred walls. At the same time, this lunar glow diffused a fresh evening mist exhaled by the Sea of Marmara. It had not been noticeable earlier, when it was diaphanous, but it, too, became pale-blue and enveloped everything, giving a vaporous look to the mosque walls, which before had seemed so heavy. The two minarets standing against the sky seemed transparent, letting the moonbeams pass through them. It made one dizzy to look at them, they were so enlarged in the haze of blue light, so insubstantial and delicate.

[44] The visit of Sultan Selim II in solemn state to the Mosque of Sultan Beyazet (Beyazet Aga Camii), in the sixteenth century; from *Le Voyage du Levant* by Philippe du Fresne-Canaye. Translated by Marina Berry.

(Philippe, Sieur du Fresne de Canaye (1551–1610), brought up a Calvinist, was sent abroad at fifteen to Germany, Italy and Constantinople, and described his journey there under the title *Ephemerides*. Henri IV made him an Ambassador on many confidential missions; he finally abjured his Calvinism (which pleased Pope Clement IV); and not surprisingly these moves helped his nomination as French Ambassador to Venice.)

The only thing there remained for us to see in Constantinople was the Gran Signor going to the Mosque. But just as with wine, this Sultan is far from sharing his father's habits, and although Soliman used to go to the mosque every Friday, during the three months I was in Constantinople, Selim only went twice.

The first time was on Good Friday, which the Turks themselves hold in great reverence. But I did not go to see him that day, as the Ambassador went to Pera with all his janissaries. The other time was on 15 May.

Warned about this by our janissary, whom we had sent to the seraglio that morning, we went to the shop of a renegade Frenchman who paints and decorates bows and is the Gran Signor's groom; and there we waited for the Sultan to pass. As we had arrived early, we saw the *tchaouchs* on horseback, the *solaks*, the *mutafarrags*, and all the other court officials with a large number of janissaries going towards the seraglio, having been warned the day before that the prince wished to go out. That is why they were gathering at the Porte. Towards noon the Gran Signor mounted his horse; the *tchaouchs* went ahead, in no particular order; holding the silver mace, they scattered everyone in front of them, and without even trotting, they followed each other at a slow, solemn pace, sometimes in threes, sometimes in fives or sixes. There were many other lords, captains and *tchaouch bachy*; and the janissary-aga, who is the commander of the militia, was escorted by a large number of janissaries without sticks, and by well-dressed slaves: they wear bonnets rather like the janissaries' (whose are white), except that theirs are not so long at the back and are tied to the head; they also carry silver horns, but not as big nor as long as the janissaries'. Their feredje and their entire garment is of red cloth.

Some men at arms rode with the *tchaouchs*, troop-leaders having under them five janissaries, or ten, or twenty; they wear egret feathers in their white bonnets: they look as if they have a couple of feather-dusters from Ferrara on their heads; they are, moreover, superbly dressed. Then we saw eight horses led by the bridle by *tchaouchs*. And although they were the most beautiful horses I have seen in my life, it did not seem to me that such magnificent and precious harnesses were appropriate; for the bridles, saddles, breastplates and reins were of pure wrought gold on gilded silver, and inlaid with so many turquoises and other stones that it would be quicker to count grains sown in Lombardy, or sand in the stream of the Val delle Donne. Their rumps were covered with a cloth of solid gold, scattered with Oriental pearls; the saddles were invisible under loose covers of crimson velvet edged with pure gold, under which were nicely folded the horses' stable blankets. The first was quite old, but one could tell he had been very beautiful, and we were told that he had faithfully and valiantly carried Sultan Soliman through several wars, and that as a reward, he would enjoy all these honours until the end of his days. The others were as many *Bayards* or *Frontins*.

With them went the Gran Signor's lackeys, whose bonnets are gilded silver vases, very tall, shaped like a chamber-pot, mostly scattered with very fine turquoises. Their *saies* are short and light, like the *solaks'*, and they wear strange, coloured shirts covered with paintings. They have rather large, curved cutlasses at the waist, with gilded silver and blue scabbards; the handle is totally white whale bone. It is true that these lackeys have no spleen, and that from youth they have it reduced, then completely removed by means of certain beverages; because they have understood that tiredness only comes from the spleen and that when it is taken away they no longer feel tired. They are really, in the Frankish tongue, *dératés*.

A short distance behind them came the Gran Signor, dressed in a Persian satin dolman and a silver and gold feredje, all embroidered like damask with crimson silk. Mehemet-pacha was on his right, talking to him, for the Turks consider the left more honourable; they say he who is on your left can prevent you from reaching your sword, but not the one who is on your right. And Mehemet-pacha was not directly beside the Gran Signor; he went a little ahead, and had his head turned back towards His Majesty. I saw on his saddle-tree (the Gran Signor's I mean) a gilded silver pommel studded with turquoises, where he holds his mace, like a *tchaouch*. At this point I do not wish to discuss the Gran Signor's horse, nor his solemn slow pace, I will only say it is no wonder he is so gentle; for the custom is to notify the head of the stable, the night before the Gran Signor goes out, which horse he will ride; the horse is promptly hoisted into the air and is not fed that night nor the next morning. Since he has had no rest and no oats, he is obliged to have the slow, weighty gait appropriate to the majesty of so great a King.

Behind the Gran Signor rode his two favourite slaves, wearing the same bonnets as the slaves of the other pashas, but without horns; and under the bonnets, one could see the damp, scented curls of their well-combed tresses falling to the middle of their cheeks. They had no trace of beard, and wore graceful, coquettish clothes. The one with the noblest rank had on his saddle-tree a rather large cloth-of-gold cushion with many pearls and precious stones. The other is Cigalo, born of a Genoese father, who became a slave after renouncing his Christian faith, and has reached this honour. He carried two beautifully painted golden bows on his right shoulder, and two very rich quivers under his left flank; in this harness he looked like the god of love following the triumphs of father Bacchus.

After them followed a few more *tchaouchs*, in no special order; then some officers who, according to custom, threw *aspres* (pennies) to the people.

While the Gran Signor was passing, the silence everywhere was extraordinarily deep: one would have said his glance alone, like Medusa's, could turn men to marble or dumb fish, for they firmly believe their lord is the shadow and breath of God on earth, having learnt nothing more in their youth in the seraglios than the obedience and respect owed to the emperor. And by this unique discipline they constantly increase their power, to the great shame of all Christians.

As I have said, none of the janissaries in Constantinople carried a stick that day. When the Gran Signor passed in front of the shop where we were, and saw Mahmout, Mehemet and Sefer with their sticks to guard us, he asked who was there; on learning they were French gentlemen, he only said, *gusel*, *gusel* (good, good).

[45] The Mosque of Selim I, 'the Grim'; from *Constantinople* by George Young.

The mosque of Bayazid's successor, Selim the Cruel, in the Phanar, can be taken in by a detour after that of the Conqueror, or it can be left out altogether. Its gloomy mass, dull without and dark within, is a suitable memorial to the tyrant; and it would be remarkable that Suleiman the Magnificent should have built such a testimonial to his father unless he too had appreciated its fittingness. The ugly forecourt and plain minarets are all in keeping. Guide-books praise the 'propriety of its proportions.' But perhaps its chief interest is that it is said to be built of the material used by Constantine when he started, a thousand years

The mosque of Selim I; from *Descrizione Topografica*, 1784 by C. Comidas de Carbognano

before, to build in the Troad the Capital which he afterwards erected on the Constantinople site.

Selim 'the Grim' was a parricide and fratricide; but his cruelty was characteristic of his age. A picturesque 'poetic justice' in his punishments appealed to public opinion. He was not unpopular, and he is known to Turkish history as 'the Just'. Corrupt judges, for example, were required to condemn themselves to death. During the eight years of his reign he decapitated seven Grand Viziers; and a 'vizierat of Selim' long survived as a proverbial term for any remunerative but risky job. He was a poet, and wrote chiefly in flowery Persian; but his more simple Turkish verses have a note of true pathos. Even in a rough rendering the lines suggest what a French critic would term 'chose vue et vécue.' It is the voice itself of imperial Constantinople.

Every morn my hosts of fancies ride o'er streams of tears to war:
O'er the one-piered, two-arched bridge my brows have builded, forth they fare.

Veiled in airy webs, bespangled with each good and evil star:
Every evening fickle fortune winds me in her wanton hair:
Still alone, a lonely stranger, in strange lands I roam afar,
While around me march the sullen guards of grief and pain
 and care.
Till I've read life's riddle, emptied its nine pitchers to the end
Never shall I, Sultan Selim, find on earth a faithful friend.

After reading this we can better understand the poet Selim sobbing over the verses addressed to him by his brother before he was bow-strung, or listening hysterically to the strangling by his deaf-mutes of his little nephews. His cruelty suggests calculation, even convention: it is not the perverted or political savagery of Mohammed who, when drunk, could murder the whole family of Notaras because he would not surrender his son to the infamy of the seraglio, could flay princes alive, have antagonist leaders sawn in two, or massacre whole populations after their conditional surrender. But to the professional wars, and peaces, of Byzantine times succeeded now an age of wars of racial and religious extermination.

[46] The Mosque of Mihrimah Sultan, built in 1562 for the daughter of Süleyman the Magnificent; from *Sinan* by Arthur Stratton.

(Sinan, architect of the golden age of the Ottoman empire, was born a Christian, but at the age of 21 was taken into the Sultan's service, became a Muslim, and served with the Janissaries as a military engineer. In about 1538, the year he built his first mosque, Süleyman the Magnificent appointed him Chief of the Imperial Architects – a post he held for 50 years, serving Süleyman's successors, Selim II and Murad III, in turn. His prodigious output of work includes 81 large mosques, 50 smaller mosques, 19 mausoleums and 32 palaces in a total of 323 buildings. Sinan was 66 when he completed the Süleymaniye Mosque, crowning glory of Istanbul's Ottoman architecture; and he died in 1588 at the age of 97, a few days after completing a new gate in the Byzantine sea walls.)

In 1562, the widow Mihrimah, the Moon of the Suns, free of her mother's and her husband's reflected phases, chose to shine in her own right. She commissioned the Royal Chief Architect to build for her a great mosque on the highest point of land in the imperial city. The Mihrimah Jami stands just within the land walls next to the Edirné Gate on top of the Sixth Hill. It serves as landmark for the Ottoman armies marching off to Holy War and returning from victory, or defeat, in Turkey in Europe.

The legend is that she paid the enormous costs out of her 'slipper money', or, as we say, pin money. But ignorant foreign chroniclers, both European and Asian, wishing to call attention either to the Grand Vezir's excessive wealth or her own excessive frivolity, read slipper money to mean that she sold a pair of shoes to build her house of God. In bad weather the Ottoman ladies wore pattens of inlaid and jewel-studded wood, six or eight inches high – how deep the mud must have been. They wore velvet slippers embellished with pearls and precious stones. Mihrimah Sultan was tiny; she could have worn no more than size three or four in shoes – apparently weighted with diamonds as big as a 'mountain of light,' the Koh-i-Noor.

Sinan built her a mosque as full of light. She must have been a merry widow at the age of forty – she did not choose to remarry. She certainly was liberal, as neither her father nor husband had been in giving Sinan a free hand to do as he saw fit for her. She had known him all her married life, and all his, since 1538. Sinan at the age of seventy-three turned revolutionary, and he began to experiment. Her mosque marks the turning point in his career from journeyman to master builder, the final period in which the architect dominates the patron. . . .

To build the mosque for the Imperial Princess Mihrimah, Sinan was under no constraint save, of course, to design and build upon the requisite formula of the circle inscribed within the square, the irreducible, insoluble equation, tense in its conditions that cannot be otherwise restated, and cannot be got around, the most vital, the most dynamic known to man. He and she understood one another, both as a powerful man and a fragile woman, the one a tall and muscular, white-bearded slave, wholly achieved; the other a Daughter of Osman, privileged, delightful, and prized; and as architect and patroness, each coming into his and her own freedoms.

In her mosque, Sinan's architecture is inseparable from his engineering, the theory from the practice, the purpose from the function, the idea from the reality, the one from the other. The Mihrimah Jami is the most architectonic of Sinan's mosques. In sculpture, outside Islam or Judaism, it would be called heroic, and it would be seen to be nude – the Apollo of Olympia or the Aphrodite of Cyrene, or both of them. . . .

The building stands high on a stone platform leveled on the top of the Sixth Hill. Sinan may have planned it on the drawing board in the perfected geometrical proportions of one to two, the globe upon the cube, and then in the construction upon the highest point of land in the imperial city, found that it would not do. He lowered the dome ten feet. It rises 37 meters, 122 feet, in height from floor to crown. In diameter, the circle measures 20 meters, 66 feet, within the square, which is 20 meters, 66 feet, to a side.

It seems to me that in this mosque Sinan put most of the intellectual symbolisms to one side. The nature of God, the nature of man; the life eternal, the life on earth; the celestial dome, the desert floor; the meaning of victory, and of failure; the inseparable and yet distinct elements, human and divine, in the sacred jurisprudence; the two aspects of power – Sinan silenced these perpetual dialogues upon the circle in the square for the time being; and he got down to facts. Let us see, he might have said to himself: what in truth does man have to go on? He then threw away the modular.

It might as well be said that the mosque of Mihrimah Sultan is a product of Sinan's passionate mind. From the outside, there they are – the essential male and the essential female principles. The single minaret is most elegant: slim, piercing, penetrating, erect, at once a finger pointing and also unmistakably the male virile member. It also has a single gallery, which fits the image only in the greatest of sophistication; and although all this is everything that is erotic, nothing can be called pornographic, not even in the abstract. The minaret towers higher than the dome and it goes up into the sky. The single great dome, and all the many, many, many smaller domes are breasts, breast-shaped, the final *alem* is the nipple; they are young breasts.

Startled by the evidence of the senses, the mind gets to work, humorously, to notice the fact of singularity among a multiplicity of ladies lying on their backs. Where is the free choice hereabouts? Or are these all remembrances? Artemis of the Ephesians! Alma Mater is the courtyard. Euclid! Come on down to earth. I find myself standing on top of the crumbling land walls. I scrambled up to get a better view. It is a matchless view.

I look across the rows of domes – yes, domes, small, twinned cupolas, the ones on the arcades and the cells of the courtyard, and the larger, but by no means matronly, domes of the porch. They are the color of the breasts of doves. Above them rises the stonemasonry of the superstructure of the mosque. There are no semidomes at all, but what a quantity of glass! Each curtain wall – it is the outline, the silhouette, of a breast – is a screen of nineteen windows in three rows, all but four of them topped by pointed arches; the four are rounds, great elephant's-eyes. . . .

Behind the mosque of the Lady as Beautiful as the Moon which rises on the top of the Sixth Hill, the triangular city of streets, of roofs, of domes, and of minarets falls away within the sea walls and the land walls. The blue water of the Sea of Marmara rises like another wall to receive the dome of the blue sky. It is a matchless sight, an urban landscape, a view of civilization, man-made. . . .

The mosque is crystalline. The eye, from inside or from out, sees clear through the building. In the four screen walls that fill the four high arches, barely pointed, Sinan made bold patterns of the fenestration. There are three levels of windows: the first of seven not quite identical rectangles, the largest in the center, pointed-arched on top; the second of five such windows with a round elephant's-eye at either end; the third, high up under the closing springers of the arch, of three pointed oblongs and two rounds.

In the exterior walls of the prayer hall . . . Sinan opened great windows. They are rectangular, not arched. He glazed those at floor level with clear glass and grilled with the Ottoman rectilinear iron bars. . . .

Today the windows are glazed with a mixture of clear and ruby glass leaded in patterns of the nineteenth-century Ottoman baroque style (in the reconstruction after the fierce winter earthquake of 1894, the interior walls of the mosque were stenciled with a bad all-over chintz design). Perhaps Sinan left the walls white and filled the windows with glass as clear as air to let in the light of the sun and the moon of the Lady Mihrimah's name. Their light compounds the space in her mosque. But if he had Drunken Ibrahim design screens of stained glass to fill the high windows with the patterns and the colors of flower beds and rainbows, then the interior must have been glorious. On a sunny day, on entering, a man might have put out his hand to find it filled with God's first gift. Let there be light! . . .

Along the parapet of the northeastern gallery, and in the east corner where ordinarily Sinan placed the Sultan's loge, he raised a gilt screen for the convenience of the Imperial Princess Mihrimah and her secluded and veiled ladies-in-waiting come in answer to the call to prayer. The women who did not stay at home to pray were specifically segregated in the mosques because, even in the act of worship, the sight of one bowing, kneeling, sitting, leaning forward upended would otherwise distract a man's attention even from God.

[47] The building of the Süleymaniye, most magnificent of the city's mosques; from *Sinan* by Arthur Stratton.

Sultan Mehmet the Conqueror took Constantinople. Sultan Bayazid the Pious worked to consolidate the empire. Sultan Selim the Grim conquered Persia, Syria, and Egypt, Tabriz, Damascus, and Cairo; and he took under the protection of the Sons of Osman the Prophet's holy cities of Mecca, Medina, and Jerusalem. Sultan Süleyman the Magnificent set himself three goals to mark his reign: for Islam, to conquer Vienna; for his people, to bring a constant flow of fresh water into Istanbul; and for his monument, to build the Süleymaniye above the Golden Horn.

In 1529 Sinan the general of the Janissary engineers breached the walls of Vienna, but the Emperor of the East failed to take the Austrian capital from the Emperor of the West. In 1550 Sinan the Royal Chief Architect began to build the Sultan's Imperial Friday Mosque and mausoleum surrounded by a *küllîyé*, that is, a sort of university city.

The pious foundation is imperial in size. Basides the mosque and tomb, it includes a *türbé*, tomb, for Haseki Hürrem, who died unexpectedly on April 15, 1558, the year after Sinan had completed the Süleymaniye. He had already built a lodge for the guardian of the cemetery garden behind the kibla wall.

The four university colleges, one each for the study of the four gospels or orthodox interpretations of the Sacred Law, stand in pairs to the northeast and the southwest of the mosque enclosure.

The Süleymaniye; from J.F. Lewis's *Illustrations of Constantinople*, 1835–6

They are classic medresés, square courtyards arcaded around a garden. To prepare the students for the colleges, Sinan built a grammar school, a higher school, a school to teach aspiring muezzins the several ways to chant the verses of the Koran, and a medical school. He built a combined hospital and insane asylum; a charitable kitchen for the poor and a refectory for the students and other members of the university city; and a guest house for distinguished visitors, in size and beauty worthy of the savants, the justices, and, it may have been, saints come to talk to the students.

Sinan and Süleyman included a public fountain (today famous for its spring water), a splendid bathhouse, and public water closets. He built a library and a playing field, the iron ground for wrestling matches. Finally, in the foundations of the terraced mosque enclosure and the basements of the buildings raised on the steep slopes of the hill, Sinan put rows of vaulted shops for the goldsmiths of the Sultan's own guild of craftsmen. There must have been a caravansary attached to the Süleymaniye; perhaps it was a building already in existence.

Süleyman and Sinan chose a magnificent terrain to build upon high up above the slopes of the Third Hill. The ground had been part of the walled gardens of the burnt-out Old Palace. . . . Under the Süleymaniye, on the slope of the hill, Sinan, who was by 1550 the custodian of all the imperial properties, bought for himself an odd parcel of the old harem's gardens, a wedge-shaped plot on which he built the great house where he died in 1588. By then he had prepared his own modest tomb of white marble. It stands in the sharp corner across the street from the terraced foundations of the mosque. His house long since has been destroyed, but in time the grounds are to be bought back and restored.

In the fine weather, probably of May, certainly in 1550, Sinan began work by laying the foundations of the walled enclosure. It is called the *sahn* and it is a rectangular 'stage' that sets the mosque, its courtyard, and its cemetery garden apart from the surrounding urban complex. Sinan dug into the top of the Third Hill and built up from the steep slope terraced foundations of solid masonry for the platform. . . .

While the mortar of the foundations hardened, Sinan assembled the mountains of limestone blocks from the quarries at Bakirkoy on the Sea of Marmara. The stone was pale yellow; it has weathered light gray. He chose the columns. He got the roughed-out capitals of white Proconessus marble from the quarries in the islands of the Marble Sea. He saw to the baking of the light-weight bricks for the domes, the semidomes, and the cupolas. And he put his assistant architects and the foremen of his teams of skilled workmen and laborers, most of them Armenians and Greeks, as well as the detachment of Janissary cadets to work on the dependencies. . . .

But surely neither for incompetence nor for failure of imagination did the royal Chief Architect and the Sultan choose to build the Süleymaniye on the floor plan of the Church of the Divine Wisdom. Both the Imperial Friday Mosque and Haghia Sophia rise from the circle inscribed in the square, extended on all four sides but roofed by a single great dome 'shouldered' by two semidomes in the main axis. The two side aisles, which rise only to the height of the four piers, are covered with cupolas and vaults. In both church and mosque, the high arches on either side are filled by fenestrated screen walls. . . .

Neither the Sultan nor the Royal Chief Architect intended to copy slavishly Haghia Sophia, nor to surpass the church – by 1550, a most hallowed imperial mosque. Instead, it becomes apparent that they planned to measure themselves, their faith, their domains, and their achievements against the Emperor Justinian the Great, the architect Anthemius of Tralles, the Christianity of the Eastern Orthodox Church, the Byzantine Empire, and the Divine Wisdom of God the One.

The dome of Haghia Sophia is larger and higher. Roughly its broken circumference measures in diameter 34 meters – (112 feet 3 inches) as against the Süleymaniye's 26 meters (87 feet 6 inches). From floor to crown, the second, higher dome of Haghia Sophia measures 56 meters (184 feet 10 inches) against 53 meters (175 feet) for the Süleymaniye. Anthemius built Haghia Sophia in no exact system of proportions, although the second dome's increased height brings it close to the golden section of 1:1.6+. Sinan designed the Süleymaniye in the exact mathematical proportions of 1:2.

The two architects were comparably supreme. The Byzantine and the Ottoman emperors are both known as lawgivers and each is called 'the Great.' The two empires, ruled from the same imperial city, were roughly equivalent in size and in power, in grandeur and in glory; and although one lasted twice as long as the other, the dynasty of the Sons of Osman, in unbroken descent in the male line for six centuries, has yet to be equaled. Oddly, the two women, the Byzantine Empress Theodora and the 'Veiled Empress' Hürrem, the one in her gynaeceum, the other in her harem, were equally powerful in their influence over their husbands. Yet the two domical buildings, the church and the mosque, each rising from the identical floor plan, are not at all the same. The one is Byzantine; the other is Ottoman. . . .

By 1550, the Sacred Law was fixed as a pure science. The dome of the Süleymaniye rises and soars. It is celestial, but it certainly does not float upon mysteriously illuminated golden air. It is held up by the law of gravity. In his building Sinan stripped bare all the technical forces at work. He revealed the structural engineering, the masonry walls, the buttresses, the

The tomb of Süleyman the Magnificent; from William J.J. Spry's *Life on the Bosphorus*, 1895

solid stone piers, the granite pillars, the voussoirs of the springing arches, the thrusts and the counterbalancing resistances of the dome and its supporting members. In the Imperial Friday Mosque there is no dialogue between man and God, no space within a space. But there is perfect, and thus infinite, unity. Through tiers and rows and banks of windows, daylight fills the space flowing through the defining masses.

In this building, Sinan first worked out his principle that engineering and architecture are inseparable; the one is the other. Therefore, in all his buildings the exterior is the outside of the interior, and the inside is the interior of the outside. As with crystalline forms, the eye looks clear through Sinan's architecture. In Islam, God gives each man his life whole at the moment of his conception. . . .

His legend, as recorded by Evliya Chelebi, gives us a story, and this one rings true. About 1556, it must have been in the last year of construction, Süleyman, as apparently was his habit, found a free moment to pay an unannounced visit to the work in progress. He had a handful of guardsmen with him, but the Sultan did not come incognito. He arrived at the side gate in the southwestern wall of the enclosure. Sinan's workmen sprang to their feet and stood at attention. Perhaps a foreman or a senior Janissary apprentice stepped up to salute the Sultan. He looked about searching for Sinan. Süleyman put the men at ease and told them to get on with their work. Although he may not have frowned, he did not smile as he walked into the finished courtyard and through the portal into the covered prayer hall. It was full of scaffolding for the plasterers, the marble-cutters, and the painters of the semidomes and the high dome. If the scaffolding of those days looked like the timbers, the crisscrossing planks, and the platforms in use during the work of restoration of 1950, Süleyman walked into a geometrical forest, a kind of very modern abstract sculpture, that cost the equivalent of fifty thousand dollars to erect. It filled the space. Silence ran ahead of Sultan Süleyman.

Then he heard his Royal Chief Architect's impatient voice cry out from the top of the scaffolding surrounding one of the gigantic granite monoliths, to say something like this: 'No! No! That's not the way to cut stalactites. Here, give me that mallet and chisel. I'll show you how to carve the capital.'

Then, standing at the base of the pillar, the Sultan had to put up his hand to shield his eyes as the chips flew and the marble dust rained down. He may then have smiled. I doubt that he interrupted Sinan as he cut the geometrical crystalline stalactites in the round to come out right.

Sinan finished the Süleymaniye in 1557. It is an enormous space, full of light by day, once lit by twenty-two thousand flames by night. In the seventeenth century, when the mosque was not a century old, Evliya Chelebi saw ten 'Frankish infidels skillful in geometry and architecture' take off their shoes and put on slippers to enter the southwestern portal. He followed them to watch the great spaces of the Süleymaniye take their effect. Heads back, the ten men shuffled along in their baboushes; they walked on thick carpets woven to Sinan's patterns at Ushak instead of on the rush matting and scatter rugs of today. Even so, the same space flows from the portal through an arch and then higher into the semidome and on up into the high dome. The head goes back, the mouth falls open. Evliya Chelebi reports that each of the ten Frankish infidels raised his right hand and laid his forefinger across his open mouth. 'They tossed up their hats and cried out . . . "Mother of God!"' . . .

[Sinan] was a robust man of sixty-eight when he climbed up onto the dome to put the burnished finial in place. According to his legend, when he got down again, he said to the Sultan, 'I have built thee, O Padishah, a mosque which will remain on the face of the earth till the day of judgment, and when Hallaj Mansur comes and rends Mount Demavend from its foundations, he will play tennis with it and the dome of this mosque!' . . .

Their mosque has the Renaissance quality of vitality. This is a building built in classic Islamic sobriety and discipline. As a whole greater than the sum total of its parts, the urban complex of the Süleymaniye, in the disposition of its components and in their proportions, has, it may be, equals in other lands. If so they are rivals – in the ruins of Greece and Rome and Egypt; at Angkor Vat; in the Gothic and the Renaissance cities; in the Moghuls' India; in the Age of Reason and in Versailles.

The Süleymaniye gives shape to the Ottoman Golden Age, within the triangular space of the walled city on seven hills, Istanbul above the Golden Horn, the Bosphorus, and the Sea of Marmara, and the lands beyond. And this mosque, according to its builder, the Royal Chief Architect Sinan, was the work of a journeyman, the Sultan's slave.

[48] A girl goes with her 'milk-mother and milk-father' to worship in the Süleymaniye at Ramazan; from *Memoirs of Halidé Edib*.

A moment's pause at the door to give one's shoes to the old man,[1] the lifting of the corner of the huge worn curtain, beside which one looked like a tiny rabbit, and then the entrance!

A gray endless upward sweep of dome, holding a hazy gray

[1] No one may pollute a mosque by walking in it with shoes dirty with the impurities of the street. Huge padded curtains hang over the mosque doorways.

atmosphere in which hung the constellation of the tiny oil lamplets.[1] The light through the coloured windows must have added a rosy hue, but the warmth of its pinkish shade was rather felt than seen. It was diffused in that gray air and added a faint tone which prevented the gray from being sad and somber, as it usually is on sea and sky. The magic of genius has given the mosque of Suleymanié the proportions which make one fancy it the largest building one has ever seen, so imposing is the sense of space and grandeur reduced to its simplest expression. Near the *mihrab*,[2] under different groups of lamps, sat various men in white turbans and loose black gowns, swinging their bodies in rhythm with the lilt of their minor chants. Everything seemed part of the simple majestic gray space with its invisible rosy hue and its invisible pulsations. In the pulpits sat men in the same dresses as the chanters. They were preaching and waving their arms in more passionate rhythm than the chanting ones, but everything became toned down and swallowed up in the conquering silence, in the invisible pulsation of the air. Nevres sat down where she could listen to some man who was chanting for the souls of the dead. Some of these chanters were old and some young, but all had the transparent amber pallor and the hectic eyes of those who are fasting. In no time I felt caught up into the general sway and began moving my body unconsciously to and fro in the same harmonious manner as the rest. I became a part of the whole and could not have moved otherwise than under the dominating pulsations of the place. No false note, no discordant gesture was possible. . . .

In the evening the great guns were fired, signaling the time to break the fast, and we gathered about the round low tray on which jams, olives, cheese, spiced meats, eggs, and all sorts of highly flavored pastries were arranged. Milk-father got back his good humor as he ate. In Ramazan the Moslem spoils his stomach as one spoils a beloved child, even the poorest allowing

[1] Until recently all mosques were lit by tiny lamps, each lamp consisting of a small, cup-like glass filled with oil on which floated a wick. From the ceiling of the dome an iron framework was hung by heavy chains, and in this framework the lamps were placed; but so slight and delicate was it that when the lamps were lit the framework was unseen and the impression was of stars hanging in the sky of the dome.

[2] The part of a mosque which shows the direction of Mecca.

himself variety and plenty.

Our evening prayers received only scant observance that night, for we had to hurry out for the Ramazan prayer, milk-father leading with a lantern in his hand; but turning back he soon lifted me on his shoulders, and swinging the lantern in his other hand, he walked by Badji's side, talking and joking. The streets were lighted by hundreds of these moving lanterns. Men, women, and children flickered forward like a swarm of fireflies, drums were sounding in the distance, and from every minaret the muezzin was calling, '*Allah Ekber, Allah Ekber. . . .*'[1] The grand harmony came nearer or grew more distant as we moved on. Then suddenly above the dimly lighted houses, above the mass of moving lights, a circle of light came into view high over our heads in the dark blue air. The tiny balcony of some dim minaret was now traced out as though by magic in a slender illusive ring of light. These light circles multiplied into hundreds, standing out in the bluish heaven, softly lighting up the picturesque masses of the wooden buildings below them, or the melting lines of the domes. And now in the same air, hanging in fact between minaret and minaret, other beautiful lines of light as if by a miracle interlaced and wove themselves into wonderful writing: 'Welcome, O Ramazan!' Belshazzar's surprise when he saw the invisible fingers writing on the wall differed from mine only in quality. I was on the shoulders of the tallest man in the crowd. Below me the lights of the lanterns swung in the dark depths of the long winding mysterious streets. Above me light circles and gigantic letterings, also in light, hung in the blue void, while the illusive tracery of the minarets, the soft droop of the domes, appeared dimly or disappeared in the thickness of blue distance as we walked on. And so once more we reached Suleymanié and plunged into the great crowd gathered inside.

The gray space was now a golden haze. Around the hundreds of tremulous oil lights a vast golden atmosphere thickened, and under it thousands of men sat on their knees in orderly rows; not one single space was empty, and this compact mass, this human carpet presented a design made up of all costumes, ages, and ranks. The women prayed in the gallery above.

Nevres Badji left me to watch it all while she found herself a

[1] God is great – the beginning of the usual call to prayer.

proper place in a regular row. Suddenly came the unique grand call – '*Sal-li-a-la Mohammed!*' and then the rise of the entire human mass. The imam stood in front of the *mihrab*, his back to the people, and opened the prayer. It is wonderful to pray led by an imam. He chants aloud the verses you usually repeat in lonely prayer. You bow, you kneel, your forehead touches the floor. Each movement is a vast and complicated rhythm, the rising and falling controlled by the invisible voices of the several muezzins. There is a beautiful minor chant. The refrain is taken up again and again by the muezzins. There is a continual rhythmic thud and rustle as the thousands fall and rise. The rest belongs to the eternal silence.

It seems as if we should go on rising and falling, rising and falling for the rest of our lives, till all of a sudden people remain longer on their knees than before, and a chorus of, '*Amin, amin*', sets the pulsing air into an almost frantic rhythm.

Then we leave the mosque.

[49] The tomb (or *turbé*) of Sultan Süleyman's second son, Mehmed Shah-Zadé; from *Constantinople, Settings and Traits* by H.G. Dwight.

There is another tomb behind another mosque of Süleïman, which is, perhaps, the most perfect monument of its kind in Stamboul. I did not always think so. But the more I look at its fluted dome and at the scheme of its interior tiling, the more I seem to see that here again Sinan, or the great decorator who worked with him, exquisitely found means to express an idea of individuality. This tomb was built, like the mosque to which it belongs, in memory of Süleïman's second and best-beloved son, the young Prince Mehmed. The mosque – so-called of the Shah-zadeh, the Prince – has lost its original decoration, but its graceful lines and its incrusted minarets combine with the smaller buildings and the trees about it to make one of the happiest architectural groups in Stamboul. As for the *türbeh*, it fortunately remains very much as Sinan left it. The design of the tiles is more abstract and masculine than those in Roxelana's *türbeh*, being mainly an intricate weaving of lines and arabesques. But there is about them a refinement, a distinction, which, it is hardly too fantastic to say, insensibly suggest the youth and the royal station of the boy whose burial chamber they beautify. For the colour – rarest of all in Turkish tiles – is a spring green and a golden yellow, set off by a little dark blue. The tomb is also remarkable, as I have already said, for the stencilling of its dome, as well as for the lovely fragments of old stained glass in the upper windows and for a sort of wooden canopy, perforated in the wheel pattern common to the balustrades of the period, covering the prince's catafalque. It is supposed to symbolise the throne which Süleïman hoped his son might inherit. Beside the prince, but not under the canopy, rests his humpbacked younger brother Jihangir. As for the unhappy Prince Moustafa, he was buried in Broussa, in the beautiful garden of the Mouradieh.

The *türbeh* of Prince Mehmed has, in my mind, another pre-eminence which perhaps its does not deserve. As in most other public buildings of Stamboul, an inscription is carved over the door. These inscriptions are generally in poetry and sometimes very long. The uninitiated reader would never guess that the last verse of many of them is also a date, for the Arabic letters, like certain Roman letters, have a numerical value. And the date of many a Turkish monument is hidden in a chronogram, always the last line of the inscription, in which the arithmetical sum of the letters is equivalent to the numeral of the year in which the monument was erected. I am not learned enough to say when this recondite fashion started, but the chronogram of this tomb is the earliest I happen to know about in Stamboul. It reads: 'Grant, Lord, to him who rests here to win the grove of Eden.' The arithmetical value of the line is 950, which year of the Hegira is equivalent to 1543 of our era.

[50] The Imperial Princess Mihrimah, widow of the Grand Vizier Rüstem Pasha, using some of the vast wealth he left to her, prevails on Sinan to build her husband an appropriate memorial; from *Sinan* by Arthur Stratton.

The Rüstem Pasha Jami, called the Tile Mosque, has no chronogram carved above the portal. That is to say, no man of letters worked out a literary conceit in which the letters of the wording in the epitaph, or the acronym of the versified eulogy, cut in stone, were given numerical values to add up to the date of the memorial. *De mortuis nil nisi bonum*, in effect, left nothing for the despised poets to say of Rüstem Pasha, deceased. Therefore, the construction cannot be precisely dated. But the charter for the pious foundation was granted in 1561, which was the year of his death.

Once again, the penny-pinching Grand Vezir had set aside a difficult parcel to build upon. It is a corner lot at a right-angled intersection of narrow cobblestoned streets in Tahtakalé. For five centuries, tinsmiths, woodworkers, rope walkers, ironmongers, potters; wholesalers in nuts, raisins, dried figs, and apricot paste; retailers and brokers in grains, the staples, dried beans and peas, seeds, olives, and spices, the oils and the cheeses, all the less perishable produce, have worked and traded in the noisy bustling quarter. It smells strong; it smells good. The market lies on the steep slopes of the Third Hill and along the littoral of the Golden Horn from the spice bazaar at Eminönü almost to the valley of the Lykos. The streets are too narrow for two carts or a single truck to pass between the stalls of merchandise offered for sale in front of the open shops. . . .

Rüstem had acquired another bargain, a ruinous Byzantine business premise. On the given vaulted substructure made of narrow, hard-baked Byzantine bricks set in rock-hard mortar, Sinan built a row of shops with storerooms behind them. He planned the pious foundation as a mosque surrounded and supported by a complex of workshops, ateliers, offices for wholesalers and retailers, and warehouses. Such a commercial building in Turkish is called a *han*, which also means 'inn' or 'caravansary'. Usually the *han* is rectangular and has two floor of massive brick masonry built around an open courtyard, arcaded, with shops below and factories or offices above. Istanbul is full of these great business premises, some of them covering whole city blocks with their many interconnecting courtyards. Sinan's palaces have all gone, but the *hans* show us his secular architecture. Those surrounding and supporting the Mosque of Rüstem Pasha are still in use – I found stacks of stiff and bloody fleeces for sale in one. The large, plain bathhouse, privately owned, has been converted into a cold-storage plant.

At Rüstem Pasha's corner in Tahtakalé, above the shops at street level, Sinan built the platform for the mosque. Three twisting and enclosed stone staircases, each occupying a minimum of valuable commercial space, lead up from the streets to the high *sahn*. This platform stands at six meters, twenty-one feet nine inches, above the cobblestones. There is no other courtyard. The edges of the level, stone-paved *sahn* are walled in and railed with pierced stone slabs.

To compensate for the loss of the suppressed courtyard arcades, Sinan more than doubled the covered space by building an outer porch around the inner porch, a sloping penthouse roof supported by right-angled arcades of slim pillars that rises to the row of five domes of the inner porch, held up by the usual monoliths and arches.

Inside, the mosque itself, again as usual, is built on the floor plan of the circle in the square, which Sinan extended on either side by an aisle roofed by three cradle vaults in a row; and, again as usual, he brought in the buttresses from the façade to widen the space behind the northwestern wall. But in the circle, Sinan drew an octagon, and built a pier at each of the eight angles. Two of the piers are engaged, as pilasters, in the kibla wall; two join the buttresses on either side of the poral. Each of the two pairs on either side, freestanding, is octagonal in section.

Sinan chose the octagon for both the Rüstem Pasha *medresé*, built ten years earlier in 1550, and for the mosque in the memorial, finished in 1561. The college and the mosque stand in different quarters of the city. Perhaps, therefore, Sinan used the octagonal plan to link the two foundations. But my belief is that Sinan saw Rüstem Pasha as a complex and complicated man of many-sided character, neither as simple as a circle nor as forthright as a square. Eight is one of the Bektashi mystical numerals. Perhaps Sinan, himself a member of the Bektashi order of dervishes, chose to stress Rüstem's liberality in religion. As Busbecq noted, the Grand Vezir, in Islam, was liberal and catholic to the point of heresy and, indeed, misbelief. In private conversation, he allowed that Christians, Jews, and even Shiite Muslims, as such, were not excluded in life or in death from God the One's salvation.

Apparently he worshiped Mammon. It may be that Sinan chose the octagon to point out Rüstem Pasha's many sides, both good and evil. Or again, Sinan may have seen the unhappy man fixed and transfixed at the top of the heap of the slave hierarchy, caught in Hürrem's spiderweb, pulled this way and that by the network of power spinning together his wife, his mother-in-law, his father-in-law, his brothers-in-law. Pinned, he spun like a

Catherine wheel. But he did not burn out, he died of water unnaturally hoarded in the cavities and tissues of his body. . . .

Rüstem Pasha bequeathed Sinan a miser's collection of hundreds and thousands of Iznik tiles, each one today worth about what each one cost to make, between two hundred fifty and one thousand paper-gold American dollars. They overwhelm the space with their impersonally perfect patterns of dark blue, light blue, leaf green, and sealing-wax red, the colours enameled upon a dead-level snow-white ground, and covered with a glaze as clear as distilled water. What is wrong with this millionaire-billionaire interior?

That, precisely, is what is wrong with it. Rüstem Pasha knew the monetary value of things. The mosque smells less of the museum than of the dealer's showroom. The Grand Vezir purchased – or, as museum curators now put it, acquired – samples of the various master potters' art from the most successful of the many kilns in Iznik. This man was famous for his floral patterns; Rüstem Pasha bought enough from him to cover half a wall with red tulips on green-leafed stems planted in rows in a vertical bed and nodding their heads this way and that. The next master was best at geometrical arrangements of mandala rosettes in dark and light blue; their interconnecting petals and crisscrossing lines, in Rüstem Pasha's mosque, surface half of another wall with a great many regimented spots. Another kiln had a more fanciful designer. He produced a field of swirling feathers blowing this way and that way in a high, obliging wind. The Grand Vezir bought up half-a-wall's worth. And so on. Only the prayer niche and its surrounds in the center of the kibla wall and the panels made to fit the spandrels of the gallery arcades reveal Sinan's sure hand at working out the appropriate patterns.

Curiously, the effect of all these disparate elements is at once static; incoherent, repetitive, and monotonous. Sadly, the individual tiles, some nine inches square, are not as good as they might be – and in another decade were to be. They look almost machine-made, mass-produced; and they have faults.

As it happened, the Grand Vezir's collector's collection does not represent the purely Ottoman art of faience at the great period. He died too soon to realize that his investment would not appreciate but instead would decline to second best.

[51] The use of colour in the Mosque of Sokollu Mehmet Pasha, built in 1571; from *Sinan* by Arthur Stratton.

Color is the glory of this mosque. Upon entering from the sunlit courtyard through the deep and dark portal that resembles the mouth of a cave, in the quiet light within the prayer hall, Sinan focuses the eye directly upon the prayer niche. This classic *mihrab* takes the shape of the monumental portal exactly opposite, of which it is the man-sized miniature. Surely, Sinan enjoyed the illusion of great distances that this juxtaposition gives the space across the floor, which he spread with carpets woven in the colors of vegetable and mineral dyes, natural substances, and in the patterns of formal gardens. Entranced, the mind behind the eye sees that Sinan once again has taken liberties, as in the optics that we call surrealism, with the laws of perspective.

Sinan framed the prayer niche in the kibla wall with a screen – it is the finest array in the world – of glowing Iznik tiles. They rise from floor level to fill the high arch between the engaged piers of the blind arcade.

In the four colors, dark blue, emerald green, light blue, and the piled-up pigment of true bolus red, enameled on a white surface like a field of snow, and glowing through the glaze that is as clear as water running in a mountain brook, Sinan drew patterns of geometrical and floral abstractions. On either side and above the prayer niche, he placed texts from the Koran in lozenges and calligraphic wheels of 'beautiful writing.' High up in the demilune that fills the 'blind' arch – twelve meters above the ground, forty feet, five times the height of a tall man's reach – he planted a garden of spring flowers, ever-blooming red-petaled tulips on nodding stalks with bladelike green leaves, carnations, roses, peonies, blue hyacinths, and sprays of fruit blossom. They are recognizable flowers but much more than ordinary everyday imitations of nature. In all ways these flowers are larger than life.

Here they are functional. In Ottoman Islam, a man who wishes to soothe the troubled mind and clear the spirit looks at a tulip or a rose so that he may stand face to face with God and with God's handiwork, himself, to pray. The flowers that Sinan designed and that the Iznik potters fired for this wall grow large on high because they do not recede into the distance, but instead grow in the gardens of Paradise, which, in Islam, is an oasis blossoming in the desert wilderness at the end of the road.

Sokollu Mehmet Pasha and Sinan could read the calligraphic verses from the Koran as most of the worshipers even in their day could not. The Grand Vezir, surely, chose them himself. In the oblong plaques above the rectangular windows at floor level and in the galleries, the enamelers wrote the ninety-nine beautiful names of God. In the discs and the lozenges of the kibla wall, the scriptural arabesques give the *Hadis*, which is the call to prayer and the declaration of faith, and which, in translation, reads, 'There is no god but God, and I bear witness that Mohammed is His slave and His Prophet.'

Then comes the First Sura of the Koran, an early one revealed to Mohammed in the desert mountains surrounding Mecca. It is called 'The Opening,' and it is the Islamic Paternoster:

> In the name of God, the Merciful, the Compassionate.
> Praise belongs to God, the Lord of all Being,
> The All-Merciful, the All-Compassionate,
> the Master of the Day of doom.
> Thee only we serve; to Thee alone we pray for succour.
> Guide us in the straight path,
> the path of those whom Thou hast blessed,
> not of those against whom Thou art wrathful,
> not of those who are astray

In the medallion surrounding the crown of the high dome, Kara Hisari, the illuminator, painted verses from Sura XXXV, 'The Angels,' that in part read, 'God holds the heavens and the earth, lest they remove. . . . Surely He is All-Clement, All-Forgiving.' Under a heavy weight of snow, the dome fell in the winter earthquake that shook the city for five days in 1894. It has gone up again upon its firm foundations.

[52] The Laleli Mosque; from *Les Peintres du Bosphore* by A. Boppé. Translated by Marie Noële Kelly.

Prince Selim himself set the example of interest in French culture. Grandson of Ahmet III, son of Moustapha III, he had been attracted by Europe since childhood, as had his three sisters, Chah Sultana, Bekhân Sultana, and Kadîdja Sultana.

The latter, known as Hadidjé, owed her birth to Adil Chah, a Circassian slave-girl who had already given the Sultan a daughter, Bydjân, who died at an early age.

The visitor, walking up the ramp leading to the Laleli Mosque, is immediately charmed by its elegance and the harmony of its interior. On the left lies the founder of the mosque, Moustapha III, in the precinct where his *turbé* (tomb) is placed. This sanctuary, dear to the Osmanlis and also containing the ashes of the reforming Sultan, Selim III, is often closed; but by peeping through an iron-grilled window one can nevertheless see, among the foliage, a small iron cupola, elegantly worked. Under this rests Adil Chah Kadin, a few yards from the Sultan's *turbé*. On the head-piece, traditionally decorated with gilded flowers and leaves, there is an epitaph that seems to commemorate only her two daughters, Bydjân and Kadîdja; for it was by their birth that Adil Chah, the Circassian girl, found her rank at Court and hence the right to be buried in the precinct of the Imperial *turbé*:

Bydjan sultane, chasteté et innocence même,
Que Dieu prolonge ta vié autant que l'Univers!
De même à sa sœur Kadidja sultane,
Que Dieu accorde une vie éternelle! . . .
Toutes deux, filles pures et angéliques d'une même mère
Qui a quitté ce séjour pour celui du Paradis,
Tant qu'elle reposera dans le Firdeos,
Jouissez d'une existence tissue de félicité, digne d'envie!
La date de son décès est tombée à point.
Adil Chah sultane repose maintenant dans le nid
[éternal du sublime Eden.

[53] An account of the founding of Eyüp Camii, Istanbul's holiest shrine, on the site of the burial-place of the Prophet's friend and standard-bearer; from *Narrative of Travels in Europe, Asia, and Africa in the Seventeenth Century*, by Evliya Efendi, translated by Ritter J. von Hammer-Purgstall.

The first is that of Khaled Ben Zeid Eba Eyyub, the Ansarite, the companion of the Prophet. When the Prophet fled from Mecca to Medina under the guidance of Gabriel, who held the bridle of his camel, it fell upon its knees before the house of Eba Eyyub, who received the Prophet as his guest, by which act he insured to himself the favour, that the Prophet's tomb now stands on the site of his house. Eba Eyyub was one of the Prophet's most faithful companions, both in time of peace and war; and has preserved many traditions from him. Under the reign of Moavia, the son of Sofian, the Ommiad, he with Moslemah twice headed an expedition against Constantinople. From the first he returned to Damascus with a rich booty; in the second he conquered Galata, and a truce having been concluded with the Emperor on the condition that he, Eyyub, should be allowed to make the pilgrimage to Aya Sofiyah to perform his devotions there, or at the place of Solomon, he was killed on his return before the Crooked gate, by a stone cast down upon him by the infidels. There is, however a tradition, which says, that he died of dysentery.

Mohommed II having laid siege to Constantinople was, with his seventy saint attendants, seven whole days searching for his tomb. At last Ak-shems-ud-din exclaimed, 'Good news, my Prince, of Eyyub's tomb,' thus saying he began to pray and then fell asleep. Some interpreted this sleep as a veil cast by shame over his ignorance of the tomb; but after some time, he raised his head, his eyes became bloodshot, the sweat ran from his forehead, and he said to the Sultan, 'Eyyub's tomb is on the very spot where I spread the carpet for prayer.' Upon this, three of his attendants together with the Sheikh and Sultan began to dig up the ground, when at the depth of three yards they found a square stone of verd antique on which was written in Cufic letters; 'This is the tomb of Eba Eyyub.' They lifted up the stone, and found below it the body of Eyyub wrapt up in a saffron-coloured shroud, with a brazen play-ball in his hand fresh and well preserved. They replaced the stone, formed a little mound of the earth they had dug up, and laid the foundation of the mausoleum amidst the prayers of the whole army. The cupola, the mosque, the college, the khan, the bath, the dining establishment and the market were built by Mohammed II and all his successors added some improvement to its splendour, so that his funeral monument resembles now a koshk of Paradise. The windows of the mausoleum look into the courtyard of the mosque, the walls are cased with china, and his tomb is surrounded by a silver grating; his banner being placed at his

Süleyman making a pilgrimage to Eyüp; from *The History of Sultan Sulayman*, 1759 – a manuscript that belonged to Sultan Murad III

head. It is full of gold and silver lamps, of candlesticks with candles of camphor as high as a man, of censers and of vases for rosewater (bokhurdan and gulabdan) set with jewels. The Korans of old writing are no where to be found in such numbers and splendor as here, unless it be at the tomb of Ali, and such precious gifts, trappings and suspended ornaments are to be met with only in the mosque of Sultan Ahmed I. At the feet of the Saint is a cistern, from which all those, who visit the tomb drink, and are with God's assistance freed from their diseases; the tablets, with inscriptions in gold, which adorn the walls have not their equal except in the mausoleum of Ali. A full description of this tomb would alone require a complete work. God bless him, and us through his interference!

[54] The keys of Mecca, recaptured from the Arabian fanatics, the Wahhabi, are received at Eyüp Mosque with thanksgiving, then taken to Sultan Mahmoud; from *Promenades Pittoresques dans Constantinople* . . . by Charles Pertusier. Translated by Marina Berry.

But what do I hear? . . . Is it the sound of a cannon echoing in my ears? . . . Yes, it is repeated; starting at Seraglio Point it gives the signal to the other batteries which echo it all along the Bosphorus. The word *Wahhabi* . . . reminds me of that schismatic sect made up of Islamic sceptics, which has suffered a notable setback in the sands of Arabia from where it had spread to the inhabited regions. The holy city [Mecca] which it had seized from the Ottomans has at last been recaptured, a clear sign of the favour granted by heaven to the fortunate Mahmoud.

Here is reason enough, as one can see, to explain such joy, which also reinforces the faith of these true believers. The heads of several leaders of this formidable sect have already been carried in triumph; but undoubtedly the best trophies are the keys to Mecca, which were handed over a few days ago at an impressive ceremony that deserves to be reported.

Ali-Pacha, the governor of Egypt who brought both the holy cities under Osmanli rule, sent his son to bring His Majesty the precious tokens of this dazzling success, and the envoy was received in the capital with all the splendour to which his mission entitled him.

The Keaya-Bey and the Mektouptchi (the Grand Vizir's secretary) after taking the precious burden from the hands of Daoud-Pacha, proceeded to the town of Eyub, where the Grand Vizir himself arrived early in the morning with all the ministers, and the grand *moufti* with the chief *ulemas*. A tremendous crowd soon followed this impressive parade, because the Osmanlis know how to be curious, or rather patriotic, when it is their interest.

The ceremony began with an act of thanksgiving to the Almighty for protecting the true sons of Mahomet; the keys were placed in the *Mihrab* [niche used as an altar] in homage to God and to restore what was His. After this, the venerated objects were carried with great pomp to the Seraglio. As in ancient triumphal marches, an enemy prisoner with a chain around his neck followed the trophies of victory. Two *tchaouchs* held the ends of this chain, so that the wretch looked like a terrifying wild beast, and this must have impressed the spectators with an even greater horror and loathing for the beliefs of his sect. When the procession reached the Seraglio, the keys were presented to the Sultan, who was awaiting them, seated on his throne. He took them to hand them to the Kislar-Agassi in his role of *nazir* [inspector] of the holy cities, who placed them immediately in the Treasury. The ceremony ended with the beheading of the Wahhabi, and his body, lying in the mud, has reminded the city for three days of the victory which the cannon is still celebrating.

[55] Aziyadé sees the investiture of Sultan Abdul-Hamid at the Eyüp Camii in 1876; from *Aziyadé* by Pierre Loti, translated by Marjorie Lawrie.

The mosque of Eyoub at the northwestern end of the Golden Horn, was built in the time of Mahomet II over the tomb of Eyoub, companion of the Prophet. Access to it has always been forbidden to Christians, for whom even its immediate precincts are none too safe.

The mosque is built of white marble and stands in a lonely spot in the open country, with cemeteries surrounding it. Its dome and minarets are almost completely hidden in the dense verdure of a grove of huge plane trees and immemorial cypresses.

The cemetery paths, which are paved with stone or marble, lie deep in shadow and are for the most part sunk. On either side stand marble buildings of great age, their yet unsullied whiteness in striking contrast to the black tones of the cypresses. Hundreds of gilded tombs with borders of flowers encroach upon these gloomy paths; they are the sepulchres of the great, of the pashas of olden days and Mussulman dignitaries. The sheik-ul-islam have their funeral kiosques in one of these dreary avenues.

It is in this mosque of Eyoub that the sultans are consecrated. . . .

I remember the day when the new Sultan went in great pomp to take possession of the Imperial palace. I was one of the first to catch sight of him as he emerged from the old seraglio, the gloomy retreat where all the heirs to the Turkish throne are lodged. Immense caïques of state had come for him, and my own caïque actually grazed that of the prince.

These few days of power have already aged the Sultan. He has lost his former look of youth and spirit. The extreme simplicity of his dress contrasted with his new environment of Oriental luxury. This man, who was called from a state of comparative obscurity to the supreme power, seemed plunged in uneasy brooding. He was pale and thin, with a melancholy, abstracted air, and there were dark rings round his great black eyes. His face bore the stamp of breeding and intelligence. . . .

To-day, September 7th, witnessed the great pageant of the Sultan's consecration.

Abdul Hamid, it seems, is all eagerness to invest himself with the prestige of the Khalifs. It may be that his accession will inaugurate a new era in the history of Mohammedanism, and lend to Turkey some lingering glamour, some last gleam of glory.

In the holy mosque of Eyoub, amid scenes of great pomp, Abdul Hamid girded on the scimitar of Osman. After this ceremony, he marched at the head of a long and brilliant procession all through Stamboul, on his way to the Palace of the Old Seraglio, pausing at every mosque and funerary kiosque in his path to pay the customary acts of worship and prayer. His bodyguard of halberdiers wore scarlet uniforms blazing with gold, and green plumes six feet high upon their heads. In their midst rode Abdul Hamid on a statuesque white steed with slow and stately-paces, caparisoned with gold and gems. Behind him went the Sheik-ul-Islam in a green mantle, the emirs in cashmir turbans, the Ulema in white turbans with golden fillets, the great pashas and dignitaries, all of them on horses glittering with gold. A solemn and interminable procession, in which the most striking looking personages filed past. With servants to hold them on their quiet palfreys, octogenarian Ulema rode by, wagging their white beards and darting at the populace brooding glances fraught with fanaticism and mystery. The whole route was lined with dense masses of spectators, those Turkish crowds, whose brilliance puts to shame the most magnificent gatherings in Western Europe. The stands erected along a frontage of several kilometres were bending under the weight of eager throngs, arrayed in all the different costumes of Europe and Asia.

On the heights of Eyoub was massed a swaying multitude of Turkish ladies, their heads veiled with the white folds of the yashmak, while their graceful forms, in vivid silken draperies that swept the ground, could hardly be distinguished from the painted and chiselled tombstones beneath the cypresses. The effect was so dazzling, so fairylike, that it seemed not so much an actual scene as the fantastic hallucinations of an Oriental visionary.

[56] A description of the glories of the Mosque of Sultan Ahmet (the Blue Mosque) in the seventeenth century; from *Narrative of Travels in Europe, Asia and Africa . . .* by Evliya Efendi, translated by Ritter J. von Hammer-Purgstall.

No mosque can boast of such precious hanging ornaments as those of this, which by the learned in jewels are valued at one hundred treasuries of Egypt; for Sultan Ahmed being a prince of the greatest generosity and the finest taste, used all his jewels, and the presents which he received from foreign sovereigns, in ornamenting the mosque. The most extraordinary ornaments are the six emerald candelabra which are suspended in the emperor's mehrab, and which were sent as a present by Ja'fer Pasha, the governor of Abyssinia. The sockets, each of which weighs eight *okkas*, are suspended by golden chains, and terminate in golden feet with green enamel. The experienced and learned have estimated the value of each of these candelabra equal to one year's tribute of Rumeili. In short, it is a most wonderful and costly mosque, and to describe it baffles the

Turkish women at the entrance to the Sultan Ahmet mosque; painting by O. Hamdy Bey, in the late nineteenth century

eloquence of any tongue. Some hundred copies of the Koran lying near the mehrab, on gilt desks inlaid with mother-o'-pearl, are presents from sultans and vezirs. The library consists of 9,000 volumes marked with the toghra of the Sultan, the care of which is entrusted to the Mutavellí (curator) of the mosque. On the outside, facing the mehrab, is a most delightful garden, where the sweet notes of a thousand nightingales give life to the dead-hearted, and the fragrant odour of its flowers and fruits gratifies the senses of the faithful assembled to prayer. The size of the mosque is the same as that of the princes of Soleïman. The court is a square paved with marble, and has stone benches running along the four sides. The windows are guarded with brass gratings: in the centre of the square plays a fountain of the purest water, for the use of the faithful: it is however only used for drinking, not for ablutions. . . .

The gate of this mosque was made under the superintendence of my father, Dervish Mohammed, at the time when he was chief of the goldsmiths. The two inscriptions on brass were engraved by his own hand. On the outside of the windows of the court there are several covered porches supported by small columns, in which, when the assembly within is too great, many of the faithful perform their devotions; and the Hindu fakirs find shelter. The six lofty minars of this mosque are divided into sixteen stories, because it is the sixteenth royal mosque of Islambol, and the founder of it, Sultan Ahmed, was the sixteenth of the Ottoman emperors. Two minars rise on the right and left of the mehrab, two others on the north and south gates of the court, each three stories high, which make in all twelve stories. The roofs and gilded crescents, which are twenty cubits high, dazzle the eye with their splendour. The two minars on the corners of the court are lower and have only two stories; their roofs are covered with lead. On the sacred nights these six minars are lighted up with 12,000 lamps, so that they resemble as many fiery cypresses. The cupolas are all covered with lead. This mosque being richly founded, has seven hundred and fifty attendants attached to it. The tribute of Ghalata and many other pious bequests (wakf) constitute its revenue.

[57] The Feast of the Prophet's Birthday in the Imperial Mosque (Mosque of Sultan Ahmet); from *Histoire de L'Empire Ottoman* by Ritter J. von Hammer-Purgstall. Translated by Laurence Kelly.

The many feast-days established during the reign of Sultan Ahmed had all been scrapped; but that of the Prophet's Birthday was still celebrated, indeed with the more solemnity and splendour as it was the only feast-day on which the Kislar Aga [guardian of the harem] (excluded from every other feast) appeared himself in all his pomp. And at that time the Kislar Aga, as we all know, was omnipotent. On that day he leaves the Saray half an hour before the Sultan, and processes to the Mosque accompanied by a fine escort of eunuchs and bodyguards. The Grand Vizier and the Mufti take their places to the right and left of the altar on raised cushions; the Viziers of the Cupola, the Aga of the Janissaries, and the Lords of the Diwan flank the Grand Vizier. On the left, by the Mufti, the senior judges of the provinces, the Mollahs, the Muderris, are all seated on little Barbary carpets like those used by pilgrims. Between these two lines, the Lords of the Bedchamber, the Reis-Efendi, and the Tsaousch Bashi all take their places, facing, however, not the altar but the Sultan's tribunal. The leading Emir is placed under a green tent facing the preacher's pulpit, and behind him there stand the Master of Ceremonies and the Captain of the Grand Vizier's bodyguard. The lieutenant-generals of the Janissaries are near the pulpit where are pronounced the Friday sermons. Two rows of Janissaries separate these great dignitaries from the public. Three Scheikhs from the Imperial mosques then follow each other in preaching eulogies for the Prophet's Birthday.

The Sultan is offered rose-essence and aloe by his sword-bearer and senior chamberlains, and the *baltadjis* spray and scent the ulemas and grandees similarly, beginning with the Grand Vizir and the Mufti.

There then follows a hymn in praise of the Prophet, and at last an anthem celebrating the birth itself, all sung by the choirs. At the same time the *baltadjis* offer sorbets and sugared sweets. Upon hearing the passage bescribing the Prophet's birth, all rise. And it is at that moment that the Sultan receives a letter from the Scherif of Mecca, in reply to the one brought to him by the bearer of the yearly gift. The messenger bearing the welcome news of the safe return of the Meccan caravan of pilgrims is entrusted with this, and he takes part in the ceremonies wearing a turban of black muslin bedecked with a heron's aigrette. He hands over (in a green satin sachet) the letter to the Grand Vizier, who hands it to the Reis; and the latter, accompanied by the Marshal of the Court and the caravan messenger, approaches the Sultan's tribunal. The Kislar Aga then takes the letter and hands it to the Sultan, who returns it to him and in turn he hands it finally to the Reis Efendi for it to be lodged in the Imperial archives. The Kislar Aga then robes himself with a sable cloak of honour, and the three singers receive kaftans of honour. A short prayer ends the ceremony.

The grandees receive cups of sweets at their houses or palaces, and the Sultan returns without an escort to the Saray. A quarter of an hour later, the Kislar Aga returns, preceded by the Aga of the Janissaries, fifty steps ahead of him. It is the Kislar Aga who is the organizer of this feast, for which he receives a modest sum for expenses. As guardian of the Imperial harem, of the two harems of Mecca and Medina, and as first officer of the Court, it is his right to be responsible for this feast to the Sultan and the great Officers of State, because it is the most solemn and most demanding of all; and as guardian of the purity and honour of the Imperial harem, and the other two sacred ones, his responsibilities symbolize, too, the solemn event of Mohammed's birth.

Topkapi Palace (the Seraglio)

[58] Verses of dedication for the Sultan Ahmet III's fountain at the entrance to the Seraglio (1723); Seyyid Vehbi's *Chronogrammatic Kaside*, from E.J.W. Gibbs' *History of Ottoman Poetry*. Newly translated by J.R. Walsh.

1

Great Lord of Lords of noblest birth,
Sovereign both in name and worth;
Arab and Turk his laws begirth,
Sultan Ahmed, World-Conqueror.

2

Fount of justice, wondrous done;
The East whence rises sainthood's sun;
The wings of soaring bliss, each one
Is panel to his palace door.

3

His person high in kings' esteem;
His sword to triumph's glades a stream;
The garden of the realm, 'twould seem,
Is watered by his pen's outpour.

4

Not only Sultan, also saint,
In whom is seen without a taint
Ali's resolve, Omers's restraint,
And all Muhammed's reverenced for.

5

The seal of state within his wield
Has brought the world entire to yield;
Inscribed thereon, divinely sealed,
The Name there is no name before.

6

All Caesars shrink from him in awe;
His like no Alexander saw.
In every land his word is law,
No king asks why, no serf wherefore.

7

It's his the House of God to mind
And serve the Prophet of Mankind.
Turks, Persians, Arabs, all we find
Subjected to him evermore.

8

The Faithful follow in his lead,
God's shadow he on earth, indeed!
In the Koran is it decreed
That no one shall his will ignore.

9

Though kings for him their kingdoms rift,
Their very crowns are in his gift.
Let once his battle-standard lift,
The foeman's head shall roll in gore.

10

That fountainhead munificent,
The pledge of human aliment;
Till graves be rent for souls' ascent
Be he the refuge kings implore.

11

What Alexander sought to find
Exploring in the darkness blind,
Lo! he that water most refined
Makes flow before his palace door.

12

This structure, of all such the best,
Rose at his Grand Vizir's behest;
The Sultan's kin by marriage blest
Whose name the Prophet's forebear bore.

13

That minister of goodly fame
The credit for this work may claim.
And blest will be the Sultan's name
By those he built this fountain for.

14

The Sultan, lavish of largesse,
Spent sums that one can hardly guess
To found this spring of kindliness.
May God reward him well therefore!

15

He carefully improved the site
And set thereon this new delight,
Outpouring waters pure and bright.
– How must the soul of Huseyn soar!

16

O pure of heart, stretch forth your hand
Unto this heavenly fountain; and
Its every drop of water bland
Will like a spa good health restore.

17

Its water all that 'pure' implies;
Its dome ascending to the skies;
No other structure wrought this wise
You'll find, though you the earth explore.

18

While sun and moon above remain
May this good Sultan ever reign!
And may God grant that he retain
His wise Vizir for evermore.

19

O Monarch, born to majesty,
Your works are boundless, verily.
Yet none so rare as this we see
In all you've compassed heretofore.

The first gate of the Seraglio, the Baba-Hamayun, and Sultan Ahmet III's fountain of 1723; from *Voyage Pittoresque de la Grèce*, 1782–1809 by M.G. Choiseul Gouffier

20

Its gilded basins coruscate;
Its waters life regenerate.
All day and night outside your gate
Its gleaming draughts of silver pour.

21

You set it in the Palace Square
And bid the thirsting hurry there.
'Twould seem you built a mansion fair
With heaven's stream outside its door.

22

Like water did you lavish gold,
And lo! this fountain we behold.
May God reward you manifold
The good that you've provided for.

23

To sing its praise my pen is dumb,
And speech thereof is cumbersome.
While waiting for the words to come,
A Voice from out the blue did roar:

24

'Be silent, Vehbi, hold your peace!
You've not the skill, so duly cease!
This task that knows of no decrease
Has challenged many pens before.

25

And tongues that ventured into speech
Have been reduced to silence, each.
But lo! this lack is in the reach
Of our great Sultan to restore.'

25

While wisest heads had not the wit
To find a chronogram for it,
'Twas then this line of perfect fit
Writ by our Lord came to the fore

26

Each word of it's a surging sea,
Its meaning pearls of purity.
Seek you style in its apogee?
Look thereupon, and seek no more.

27

Sultan Ahmad Khan's chronogram
Flows fluent from the faucet's tongue:
Aç besmeleyle iç suyu
Hân Ahmede eyle du'â.[1]

1141a.h. (AD *1723*)

[1] 'Invoking God's name, drink the water and say a prayer for Sultan Ahmet.'

[59] The bed-chamber of Sultan Murad III and his chief *Kadine*, Saffieh Baffo, in the Seraglio; from *Pavilions of the Heart* by Lesley Blanch.

Safieh Baffo, the beautiful Italian concubine who was for many years Sultan Murad's only, and adored, Kadine, she who shared with him the loveliest of all rooms for loving, had no need to better herself. Luxury and rank were her birthright. She came of a noble Venetian family, rich and proud in their splendid palazzo. To her, the opulence of the Seraglio must have seemed almost barbaric; and we can imagine the despair of her family when they learned she had been abducted by corsairs and sold into the Seraglio of the Grand Turk. It is not known how she came to be seized, for young girls of her kind were strictly kept: though abduction by corsairs was one of the hazards of earlier centuries. . . . I know of no existing portrait, such as that of the Russian Kadine Roxelane, by which we could gauge something of her beauty. But it is certain she enslaved the Sultan to the exclusion of every other woman. It was for love of her, I like to think, and for the purposes of this book maintain, that he built that perfect room known as Sultan Murad's Bedchamber. . . .

By tradition, it was the Sultane Validé who, on the Night of Power, at Baïram, personally selected the virgin whom she conducted in state to her son's bed, in the expectation that his ardours, agreeably renewed after long abstinence, would ensure a lusty heir. The trembling aspirant was always well coached: she knew that she must approach Allah's Shadow on Earth with proper humility, it is said, by entering the Imperial bed symbolically, from the foot only, inching up by degrees. Etiquette even here, between the sheets.

No doubt Safieh Baffo followed this formalized beginning to her days of love and power.

Let us look now at the setting of her life. This room, an expression of romantic genius, was conceived by Sinan Agha, supreme architect of Ottoman glories, of the greatest mosques and secular buildings of the sixteenth century. . . .

When Sinan Agha designed Sultan Murad's room he seems to have been inspired by some special grace, as if he were aware that he was building for love rather than majesty. For all its stateliness, this room retains, to an extraordinary degree, a sense of emotion, as opposed to the sensuality of the kiosks. It is a secret enclosure 'in palace chambers far apart'. Sinan Agha probably built this room when he was rebuilding much of the Seraglio after the fire which ravaged the earlier palace in 1574. It lies at the heart of the *haremlik*, as it were embedded in successive layers of mystery, secrecy and silence, and is reached either through the Corridor Where The Djinns Hold Consultation, or by the majestic Vestibule of the Fountain, also by Sinan's hand. . . .

Two vast *lits à baldaquin*, the canopied beds which served as such, or as thrones, are the dominant feature, and have given the room its name. They are placed symmetrically flanking a huge chimney-piece, hooded in bronze, one of those tall, pointed, helmet-shaped structures, the *achmak*, found in old Turkish houses and recalling the headgear of Asiatic conquerors. . . . The canopied beds are carved and gilded, and must once have been spread with innumerable cushions. Their hangings, or some similar ones used elsewhere in the Seraglio are described as being particularly magnificent, 'of black Velvet, with an Embroydery of great Pearls, whereof some are long and others round, and in the form of Buttons. . . . There is another of white Velvet set out with Rubies and Emeralds . . . a third of a Violet coloured Velvet, embroyder'd with Turquoises and Pearls'. The posts supporting the baldaquins were gilded and painted, and also worked with precious stones, the curtains roped back with swags of pearls, while coverlets of tufted velvet or cloth-of-gold lined with lynx or sable were flung about among the cushions. Even without these furnishings, or the wonderful carpets, Ouchaks, Karabaghs or Konias to make the mouth water, this room is never bleak in its present abandonment. The textures of its lost glories are still sensed, for with all its spacious splendour there is warmth and harmony too. The soaring ceiling is domed, yet it does not seem remote, for the walls rise to meet it without straining, their lofty proportions, which might chill, are rendered intimate, or brought to living level by a deep gilded dado of Koranic inscriptions which circle the entire room and are set above panels of superb faïence. Almond blossom, carnations or tulips bloom here on a background of burning blue, edged with that thread of coral red which is the signature of faïences made at Iznik, the old Nicaea. There are double rows of windows: those placed high – very high, above the dado and almost merging with the dome – do not shed that chilling top-light found in studios, for they have panes of jewel-coloured glass and cast pools of colour on the stone floor, though since this was certainly once criss-crossed with carpets overlaid one on another in that prodigal fashion peculiar to the East, the shafts of light streaming down from the windows must have overlaid colour on colour most sumptuously. The lower lines of windows are deeply embrasured and typify those low-set, door-like apertures, almost at ground level, which are so significant a feature of Eastern architecture, whether domestic or religious.

Such low-placed windows, precursors of the modern picture window, always remind me of the raised tent flap in encampments, where the desert's rim is ever visible to those inside. It was from such nomads, roaming the steppes, that the pattern of living and so many tenets of Eastern taste developed.

Throughout the arid East, water is regarded as the ultimate luxury, venerated for its scarcity and man's thirst. The finest gesture of hospitality is to offer a glass of pure water, while fountains and pools obtain almost mystical qualities. Thus, in placing a wide, three-tiered marble fountain stretching the length of one wall in Sultan Murad's room, Sinan Agha set the seal of splendour and pleasure on this room . . . it is the fountain – the marvellous wall-fountain – which is the supreme symbol of luxury. Two tiers of white marble stretch almost the entire length of the wall facing the throne beds, and each tier is set with a row of nine bronze taps, so that cascades of water fall in a shimmering curtain. Moreover, each tap is contrived to sound a different note, thus making a sort of liquid symphony to lull the Sultan's slumbers. Here moonlight, starlight or firelight glittered across the water as it fell, or shafts of sunlight from the jewel-coloured windows above played over it in rainbow arcs. Here is a setting worthy of true love. Here the silences and sighs of passion must have lost themselves in the shadowy dome, or sunk, muffled by the murmuring splash of the fountain. Here the Sultan and his Italian Kadine lived becalmed, shut away from the terrors and tragedies of the Seraglio, indifferent to the extravagance of their setting, perhaps, but figures of unparalleled magnificence themselves. Veronese should have painted them in all their splendour.

I like to imagine the scene and the figures for whom this pleasance was made. They are couched among the tufted velvets and lynx skins. Sultan Murad is a bearded, beetle-browed, long-nosed man, his gigantic turban, heron-plumed, is laid aside, like his jewelled dagger, as he puffs at his turquoise-studded *tchibouque* and fondles the woman at his side. He wears the traditional caftan or surcoat, which changed little through thirty successive Sultanships, only in the nineteenth century giving place to the Western frock-coat, or 'Stambouline', as its local variation was known. Caftans were always monstrously stiff and heavy, in cut velvet and brocades, often lined with sable and fastened by a line of jewelled clasps. . . . His feet are thrust into yellow leather slippers; his hands are heavily ringed, and while the buttons of his outer caftan are diamonds, the size of gooseberries, those of his under-caftan are gigantic sapphires.

Beside him, Safieh Sultane, as splendidly arrayed. She sits cross-legged, so that her crimson taffeta *chalvari* emerge from beneath a flowing lemon-coloured damask robe, or *entari*, the basic garments of every Turkish woman of quality, worn loose over under-shifts and tunics, its sleeves trailing almost to the floor. It is buttoned with topazes, and belted by a wide, heavy girdle, a mosaic of precious stones, the stomacher-clasp fashioned of enormous diamonds. Her gauze chemise is left open to the waist, revealing her breasts: between them dangle chains of pearls and rubies. . . . Her feet are bare, and tinted with henna. On her head she wears the traditional *talpock*, a little flat round tasselled-cap, studded with peals and worn rakishly to one side. . . . Her long blonde hair is left unbound, and falls over her shoulders in a molten shower where diamonds glitter, for they are attached to fine gold chains threaded through her locks. She is painted in the bold manner of the Seraglio, her lips crimsoned, her eyes darkened by kohl, and her eyebrows marked emphatically, being joined in one ebony sweep, for this is the fashion from Samarcand to Cairo. We must hope, in the interests of romance, that her teeth were not also blackened in that manner admired and followed for some centuries by ladies of the *haremlik*.

She holds a lute of Venetian workmanship, tulipwood inlaid with ivory, but now she puts it aside and turns towards her lord and master. On a signal from the Sultan a eunuch steps forward and draws the silk curtains round the throne, which, on the instant, becomes their bed. Eunuch, pages and buffoons steal away; it is quite silent in the great room: only the shift of smouldering logs and the faint music of the fountain sounds. Moonlight streams down from the high windows above, and outside, silvers the dark spears of the cypress groves where there nightingales. Firelight, moonlight, bird-song and the sound of a fountain. . . . Such was the Pavilion Sinan had devised for these lovers.

[60] Thomas Dallam presents an organ to the Sultan Mehmet III, on behalf of Queen Elizabeth I in 1599; from *The Day of the Crescent* by G.E. Hubbard.

At a certain point in her struggle with Philip, Elizabeth harboured the notion of a Turkish alliance. The Ottoman fleet, though well past its prime, could do much to embarrass the Spaniards, and the Queen went so far as to appeal to Mohammed III for assistance in the name of religion, on the grounds that Moslem and Protestant were united in their hatred of 'image-worshippers'. She thought well, however, to back up the appeal with a more material argument and so arranged with the Levant Company – then a close corporation for trading with Turkey – for the purchase and despatch to Constantinople of a gift to the Sultan in the form of an organ.

Dallam, who had just finished the erection of the organ in Kings' College, Cambridge, was entrusted with the work and in the year 1599 the organ was completed (it was the Levant Company, one need hardly mention, who had to pay for it!) and, having been packed in sections, was shipped together with Dallam to Constantinople.

The room in the Seraglio which was set aside for the erection of the instrument was a beautiful kiosk with walls of porphyry topped by a course of lattice work fitted with awnings to moderate the heat and a fish pond in the centre with silk carpets all round. It had – so Dallam at any rate was made to believe – been specially constructed as a theatre for the strangling of members of the royal family, for whose comfort in their last moments these pleasant features were considerately provided. Here in the course of a week or two Dallam reconstructed his organ and a day was fixed for the Sultan to come and hear it play. . . . Let him from this point take up the narrative himself:

'When I came within the Dore that which I did see was verrie wonderful unto me. I came in direcktly upon the Grand Sinyori's ryghte hande, but he would not turne his head to louke upon me. He satt in greate state, yeate the sighte of him was

Thomas Dallam's organ; from the *Illustrated London News* of October 1860, and said there to have been taken from the original specifications

nothinge in Comparison of the traine which stoode behind him and made me almost to thinke that I was in another worlde. I stood dazlinge my eyes with loukinge upon his people, the which was 4 hundrethe persons in number. . . .

'When I had stode nearly $\frac{1}{4}$ of an houre behouldinge this wonderful syghte I hearde the Grand Sinyori speake unto the Cappagan (viz. Capuji) who then came to me and touke my cloake from aboute me and layed it downe upon the carpetes and bid me go playe on the organ; but I refused because the Grande Sinyori satt so neare that I coulde not come at the place and muste needes turne my backe towards him and touche his knee with my britchis, which no man in paine of deathe myght doo save only the Cappagan.

'So he smyled and let me stande a litle. Then the Grand Sinyori spoake again and the Cappagan with a merrie countenance bid me go with goode curridge and thruste me on.

'When I came verrie neare the Grand Sinyori I bowed my heade as low as my knee and turned my backe righte tow him. He satt so righte behind me that he could not see what I did; Therefor he stoode up and the Cappagan removed his chaire to one side wher he myghte see my handes, but in his risinge from his chaire he gave me a thruste forwardes and I thought he had bene drawinge his sorde to cut off my heade.

'I stood thar playinge suche things as I could until the cloke strouke. Then I went close to the Grande Sinyori againe and bowed myself and wente backwardes to my Cloake. When the Company saw me theye seemed to be glad and laughed. Then the Grande Sinyori put his hande behind him full of goulde which the Cappagan receved and brought unto me fortie and five peeces and then was I put out againe wheare I came in, beinge not a litle joyfull of my good suckses.' . . .

One day his palace friends took Dallam all round the palace. They came in the course of their tour to a blank wall with a small iron grille in it which they told him to look through, though they would not themselves go near. On looking he saw thirty or forty persons playing at ball. 'At the firste syghte of them I thoughte they had bene yonge men, but when I saw the hair of theire heades hange doone on their backes platted with a tasle of small pearles and by other plaine tokens I did know them to be women and verrie prettie ones in deede.

'They wore a litle capp which did but cover the crowne of the heade, faire chaines of pearls and juels in their ears, coats like a souldier's mandilyon some of red sattan and som of blew, britchis of fine clothe made of coton woll as whyte as snow and as fine as lawne. Som did weare fine cordovan buskins and som had their leges naked with a goulden ring on the smale of her legg, on her foute a panttoble 4 or 5 inches hie. I stoode so long loukinge upon them that he which had brought me began to be verrie angrie with me and made a wrye mouthe and stamped with his foute to make me give over loukinge; the which I was verrie lothe to dow, for the sighte did please me wondrous well.'

He subsequently learnt that he had been watching the ladies of the sultan's own harem, an offence only to be expiated by instant death or worse.

[61] The Seraglio: a description of the ladies of the Sultan's harem in the early seventeenth century; from 'The Description of the Grand Signior's Serraglio' by Robert Withers, in *Purchas, his Pilgrimes*.

(According to N.M. Penzer's *The Harem*, Robert Withers was attached to the suite of Sir Paul Pindar, British Ambassador to the Porte from 1611 to 1620; Withers probably arrived in Constantinople in 1610. The essence of his account comes from the eye-witness material of Ottaviano Bon, written between 1604 and 1607 when he was Venetian Ambassador to Ahmed I (and from whom Michael Baudier also 'borrowed' extensively). This account of the inmates of the Seraglio is thus reasonably trustworthy, being by two seasoned diplomatic residents of the Porte over several years.)

First, I say that all they which are in the *Serraglio*, both men and women, are the *Grand Signiors* slaves, and so are all they which are subject to his Empire: for as hee is their onely Soveraigne, so they doe all of them acknowledge, that whatsoever they doe possesse or enioy, proceedeth meerely and simply from his good will and favour.

This *Serraglio* may rightly bee termed the Seminarie or Nurcerie of Subjects; for, in it all they have their bringing up, which afterward become the principall Officers, and subordinate Rulers of the state and affaires of the whole Empire. They which are within the third Gate, called the Kings gate, are about two thousand persons, men and women, whereof the women (old and young one with another, what with the Kings Concubines, old women, and women servants) may bee about eleven or twelve hundred, Now, those which are kept up for their beauties, are all young Virgins taken and stollen from foreign Nations, who after they have beene nurtured in good manners, and can play on Instruments, sing, dance, and sew curiously, they are given to the *Grand Signior* as Presents of exceeding great value . . .

These Virgins, immediately after their comming into the *Serraglio* are made *Turkes*, which is done by using this ceremonie onely, to hold up their fore-finger, and say, *Law illaw-heh it, Allawh Muhamed resull Allawh*, that is, there is no God but God alone, and *Mahomet* is the Messenger of God: and according as they are in age and disposition (being proved and examined by an old woman called *Cahiyah Cadun*, that is, as wee say, *the Mother of the Maides*) so they are placed in a Roome with the others of the same age, spirit, and inclination, to dwell and live together. Now, in the Womens lodgings, they live just as the Nunnes doe in their great Monasteries; for, these Virgins have very large Roomes to live in, and their Bed-chambers will hold almost a hundred of them a piece: they sleepe upon *Sofaes*, which are built long wise on both sides of the Roome, so that there is a large space in the midst for to walke in. Their Beds are very course and hard, and by every ten Virgins there lies an old woman: and all the night long there are many lights burning, so that one may see very plainely throughout the whole Roome; which doth both keepe the yong Wenches from wantonnesse, and serve upon any occasion which may happen in the night: neere unto the said Bed-chambers they have their *Bagnoes*, and Kitchins for their use at all times, with a great abundance of Fountaines of which they are served with water. Above over the said Bed-chambers there are divers Roomes, where they sit and sew, and keepe their Chists in which they lay up their apparell. They feed by whole Camaradaes, and are served and waited upon by other women; so that they doe not want any thing whatsoever which is necessary for them. They have other places likewise where they goe to schoole, to learne to speake and reade the *Turkish* tongue, to sew, and play on Instruments; and so they spend the day with their Mistresses which are ancient women: some houres notwithstanding being allowed them for their recreation, to walke in their Gardens, and use such sports as they familiarly exercise themselves withall.

The King doth not at all frequent or see these Virgins, unlesse it be at the instant when they are first given him, or else in case that he desire one of them for his bed-fellow, or to shew him some pastime with Musike and tumbling trickes: and then hee giveth notice to the aforesaid *Cahiyah Cadun* of his purpose, who immediatly chooseth out such as shee thinketh to bee the most amiable and fairest, and having placed them in good order in a Roome, in two rankes, halfe on the one side and halfe on the other, shee forthwith brings in the King, who walking foure or five turnes in the midst of them, and having viewed them well, taketh good notice of her which he best liketh, but sayeth nothing, onely as he goeth out againe, he throweth a Handkerchiefe into that Virgins hand, by which shee knoweth that shee is to lie with him that night; and she being wondrous glad of so good a fortune, to be chosen out from among so many to enioy the societie of an Emperour, hath all the art that possible may bee shewen upon her by the *Cadun*, in attiring, painting, and perfuming her, and so at night shee is brought to sleepe with the *Grandsignior* in the womens lodgings: (there being divers Chambers appropriated for that businesse onely: and being in bed they have two great Waxe lights burning by them all night, one at the beds feete, and the other by the doore; and there are appointed (by the *Cadun*) divers old *Blacke-moore* women, which watch by turnes that night in the Chamber, two at a time, one to sit by the said light at the Beds feet, and the other by the doore, and when they will they change, and other two supply their roomes, without making the least noise imaginable, so that the King is not any wise disturbed. And in the morning when his Highnesse riseth (for he riseth first) he changeth all his apparell from top to toe, leaving those which hee wore to her that he lay withall, and all the money that was in his pockets were it never so much; and so departeth to his owne lodgings, from whence also he sendeth her immediately a Present of Iewels, Vests and Money of great value, according to the satisfaction and content which hee received from her that night: in the same manner he is to deale with all the others which hee maketh use of in that kind, but with some he continueth longer, and enlargeth his bounty more towards some then to others, according as his humour and affection to them encreaseth; by their fulfilling his lustfull desires. And if it so fall out, that any one of them doe conceive by him and bring forth his first begotten child, she is called by the name of *Sultana* Queene, and if the child bee a sonne, then shee is confirmed and established by great Feasts and Solemnities; and hath a dwelling apart assigned unto her, of many stately Roomes well furnished, and many servants to attend upon her: The King likewise alloweth her a very sufficient Revenue, that shee may give away and spend at her pleasure, in whatsoever shee may have occasion; and all they of the *Serraglio* doe acknowledge her for Queene, shewing all the respect and dutie that may bee, both to her and hers. . . .

The Women of the *Serraglio*, are punished for their faults very severely, and extreamely beaten by their Over-seers: and if they prove disobedient, incorrigible and insolent, they are by the Kings order and expresse commandment, turned out and sent into the old *Serraglio*, as being reiected and cast off, and most part of that they have is taken from them. But if they shall be found culpable for Witchcraft: or any such hainous offence, then are they tyed and put into a Sacke and in the Night cast into the Sea: so that by all meanes it behooveth them to bee very obedient, and containe themselves within the bounds of honestie and modestie, if they meane to come to a good end.

Now it is not lawfull for any one to bring ought in unto them, with which they may comit the deeds of beastly uncleannesse; so that if they have a will to eate Cucumbers, Gourds, or such like meates, they are sent in unto them sliced, to deprive them of the meanes of playing the wantons; for, they being all young, lustie, and lascivious Wenches, and wanting the societie of Men (which would better instruct them) are doubtlesse of themselves inclined to that which is naught, and will be possest with unchast thoughts.

Now as concerning the Blacke Eunuches, and Black-moore Wenches, which serve the *Sultanaes* and the Kings Women; It is to bee noted that the Blacke Eunuches, whilst they are Boyes, are for the most part kept and taught among the other youthes of the *Serraglio*, until they bee come to age and made fit for service; and being taken from thence they are appointed for the Women, and set to serve with others at the *Sultanaes* Gate (all under command of the *Kuzlar Agha*, that is to say, the *Master of the Virgins*) being allowed a Pension of fiftie or sixtie Aspers *per Diem*, and two Vests of Silke *per Annum*, with Linnen and other necessaries sufficient for their use, besides divers gifts they receive from Women strangers at such times as they let them goe in to the Kings women: they are named by the names of Flowers, as *Hyacinth, Narcissus, Rose, Gilly-flower*, and the like; for that, serving the Women, their names may bee answerable to their Virginitie, sweet and undefiled.

[62] The Great Review of the Merchant Corporations of the city before Sultan Murad IV at the Alay Kiosk in 1638; from *Narrative of Travels in Europe, Asia, and Africa* . . . by Evliya Efendi, translated by Ritter J. von Hammer-Purgstall.

[The Sultan said] 'I desire that all guilds of Constantinople, both large and small, shall repair to my Imperial camp. They shall exhibit the number of their men, shops, and professions, according to their old constitutions, they shall all with their Sheikhs, Nakibs, Pirs, Aghas, Kyayas, Yigit-bashi, and Chaushes, on foot and on horseback, with their complete eightfold music, pass before the Alaikoshk, that I may see how many thousand men and how many guilds there are. It shall be an Alai (procession) the like of which never was seen before. A general description shall be made of all the Imperial mosques, of the Vizirial mosques, of the mesjids, colleges, houses for reading the Koran, and houses for reading the tradition, schools, convents, khans, baths, magazines, caravanserais, palaces of the vezirs and great men, fountains, establishments for distributing water, conduits, cisterns, quarters of Moslims, Christians, and Jews, churches and synagogues, ovens for bread and biscuits, water, wind and horse-mills, halls and repositories, of all the houses, gardens, koshks, yallis, and all the monuments to be found in the four districts, ruled by the four great Mollas of Constantinople. The inhabitants of all the quarters, the guilds, the Imams, Khatibs, and Kyayas of the quarters shall assemble and note down every thing, and then send the complete description to my sublime Porte. Those who make the description shall be men of impartial character, if the contrary should be found I shall order them to be quartered.' . . .

[*The description of Constantinople and all its suburbs and villages on both sides of the Bosphorus was completed in three months . . .*]

Most Humble Report to the Sublime Porte.

According to the Imperial rescript, the following is the description of the excellent town of Constantinople. May God preserve her from decay and fall!

Under the four Mollas of Constantinople, Galata, Eyyub and Scutari, justice was transacted at six hundred and seventy tribunals. Great mosques of the Sultans (Jamii Selatin) 74. Great mosques of the Vezirs (Jamii Wuzera) 1985. Small mosques of the town-quarters (Mesjid) 6990. Other mosques great and small, 6665. . . .

Of all the Guilds and Professions existing in the Jurisdiction of the Four Mollas of Constantinople; with the Number of their Shops, their Men, their Sheikhs and Pirs.

They are distributed into fifty-seven sections and consist altogether of a thousand and one guilds. . . .

(12) The Executioners (Jellad). Their patron is Job, from Bassra, who was girded by Selman in the Prophet's presence. He was the first, who, according to the text of the Koran, cut off the head of a murderer, and so became the patron of hangmen. His duty was to prepare those, who were condemned to death, to comfort them by exhortations, to direct their faces towards the Kibla, to fix the head of the man about to be killed with his right hand, then to take the sword in both hands and to sever the head from the body, to read a fatihah, and to admonish all those present, that they might take warning from the culprit. This patron of executioners died at an hundred and seventy years old; he himself brought the corpse of Moavia to Damascus, where he buried it, near the Pasha's gate, built a cupola over it, and was himself buried there. A son of my gracious Lord, Melek Ahmed Pasha is also buried there, and culprits are even now executed in face of his tomb. It is a place of general pilgrimage. The executioners are the men to whom the verse is applied: 'If it was not the Sultan's command, the executioner would commit no cruelty.' The greatest model of hangmen was the executioner of Sultan Murad IV, Kara Ali, who was girded with a fiery sword, and wore in his girdle all the instruments of torture and of his profession, nails, borers, matches, razors for scorching, steel-plates, different powders for blinding, clubs for breaking the

hands and feet, hatchets, and spoons, and was followed by his servants carrying the rest of the seventy-seven instruments of torture. Then by other servants with gilt, well carved, well greased, and well perfumed pales, with ropes and chains on their waists, and drawn swords in their hands. They pass with great vehemence, but no light shines from their faces, for they are a dark set of people. . . .

(58) The Merchants of rose-water (Gulabjian) are seventy, with forty-one shops. Women of Adrianople sell rose-water in large vessels of bronze before the old Bezestán. Others sell water of frankincense, of amber, of jasmine, and many other perfumed waters of this kind. Their patron is 'Atr-ud-din, the Indian, who is buried in India, at the town of Div. The Prophet liked extremely all kinds of scents and perfumes, and 'Atr-ud-din (the essence of religion), therefore presented him always with such. He received the girdle from Alí, and was created by him a Pír, or patron. They pass at the public procession, pouring on both sides rose-water and frankincense-water in large streams on the spectators.

(59) The Perfumers or merchants of essential oils (Debhan), are one hundred and fifteen, with eighty shops. . . . The perfumers extract the essential oils from almonds, cypress-nuts, pistachios, hazel-nuts, and other similar fruits. With the bottles full of such oils and essences they adorn their shops and their litters on public processions, and, in passing by, perfume the crowd with essences of roses, jasmine, basilicon, hyacinths, &c. They pass in the suite of the Proto-medicus or Hekim-bashi, who is followed by the Kohhal-bashi (the head of the oculists), the Jerrah-bashi (the head of the surgeons), and the substitutes or assistants (Khalfa) of the Protomedicus, who carry sticks in their hands. . . .

(195) The Snow and Ice merchants (Karji) have an establishment near the vegetable-market, where the chief of the Imperial ice-porters resides summer and winter. Three hundred boatmen under his direction are always on excursions to the mountains of Katirli, Modania, and Olympus. They embark the snow, ice, and fresh water, from these mountains, and carry them to the Imperial kitchen, to the confectionary, to the Harem, and to the houses of the grand vezir and other great men. The porters who carry the ice and snow from the mountains down to the sea are the muleteers of Madonia, the yuruks (wandering tribes) of

Procession of the Silver-Threadmakers, Blacksmiths, Shipbuilders, Embroiderers, Saddlers and Feltmakers; from the *Surname-i Vehbi*, commemorating the circumcision of the sons of Ahmet III, 1720

Brussa and stone-cutters. . . . In the winter, when it snows, the grand Vezír, the Agha of the Janissaries, the Bostanjí-bashí, the Kapudan-Pasha, with a crowd of two hundred thousand men, carrying shovels, assemble at the Ok-maidan, and heaping up the snow in large masses throw it into the snow magazines. They then collect the snow of the vallies of Diodar-dereh, Buyuk-dereh, Ghanizadeh-dereh, Aineh-dereh, Tuzkoparan-dereh, Choban-dereh, and Kanli-dereh, which they press together, so that it all freezes to ice. The Kapudan Pasha then gives at the convent of Ok-maidan a feast to the grand Vezir and the other ministers of state. . . . The next morning the whole army proceed to Eyyub, where they collect the snow on the fields of Edris, and fill the snow magazines of that place. There are seven such snow-pits, the upper part of which are covered. . . . In the summer these pits are emptied by the Karji-bashi who delivers the snow and ice when it is wanted for the Emperor's and the Valideh's service. At the public procession these snowmen pass with turbans of different shapes and sizes, all made of snow; they throw snow balls at one another and at the spectators, playing many other tricks. They drag also on wagons loads of snow of the size of the cupola, and from seventy to eighty files of mules loaded with the purest snow from Mount Olympus close their train. The ice-men, half naked, hold in their hands clubs made of ice, some of them run wire through their ears, and some perforate their limbs and run sticks into them. The number of covered ice-pits amounts to seventy. . . .

(253) The Flower merchants, who at the same time sell fruit, are three hundred persons, with eighty shops. Their patron is Khabil Irmaghani, who was girded by Ins Ben Malek. He used to bring baskets of flowers and fruit as presents to the Prophet and to his family. He is buried at Taif. The shops of these Flower-merchants (Jejekjian, the former Shukufehjian) are in the part of the town called Takt-ul-kala'a, Ak-seraï, Sultan Mohammed, and Aya Sofiyah, before the gate of the Jebeh-khanah. Here at all seasons of the year are found dishes full of flowers and fruits, which are offered as presents to the vezirs and great men. They make a great show, being an exquisitely armed troop. They carry on poles koshks, which are imitations of the koshk of the Mohtessib and of the koshk at the fruit market, wherein fine boys reclining on golden cushions do service. . . .

(268) The Firework-makers (Fishekjian) are one hundred

men, with eighteen shops. Their patron is Jemshid; the greatest part of them belong to the armourers. They exhibit their skill in fireworks on the occasion of public rejoicings, on the birth of princes, and on the feast of circumcision. Their manufactory is outside of the hospital of the Suleimanieh, where they have the repository of their tools and their magazine. They have also shops at Eyyub, Galata, Top-khanah, and Beshiktash. The first artist in fireworks was Avicenna (Abu sina) who is the master and patron of all firework-makers. On the occasions of rejoicing for victories, these firework-makers set on fire some hundred thousand rockets of different colours, some of which mount straight into the sky, and some go in an oblique direction, spreading stars around them. Some of these rockets, divided into three parts, ascend at three different times, so that when the first, having burned out, falls to the ground, the second is lighted, and then the third, which at last explodes with a noise that seems to rend the clouds. It is probable that the Cherubim, hearing this dreadful report, recite the verse of the Koran, 'O God guard us from the evil of mankind!' In the days of my youth when I, poor Evliya, mingled with all sorts of company, I made, for my master, Ali Agha, the inspector of the Custom-house, one of these rockets with seven divisions. It was made of a sprig of fir-tree hollowed out, at the top of which was fixed a kind of cap filled with seventeen occas of powder, and below it was carried by pinions made of eagles' wings. On the night of the birth of Kiasultán (afterwards the wife of Evliya's patron, Malek Ahmed Pasha), I launched out to sea in a boat, and thence the rocket ascended into the sky at seven times to such a height, that the report of the seventh was heard on earth with so stupendous a noise that people hearing it lost their courage. Each of the seven divisions exploding, showered on the grounds a fiery rain of Nafta-balls and stars, as if the seven planets and all the fixed stars had fallen from heaven. Seeing this stupendous sight, I began to repent, and as the tradition says, 'Whosoever repents of a fault shall be considered as if he had not done it,' I hope this my trick shall be considered as not having happened; it was, however, a strange spectacle. The firework-makers of Constantinople also make another kind of large rocket, which in exploding, vomits forth forty small rockets, some of which mount into the air, some go to the right, some to the left, and some fall amongst the crowd of spectators, burning them, which causes great noise and riot. On the nights of the feast of circumcision, some hundred thousand rockets of every description are set on fire, covering the surface of the sea, some of them dive and come up again, and put the whole sea into a blaze and the fish into an uproar, so that they jump out of the water and dive again, which is also a spectacle worth beholding. . . . At the same time different sorts of rockets, fire-wheels, and engines . . . fire-suns, dragons, serpents, thunder-bolts, &c. are burning on all sides, and produce a spectacle, which borders on the miraculous. They pass at the public procession with similar exhibitions before the koshk of the Emperor. . . .

(716) The Fools and Mimics of Constantinople. Whenever there is a feast of Imperial circumcision, nuptials, or victory, from two to three hundred singers, dancers, comics, mimics, with mischievous boys of the town, who have exhausted seventy cups of the poison of life and misrule, crowd together and play day and night. At some private weddings they gain in a night the sum of a thousand piastres, collecting the money in the half-drum after each dance. . . .

(727) The twelfth company of Semúrkásh are two hundred boys, who are all Jews, and all tumblers, jugglers, fire-eaters, ball players, and cup-players, who pass the whole night in showing their tricks, and ask more than one hundred piastres for a night's performance; as these Jewish boys have the greatest antipathy to the gipsies, who compose the first company, they generally set a band of these Jewish boys against a band of gipsies, which produces the strangest scenes. Thus, they represent the play of a Jew surprised in flagrante with a Gipsy girl, the girl is seated on an ass, and conducted through the street with nasty intestines on her head, which makes the people nearly die with laughing. . . . They are all dressed in gold stuff, and endeavour to excel while passing under the Alaï-koshk, where the Emperor is seated, so as to attract his attention by their fits and tricks. Since Adam descended from Paradise on earth, never was there seen such a crowd of tempting boys than under Sultán Murád IV.

[63] The relics of the Prophet, kept at Topkapi; from *Histoire de l'Empire Ottoman* by Ritter J. von Hammer-Purgstall. Translated by Laurence Kelly.

Hasan Pasha had been ordered to strengthen the pillars of the Kaaba, to provide a new cover for the holy building, and to replace the 'star of pearls' (or "Kewkeb dürrer" pearl) placed on the inner wall of the temple with a valuable diamond. He was received on return to the capital by the Sultan Ahmet, and to him he delivered the sacred relics from Mecca. Hasan had replaced the pearl by a plaque made of gold, on which was fixed a diamond of superb quality, which had cost Ahmet's father 50,000 ducats. There were also 227 other less valuable diamonds. Hasan brought back to the Porte the old cover of the Kaaba, the kewkeb dürrer pearl, and also a staff cut from the roof top of the temple which he offered to the Sultan, saying that he hoped it would be a support to him in his old age. Within the harem there was the 'room of the noble habit' where the Prophet's mantle was kept, and there the staff and pearl were put. When Mohammed III had gone to besiege Erlau, he had taken the holy mantle with him, and at the battle of Kersztes at the most dangerous moment he had put it on. As well as the mantle (to which Kaab ben Soheir and Boussiri have dedicated two immortal poems) the Prophet's bow and sword are venerated; and also a carpet of Ebubeker, and the swords of the Prophet's companions. The standard and mantle are the most precious of these relics, which themselves are the most precious of the Ottoman Empire.

The standard of Mahomet is wrapped up in forty silken covers, and his mantle is packed in forty layers of rich fabrics. Every year, on the fifteenth day of Ramadan, the holy mantle is unwrapped and shown to the whole fasting Court; those present kiss it. The senior Chamberlain, standing next to the holy relics and holding a piece of muslin, wipes the place where each person has kissed it, and then gives the piece of muslin to each person in memory of this holy duty. The Kislar Aga then washes, in a large silver basin, that part of the mantle where the faithful have kissed it. He then pours the holy water into little phials, which he seals and gives to those present. A few drops of the holy water should also be poured into the glasses of water drunk in the evening at the end of the fast on the feast day, giving sovereign balm against illnesses and fires, and assuring divine salvation.

The door of the Chamber of Relics is studded with silver; and indeed in the Palace of Byzantine Emperors a spectacular door, also covered in silver, led into the Hall of Gold where the Crown jewels and other relics were kept, such as Moses' staff, and the Holy Cross brought by the Empress Helena from Jerusalem to Constantinople.

[64] Mutinous Janissaries invade the Seraglio in 1622, depose Sultan Osman II and restore Sultan Moustafa in his place; from *Histoire de l'Empire Ottoman* by Ritter J. van Hammer-Purgstall. Translated by Laurence Kelly.

The Ulemas asked the mutineers what evidence they had as to the crimes of the others [*for whose heads they had asked*]. They were told that the Grand Vizier had showered the troops with a hail of arrows from his house; that the Treasurer only paid in debased coinage; that the Kaimakam was not paying the pensions of retired soldiers; and that Nassouh Aga was the Kaimakam's crony. The Ulemas then went to the Saray to present the petition to the Sultan. Osman refused to approve such a bloody proposal. The Ulemas, undeterred, advised that it was a choice of the lesser of two evils. 'Don't meddle with such matters,' cried Osman. 'They are a leaderless rabble which will soon melt away.'

The Ulemas stressed that the troops, once assembled, had a way of taking for themselves what they wanted, and that the Padishah's illustrious ancestors in such cases had pre-empted their desires. Hearing this, and much angered, the Sultan cried back: 'You speak as if you were the fomenters of this mutiny, and I will put you to death as well as the rebels.' The Ulemas fell silent.

The retired Grand Vizier, Husein Pasha, then threw himself at the feet of the Sultan. 'My Padishah,' he said, 'if they want my head, give it to them but think of your own salvation'. The Ulemas repeated in vain their advice and wanted to retire from the royal presence, but they were ordered to stay in the Saray.

The rebels were still waiting in the Hippodrome for the Ulemas to return, and as they did not, they came to the conclusion that their demands had been rejected. There was general uncertainty as to whether or not the *bostançis* [gardeners] had been armed to defend the Saray, and one of the rebels climbed the minaret of Aya Sofya to clear matters up. He saw neither *bostançis* nor Ulemas. At this news the whole mob rushed towards the Imperial gate and got through into the First Court of the Seraglio. Warned by the gatekeepers to beware of the *bostançis*, the rebels manned the battlements with some hundreds of musketeers. Other soldiers (the *djebedjis*, the *topdjis*, the *adjemoglans*) who had come without arms took stakes from the woodsheds. For some hours, the crowd stayed in the First Court, calling loudly for the heads of the Hodja, the Kislar Aga, and that of the Grand Vizier. There was no reply. Then the mob pressed through the second Gate into the Second Court where for two hours they besieged the Divan with the same cry. In front of the Gate of Felicity, the Ulemas were seated on stone benches. According to some, the head of the Scherifs (Ghoubari Efendi) told the troops: 'Our speeches led to nothing, go and speak for yourselves.' Some White Eunuchs, guarding the Gate of Felicity, had fled to the Inner Court, and the waves of invading soldiery rushed after them.

At this moment, one of those insignificant events which often settle the fate of governments in a revolt, diverted the ideas of the mob to another end. A voice cried out in the Inner Court: 'We want Sultan Mustafa!' The cry was immediately repeated a thousand and one times. The rebels rushed towards a part of the palace where none of them had ever been, and began to run through the Great Room, the Little Room, the inner room of the Forty Pages, all the while shouting, 'We want Sultan Mustafa!' An Ulema in the Third Court showed the soldiers where the Harem was. But they could find no door, and so they built up a pile of wood over which they could get in through a dome; and still the cry went up, 'We want the Sultan Mustafa!'

Suddenly a feeble voice was heard from below, saying: 'Sultan Mustafa is here!' The roof was forthwith demolished. Some negroes firing arrows at them were killed. As there were no stairs leading down from the dome, they cut the cords of the curtain of the Divan, and one of the rebels was lowered down by this means. He found the Sultan Mustafa sitting on an old mattress, attended by two slaves. 'My Padishah, the Army awaits you outside,' he said. Instead of a formal reply, Mustafa simply said: 'I am thirsty.' For three days he had been left without food or drink. The Janissaries sent him water in a leather bucket, and some of them ran to the old Saray to tell Mustafa's mother that her son had been found. Mustafa was then lifted out through the dome and into the Court, where he was placed on the Mufti's horse. But he was too weak to remain mounted, and so he was carried into the Throne Room. He was shaking with fear at the sight of cold steel, and was hardly comforted by being told he had nothing to fear.

As soon as Osman had seen his palace being invaded, he brought back from Scutari the Grand Vizier Dilawer Pasha (who had gone into hiding in the cell of the Grand Sheikh Mahmud) and had him brought to the Saray. At the same time as the dome, under which Mustafa was languishing, was being destroyed, a door of the Harem had been opened; the Kislar Aga and the Grand Vizier had been pushed out and the door immediately closed again. The troops to whose fury this sacrifice had been offered immediately hacked them to pieces.

The Ulemas were then asked by the troops to swear loyalty to Sultan Mustafa, but replied: 'Calm yourselves down; you have got what you wanted, and what more can you ask? Leave the Padishah Osman in peace. . . . Sultan Osman greets you and he has yielded to your demands . . . But if you place Sultan Mustafa on the throne, you will live to regret the day.' . . .

At this refusal a thousand swords flew from their scabbards, and before such a threat the Ulemas were forced to swear their oath to the new Sultan. One of them died of fear. From all the minarets Mustafa was proclaimed reigning Sultan. As he was too weak to ride a horse, he was placed in a carriage with his two companions, and his Mamluk who was his equerry. Thus the people dragged him to the old Saray. . . .

[The next afternoon] the [new] Grand Vizier, Daoud Pasha, and the Kiaya, Omer, and the lieutenant of police, Kalender Oghri, took Osman away to the Castle of the Seven Towers. A huge crowd watched the dethroned sovereign's procession. As soon as the gates of the fortress had closed behind them, and the people dispersed, the Grand Vizier and his henchmen tried to kill Osman. But he struggled like a young tiger, and fought long and hard the four attackers who were weaker than he. At last, however, the Djebedgi Bashi managed to get the bowstring round his neck, whilst Kalender Oghri crushed his testicles. Thus took place the first murder of a Sultan, which disgraces Ottoman history. His ear was cut off, and delivered to Mustafa's mother, the Sultana. Osman was eighteen, and the sixteenth Osmanli Sultan.

[65] The accession of Sultan Ibrahim in 1640; from *Histoire de l'Empire Ottoman* by Ritter J. von Hammer-Purgstall. Translated by Laurence Kelly.

Murad [IV] was dead, and the Court grandees rushed with joyful shouts to the Kafes (or Cage of the Princes) to tell the new Sultan of his accession. Ibrahim bolted his door, fearing that the old tyrant was still breathing and was exploiting this ruse as a way to claim his head and thus make him pay the price for being the sole survivor of all his brothers. The door – with every possible courtesy – was broken down. Ibrahim only accepted the chorus of congratulations when his mother, the Sultana Koesem, herself confirmed Murad's death by placing the late Sultan's corpse, as irrefutable evidence, before his brother's door.

Ibrahim then went to the Throne Room where he received the allegiance of the Diwan, the Ulemas, and the Agas. He had his brother's corpse taken to the Gate of the Saray. Following ancient custom, the Sultan was then girded with the Sword at the Mosque of Eyüp. The Validé Sultana Koesem kept her word, and not a Vizier was deposed from office.

[66] The tastes of Sultan Ibrahim; from *Histoire de l'Empire Ottoman* by Ritter J. von Hammer-Purgstall. Translated by Marina Berry.

At the beginning of his reign, when he was still the only descendant of the race of Osman, all the vizirs felt they should encourage his fondness for women, and competed in their eagerness to offer him beautiful slaves. He himself would give four or five purses to the guards at the gates, whenever he rode outside the city or went on an outing, so that they would pray to God to give him children. Later the birth of half a dozen princes disposed of his fear of dying without descendants, but did not reduce in the least his love of pleasure; and as the influence of women increased his own diminished. At the age of twenty-four, the passionate and robust young man had a large harem, and his strength so faithfully kept pace with his immoderate desire that twenty-four slaves could visit his couch successively in the space of twenty-four hours. His whole system soon began to feel the results of such excesses. Ibrahim consulted Doctor Hammalzade-Efendi about his irritability, melancholia and other complaints following such debauchery, but he was banished in disgrace to the Isle of Princes for prescribing no other remedy than moderation and rest. Hammalzade's position was given to Isa-Efendi, whose science was no doubt more obliging. The Prophet Mohammed used to say that God had placed his joy and delight in three things: prayer, perfume and women. Commenting on these words of Mohammed, a poet said that just as prayer and perfume rise to heaven, women, who live among perfumes and prayers as devout beings veiled in clouds of sweet scent, raise men to the celestial regions. Ibrahim agreed more or less with the Prophet; above all he loved women, perfumes and furs. For him the harem was a bed of sensuousness, giving out intoxicating emanations, and covered with rich soft furs. Ibraham ignored the cost when it came to buying slaves, amber or pelts; the price of slaves rose so high during his reign that none sold for less than five hundred piastres, and the most beautiful could fetch up to two thousand; amber, which he breathed in like scent, or drank dissolved in scalding coffee to steady his nerves, reached the enormous price of fifteen to twenty piastres a miskal (one and half drams).... Ibrahim took the luxury of fur to such an extent that Siberian squirrel, lynx and ermine went out of fashion, and the price of sable increased tenfold. The Sultan's passion for women, perfumes and sables, as well as for flowers, sumptuous clothes and games continued to increase. Ibrahim loved flowers which symbolized women, with their delicacy, their brilliance and their sweet scent. Instead of wearing heron plumes mounted on diamond clips, the usual ornament of the imperial turban, he wove flowers in his hair and behind his ears, which was considered improper in Turkey, as it was the fashion of the Cynedes.

Ibrahim designed a robe for orgies with sable outside and inside; he created another for his use only, the buttons of which were inlaid with precious stones, each one worth eight thousand piastres. The lavishness of the harem women's dresses outshone anything ever seen before or since; the finest English cloth, the softest French silk, the richest Venetian velvet and gold brocade were spread about the harem with splendid liberality. Whenever the news reached Constantinople that a ship loaded with beautiful material had reached the Dardanelles, if by chance the north wind prevented it from entering the port, the Sultan's slaves rushed to send messengers to the long-awaited ship, who often took the merchandise by force, without paying. The English ambassador had to complain of such acts of violence carried out against some traders of his nation, and sought satisfaction. . . .

All the time he was not with women, Ibrahim spent with fife, flute and tambourine players, singers and jesters . . . at night he would leave the seraglio of Daoud-Pasha with torch bearers, wander through the streets of the city to the grand seraglio, flitting from one place to another, from one pleasure to a new one. . . . Although the Sultan's pleasures were constantly renewed, his imagination was insatiable. Once, while riding near Scutari, he decided that the degree of sensuous delight must be in proportion to physical size. Messengers were immediately sent out to find the biggest and fattest woman possible; they found a gigantic Armenian whom they brought back to the seraglio. The new favourite rose so fast in the Sultan's favour that she soon overtook her rivals. She asked for and received the governorship of Damascus, which she ruled through a delegate. But the Validé Sultana, jealous of the increasing influence of the Armenian, invited her to a feast, and had her strangled.

[67] The custom of insulting foreign envoys begins with the humiliation of the French Ambassador, the Marquis de Nointel, at the court of Mehmet IV in 1677; from *Under the Turk in Constantinople* by G.F. Abbott.

On arriving at the Porte on the appointed day (Sunday, April 22nd), Nointel had to wait three whole hours in the room of the Kehayah – a surly Turk – without conversation or any other entertainment; and when at last he was called in, he found the narrow corridor that led to the Audience Chamber crowded with chaoushes who jostled him most rudely. Truth to tell, this rudeness, at all events, was not premeditated. The poor chaoushes had come in the turbans of ceremony worn on such occasions, but had been ordered by the Vizir to go and exchange them for their ordinary headgear: hence their hurry to get back to their places before the Ambassador made his entry. Nointel, however, whose nerves were already on edge with the long waiting, saw in their behaviour a fresh insult, and he elbowed his way down the passage fiercely flinging the chaoushes to right and left against the walls. In this temper he entered the Audience Chamber, and there he observed something at which his resentment reached the height of exasperation: the stool destined for him was not upon the Soffah, but on the floor below! He ordered his Dragoman to set it where it should be; one of the Vizir's pages brought it down again. Then the Ambassador, in a towering rage, seized the stool with his own hand, carried it to the Soffah, and sat upon it.

When this act was reported to the Vizir, who was in an adjoining apartment, he sent for the Ambassador's Dragoman and commanded him to tell his master that he must move his seat back where he had found it. The trembling Dragoman delivered the message and was bidden by the angry Ambassador to hold his tongue. Next the Vizir sent his own Dragoman, Dr. Mavrocordato, with whom Nointel maintained the closest friendship. In vain did the Greek try to soothe the enraged Frenchman, imploring him to moderate his temper and yield gracefully to the inevitable. Nothing could prevail over M. de Nointel's obstinacy: the pride of the wig was pitted against the pride of the turban, and it must be remembered that both wigs and turbans were then at their zenith. In the end, Mavorcordato, finding argument useless, changed his tone and said, in Italian: 'The Grand Vizir commands the chair to be placed below.' Nointel replied: 'The Grand Vizir can command his chair: he cannot command me.' At that moment the Chaoush-bashi burst into the room, roaring, '*Calder, Calder* – Take it away, take it away!' – and before he knew what was happening, Nointel found the stool snatched from under him. In an access of fury, his Excellency dashed out of the room, sword on shoulder, pushed his way through the throng, and, ordering the presents which he had brought to follow him, mounted his horse and departed, exciting, as he boasted, by his firmness, 'the astonishment of the Turks and the joy of the French'. Kara Mustafa alone remained calm. His comment, when he heard that the Ambassador was gone, was one word: '*Gehennem*' (Let him go to Hell).

One barbarous word, that can be shown to be authentic, is worth volumes of descriptive writing.

Such was the beginning of the celebrated 'Affaire du Sofa' – a quarrel which drew the attention of all Europe and nearly led to a rupture between France and Turkey.

[68] J.C. Hobhouse and Lord Byron accompany the British Ambassador to an audience with the Sultan Mahmoud II in the Seraglio; from *A Journey through Albania . . . to Constantinople during the years 1809 and 1810* by J.C. Hobhouse.

(John Cam Hobhouse (1786–1869) travelled with Lord Byron across Portugal, Spain and via Greece and Albania to Constantinople in 1810. He was best man at Byron's ill-fated marriage; and his was the hand, as literary executor, that burned Byron's memoirs. Created Baron Broughton in 1851, he had a long, interesting political career.)

A short time after the passage of the Caimacam we moved forwards, and in nearly half an hour arrived at the entrance of the Seraglio, the Baba-Humayun, or Sublime Gate . . . We dismounted about a hundred yards from Baba-Salàm (*the gate of Health*), upon entering which all our state vanished, for we were shown into a dirty chamber on the left hand of the porch, where we remained in darkness for some time, all huddled together in this and another room, appropriated to very unsavoury purposes. This is the executioners' lodge, and it seems that we were detained here in order that we might enter the second court at the instant that the Janissaries run for their pilau, which is placed in innumerable little pewter dishes, and, at a given signal, scrambled for and seized upon by the soldiery assembled for the occasion, to the number generally of four thousand.

The second court is considerably smaller than the first. It is colonnaded on three sides, and the middle space is a green, thickly shaded with rows of cypress trees. On the right are the Seraglio kitchens, and on the left is an open walk, with a fountain and the hall of the Divan.

The third gate, Baba-Saadi (*the gate of Happiness*), and the walls of the interior palace, front the entrance to the court. The

The Sultan (above) and the Bostanji-bashi (below), 1787; from *Voyage Pittoresque de la Grèce*, 1782–1809 by M.G. Choiseul Gouffier

Divan is a small vaulted saloon, with three windows in the dome which admit but little light; it is richly ornamented and wainscotted with a plaister or stucco well polished, and representing a pink variegated marble. On the left of the saloon is a second chamber, also vaulted, and about the same size as the first, divided from the council-hall by a division only breast-high: this is filled by the clerks and attendants of the court. A cushioned bench, something like that of our Court of Chancery, ranges along the back of the chamber, and in the middle is the seat of the Grand Vizier, and little raised and immediately under a small latticed casement, through which the Sultan himself inspects, or is supposed to inspect, the transactions of the Divan. On the left side of the room is another cushioned bench, and on the right a lower bench without any covering, attached to the wall. On entering we found the Caimacam in his seat; on his left hand, at a little distance, were the Cazy-askers of Romania and Natolia, and on the bench on the same side, were the Tefterdar-Effendi and two other officers of the treasury. . . .

At ten the dinner was served, and the Ambassador, attended by Prince Maroozi, sat at a table with the Caimacam. Some of the gentlemen of the embassy, with my fellow-traveller and myself, were placed at another table with Cheliby-Effendi. There were one or two other tables and some seats brought into the room, but the greater part of the company were obliged to stand. Any person may join an Ambassador's suite on these occasions, and there were several raggamuffins in the Frank habit amongst the crowd, who seemed to have been collected purposely to disgrace the embassy. The table-furniture consisted of a coarse cloth, on which a wooden spoon and a crumplet were set before each guest. The first we dipped into the soups and sherbets promiscuously; the latter article served us instead of a plate, after we had torn off the meat with our right hands. Two-and-twenty dishes were served up, one after the other, and we tasted of each; but some of them were suffered to remain scarcely an instant on the table, and were borne off as if under the influence of Sancho's dread doctor and his wand. Rising from dinner, we were sprinkled with rose-water, and the Ambassador was served with an ewer to wash his hands.

In a short time a message arrived from the Sultan, intimating that he would receive the Eltchi, whose arrival and humble request of an audience had been before communicated by an officer of the Divan. The Ambassador accordingly, and the whole party, left the council-chamber, and were conducted towards the third gate of the Seraglio. . . .

Just as we entered the gate, there was much unseemly squeezing and jostling, and those who had not pelisses of fur were pushed away by the attendants. We afterwards moved forwards with more regularity, each of us being accompanied and pressed upon the shoulder by one or two of the guard. My attendant was one of the White Eunuchs, a crowd of whom were standing within the gate. We went through a court, or rather a large saloon, open on both sides, and passing on our right several rows of the Solak guards, in white robes and pointed caps of gold, mounted a low step into a passage, covered with rich carpets, which brought us into the presence-chamber. The room appeared quite full when we entered, but my Eunuch pushed me quickly forwards within ten paces of the throne, where he held me somewhat strictly by the right arm during the audience. He had not forgotten the assassination of Amurath.

The chamber was small and dark, or rather illumined with a gloomy artificial light, reflected from the ornaments of silver, pearls, and other white brilliants, with which it is thickly studded on every side and on the roof. The throne, which is supposed the richest in the world, is like a four-posted bed, but of a dazzling splendour; the lower part formed of burnished silver and pearls, and the canopy and supporters encrusted with jewels. It is in an awkward position, being in one corner of the room, and close to a fire-place.

Sultan Mahmoud was placed in the middle of the throne, with his feet upon the ground, which, notwithstanding the common form of squatting upon the hams, seems the seat of ceremony. He was dressed in a robe of yellow satin, with a broad border of the darkest sable: his dagger, and an ornament on his breast, were covered with diamonds: the front of his white and blue turban shone with a large treble sprig of diamonds, which served as a buckle to a high straight plume of bird-of-paradise feathers. He for the most part kept a hand on each knee, and neither moved his body nor head, but rolled his eyes from side to side, without fixing them for an instant upon the Ambassador or any other person present. Occasionally he stroked and turned up his beard, displaying a milk-white hand glittering with diamond rings. His eye-brows, eyes, and beard, being of a glossy jet black, did not appear natural, but added to that indescribable majesty which it would be difficult for any but an Oriental sovereign to assume: his face was pale, and regularly formed, except that his nose (contrary to the usual form of that feature in the Ottoman princes) was slightly turned up and pointed: his whole physiognomy was mild and benevolent, but expressive and full of dignity. He appeared of a short and small stature, and about thirty years old, which is somewhat more than his actual age.

On each side of the throne was an embroidered cushion: that on the left supported a silver purse, containing the letter from the Grand Signior to the King of England, and near it was a silver inkstand adorned with jewellery: a sabre, partly drawn from a diamond scabbard, was placed nearly upright against the cushion on the other side of the Sultan.

It seems from Busbek, and other authorities, to have been the custom formerly for Ambassadors and their suite to kiss the Sultan's hand; and that their whole reception was more courteous than at the audiences of the present day: amongst other points, it was usual for the Sultan to address a word or two to the minister, which he now never deigns to do.

The Ambassador stood nearly opposite, but a little to the left of the throne; and on his left was the Prince Maroozi, who acted as his interpreter. On the right of the Sultan the Caimacam was standing between the throne and the fire-place, with his head bent, and his hands submissively crossed in front of his vest. There were only a few feet of an open circular space between the Grand Signior and the audience, the rest of the apartment being completely occupied by the crowd. His Excellency laying his hand on his breast, and making a gentle inclination of the head, now addressed the Sultan, in a speech delivered in a low tone of voice, which was interpreted still less audibly by the Prince Maroozi. The Sultan then said a few words to the Caimacam, who proceeded to speak to the Ambassador, but hobbled repeatedly, and was prompted aloud several times by the Grand Signior. He seemed also to stop before he had concluded his oration, which, however, was a very immaterial circumstance, as the Dragoman was previously acquainted with it, and had learnt it by heart. . . .

Immediately afterwards his Excellency bowed and withdrew, the audience having lasted twelve or fifteen minutes. On retiring, my attendant Eunuch hurried me briskly along, and dismissed me with a gentle push down the step of the antichamber. The embassy, and the whole suite, then passed through the third and the second gate of the Seraglio, where we mounted our horses, and waited for nearly an hour under a scorching sun covered with our fur robes; and were not permitted to move before mid-day, nor until the Caimacam with his suite had proceeded from the Divan on his return to the Porte, and all the Janissaries had issued from the second court. They came out roaring and running, many of them being children, and all, in appearance, the very scum of the city.

[69] The tulip festivals of Sulvan Ahmet III in the Seraglio in the eighteenth century; from *The Ottoman Centuries: the rise and fall of the Turkish Empire* by Lord Kinross.

The Seraglio during the winter was regaled with *helva fêtes*, social gatherings in which philosophical symposia, together with poetry recitals, dancing, Chinese shadow plays, and prayers were accompanied by the distribution of sweets, otherwise helva. But when the winter was over there was now introduced for the Sultan's delectation a spring fête which developed largely into a festival of tulips. Ahmed had a great love for flowers – for the rose, the carnation (which his moustache was said to resemble), the lilac, the jasmine. But it was eventually the tulip that captured his fancy above all the rest. Its name in Turkish was *lale*, held to have a sacred significance from its resemblance to 'Allah', and the reign of Ahmed III became known to posterity as *Lale Devri*, or the Reign of the Tulip.

The tulip was a wild flower of the Asiatic steppes which had strewn the path of the Turks throughout their centuries of westward migration. It was Busbecq, the Austrian imperial ambassador of the sixteenth century, who as a keen botanist first introduced the tulip to the West, taking tulip bulbs back to Flanders on his journey home. Its European name was derived from the nickname the Turks gave it: *tulbend*, or 'turban' in the Persian language. Not long afterward the tulip was imported by European merchants and propagated in large quantities in Holland, where in time some twelve hundred varieties of it were known. This gave rise in the seventeenth century to a craze of tulipomania among the Ottoman elite, in the course of which fortunes were made and lost from rare tulip bulbs, and the tulip became known as 'the gold of Europe'.

It was Mehmed IV, the father of Ahmed, who first reintroduced the tulip into Turkey, making a tulip parterre, which comprised several varieties, in the gardens of the Seraglio. But it was Ahmed himself who first imported tulips in large quantities, not only from Holland but from Persia. Their cultivation in his gardens was carefully planned, with only a single variety to each bed.

Ahmed III's fête of spring, the Tulip Fête, in the gardens of the Grand Seraglio came for a while to outshine in importance the established religious feasts of Islam. It was held always in the month of April on two successive evenings, preferably by the light of a full moon. The Sultan covered over like a conservatory a part of his gardens where the parterres of tulips were planted. Here ranged on shelves were countless vases of the flowers, carefully chosen and placed for their harmonizing colours and shapes, interspersed with minute lamps of coloured glass and glass globes filled with liquids of different colours, so as to shine as it were with their own light. On the branches of the trees, combining aviary with conservatory, were cages of canaries and rare singing birds. The Sultan sat throned in the center beneath an imperial pavilion, receiving homage. On the second evening the entertainment was for the ladies of the harem, whom he received alone, entertaining them with music and poetry and song and the dancing of his slaves, while turtles wandered through the gardens with candles on their backs, to light up the tulips. Sometimes there was a treasure hunt – as for Easter eggs in Europe – with coloured bonbons and trinkets concealed amid the flowers, and the concubines fluttering hither and thither, 'tiptoeing through the tulips', as it were, in search of them. Ibrahim Pasha himself admired above all a variety named 'Blue Pearl', offering handsome rewards to anyone who could acclimatize it, and covering it with white veils to protect it from the sun in hot weather.

Not only did the tulip become a prominent feature in the tiles and other decorative arts of the Ottomans; with its accompanying cult of the spring it became a source of inspiration to the Ottoman poets at a time when they were shedding Persian influences to evolve a new muse of their own. The leading poet of the reign of Ahmed III, with its gaiety and luxury and *douceur de vivre* in these elegant surroundings, was Nedim, 'the Boon Companion', a poet of pleasure with a lighthearted philosophy: 'Let us all laugh and play, let us enjoy the world's delights.'

The tulip was to survive as an image in Turkish poetry right up to the republican era of the twentieth century. 'Victory', wrote a contemporary poet, Yahya Kemal, 'is a shattering beauty with a rose face and tulip kisses'.

For the Tulip Age was more than a mere passing fashion. In its essentials it marked the birth of a modern era in the Ottoman Empire. Here was the dawn of a new worldliness, a new enlightenment, reflecting a spirit of rational inquiry and liberal reform. It looked for inspiration to the West, in its own new phase of scientific progress, economic wealth, and military power, to provide a secular counterpoise to the traditional religious values of the Islamic East. In Western civilization lay the pattern of that social and cultural reform which was increasingly seen to be necessary, if only still by a relatively small element among the Ottoman elite. Thus the tulip became a symbol, that of a dawning Turkish renaissance under the influence of Western civilization.

[70] The investiture of the last Caliph, Abdul Mecit, in the Seraglio in 1922; from *Constantinople* by George Young.

Let us pay a last visit to the Old Serai to attend the ceremony. As we cross the bridge there passes us at a trot an escort of Lancers, mounted lackeys in red, and a carriage and four with postilions. In it sits a portly person in a fez, frock-coat and green ribbon. It is Abdul-Medjid, son of that Abdul-Aziz who cut the tangled knot of his fortunes with a pair of scissors. Abdul-Medjid is on his way to be invested as Caliph. The carriage whirls into the inner court of the Old Serai. On the one side are the mediæval kitchens with their conical chimneys, on the other the cupolas of the hareem, at the end a Byzantine portico of marbles and coloured tiles, still delightful in its dilapidation. On the pavement in front of the portico stands the Golden throne studded with jewels, looted from Egypt by Selim, the first Ottoman Caliph. In a circle round it stand a few reporters, some sight-seeing French and Italian officers, and some American ladies. No Britisher is there but myself. I venture to slip past the chamberlains through to the

Bagdad Kiosk and so get a glimpse of that most sacred of ceremonies, the Investiture of a Caliph.

But what a travesty it is! Instead of the solemn ritual in the Mosque of Eyoub and a Sultan girded with the Sword of Osman receiving from the Sheikh of Islam the emblems of his spiritual power, here is a delegation of Angora deputies notifying an elderly dilettante that he has been elected by a majority vote like any Labour leader. There are the sacred relics, but the Sword of Othman remains at Eyoub to show that, though Abdul-Medjid is Caliph, he is not Sultan.

The new Caliph comes out to the portico for his Selamlik. A little ring of curious sightseers and correspondents crowds round, there is a short prayer, and a comic Palace dwarf, with some eunuchs, give a note of local colour. The chamberlains dislodge the American ladies from coigns of vantage where they would spoil the film; some undistinguished frock-coats and fezzes, princes of the House of Othman, defile across with hurried salaams to a whir of cinemas. Dingy, pot-bellied officials trot across, muftis and dervishes follow, and the operators pack up. As soon as they do so, the ring is broken, the carriage drives up, and the eunuchs begin to take the throne to pieces. The Caliph climbs into his carriage, but this time not alone. Facing him sits a soldierly little figure, spare and spruce, with the profile of a sparow-hawk – Rafet Pasha, the Nationalist Governor of Constantinople. The Caliph has been denied his Sword of Othman, but he has been given his Sword of Damocles.

The Dolmabahçe Palace

[71] The death of Atatürk in the Dolmabahçe Palace on 29 October 1938; from *Atatürk* by Irfan and Margarete Orga.

Celal Bayar remained at Dolmabahçe Palace, but as October 29 drew near – the fifteenth anniversary of the Turkish Republic – Atatürk became almost unmanageably restless. He wanted to deliver his usual anniversary speech to the nation. He wanted to talk to the Army especially. It was obvious, however, that he would never reach Ankara alive. He complained querulously to Celal. 'For fourteen years I have made my speech, and now you must do it for me. Read me my speech.' Celal protested, 'Not now, later. You are tired now.'

However, seeing the resignation on the dying face, Celal weakened. 'That resignation,' he wrote afterwards, 'affected me like a clap on the head . . . if he had only protested a little! But I had never seen him resigned before, never so helpless before my will . . . so I read the speech to him, and when it was over I took his hand in mine and kissed it. Then I had to leave him, for already he was past even exhaustion. As I reached the door he said, "Give my regards to our friends in Ankara." And I think I wept a little hearing that small, small voice . . .'

The Turkish Republic was fifteen years old. It was the night of 29 October 1938, and while the awakening adolescent was just beginning to have some idea of its importance in the world, its progenitor, its father-figure lay dying in a forgotten Sultan's palace.

He lay in a vast walnut bed in a room on the second floor, whose windows overlooked the Bosphorus. He dozed fitfully. He made occasional restless, agitated movements which brought the doctors to his side. During the day the usual Military Parades, the Youth Parades and the Sports contests had been held in towns and cities across the country. . . . Now with night standing in the long windows of the Palace, the streets of Istanbul were illumined with the brilliant, incessant tracery of fireworks, and noisy with the merry-making throng. But no shouts from the roistering crowd reached the room on the second floor of the Palace. Here all was silence, the unearthly silence of death lurking. The echoing corridors of the Palace, the vast, empty *salons*, the beautiful staircase were dimly lit. The footsteps of doctors or servants moved softly in the deep pile of the carpets.

The room where Atatürk lay was lit by a small night-lamp so that he was in perpetual shadow, already half-dissociated from this world. His doctors kept vigil by the windows. They stared across the black night water of the Bosphorus to the Anatolian side of the city. Fireworks lightened the skyline and, for an instant, etched minarets sharply against their feverish glow. The sound of their explosions travelled ever nearer to the quiet room, and the doctors eyed each other anxiously hoping their quiescent patient would not ask questions. He was not supposed to know that this was the anniversary he had hoped to see, or that his people were *en fête* down in the streets below. But Atatürk was not deceived by their conspiracy of silence. He knew what day it was, and as he moved restlessly a doctor bent above him reassuringly. 'What is that noise?' Atatürk asked in a thread of voice. The doctor replied that it was nothing at all, and attempted to soothe him. Atatürk turned his face to the dark windows. 'It is the fireworks from Usküdar. Why do you say you do not know? They are the fireworks. It is my people celebrating the Republic, and I am here . . .'

He died on the morning of November 10, 1938.

It was the surgeon, Kemal, who, since the first grey light of dawn crept in at the windows, had noted his rapid decline. At five minutes past nine o'clock, when the crowds were hurrying to their work, he drew his last, rasping breath. Kemal noted the time on a chart, and then moved forward to close the fierce blue eyes for the last time.

The rest of the city

[72] The Bazaar, in the second half of the nineteenth century; from *Constantinople* by Edmondo de Amicis.

The Great Bazaar has nothing exteriorly to attract the eye, or give an idea of its contents. It is an immense stone edifice, of Byzantine architecture, and irregular form, surrounded by high grey walls, and surmounted by hundreds of little cupolas, covered with lead, and perforated with holes to give light to the interior. The principal entrance is an arched doorway without architectural character; no noise from without penetrates it; at four paces from the door you can still believe that within those fortress walls there is nothing but silence and solitude. But once inside you stand bewildered. It is not an edifice, but a labyrinth of arcaded streets flanked by sculptured columns and pilasters; a real city, with its mosques, fountains, crossways and squares, dimly lighted like a thick wood into which no ray of sunlight penetrates; and filled by a dense throng of people. Every street is a bazaar, almost all leading out of one main street, with an arched roof of black and white stone, and decorated with arabesques like the nave of a mosque. In this dimly lighted thoroughfare, carriages, horsemen, and camels are constantly passing, making a deafening noise. The visitor is apostrophized on all sides with words and signs. The Greek merchants call out in loud voices and use imperious gestures. The Armenian, quite as cunning, but more humble in manner, solicits obsequiously; the Jew whispers his offers in your ear; the silent Turk, seated cross-legged upon his carpet at the entrance of his shop, invites only with his eye, and resigns himself to destiny. Ten voices at once address you; Monsieur! Captain! Caballero! Signore! Eccellenza! Kyrie! My Lord! At every turn, by the side doors, are seen perspectives of arches and pilasters, long corridors, narrow alleys, a long confused perspect of bazaar, and everywhere shops, merchandise piled up or hanging from wall and ceiling, busy merchants, loaded porters, groups of veiled women, coming and going, a perpetual noise of people and things enough to make one dizzy. . . .

You may linger a whole day in one bazaar, unconscious of the flight of time; for example, the bazaar of stuffs, and clothing. It is an emporium of beauty and riches enough to ruin your eyes, your brains, and your pocket; and you must be on your guard, for a caprice might bring upon you the consequence of sending for help by telegraph. You walk in the midst of towering heaps of brocades from Bagdad, carpets from Caramania, silks from Broussa, linens from Hindustan, muslins from Bengal, shawls from Madras, cachemeres from India and Persia, many tinted tissues from Cairo; cushions arabesqued in gold, silken veils woven with silver stripes, scarfs of gauze in blue and crimson, so light and transparent that they seem like sunset clouds; stuffs of every kind and every design, in which red, blue, green, yellow, colors the most rebellious to sympathetic combination, are brought together and interwoven, with a happy audacity and harmony, that makes one stand in open-mouthed wonder; table-covers of all sizes, with red or white grounds embroidered all over with arabesques, flowers, verses from the Koran, and imperial ciphers, worthy of being admired for hours, like the walls of the Alhambra. Here may be found, one by one, each separate part of the Turkish lady's dress; from the mantle green, orange, or purple, that covers the whole person, down to the silken chemise, the gold-embroidered kerchief, and the satin girdle, on which no eye of man is permitted to fall, save that of the husband or the eunuch. Here are caftans of crimson velvet, bordered with ermine, and covered with stars; corsets of yellow satin, trousers of rose-coloured silk, under-vests of white damask embroidered with golden flowers, bride veils sparkling with silver spangles; green cloth jackets trimmed with swans-down; Greek, Armenian, and Circassian garments, of the oddest shapes, overloaded with ornament, hard and splendid like a cuirass; and with all this, the prosaic stuffs of France and England, of dull colours, reminding one of a tailor's bill among the verses of a poem. No one who loves a lady can pass through this bazaar without cursing fate that has not made him a millionaire, or without feeling his soul on fire with the fury of sack and pillage. . . .

From this, one falls again into temptation upon entering the bazaar of perfumery, which is one of the most completely Oriental, and dear to the Prophet, who said:— 'Women, children, and perfumes' – naming his three most beloved pleasures. Here are found the famous Seraglio pastilles, for perfuming kisses, the capsules of odoriferous gum which the robust girls of Chio make for the reinforcement of the mouths of the soft Turkish ladies; the exquisite essence of jasmine and bergamot, and that most potent essence of roses, shut in cases of gold-embroidered velvet, and of prices to make your hair stand on end; here is *kohl* for the brows and lashes, antimony for the eyes, henna for the finger tips, soaps that soften the skin of the lovely Syrians, pills that cause the hair to fall from the faces of Circassian men, citron and orange waters, little bags of musk, oil of sandal wood, grey amber, aloes to perfume pipes and coffee cups, a myriad of powders, waters and pomades; of fantastic names and mysterious uses, that each represents an amorous caprice, a purpose of seduction, a refinement of voluptuousness, and that all together, diffuse an acute and sensual fragrance, which invokes a vision of languid eyes and caressing hands, and a suppressed murmur as of sighs and kisses.

[73] Arrival by train at Sirkeci Station in the 1890s; from *Diary of an Idle Woman in Constantinople* by Frances Elliot.

The terminus is an elongated shed built on a barren waste. I am bound to say the unspeakable Turk is building another of stone close at hand. In a moment we are surrounded by a scarecrow crowd, screaming in Greek, Italian, Turkish, French (to live here you must be a polyglot, and command the idioms of the East and West, or be silent for ever), out of which advance the Turkish officials, quite European save for a fez; a scene of absolute squalor backed by the foul station.

A pale little man vainly struggles among the dark-skinned Armenians and big-nosed Greeks, trying to board the train. Not succeeding, he stands apart and calls out in a shrill voice, high over the eastern gutturals making a chorus round, 'I am Cook's man; I can speak English.'

Blessed little man! What a boon to travellers who arrive without friends or preparation! I am told the *douane* is a fearful struggle, and the Turk quite mediæval in boorish stupidity.

But I who write suffered none of these things. Cook's excellent little agent was to me as naught, for had I not there, before my eyes, the stalwart form of the *kavass* of the English Embassy, a fine dark-complexioned Greek, of excellent presence, in a close-fitting jacket, covered with gold lace, a richly-worked dagger at his waist?

With what a sense of command he kept off the rabble, and how proud I felt of belonging to him! Here, amid the surging waves of that ill-smelling mob (now increased by the passengers who had descended), I blessed the kindness of the Ambassador, who extended the flag of our Empire to me, a lone woman with a maid, in the middle of dirty Stamboul!

All make way before me; no question is asked. The kavass puts all back with a lordly motion of his hand, and at once places me in an excellent landau in waiting. Aloft, on the shoulders of broad porters in long petticoats, with bare legs and feet, a coloured sash round their loins to hold all together, soar my boxes (all accomplished in a chorus of incredible screams) to be deposited in a two-horse fiacre which follows my landau. I am the more particular in detailing this, because I find a certain terror exists as to arriving at Constantinople.

The god-like calm with which the kavass treats everyone, including myself, whom he evidently looks on as a being of an inferior order whom he is sent to convey – in the sense that a lion may take care of a poor little mouse – greatly impresses me.

With the same sublime repose (all arrangements having been made and *bakshish* duly distributed) he mounts the box of my landau, to my extreme surprise (I was prepared to give him the best place inside), and gives the signal of departure without cracking of whips or other ceremony, on the most execrable road I ever was shaken on in my life. There are holes in Spanish highways in which a small cart could be accommodated, but in Turkey freshly split rocks are a novelty one would willingly dispense with.

[74] The revolt of the Janissaries on the At Meydani (once the Hippodrome), and an eye-witness account of their destruction by Sultan Mahmoud II in 1826; from *Précis Historique de la Destruction du Corps des Janissaires par le Sultan Mahmoud en 1826* by Mahammad As'ad Safvat. Translated by Laurence Kelly.

Suddenly the revolt exploded. On the night of Thursday 15 June 1826, the conspirators made their way in twos and threes to the Et-Meidan which they had chosen as their headquarters. With the exception of a few captains and Oustas whom they considered unreliable, they invited all officers and soldiers to join them. Soon the square was filled with rebels. Their leaders sent one unit to attack the Agha in his palace, and sent repeated messengers to the Quartermaster-General, Hassan Agha, to seduce him into joining them. The latter replied to them, 'I cannot come alone to the meeting but I have alerted all the company commanders and when they arrive we will all come together.' With this answer he got rid of them and escaped the trap; he stayed at home waiting for the company commanders, crushed by worry and petrified with amazement.

As for the rebels who went to find the Agha, they arrived at his palace just as he was returning from a tour of inspection of the district of the Castle of Seven Towers, and was preparing for bed. Luckily for him, he was in the lavatory when they arrived, and the men – anxious to loot, which was the principal aim of the rebellion – rushed back to the Et-Meidan as they did not find him. Even so, in their frustration at not finding him they smashed the doors and windows with their muskets, and set the palace on fire. Fortunately the fire fizzled out, as if symbolizing the forthcoming extinction of the rebels themselves.

At dawn the rebels brought out their kettles from the barracks on to the Et-Meidan. They ran off to the barracks of the *Djebedjis* [armourers] and *Serradjis* [saddlers] to seize their kettles. The 5th Company of armourers surrendered theirs, thus committing those fine men to the rebellion. At the same time the rebels sent under-officers to the districts around the Castle of Seven Towers, where lived every kind of hot-head and disaffected person, to get them to join the Janissaries. They spread the rumour that the Grand Vizir, Hussein Pasha the Agha, and all the chief officers of state had been captured or killed, and by means of these rumours sought to excite the mob to loot. Soon porters and other miserable mercenaries lounging in the streets of Constantinople rushed to join them, swelling their numbers to an impressive total. One enraged party marched off to the palace of the Grand Vizir under the leadership of Mustafa the fruiterer; another, under Mustafa the drunkard, went off to catch the teacher Daoud Pasha, and also to sack the house of the Egyptian Pasha's agent, Nedjib Efendi, whom the Janissaries cordially loathed.

By good luck, the Grand Vizir had spent the night at his country estate at Beylerbey. But his wives, hearing the noisy arrival of the rebels within the house, took refuge in terror in a

The At Meydani; from *Voyage Pittoresque de la Grèce*, 1782–1809 by M.G. Choiseul Gouffier

room under the garden. So they were neither seen nor violated. The men looted the palace and took about 6,000 money-purses and other valuables.

At the same time the Janissaries were crying in the streets: 'Death to the makers of *Fetvas* [religious edicts], to the scribblers of legal orders, to those resisting us, and to all wearing the *Caouk* (i.e., the headgear of lawyers, civil servants, men of the pen, etc.). We shall take their women and their children, and we shall sell the boys and girls for ten piastres each, and their clothes for five. But let all the merchants open their shops, and if even a piece of glass is stolen we will return to them a diamond; and if one of our men causes them any damage, we will cut him to pieces.'

The news reached the Grand Vizir in a flash; and, entrusting himself to Providence, he returned by boat to the Kiosk-by-the-Water [in the Saray], accompanied only by his coffee-maker, Osman Agha. Once there, he called the Palace Treasurer to inform immediately his Highness [i.e., the Sultan] of these events, to ask his permission to display the Prophet's standard, and to beg him to show himself to the troops. . . .
The Grand Vizir, the Mufti, the Ridjals and the Ulemas all met at the Mosque of Sultan Ahmed. Their arrival, and that of the two Vizirs Hussein Pasha and Mohammed Pasha with their troops, had given the greatest heart to the people thronging the inner precincts and surroundings of the Mosque. From the *Mihrab* (or altar) the Vizirs and Ulemas were debating what orders to give to the brave troops assembled under the Prophet's standard. Some officers argued to the Ulemas: 'If guilty men have broken into the harem of the Sultan's first minister, and other ministers, looted their houses, trampled underfoot our holy laws, and befouled their oath of allegiance to the lawful Sovereign, and to the head of our religion, should they not be crushed by force of arms?' 'Yes,' answered the Ulemas. But others said, 'Would it not be the sensible thing to send a wise spokesman to the rebels, and find out what their grievances are? If they then persist, we will use force.' Those proposing this wanted Professor Ahmed-Efendi to take on the highly tricky mission. 'I am ready to try,' he said, 'but you know well their obstinate and implacable attitudes. They will hold me prisoner, and all you will have achieved is to delay the crushing of the revolt which it is our duty to do.' 'That is true,' cried Mohammed Pasha; 'no time should be lost in debate. Arguments

will not settle their doubts; they must be cut through by the sword'.

The Grand Vizir remained at the Mosque; Hussein Pasha and Mohammed Pasha left it. With the regiment of gunners and that of marines, they went down the Great Street of the Divan. The sappers and bombardiers marched off down the arcade of the Bouzdoghan (or the Aqueduct of Valens) and the horse-market. Captain Ibrahim Agha also had two cannon from the *Infernal* under his command, and these preceded the two Pashas. When they reached the Khorkhor Fountain, they found some Janissaries ready to resist them, and fire was exchanged. Two gunners died in this first shedding of blood, but, frightened by the determination of the attackers, the rebels fell back and regrouped on the Et-Meidan, where they closed the Great Door and blocked it with a great pile of stones.

The Pashas, reinforced by fresh troops from the Saddlers' barracks, and soon by those arriving from the Sultan Ahmed Mosque (under Nedjib Efendi), blocked off every access to the Et-Meidan and the Janissaries' barracks. Before starting the blockade, Captain Ibrahim Agha went close to the Great Door, and speaking to the men within it, said:

'Lads, you had accepted and promised to carry out the Sultan's order that seeks to teach you the martial arts which the Koran itself tells you is your duty. Today you are rebelling against this and risking your lives to no purpose. Return to your duty, ask the Sultan's forgiveness, and carry out his orders. The two Vizirs here will intervene for you with him and he is a generous Sovereign. His Highness with his mercy will overlook this new error in your ways.'

Ibrahim repeated these arguments several times, but the Janissaries rejected the advice with imprecations that sounded like the barking of dogs. Then the Pashas ordered the guns to be lit, and – to deceive the rebels – the gunner General Naman Agha and Ibrahim Pasha shouted: 'The powder has not yet arrived, how will we fire?' Some of the ringleaders, hearing this and being cleverer than their comrades and well foreseeing the end of the matter, said to the others: 'Stay here to guard the kettles, and we will go out through the drill door [*Talim-capouçou*] and capture the cannon from behind.' They hoped to save their lives by fleeing into the neighbouring streets. Those who remained, buoyed up by false hopes, were massed behind the

Gate when a cannon-shot smashed a panel of the Gate and knocked down several of them. Mohammed Pasha advanced immediately, and a gunner called Mustafa – to whom he gave 2,500 piastres – was first over the barricade and managed to open the Gate. At this moment a bullet wounded Ibrahim Agha in the ankle, and slowly dropping back and seeming not to suffer from this wound, he continued to encourage the soldiers by word and deed.

Soon the rebels were thinking only of flight. Some re-formed in the miserable place in the middle of the Square called the convent [or *Tekié*]. Some sought shelter in their huge barracks, hurling recriminations at one another. Whilst chaos and dissension racked them, Mustafa the gunner took one of those fuses called 'by moonlight' whose flame resembles a glittering star, and set fire to the butchers' stalls adjoining the barracks. Ten or twelve volleys of grapeshot fell on the building in succession; and tongues of flame licked it on all sides. The haven of the rebels was consumed within a few minutes.

[75] Seventeenth-century festivities in the At Meydani for the circumcision of the Sultan's son; from *The History of the Serrail and of the Court of the Grand Seigneur, Emperour of the Turks* by Seigneur Michael Baudier of Languedoc.

(Seigneur Michael Baudier (c. 1589–1645) was born in Languedoc where he commanded a company of 50 men at arms. He knew Greek, Latin, Hebrew, Arabic, Italian and Spanish, and was a passionate collector of medals, manuscripts and antiquities, as a result of which he died almost ruined. Historian to Louis XIII, he published his *History of the Serrail* in 1624. It ran into many editions, and was translated into English in 1635.)

The day being come when they are to begin the Feast, the Emperour goes on horsebacke from the *Serrail*, to come to the *Hippodrome*; the young Prince his Sonne is on the right hand, (which is the lesse honourable among them) attired in a rich Robe of Cloth of Gold, covered with an infinite number of Diamonds, and great round Pearles of inestimable value: The point of his Turbant glistered with precious stones: He was mounted upon a goodly Horse, with the richest Caparison that could be found in the *Sultans Serrail*: The Bitt was of massive Gold set with many Diamonds, the Stirrops of the same metall covered with Turquoises, the Buckles were also of gold enricht with Rubies, and the rest of the stately Furniture accordingly: The *Grand Vizir*, the *Beglierbeys* of *Asia*, and *Europe*, with other *Basha's* of the Port follow their Lords, the *Ianizaries*, *Solaquis*, *Spahis*, *Capigis*, and the other Guards and Officers of the Court accompany them, all of them attired with so great lustre and pompe, as it seemed that all the wealth not only of the East, but of the whole World had beene transported to *Constantinople*, to adorne the Men which shewed themselves in this Solemnitie. . . .

The *Sultans* having crost the place entred the Pallace of *Hibraim Bassa*, where the pavement of the Court was all covered with Cloth of Gold . . . The Father entred into a Pavillion which was prepared for him, having a Portall adioyned beautified with rich pictures of *Arabia*, which looked towards the place: The Sonne went into a Chamber upon the left hand, where his feast was prepared. The *Sultanaes* place was ioyning to the Pavillion, In the which were only the Mother of the young Prince and Wife to the Emperour, his Sister the young Princesse, and the women of their Traine: Their Robes and glorious lustre of pearles and precious stones which they carried were worthy of the wife & Daughter of the most powerfull and rich Monarch of the Earth. All the *Agaes* and Captaines of the Port were in a Gallery neere unto them . . .

The Ranckes . . . distributed, and the order carefully observed, the Embassadours went to the *Baisemain* of the *Sultan*, or to kisse his Robe, and made him rich Presents: For they never goe unto him emptie handed . . . All . . . made their Presents according to the order and rancke of the Princes which sent them . . .

These Homages and Presents being thus ended, the Combats of warre, did shew the force of their art, and the sports the pleasure of their braverie: The *Grand Vizir* would have the honour to expose unto his Masters eyes, the representation of his victories against the Christians. He caused to be drawne into the place two great Castles of Wood, diversly painted, mounted upon Wheeles, garnished with Towres, fortified with Rampiers, and furnished with Artillerie: The one was kept by Turkes, who had planted upon their Tower, many Red, White, and Greene Ensignes: The other was defended by Men, attired and armed after the French manner, who seemed Christians: Their

Ensignes carried white Crosses; without doubt they had beene taken in some encounter, or at the sacke of some Towne of the Christians . . . The Turkes forced the others to make their last retreate into their fort, where they shut them up, besieged them, battered their walls, made a breach, sent to discover it, and marched to the assault with their usual cries and howlings . . . As soone as they were entred, they abandoned the place to their cruelty, put all to the sword, cutting off the heads of the principall, and lifting counterfeit heads above the walls. The contempt which they make of us ended the triumph; They let slip into the place about thirty Hogs which they had shut into a Fort, and ranne after them crying and howling in mockerie: Thus the Turkes doe not sport but in contemning the Christians, nor labour seriously but in ruining them . . .

Occhiali Bassa great Admirall of the Sea, exceeded by his industrie, the Vizirs invention. Hee caused to come rowling into the place, a great Island, admirably well made of boords and pastboord, which represented *Cypres*: Two powerfull Armies held it besieged, the one by Sea and the other by Land: There was artificially seene their descent into the Island, the siege of *Famagouste*, the sallies, skirmishes, batteries, counter-batteries, mines, counter-mines, breaches, assaults upon assault, fire-workes, and whatsoever the furie of Warre could invent . . . The wonder of this artificial representation did much please the *Sultan*, reioyced the people, and revived in the Christians minds the griefe of their losse . . . The Cannonadoes, where there was nothing but Powder, slue many of these takers of the Island in Picture upon the place, & wounded a great number . . .

A goodly troupe of Archers on horsebacke arrived soone after with a more generall joy; They Activities which they shewed are admirable. After they had finished their courses, with a Target in the left hand, and a long Dart or halfe Pike in the right, sometimes ranged in battaile, sometimes disbanded, casting them one at another, and taking them up from the ground in running: They ranne their Horses with their full speed, and in the swiftnesse of their course, drew their Semiters thrice out of their Scabbords, and put them up as often without any stay: In like manner they shot thrice with their Bowes, with the first they hit an Iron on the hinder part of the horse; with the second they strooke an Apple of gold, which was upon the top of a great Mast of a Ship set up in the midst of the place: with the last they hit the Ring at which the *Albanois* had runne: Then standing upright in their Saddles, they did run their Horses with full speed, and did mannage their Armes as before. . . .

The day following the Feast was continued. A troupe of excellent Tumblers and Mountebankes (whereof Turkey abounds above all the Regions of the Earth) did to the common amazement of all the Spectators these things which follow. The first which shewed himselfe in the place, shut a young Boy naked into a Hogshead, with five and twenty or thirty great Serpents, and rowled it about the place, and then drew out the Boy whole and sound: The same Serpents stinging and biting others which came neere them. After this they buried a young Boy deepe in a Ditch, and covered him with Earth as if hee had beene dead, and yet he answered as distinctly and intelligibly to that which they demanded of him, as if hee had been out of the ground. Another presented himselfe naked without shame, but not without more than humane force, hee layed himselfe flat on his backe upon the edge of two Semiters; being in this posture, they laid upon his Belly a great Anuile of Iron, whereon foure men did beate with great Hammers, and moreover they did rive many great pieces of wood without any offence to him . . . Another shewed the force his jawes, and his hands: he held a horseshoe betwixt his teeth, and puld it in pieces with his hands . . . Another band came after, whose feet were so hardened, as they went bare upon a Harrow full of sharpe Pikes and cutting Knives: There was one followed them, who with a cord, tied to his haire without the helpe of his hands, did lift up a stone of a hundred and fifty pound weight. Many Beasts instructed in this Art of tumbling augmented the pleasure of the Assistants: little Birds, went to fetch a piece of silver as farre as they directed them, and brought it to their Masters, Asses danced, Dogges and Apes shewed a thousand pleasant tricks. The *Grand Seigneurs* Wrestlers, came to shew their force and activitie, being oyled and greased to avoid the surprize of their Enemies: These are the most continent men in Turkey, they keepe their Virginity pure and untoucht, and say with reason that it doth entertaine and preserve the force of their bodies . . .

Such were the pomps of the day, the night wanted not hers, if there were any night during the solemnity of this royall Circumcision: For at such time as the Sunne did not shine in their Hemispheare, they had raised a ship Mast in the *Hippodrome*, whereon there was a great Circle like a Crowne furnished with burning Lamps: and neere unto the Obelisque which is the ancient ornament of this place, there was a huge wheele set up, the which did turne continually, and made twelve other smaller to move, all which were invironed with lights, which remayning firme, seemed notwithstanding to follow the motion of the wheeles, not without a wonderfull content to the eyes of those which beheld them: Besides this there were many ship Masts with their tops and tacklings, all covered with lamps, which gave so cleer a light, as in the dark night they made an artificiall day; by the favour of which light, most of those goodly things which had appeared in the day, came after Supper to give contentment to the company by their shew. . . .

But if the description of this Royall Feast hath beene a pleasing diversion unto us in the toile of this Historie, let us end it according to the naturall course of pleasure, by the griefe which followes . . . During the spectacles of this solemnity, the wretched Grecians ran by troupes in this place to make themselves *Mahometans* . . . This hope of better fortune drew the Idlenesse of many young men, so as they could hardly find Masters enough to cut them: This detestable troupe of Rascals, went to shew themselves before the *Grand Seigneur*, their Bonnets under their feet, in signe that they did tread their law and honour under foot: There is a Turkish Priest did cause them to lift up the demonstrative finger of the right hand, in signe that they did not beleeve but one God in one person, & to say with a loud voice, *La illa ey lala* Mehemet *rafoulialla*; Then they led them into certaine Pavillions, which were erected expresly at the end of the place where they were circumcised: The number of these cast-awayes was found to bee above foure thousand soules.

These sports and triumphs being thus miserably ended, the young Prince for whom they had beene made, was brought into his Fathers Chamber, where hee was circumcised by one of the great Men of the Court in the presence of all the *Basha's*. His wound being cured within a few dayes, hee goes to take his last leave of the *Sultana* his Mother, whom she shall see no more untill hee comes to take possession of the Empire, after the death of his Father, if hee be the eldest, or to end his life with a halter if hee be a younger brother, when his elder shall Raigne. She gives him presents: and the other *Sultana's* doe the like: All the *Basha's* present him, and the Emperour his Father appoints his Family, gives him a *Preceptor*, an Eunuch for Governour, with many other men to serve him, and sends him into *Asia* . . .

Yildiz, Pera and Galata

[76] The Sultan's Selamlik, or Friday Prayers, at the Mosque of the Yildiz Palace in 1898; from *Turkey in Europe* by Sir Charles Eliot, KCMG.

Every Friday in Constantinople is performed a ceremony called the 'Selamlik' or public visit of the Sultan to a mosque for the mid-day prayer. Farmer sovereigns usually discharged this duty at St Sophia or one of the principal religious edifices, in each of which is a Mahfil or Imperial pew. Abd-ul-Hamid II, however, has since the beginning of this reign shown a preference for the mosques in the immediate vicinity of Yildiz, and of late years has had one constructed for his special use, and to all intents and purposes in the palace grounds. From the gate of Yildiz descends a steep road bordered on one side by annexes of the palace, which terminate in two pavilions, one devoted to the reception of distinguished persons and ambassadors, while in the other are accommodated the common herd of sightseers. On the other side are a garden and a mosque, white, new, and unpretentious, but deriving a certain grace and dignity from the background, where the coast of Asia and Mount Olympus are seen rising from the Sea of Marmora.

Long before mid-day on Friday soldiers, and spectators, among which latter are hundreds of Turkish women, occupy all the available space. Cohort after cohort of muscular peasants, drawn from every district of this variegated empire, marches up to the clang of barbarous music and takes its place. As a military display the spectacle is remarkable; as a pageant, disappointing. Turkish ceremonies lack order and grandeur. Detectives thread their way through the crowd, and now and then arrest some poor innocent. Dirty-looking servants from the palace, wearing frock-coats, no collars, and white cotton gloves, hurry hither and thither, carrying dinners wrapped up in cloths, which are sent to various persons as complimentary presents from the Imperial kitchen. Fat men of great rank and girth drag about laboriously black Gladstone bags in which they have brought uniforms stiff with gold. Tourists in strange headgear peep and gibber. Ultimately – for the Caliph avails himself of the letter of the law which says that the mid-day prayer must be said after the sun has begun to decline – ultimately a trumpet sounds. The troops salute and officials hastily confiscate the opera-glasses of the tourists, who are generally so surprised and indignant that they fail to notice what little they might have seen with their eyes. The trumpet sounds again, the soldiers shout 'Long live our emperor!' and a victoria with the hood up comes slowly down the steep road. An old man in uniform, Field-Marshal Osman Pasha, the hero of Plevna, sitting with his back to the horses, speaks with deep respect to some one seen less distinctly under the hood. The carriage stops at a flight of steps leading to the private door of the mosque. The hood is lowered by a spring, and he who sat beneath it alights, mounts the steps, and, in a moment of profound silence, turns and salutes the crowd. He has not come as the chief of a military race should come, on a prancing steed or with any dash and glory. There is no splendour in his dress or bearing; but for the moment that he stands there alone a solemnity falls over the scene, the mean and comic details disappear, and we are face to face with the spirit of a great nation and a great religion incarnate in one man. Of all his subjects assembled there before him, there is not one whose life and fortune do not depend on his caprice; of all those wild men gathered together from Albania, Arabia, and the heart of Anatolia, there is not one but would fall down and kiss the hem of his garment did he deign address them, or cheerfully die to preserve his tyranny; of all those women, there is not one but would account his slightest and most transient favours her highest glory; of all those Liberals and Young Turks, there is not one who, when the time for talking is over and the time for action comes, will not submit to his will: for all that the Osmanlis can do, all they may suffer, all the ideas they can form of politics or statecraft are centred in that one personality, and they who would depose him can think of no better expedient than to appoint another like him as his successor.

[77] Sultan Abdul Hamid's views on animals, birds, the telephone and electricity in the Yildiz Palace; from *Abdul Hamid Intime* by Georges Dorys. Translated by Laurence Kelly.

The Sultan has a distinct liking for animals, and at Yildiz he keeps a complete mini-zoo, including wild beasts and a wide variety of tame and trained ones. During his walks he feeds fruit and other delicacies with his own hands to gazelles, Highland goats, mouflons and chamois. In characteristic Oriental contrast, the Sultan also greatly enjoys fights between rams, just as Abdul Aziz liked cock-fights.

A special place in the park is set aside for a dogs' hospital and splendid kennels. The handsomest species of every dog are comfortably installed there, in stark contrast to their wretched cousins in the streets of Constantinople.

Abdul Hamid's love of animals even takes priority over the most serious of diplomatic questions. In 1882 Gladstone had an important request about Egypt to put to the Turkish Ambassador in London, Mussurus Pasha, which the latter immediately telegraphed to the Sultan, urgently requesting an answer. A worried man, he waited three days for the Sultan to come to life. At last, the following night, he was woken up to be given a long cipher despatch which – now a much relieved man – he thought would provide him with his master's answer. In fact, it was an order from Abdul Hamid for mouflons to adorn the Imperial park.

The Sultan is also a great collector of birds, and the Mikado last year had the happy inspiration of sending him a present of the most exotic and rarest birds from the Empire of the Rising Sun. He likes pigeons and parrots best of all, possessing hundreds of pairs of these. There are aviaries of every sort in Yildiz. But bird-lover though he is, Abdul Hamid is nevertheless Sultan first. One day one of his favourite parrots, at the window of his room, cried out 'Djafer Aga!' The eunuch Djafer Aga immediately rushed in, thinking it was his master's voice. But the Padishah had not called him; and the latter so far lost his temper with the wretched bird that he wrung its neck himself, saying that in his palace there could only be one voice giving orders....

Abdul has the telephone and electricity in his apartments but has not yet allowed these conveniences in the city, however essential they are to a great capital. He thought that the telephone, invisible and loyal messenger defying all supervision, would greatly encourage plots. For the same reason, the breeding of carrier pigeons was forbidden. The Ministers of the day supported this absurd belief in their master, and even told him that a stick of dynamite connected with the end of the wire might – at long range – kill him. Of course Their Excellencies also had every incentive to prevent him from summoning them at every moment to the Palace. So frequent were the political crises that terrified their sovereign, they feared this form of torture most of all. He suffered the same horror of electric light, and though using it in his own rooms would not even countenance electricity elsewhere in the palace, and certainly not in the capital.

[78] The deposition of Sultan Abdul Hamid at the Yildiz Palace in 1909; from *The Fall of Abd-ul-Hamid* by Francis McCullagh.

On the morning of April 24, when the Macedonians closed in on the city, Yildiz attempted for a moment a feeble offensive. The Palace troops advanced, but, on catching sight of 1500 Macedonian infantry and three batteries on a height at Shishli they fell back again. After that there was no need to reconnoitre, for the Macedonian cavalry screen on the distant hills was visible from the upper windows of the Palace.

It was asserted at the time that the Macedonians had cut off Abd-ul-Hamid's gas and water, as if he had merely been an obdurate citizen who had refused to pay his gas and water rates, but Mahmud Shefket Pasha has assured me that there is no truth in this story.

I knew for a fact, however, that there was a terrible panic in Yildiz, for on April 24 I met soldiers and servants running away from it. This panic probably led to a general disorganization in the Palace, which resulted in turn in the electric light failing, the kitchen fires remaining unlighted, and the rumour getting abroad that the Macedonians were starving the Sultan into submission. . . .

The very multitude of servants and dependents in this overgrown household served to heighten the confusion. There were chamberlains, secretaries, body-guards, and *aides-de-camp* (350 persons), ladies and slaves (370 persons), sons and daughters of the Sultan with their respective suites (160 persons), eunuchs in the service of the harem (127), the *personnel* of the kitchens (390), the *personnel* of the stables (350), doorkeepers and other servants (250), troops forming the immediate Palace guard (1450).

On Saturday night all these thousands of people had to struggle in the darkness for food as best they could. More unnerving, however, than want of food was the want of a master to inspire confidence in this herd of dependents. . . . Abd-ul-Hamid was not visible or accessible, and in horrified whispers his people asked one another if perchance he were drugged, or in a fit, or dead. These whispers reached the soldiers, who gradually lost confidence and deserted. In proportion as the Palace was thus denuded of its guards, who streamed away from it unchecked like blood from an open wound, the panic increased among the helpless inmates of the Harem, into which some of the eunuchs carried from the outer world exaggerated accounts of the danger in which Yildiz stood. The hundreds of hapless ladies believed that the Palace might at any moment be stormed by a licentious soldiery. Some of them fainted, some fell down in hysterics, and once during the night the rest began to scream until the place seemed like Bedlam. Saturday night was as still as death and the screams were consequently heard by some of the Macedonians, 10,000 of whom, with a powerful artillery, now surrounded the Palace. They must also have been audible in the Imperial Kiosk, but no sign was made, and mystery continued to brood over that mysterious retreat. . . .

The Roman tradition, inherited by the Osmanli, makes building the work of kings. In the second place, there was the traditional Oriental superstition that the more a man builds the longer he will live. Moreover, the necessity for seclusion, in the case of a man like Abd-ul-Hamid, made the erection of new Palaces advisable. Hence Abd-ul-Hamid built. And as he was wealthy he could make this Palace an accurate representation of his own mind, could knead it like clay in his hands, could tumble down, rebuild, and alter as much as he liked – just as a painter might efface line after line until he had got exactly what he wanted – without fear of encountering the faintest opposition from any quarter. The result was an architectural horror such as the world never saw before – not even in the days of decaying

Rome, for Diocletian's villa is even yet beautiful and imposing. The wilderness of ugly kiosks, pavilions, chalets and *belvédères* which go under the general name of Yildiz has no master thought, no dominant inspiration unless it be – Fear.

Everything in Yildiz bears the imprint of the curious and crooked mind which called it into existence. Safety from pursuit and assassination seems to have been the main object in view. 'It is not a Palace,' said one of the deputies who took part in the examination of it, 'it is a labyrinth. It has the air of having been constructed with the unique object of rendering pursuit along the corridors impossible.'

No one can examine the Sultan's residence without coming to the conclusion that it was the production and the abode of fear unutterable. Like the Caligula and Domitian described for us by Suetonius, Abd-ul-Hamid was almost insane. Fundamentally, indeed, he was neither a Caligula nor a Domitian, but he curiously resembled the latter in his suspiciousness, his elaborate precautions against assassination, and his intense dread of conspiracies directed against his life. To guard against conspirators getting a plan of his residence, he was continually changing its internal arrangements, walling up doors, opening new ones, narrowing passages, dividing rooms by partitions, making windows and closing them again. The iron door which communicated with the garden was of great strength, and was capable of being very firmly bolted inside. . . .

The windows were not properly painted, there was a large hole in one of the carpets, and the furniture was at once extraordinarily incongruous and extraordinarily abundant. Sometimes in one and the same room you had imitation Louis XVI., Empire, Japanese, *art nouveau*, and several other styles. The only thing you had not was the old Turkish style. Despite all his efforts to pose as the religious chief of Islam, Abd-ul-Hamid furnished his house in what he conceived to be European fashion, and as he was, after all, little more than an ignorant peasant, the whole effect was tasteless and vulgar. . . .

Like everything else in Yildiz, this array of old furniture in the corridors had a meaning. It meant that the Padishah, fearing that these particular corridors were not sufficiently narrow, had determined to narrow them in this way. Sometimes he attained the same object by moving the walls more closely together, his aim being to prevent two or more assassins from coming abreast into his presence. Of one man at a time he was not, apparently, afraid, for as the bullet-holes in the bull's-eyes and movable man-shaped targets in his private revolver range indicated, he was a very good shot, and besides the revolver which he continually carried in his breast-pocket, he always had numbers of loaded pistols and revolvers lying within reach of his hand. When the Macedonians entered Yildiz they found loaded firearms lying about almost everywhere – in the bathroom, cupboards, at the bed-sides and on the writing-tables. In the Sultan's residence alone over one thousand revolvers were discovered. . . .

The 'famous' garden of Yildiz, whereon look out the reception-room in which Abd-ul-Hamid heard of his deposition and the study where he used to sit on an insulated chair consists of about ten acres of park containing some fine old trees, well-kept gravelled paths, imitation and real flowers, little arbours (provided, like every room in the Palace, with match-boxes and ash-trays, for the ex-Sultan is a great cigarette-smoker) and a canal, traversed by a little treadmill boat and provided with toy landing-stages corresponding to the different landing-stages on the Bosphorus. . . .

While the attack was being made on the city, Abd-ul-Hamid remained entirely in the Little Mabeïn, passing his time between his bedroom and the small ill-lighted sitting-room adjoining it, smoking innumerable cigarettes, and accompanied all the while by his favourite boy, Prince Abdurrahmin. Despite his brave attempt to keep up appearances and his hope that he would be allowed to remain on the throne, he must have been very uneasy, for he could not intrigue any longer and had only to wait, helpless and passive, to see what the Macedonians would do with him. He was handicapped, not only by his age, his infirmities and his unmilitary disposition, but also by his superstition, for he had been long aware that a venerable sheikh of Kurdistan had prophesied that he would only reign thirty-three years and as everybody knows, he mounted the throne in 1876.

The disorder which prevailed in the Palace and the flight of some soldiers and servants were all calculated to upset him. . . . Since they [the deputation] had got to discharge their mission whatever the risk, the secretary brought them across to the Little Mabeïn and knocked on the outer door.

He had to knock a long time, however, before the door was

The grounds of the Yildiz Palace at the end of the nineteenth century; from William J.J. Spry's *Life on the Bosphorous*, 1895

opened, and meanwhile the party had been surrounded by thirty black eunuchs. On being finally admitted, they were brought directly to a saloon which is situated a few paces from the entrance and which I have since been privileged to examine, while all the furniture, screens, ornaments, &c., were still in exactly the position which they had occupied on the occasion of this momentous interview. . . .

A great many clocks ticked all round the apartment, one of them a mother-of-pearl clock, and another shaped like a mosque. There were four or five arm-chairs and several large mirrors placed along the walls. Abd-ul-Hamid was particularly fond of mirrors, because they could tell him if assassins were approaching him from behind.

Beside the Padishah sat his little boy, Abdurrahmin Effendi. The father wore a black civilian coat and a military overcoat buttoned up. The son wore the Palace uniform and had his two hands on his breast, after the beautiful fashion of a Turkish child in the presence of superiors.

The deputation advanced into the centre of the room. The Sultan's secretaries, Galib Bey, Djevad Bey, and a number of eunuchs and valets remained near the door. Looking haggard and worn, Abd-ul-Hamid rose and, advancing from behind the screen, said, 'Why have you come?' whereupon General Essad Pasha gave the military salute, took two steps forward and replied:

Essad Pasha: In conformity with the *fetva* that has been pronounced, the nation has deposed you. The National Assembly charges itself with your personal security and that of your family. You have nothing to fear from anybody. Be reassured!

Abd-ul-Hamid: I am not guilty. . . . It is my destiny (*Kismet*). . . . Is my life, at least, in safety?

(Carasso Effendi says that Abd-ul-Hamid had tears in his eyes as he asked this question.)

Essad Pasha: The Ottomans are noble and magnanimous. They never commit injustice.

Abd-ul-Hamid: Swear to me on what you say, for your declarations may soon be modified. Swear to me, then, in person that you shall not go back on what you say.

Essad Pasha: I repeat to you that the Ottomans are noble and that they do not commit injustice. Your life is in every way guaranteed by the National Assembly. Do not, therefore, be uneasy.

Abd-ul-Hamid: You will not let me stay here any longer? I desire that the Teheragan Palace be allotted to me as my residence. . . . I am ready to at once make preparations to go thither.

Essad Pasha: We shall submit your desire to the National Assembly, whose decision will be communicated to you later on. I hope very much that your desire will be granted.

Abd-ul-Hamid: I gained the Turko-Greek war, and history will bear witness to the fact that I have done much for the interests of the nation. I am by no means guilty.

Essad Pasha: It is impossible, under the constitutional *régime*, to punish any one unless he is guilty. Condemnation can only be pronounced after a careful investigation.

This scene, like the climax or culminating-point of most great historical scenes, only took a few moments, and as the deputation left, Abd-ul-Hamid saluted them in the Turkish fashion by raising his hands first to his mouth and then to his forehead. As was only natural, he was in a state of agitation, almost of collapse, and looked years older than he had looked at the Selamlik only four days earlier, his undyed beard having become greyer and the wrinkles on his face having now become deeper. But considering how terrible was the blow he had just received, and how great his suffering must have been during the preceding few days, the wonder is that he bore up so well.

The last sound which the deputies heard as they left the house was the boyish voice of little Abdurrahmin Effendi, who was crying as if his heart would break.

Thus fell Abd-ul-Hamid, the twenty-fourth Sultan of the House of Othman, and by a strange coincidence he was dethroned by the very force which he had called into activity in order to smash the Constitution. On April 18 his mutinous soldiers had cried out for the *Sheriat*, the Sacred Law of Islâm. On April 27 the *Sheriat* broke them and their Sultan together.

[79] Lord Stratford de Redcliffe gives a Christmas Day ball at the British Embassy in 1855, attended by Florence Nightingale; from *Constantinople during the Crimean War* by Lady Hornby.

(Lady Hornby's account of Constantinople was written while her husband Edmund (at that time still to be knighted) was a Loan Commissioner to the Ottoman government. With two colleagues, Mr Cadrossi (a Frenchman) and Caboul Effendi, he was supervising the spending of a gold loan of £5 million, to the displeasure of many Turks 'furious at the idea of not being able to finger some thousands for their private purses', writes Lady Hornby. Mr Hornby, despite this, was awarded the Order of the Medjidi.)

The palace looked very beautiful – its spacious white stone corridors, richly and warmly carpeted, and an air of *perfectness* very striking here. Beautiful orange and lemon trees, bearing both flowers and fruit; bright, shining myrtles, and gorgeous scarlet cacti, had a charming effect. There were a few branches of

Turkish holly, which is small and stunted, but not a single berry of the cherished scarlet. Mistletoe is found on many of the old oak-trees in the Crimea, but I have never seen any here. The ladies at the Embassy have great taste in the arrangement of flowers and shrubs, and the drawing-rooms seem so beautiful to me after our savage little kiosk, that I feel like an Esquimaux suddenly imported into Belgravia, and, seated on a low sofa canopied with orange and myrtle, delight mine eyes exceedingly. I never thought to have looked with so much interest at a blazing fireplace as I do now, not having seen one for months.

Lady Stratford was not in the drawing-room when we arrived. . . . But by-and-by the drawing-room doors are thrown open, and the ambassadress enters, smiling a kind welcome. Behind her are her daughters; by her side, a tall, fashionable, haughty beauty. I could not help thinking how lovely a person; but the next instant my eyes wandered from her cold unamiable face to a lady modestly standing on the other side of Lady Stratford. At first I thought she was a nun, from her black dress and close cap. She was not introduced, and yet Edmund and I looked at each other at the same moment to whisper, 'It is Miss Nightingale!' Yes, it was Florence Nightingale, greatest of all now in name and honour among women. I assure you that I was glad not to be obliged to speak just then, for I felt quite dumb as I looked at her wasted figure and the short brown hair combed over her forehead like a child's, cut so, when her life was despaired of from fever but a short time ago. Her dress, as I have said, was black, made high to the throat, its only ornament being a large enamelled brooch, which looked to me like the colours of a regiment surmounted with a wreath of laurel, no doubt some grateful offering from our men. To hide the close white cap a little, she had tied a white crape handkerchief over the back of it, only allowing the border of lace to be seen; and this gave the nun-like appearance which first struck me on her entering the room, otherwise Miss Nightingale is by no means striking in appearance. Only her plain black dress, quiet manner, and great renown, told so powerfully altogether in that assembly of brilliant dress and uniforms. She is very slight, rather above the middle height; her face is long and thin, but this may be from recent illness and great fatigue. She has a very prominent nose, slightly Roman; and small dark eyes, kind, yet penetrating; but her face does not give you at all the idea of great talent. She looks a quiet, persevering, orderly, ladylike woman. I have done my best to give you a true pen-and-ink portrait of this celebrated lady. I suppose there is a hum all over the world of 'What is she like?'

Many officers now arrived, and the new ball-room, which is a very beautiful one, was thrown open. Several Christmas games were played, in which almost every one joined. . . .

Miss Nightingale was still very weak, and could not join in the games, but she sat on a sofa, and looked on, laughing until the tears came into her eyes. There was afterwards a dark room, with a gigantic dish of snap-dragon, and we all looked dreadfully pale in the blue light. The red coats of the officers turned orange-colour, their stars and orders of the most unearthly hue; and each wondered at the other's spectral looks, except the 'middies', who showed a marvellous capacity for eating fiery plums.

[80] The Sultan Abdul Mecit attends the British Ambassador's fancy-dress ball; from *Constantinople during the Crimean War* by Lady Hornby.

The Sultan had, with very good taste, left his own Guard at the Galata Serai, and was escorted thence to the palace by a company of English Lancers, every other man carrying a torch. Lord Stratford and his Staff, of course, met him at the carriage-door, and as he alighted, a communication by means of galvanic wires was made to the fleet, who saluted him with prolonged salvos of cannon. Lady Stratford and her daughters received him at the head of the staircase. Then, after the usual royal fashion, his Majesty retired to one of the smaller drawing-rooms to repose himself a little after his jolting. I never shall forget the splendid scene when we entered the ball-room. Anything more beautiful it would be difficult even to imagine. . . .

In fact, every costume in the known world was to be met with: Queens and shepherdesses; Emperors and caïquejees; Crimean heroes; ambassadors, attachés, and diplomatists. The flash of diamonds was something wonderful, especially among the Armenians and Greeks, who pride themselves, when wealthy, on the splendour of their wives.

We were noticing and admiring all this, and had shaken hands with M. de Thouvenel, and spoken to the few of the crowd whom we knew, when it was whispered that the Sultan was coming. Every one of course made way, and Abdul Medjid quietly walked up the ball-room with Lord and Lady Stratford, their daughters, and a gorgeous array of Pashas in the rear. He paused with evident delight and pleasure at the really beautiful scene before him, bowing on both sides, and smiling as he went. A velvet and gold chair, raised a few steps, had been placed for him in the middle of one side of the ball-room; but, on being conducted to it, he seemed too much pleased to sit down, and continued standing, looking about him with the undisguised pleasure and simplicity of a child. He was dressed in a plain dark-blue frock-coat, the cuffs and collar crimson, and covered with brilliants. The hilt of his sword was entirely covered also with brilliants. Of course he wore the everlasting fez. There is something extremely interesting in his appearance. He looks languid and careworn, but, when spoken to, his fine dark eyes brighten up and he smiles the most frank and winning of smiles.

I am quite charmed with the Sultan, so different to most of the Pashas by whom he is surrounded, so touchingly kind, and simple, and sorrowful! The Pashas behaved very badly, forcing themselves violently in a double row on the Sultan's right-hand, and pushing every one right and left, like policemen when the Queen is dining in the City; just as if they thought that the ladies were going to carry off the Sultan at once. We were accidentally close to the dais, and got a terrible squeezing. My lace mantilla was caught in a Pasha's sword, and I thought that nothing could save its being torn to pieces. However, Lord Dunkellin very kindly rescued me, and, thanks to his strong arm, I was able to keep my place and see Miss Mary Canning and the Ministers' wives presented to the Sultan. A quadrille was formed, as well as the crowd would allow, which the Sultan watched with great interest, and then a waltz. After that his Majesty walked through the rooms, took an ice, and then departed, expressing, I must not forget to tell you, the greatest admiration of the Highlanders and Lancers who lined the grand staircase, one on each step, and of the Light Dragoons and Royals, who presented arms to him in the hall: most of the cavalry men wore the Balaklava clasp. He certainly seemed much struck and gratified, as the papers say, at this splendid scene. Colonel Ebor, the handsome 'Times' correspondent, was there, and saw everything, but was obliged to keep out of the Sultan's sight, being attired in the magnificent dress of a Janissary Aga. . . .

Most of the Pashas eat enormously at a ball. They are for ever paying visits to the refreshment-room, and drink vast quantities of champagne, of which they pretend not to know the exact genus, and slyly call it 'eau gazeuse'. The English papers talk of Turkish prejudices; generally speaking, your modern Turk has none, either religious or political, unless it suits him. The word 'prejudice' means their dislike of anything which will prevent their living in splendour on the misery and oppression of the people. They drink champagne and brandy, and defy the laws of the Koran, comfortably enough, in secret. Of course this does not apply to the real Turkish gentleman and strict Mussulman, who is seldom heard of now, and never mentioned in the same breath with 'reform' or European manners. It is curious, too, that among the Turks the rich represent the bad; the poor seem almost invariably to be honest, temperate, patient, hard-working, and religious. A poor man here has a strikingly noble countenance; you may know rich ones only too frequently by the sensuality and ferocity of their expression. Here a man can hardly be wealthy and virtuous; if he keeps a place it must be by dishonest means, and so he goes on from bad to worse. . . .

A most horrible-looking creature is the Chief of the Eunuchs. He is a Black, and hideous to a degree positively revolting; yet he is the second man in the kingdom, and the Sultan dares hardly go anywhere without him. He walked about leaning on the arm of a Negro but little less frightful than himself, their long swords clattering as they went. I am told that this creature walks about the Seraglio with a thong of leather in his hand, ready to strike any rebellious lady who may offend him. They say that the Sultan would be very glad to give up his Seraglio if he dared. He is much attached to the Sultana, the mother of his children, and seldom visits the seven hundred women shut up in the great cage near him.

[81] The Whirling Dervishes of Pera; from J.C. Hobhouse's *A Journey through Albania . . . to Constantinople during the years 1809 and 1810.*

Attempts have been made to abolish the institution, but the Janissaries still retain eight Dervishes of the order of Bek-tash, as

Whirling Dervishes; from *Stamboul Souvenir d'Orient*, 1861 by A. Preziosi

chaplains to the army; and the people of Constantinople run in crowds to amuse themselves (for no other motive can be assigned to them) at the exhibitions of the turning and of the howling Dervishes, to which all strangers are carried, as to the theatre or other places of entertainment in the cities of Christendom.

There is a monastery of the former order, the *Mevlevi* (so called from Mevlana their founder) in Pera, and we were admitted to the performance of their ceremonies on Friday the 25th of May. We were conducted by a private door into the gallery of the place of worship, a single octagonal room, with the middle of the floor, which was of wood highly polished, railed off for the exhibitors. A red carpet and cushion were placed at the side opposite the great door near the rails, but there were no seats in any part of the chamber. We waited some time until the great door opened, and a crowd of men and boys rushed in, like a mob into a playhouse, each of them, however, pulling off his shoes as he entered. The place without the rails, and our gallery, were filled in five minutes, when the doors were closed. The Dervishes dropped in one by one, and each of them crossing his arms, very reverently and with the utmost grace bowed to the seat of the Superior, who entered at last himself, better dressed than the others, and with his feet covered. With him came in another man, who was also distinguished from the rest by his garments, and who appeared afterwards to officiate as a clerk. Other Dervishes arrived, and went into the gallery opposite to the Superior's seat, where there were four small cymbal drums. The Superior now commenced a prayer, which he continued for ten minutes; then a man stood up in the gallery, and sang for some time from a book: the cymbals began to beat, and four Dervishes taking up their *neïh* or long cane pipes, called by Cantemir the sweetest of all musical instruments, played some tunes which were by no means disagreeable, and were, indeed, something like plaintive English airs. On some note being struck, the Dervishes below all fell suddenly on their faces, clapping their hands with one accord upon the floor.

The music ceased, and the Superior began again to pray. He then rose, and marched three times slowly round the room, followed by the others, who bowed on each side of his cushion, the Superior himself bowing also, but not to the cushion, and only once, when he was half way across it. The Superior reseated himself, and said a short prayer. The music commenced a second time, all the Dervishes rose from the ground, and fourteen out of the twenty who were present, let drop a long coloured petticoat, round the rim of which there were apparently some weights; and throwing off their cloaks, they appeared in a tight vest with sleeves. The clerk then marched by the Superior, and bowing, retired into the middle of the room. A Dervish followed, bowed, and began to whirl round, his long petticoat flying out into a cone. The rest followed, and all of them were soon turning round in the same manner as the first, forming a circle about the room, with three or four in the middle. The arms of one man alone were held straight upwards, two of them crooked their right arms like a kettle-spout, the rest had both arms extended horizontally, generally with the palm of one hand turned upwards, and the fingers closed and at full length. A very accurate and lively representation of this curious scene may be found in Lord Baltimore's Travels. – Some of them turned with great speed; they revolved round the room imperceptibly, looking more like automatons than men, as the petticoat concealed the movement of their feet: the clerk walked with great earnestness and attention amongst them, but without speaking, and the Superior remained on his cushion moving his body gently from side to side, and smiling. The performers continued at the labour for twenty-five minutes, but with four short intervals; the last time they turned for ten minutes, and notwithstanding some of them whirled with such velocity that their features were not distinguishable, and two of them were boys of fifteen and seventeen, apparently no one was affected by this painful exercise. The clerk, after the turning and music ceased, prayed aloud, and a man walking round, threw a cloak upon the Dervishes, each of whom was in his original place, and bending to the earth. The Superior began the last prayer, and the company withdrew.

The ceremonies just described are said by Volney to have a reference to the revolution of the stars, and whether or not they are to have credit for any superior astronomical science, these Dervishes certainly possess some literary merit, as all of them are instructed in the Arabic language, and make it their study to become critically acquainted with its beauties. Their monasteries contain many rare books, collected at considerable pains and expense in all the countries of the East where they have any establishments, or which are visited by any of their fraternity.

The Mevlevi are rational worshippers, when compared with the Cadrhi, or Howling Dervishes, whose exertions, if considered as religious ceremonies, are more inexplicable and disgusting than those of any enthusiasts in the known world, and if regarded merely as jugglers' feats, are legitimate objects of curiosity.

[82] The diversity of the Ottoman Empire passing over the Galata Bridge, towards the end of the nineteenth century; from *Constantinople* by Edmondo de Amicis.

To see the population of Constantinople, it is well to go upon the floating bridge, about one-quarter of a mile in length, which extends from the most advanced point of Galata to the opposite shore of the Golden Horn, facing the great mosque of the Sultana Validé. Both shores are European territory; but the bridge may be said to connect Asia to Europe because in Stamboul there is nothing European save the ground, and even the Christian suburbs that crown it are of Asiatic character and color. The Golden Horn, which has the look of a river, separates two worlds, like the ocean. . . . The crowd passes in great waves, each one of which is of a hundred colors, and every group of persons represent a new type of people. Whatever can be imagined that is most extravagant in type, costume, and social class may there be seen within the space of twenty paces and ten minutes of time. Behind a throng of Turkish porters who pass running, and bending under enormous burdens, advances a sedan-chair, inlaid with ivory and mother of pearl, and bearing an Armenian lady; and at either side of it a Bedouin wrapped in a white mantle and a Turk in muslin turban and sky-blue caftan, beside whom canters a young Greek gentleman followed by his dragoman in embroidered vest, and a dervise with his tall conical hat and tunic of camel's hair, who makes way for the carriage of a European ambassador, preceded by his *running footman* in a gorgeous livery. All this is only seen in a glimpse, and the next moment you find yourself in the midst of a crowd of Persians, in pyramidal bonnets of Astrakan fur, who are followed by a Hebrew in a long yellow coat, open at the sides; a frowzy-headed gypsy woman with her child in a bag at her back; a Catholic priest with breviary staff; while in the midst of a confused throng of Greeks, Turks, and Armenians comes a big eunuch on horseback, crying out, *Larya!* (make way!) and preceding a Turkish carriage, painted with flowers and birds, and filled with the ladies of a harem, dressing in green and violet, and wrapped in large white veils; behind a Sister of Charity from the hospital at Pera, an African slave carrying a monkey, and a professional story-teller in a necromancer's habit, and what is quite natural, but appears strange to the new comer, all these diverse people pass each other without a look, like a crowd in London; and not one single countenance wears a smile. The Albanian in his white petticoat and with pistols in his sash, beside the Tartar dressed in sheepskins; the Turk, astride of his caparisoned ass, threads pompously two long strings of camels; behind the adjutant of an imperial prince, mounted upon his Arab steed, clatters a cart filled with all the odd domestic rubbish of a Turkish household; the Mahometan women a-foot, the veiled slave woman, the Greek with her red cap, and her hair on her shoulders, the Maltese hooded in her black *faldetta*, the Hebrew woman dressed in the antique costume of India, the negress wrapped in a many-colored shawl from Cairo, the Armenian from Trebizond, all veiled in black like a funeral apparition, are seen in single file, as if placed there on purpose, to be contrasted with each other.

It is a changing mosaic of races and religions that is composed and scattered continually with a rapidity that the eye can scarcely follow. It is amusing to look only at the passing feet and see all the foot-coverings in the world go by, from that of Adam up to the last fashion in Parisian boots – yellow Turkish babouches, red Armenian, blue Greek and black Jewish shoes; sandals, great boots from Turkestan, Albanian gaiters, low cut slippers, leg-pieces of many colors, belonging to horsemen from Asia Minor, gold embroidered shoes, Spanish *alporgatos*, shoes of satin, of twine, of rags, of wood, so many, that while you look at one you catch a glimpse of a hundred more. One must be on the alert not to be jostled and overthrown at every step. Now it is a water-carrier with a colored jar upon his back; now a Russian lady on horseback, now a squad of Imperial soldiers in zouave dress, and stepping as if to an assault; now a crew of Armenian porters, two and two, carrying on their shoulders immense bars, from which are suspended great bales of merchandise; and now a throng of Turks who dart from left to right of the bridge to embark in the steamers that lie there. There is a tread of many feet, a murmuring, a sound of voices, guttural notes, aspirations interjectional, incomprehensible and strange, among which the few French and Italian words that reach the ear seem like luminous points upon a black darkness.

The approaches to the city by water

[83] Fishing at the Island of Prinkipo (Büyükada) in the sixteenth century; from *Travels into Turkey* . . . by A.G. Busbequius.

(Augier-Ghislain de Busbecq (1522–1592) was born in Flanders, legitimized (fortunately for him) by his father, educated at several universities in Europe, and professed seven languages. Ferdinand, King of the Romans, sent him as Ambassador to Suleiman II in 1555, and he stayed there seven years, returning honourably with useful treaty terms, and some hundred Byzantine manuscripts which are now the backbone of the Vienna State Library.)

I lived there very pleasantly for three Months. It was a private Place, without any Crowd or Noise. There were only a few *Greeks*, with whom I diverted myself; but never a *Turk* to interrupt my Mirth. As for the *Turks* of my Household, they created no trouble to me; I might go whither I would, and pass from one of these Islands to another at my pleasure, without any molestation from them. There grew several sorts of Plants, as *French* Lavender, sharp-pointed Myrtle, Cotton-weed, and abundance more. The Sea is full of divers sorts of Fishes, which I took sometimes with Net, sometimes with Hook and Line. Several *Grecian* Fishers with their Boats attended me, and where we had hopes of the greatest sport, thither we failed and cast our Nets. Sometimes we played above board, and when we saw a Crab or a Lobster at the bottom, where the Sea was very clear, we ran him through with a Fish-spear, and so halled him up into a Vessel. But our best and most profitable sport, was with a drag-Net; where we thought most Fish were, there we cast it in a round; it took up a great compass, with the long Ropes tied to the ends of it, which were to draw it to Land. To those Ropes the Seamen tied green Boughs very thick, so that the Fish might be frightened, and not seek to escape. Thus we brought great Sholes of trembling Fishes near the Shore. And yet in this danger they were naturally instigated how to save themselves; some would leap over the Net, others would cover themselves in the Sand, that they might not be taken; others strove to bite the Meashes of the Net, though made of coarse Flax, or Hemp, of which kind were the *Synodontes*, Fish armed with strong Teeth; and if one made way for himself, all would follow him, and so the whole

Draught would escape, and not a fish left for the Fisher. To remedy this Inconvenience, (for I was aware of it) I stood with Pole in my Hand, beating the Water, that I might keep the Fish from biting the Net. At which my Attendants could not choose but laugh; yet, for all this, many of them escaped: So sagacious are Fishes where they are in extream danger! But notwithstanding the Fugitives, we brought a great many Fishes ashore, a Sea-Bream, Scorpion-Fishes, Dragon-Fishes, Scare-Fish, Jule-Fish, Chane or Ruff-Fish, whose Variety did delight my Eye, and the enquiry into their Nature, did hugely please my Fancy: So that at Night I return'd home with my trimphant Vessel laden with Prey. The next Day I presented *Hali Bassa*, and his Chief Steward, with Part of what I had taken, who thought it a very acceptable Present.

[84] A Victorian lady visits the Island of Prinkipo and St George's Monastery in 1856; from *Constantinople during the Crimean War* by Lady Hornby.

The Greeks of Constantinople consider Prinkipo as their paradise on earth, and begin a regular course of monotonous amusement from the first moment of their arrival; which is scarcely varied for a single day, up to the last instant of their stay. About seven in the morning all the visitors who have not departed for Pera by the early steamer, are to be seen (if you take caïque toward the village) wending to the little wooden bathing-houses on the shore. Some of these people have returned from an early donkey-ride up the mountain – most from the divan and cup of coffee. Through all the sultry hours, until about four or five o'clock, everybody lies *perdu*; not even Signor Giacomo's Croat gardeners are to be seen, not even his sun-burnt children, – scarcely a single caïque moving about on the water; only under a large fir-tree opposite our windows a red-capped shepherd, fast asleep, with three or four drowsy goats about him, and a large, dark eagle or two soaring majestically about. The only sound is the ceaseless chirp of the cicala, a deep-toned grasshopper which here dwells principally in the fir-trees. A dark cloud of heat hangs over distant Constantinople. I fancy that, if even we were nearer, we should hear no 'city's hum' at midday. My caïque is the only busy thing about.

But I must hasten to tell you what you wished to know, – how one passes a long summer's day in the 'Islands of the Blest'. Well, sometimes I point to a small bay, about half-way round the island. My sturdy rowers pull rapidly in. The Monastery of St George, perched on the very highest peak of mountain above, looks no bigger than a doll's house, left there by some spiteful fairy, to be shaken by winter tempests and scorched by summer glare. Walking a few paces over the white sand of the creek, you cross a low hedge-bank into the deep shade of some ancient fig-trees. This is the garden of the Monastery. The lay Brother must be an active person I should think, if he descends the mountain every morning for the ascetic salads. The gardener is a remarkably fine, picturesque old Greek; he always comes to meet me, attended by his two wild, shaggy dogs, helps the boatmen to bring the cushions from the caïque, and carefully picks out the coolest bit of shade under the wide-spreading fig-tree. He keeps a nice piece of matting, and some antique-shaped earthen water-jars of spring water, always ready for the use of occasional visitors to his creek. . . . Johannachi spreads the luncheon with great glee, Janko and Pandalij search with the old gardener for the finest figs, while I stroll away to the hedgerow on the beach, in search of specimens for my collection of island plants. . . . After luncheon I sit and read. What thorough enjoyment it is, and how often I wish it were possible you could spend a morning with me! Having risen so early, by eleven o'clock I begin to feel tired, and generally enjoy a sound sleep on the cushions under the fig-tree; the caïquejees slumbering profoundly meanwhile in the 'Edith Belina', and my tiny guard Johannachi either discussing melons and figs, or playing in the garden with the old man's dogs. . . .

Miss Barker and I spent yesterday at the Monastery [of St George], riding up the mountain on donkeys. We walked through the pretty French camp [*a sanatorium for Crimean wounded*], and admired the neat wooden houses which the soldiers have built for their sick officers in the most lovely situations among fir-trees overhanging the sea. At a little distance in the valley below is their cemetery, which is carefully walled round, and planted with rows of simple wooden crosses, like those in the Crimea. The East has gathered many dead from distant places since the war began. . . .

Having kind Miss Barker to interpret, made the visit so much pleasanter. We found the Superior standing before the old gateway of the courtyard of the monstery, throwing a few dried leaves to the flock of goats which came bounding over the vast piles of rock which lie heaped around. He is a fine, stern-looking man, his active energetic movements and long beard contrasting strangely with the old dark-blue satin petticoat peeping out from beneath his black outer robe. A few rough tools were lying on a bench beside him: he had been patching up a little, he said apologetically, against the winter storms, for the place had not been repaired for years, and the brotherhood here was too poor to spend any money on workmen. Their goats, he said, were almost all they had to depend upon in winter, besides the produce of the garden at the foot of the mountain, of which an immense heap of tomatas were drying in the sun: it must be a hard and lonely life. . . . We went into the church, and he showed us a very curious cross, of great antiquity. It is about seven inches in length, and the frame is of light and delicate filagree-work, exquisitely wrought and designed. The hollow centre is composed of minute figures in carved cedar, of our Saviour, the Virgin Mary, and the Apostles on one side, and of several Saints and Martyrs on the other. There are holes for jewels all round, and a few small ones still remained. On particular days this cross is placed on the altar of St George, above the old tomb, where a lamp is always burning. We were particularly amused by an old picture in honour of St George, which hangs in a remote part of the church. Crowned kings, pilgrims, queens in gorgeous array, children, and beggars, are seated stiffly round the tank of water, supposed to have sprung from the favourite well of the Saint. Some of the ladies certainly look rather tipsy, especially one seated near a very jolly-looking and roysterous king, whose crown is too big for him, and set all on one side, in a very jaunty manner. All are lifting up their hands and eyes, or in some way or other expressing a comical kind of surprise in the miraculously healing effect of the draughts they are quaffing.

This picture, offered to St George after a cure performed at his shrine here, cost a great deal of money, and was considered a very fine one, the monk said. . . . Though you will have had enough by this time of Greek pictures, I must tell you about the St George in this place. The whole of the picture, except the swarthy face of the saint, is covered with silver, barbarously enough laid on. It is said to be the original picture belonging to Irene's church; and the legend adds, said one monk, that it was buried by one of the

Leander's Tower (the Kiz Kulesi); from *Descrizione Topografica*, 1784 by C. Comidas de Carbognano

ancient brotherhood, when Constantinople was taken and its Christian churches razed. Many sacred treasures were so preserved in those days. A young shepherd of Prinkipo, two or three centuries later, sleeping on the mountain, dreamed that St George appeared to him, and directing him to dig on the exact spot where he lay, assured him that he would there find the long-lost picture of his shrine. Of course the shepherd dug, and of course he discovered the picture, which he restored to the present church, since which time it has been famous for miraculous cures, especially in all kinds of madness. The shepherd left his flock, turned monk, and ultimately died Superior of this Monastery, and in great odour of sanctity.

[85] Leander's Tower (Kiz Kulesi) – the Turkish legend of the Maiden in the Tower; from *Un Parisien à Constantinople* by Vicomte René Vigier. Translated by Marina Berry.

A certain Sultan had a daughter who was as beautiful as the dawn. He consulted his astrologer as to her future, and received the following laconic and deadly reply: 'O great Lord, your daughter will be stung by a snake.'

In a desperate attempt to avert destiny, the Sultan ordered a tower to be built in the middle of the sea beyond the reach of all reptiles. When it was finished this tower became the girl's prison. Now the maiden had a tender heart, and she had noticed in her father's household a young Persian prince. I have said that she was beautiful, so it is only natural that the prince, who was no less pleasing and charming than a prince in Perrault's fairy tales, should lose his heart to her, as is fitting in an Oriental fairy tale. You can imagine his sorrow when he learnt of his beloved's exile, as the Sultan insisted that in her new refuge she see only her ladies and her eunuchs.

Love knows no bounds; one can stretch chains across the Bosphorus and separate two seas, but not two hearts that adore each other. The prince soon won over the eunuchs and the ladies; every evening he would come to the foot of the tower by boat, and give the princess flowers which he had picked with his own hands. (It is even said that this is when the sweet language of flowers was born, which ever since has been so widespread in Constantinople.) Yet orders were strict and he was never allowed to cross the threshold. He would bring his gifts, and she would thank him with a smile through half-open windows. One evening, one summer's evening as beautiful as this one, it happened that the prince brought lovely Niloufer (for she was called Niloufer, meaning lotus flower), it happened, as I was saying, that the prince brought her a basket of roses and lilacs.

Carried away by joyous love, she clasped them to her bare breast when, O horror! an asp, a hideous asp, emerged from a rose and stung her. At the foot of the tower the prince heard an anguished cry – he remembered the prophecy, he guessed everything, and, crazy with anguish, impotent against fate, he sought to put an end to his life in the deep waters of the sea.

But a *houri* was passing by on a cloud; she saw his dark despair and was touched by such passion and constancy. Taking the young man's hand, she lifted him through the air, and placed him in the room where Niloufer lay ashen with fear.

You have guessed what he did. Placing his lips on the wound, he drank the venom which the reptile had injected. The princess was cured, and gave back to him with kisses what he had given to her with flowers.

[86] The Bosphorus; from Canto V of *Don Juan* by Lord Byron.

III.

The European with the Asian shore
  Sprinkled with palaces; the Ocean stream
Here and there studded with a seventy-four;
  Sophia's cupola with golden gleam;
The cypress groves; Olympus high and hoar;
  The twelve isles, and the more than I could dream,
Far less describe, present the very view
Which charm'd the charming Mary Montagu.[1]

V.

The wind swept down the Euxine, and the wave
  Broke foaming o'er the blue Symplegades;
'T is a grand sight from off 'the Giant's Grave'[2]
  To watch the progress of those rolling seas
Between the Bosphorus, as they lash and lave
  European and Asia, you being quite at ease:
There's not a sea the passenger e'er pukes in,
Turns up more dangerous breakers than the Euxine.

[1] ['The pleasure of going in a barge to Chelsea is not comparable to that of rowing upon the canal of the sea here, where, for twenty miles together, down the Bosphorus, the most beautiful variety of prospects present themselves. The Asian side is covered with fruit trees, villages, and the most delightful landscapes in nature; on the European stands Constantinople, situated on seven hills; showing an agreeable mixture of gardens, pine and cypress trees, palaces, mosques, and public buildings, raised one above another, with as much beauty and appearance of symmetry as you ever saw in a cabinet adorned by the most skilful hands, where jars show themselves above jars, mixed with canisters, babies, and candlesticks. This is a very odd comparison; but it gives me an exact idea of the thing.' – LADY M.W. MONTAGU.]

[2] The 'Giant's Grave' is a height on the Asiatic shore of the Bosphorus, much

VI.

'T was a raw day of Autumn's bleak beginning,
When nights are equal, but not so the days;
The Parcæ then cut short the further spinning
Of seamen's fates, and the loud tempests raise
The waters, and repentance for past sinning
In all, who o'er the great deep take their ways:
They vow to amend their lives, and yet they don't;
Because if drown'd, they can't – if spared, they won't.

[87] The Bosphorus at night; from *The City of the Sultan and the Domestic Manner of the Turks in 1836* by Miss Pardoe.

(Julia Pardoe (1806–1862) precociously published poems at the age of fourteen, which went into two editions. She accompanied her father, a Yorkshire major who had served at Waterloo, to Constantinople in 1835, and published so much that in 1860 she was awarded a Civil List pension 'in consideration of thirty years' toil in the field of literature'. Amongst other Orientalia she wrote *The Romance of the Harem* (1839) and *The Thousand and One Days*, a companion to the *Nights* (1857).)

To be seen in all its beauty, the Bosphorus should be looked upon by moonlight. Then it is that the occupants of the spacious mansions which are mirrored in its waters, enjoy to the fullest perfection the magnificence of the scene around them. The glare of noonday reveals too broadly the features of the locality; while the deep, blue, star-studded sky, the pure moonlight, and the holy quiet of evening, lend to it, on the contrary, a mysterious indistinctness which doubles its attraction. The inhabitants of the capital are conscious of this fact; and during the summer

frequented by holiday parties; like Harrow and Highgate. [In less than an hour, we were on the top of the mountain, and repaired to the Tekeh, or Dervishes' chapel, where we were shown, in the adjoining garden, a flower-bed more than fifty feet long, rimmed round with stone, and having a sepulchral turban at each end, which preserves a superstition attached to the spot long before the time of the Turks, or of the Byzantine Christians; and which, after having been called the tomb of Amycus, and the bed of Hercules, is now known as the Giant's Grave. – HOBHOUSE.]

View of the Bosphorus; drawing by William H. Bartlett in Julia Pardoe's *The Beauties of the Bosphorus*, 1861

months, when they occupy their marine mansions, one of their greatest recreations is to seat themselves upon the seaward terraces, to watch the sparkling of the ripple, and to listen to the evening hymn of the seamen on board the Greek and Italian vessels; amused at intervals by a huge shoal of porpoises rolling past, gambolling in the moonlight, and plunging amid the waves with a sound like thunder: while afar off are the dark mountains of Asia casting their long dusky shadows far across the water, and the quivering summits of the tall trees on the edge of the channel sparkling like silver, and lending the last touch of loveliness to a landscape perhaps unparalleled in the world.

Shakespeare must have had a vision of the Bosphorus, when he wrote the garden scene in Romeo and Juliet!

All the Orientals idolize flowers. Every good house upon the border of the channel has a parterre, terraced off from the sea, of which you obtain glimpses through the latticed windows; and where the rose trees are trained into a thousand shapes of beauty – sometimes a line of arches risen all bloom and freshness above a favourite walk – sometimes the plants are stretched round vases of red clay of the most classical formation, of which they preserve the shape – ranges of carnations, clumps of acacias, and bosquets of seringa, are common; and the effect of these fair flowers, half shielded from observation, and overhung with forest trees, which are in profusion in every garden, is extremely agreeable.

Another peculiarity of the Bosphorus is the great depth of the water to the very edges of the channel. The terraces that hem it in are frequently injured by their contact with the shipping which, in a sudden lull of wind, or by some inadvertence on the part of the helmsman, 'run foul' (to use a nautical expression) of the shore; nor is it the terraces alone that suffer, for the houses whose upper stories project over the stream, which is almost universally the case where they are of any extent, are constantly sustaining injury from the same cause.

We had occupied our summer residence only two days, when an Imperial Brig in the Turkish service, in attempting a tack, thrust its bowsprit through the centre window of the magnificent saloon of an Armenian banker, with whose family we were acquainted. The master of the house, exasperated at the evident carelessness in which the accident had originated, rushed out upon the terrace to remonstrate, but his remonstrances were unheeded; and he had scarcely re-entered the house when the Turkish captain, who was intoxicated, landed, and without ceremony passed into the outer court, accompanied by some of his crew; and, seizing the brother of the gentleman, and several of his servants, gave them a severe beating, and then quietly returned on board. The vessel was extricated after a time, carrying away with it nearly the whole front of the saloon, and a large portion of the roof; after which, the gallant commander again entered the house, and insisted upon conveying its master to Constantinople, there to expiate the sin of insolence to a Turkish officer. The Saraf, however, having business in the city, had already departed, and consequently escaped the inconvenience and insult destined for him.

[88] The execution of a naval officer by the Capitan Pasha on his own ship; from *Records of Travels in Turkey, Greece, and of a Cruise in the Black Sea* by Captain Adolphus Slade, RN, FRAS.

(Sir Adolphus Slade KCB (1804–1877) rose to be both British Vice-Admiral and an Admiral in the Ottoman Navy. After attending the Royal Naval College at Portsmouth in 1815, he served in South America, Algiers, and at the Battle of Navarino in 1827. He first visited Constantinople in 1829 whilst on half pay, cruising in the Black Sea on the *Blonde*. In 1849 he was seconded to the Porte, and for seventeen years (including the Crimean War) was administrative head of the Ottoman Navy. He never married, and retired to England in 1866.)

Poor Hamid! peace to his errors! I knew him well; a merry, mellow-eyed mortal, who, though a true Osmanley, preferred punch to sherbet, and the daughters of Eve to the Houris in reversion. The evening before his catastrophe we smoked a pipe together, when he little thought that the rustling of Azrael's wings fanned the cool breeze in our faces. Late that night the capitan pasha returned from Constantinople, where he had been assisting at a divan, with the fatal firman in his bosom; and the next morning, the sun just peeping above the Asiatic hills, I saw a barge row swiftly from the flag-ship to the nazir's house, which overhung the water. Suspecting something, I put a question to the officer of the boat, as he passed my window; he shook his head in reply. The nazir was still reposing. 'The pasha wants you,' was the pithy message. 'Why, what can he require?' 'You will soon learn; rise.' He adjusted his dress, performed his ablutions, prayed, and then, without making any arrangement, stepped into the barge. I was already dressed and on the quay; passing which, he waved his hand to me, and said something, I thought farewell, so I took a caique and followed. The principal officers of the fleet received him on the quarterdeck; the man whose smiles they courted the day before, on account of his intimacy with the capitan pasha, they received with insults. Hassan, riala bey, gave him a kick. At this he crossed his hands and exclaimed, 'I understand'. He was then conducted down on the main deck: there his accusation was read to him, enumerating, with other charges, the unjust one of grinding the poor. So false an accusation, without the power of refuting it, must have added a pang to the bitterness of death; that is, if he felt any, for he betrayed no fear, neither probably, with true Ottoman stoicism, would he have said one word, had not the capitan pasha at that moment come out of his cabin to look at his old friend, who, one little spark yet burning among the embers of hope, cried once 'Aman'. He might have spared his breath. The pasha answered by a slight wave of the hand, the usual signal in such cases; the guards understood it, and taking the nazir by the arms, led him below to the prison, where two slaves attended. Not thinking for a moment that he was going straight to death, I was about to follow, moved by an impulse of pity, or of curiosity, when the pasha motioned me to come into the cabin. The bowstring soon did its task, and in a few minutes, the receipt, poor Hamid's head (the countenance calm as in sleep) was brought up to be shown to the pasha, before being transmitted to the seraglio. It is startling to see a human head carried in a platter up the ladder, down which you had seen it descend, just before, sentient and well posed on a pair of shoulders; this had an effect even on the cold-blooded Osmanleys, under the half-deck; they involuntarily shuddered, as well they might: the reign of terror was begun, when no man might say that his turn would not come next.

An officer was sent to seal up the nazir's effects, and to seize his secretary; and the pasha, having first breakfasted with as good an appetite as ever, rode to the outer castle of Europe to hold a summary trial on the garrison, which ended by twenty of its members being strangled and thrown into the Bosphorus. After this pastime, he took his siesta at the castle, and then, having first installed his kiaja as governor, returned in the evening to Sariery. A moving scene awaited him on landing, in the wife and children of the nazir's secretary, who, with dishevelled hair, and weeping, implored mercy at his feet, for an innocent husband and father. The pasha passed on without deigning to notice them, but the following morning I was happy to find that the man was released, as being innocent of his master's guilt; in other words, that there was neither wealth nor secrets in the case to extract. Poor Hamid! he did not leave much; his favourite female slave was given to one of the capitan pasha's retainers, and his personal chattels were sold by auction.

[89] The British Ambassador's reception by the Sultan at Büyükdere, opposite Tarabya, in 1828; from *Records of Travels in Turkey, Greece, and of a Cruise in the Black Sea* by Captain Adolphus Slade, RN, FRAS.

In the forenoon the ambassador landed from the *Blonde*, which had anchored for the occasion within musket-shot of the plain, accompanied by a numerous suit of officers and gentlemen, forming altogether the most respectable Frank show ever exhibited to the Osmanleys. He mounted a richly caparisoned horse, and escorted by the marines of the frigate, her band playing before him, proceeded to the second tent, where sat the caimacan with the cazi-askers of Europe and of Asia, the latter of whom were interesting to look on, considering that, as the chief judges of Turkey, they could be excelled by none in duplicity. The caimacan relaxed his unmeaning countenance as his guest approached, and motioned to a low stool; but the ambassador disregarding this little assumption of superiority, so consistent with Ottoman etiquette, placed himself on the divan beside him. No notice was taken; the important stool was quietly removed; the dragomans knelt on the carpet beside their respective masters, and the usual insipid string of compliments ensued. The *Blonde's* band performed lively airs, and her fine body of marines drew up quarter facing the imperial tent, affording, in our eyes, a gratifying contrast to the slouching, ill-dressed nizam dgeditt.

A banquet followed the preliminaries of pipes and coffee. . . . We were then conducted to another tent to be clothed. 'Feed and clothe the infidels' is the ancient expression; the custom remains, but it must be considered an honour in the present day rather than an insult, as formerly. Our clothing consisted of Spanish mantles, made of inferior cloth, of scarlet, red, or yellow, according to the wearer's rank. They gave us a grotesque appearance, increased by our hats, which, there being several military and fancy uniforms among us, were extremely varied in shape.

Presently tremendous firing and cheering from the Turkish fleet, which manned yards in the bay, announced the sultan's departure from Therapia. In six minutes his twelve-oared caique, distinguished by a gold eagle in the prow, traversed the mile between the palace and the plain. He then mounted a superb Arabian whose trappings were covered with jewels, (not so loose, as some sultans have fancied, as to fall out for the benefit of the crowd,) and advanced slowly to his tent, pages walking on either side with high peacock plumes to conceal his resplendent visage from profane eyes. The troops salaamed to the ground as he passed along, and drowned the notes of the bands with cries of 'Live a thousand years!'

He reposed an unreasonable time, considering that the embassy was waiting, ready 'clothed and fed'. At length, a capidgi informed us that he was ready. On our entering the audience tent, a remnant of ancient prejudice in regard of Christians was displayed in an equal number of dismounted cavalry mingling with our ranks by way of precaution; yet, so quietly was the manœuvre performed, that, had not the cause been present to our minds, it would scarcely have attracted notice. It is to be remarked that the whole party wore swords, an honour which no Christian, except General Sebastiani, to whom Selim III accorded it, has enjoyed since Amurath I was stabbed in his tent by a Servian after the battle of Cossova; since when ambassadors have always been disarmed and held while in the presence.

The sultan received the embassy with great simplicity; his selictar and his serrkiatib were the only individuals present. In person he was equally divested of sultanic pomp. Instead of robes of golden tissue, and a cashmere turban concealed by precious stones, he wore a plain blue military cloak and trowsers, with no other ornament than a diamond chelengk in his fez, and steel spurs on his Wellington boots.

[90] The Sweet Waters of Asia in 1855; from *Constantinople during the Crimean War* by Lady Hornby.

Therapia, October 26th, 1855.

My dear Julia,

On Friday we went in a caïque to the 'Valley of the Sweet Waters of Asia,' – The Turkish Hyde Park. It is a charming spot, shut in by ranges of hills on three sides, with the Bosphorus glittering before it, and a fine view of the opposite castles of Europe, with their ivy-covered walls and towers. We landed on a kind of terrace, beyond which was a very large white marble fountain, looking, as all fountains do here, like a square-built temple, ornamented with inscriptions in coloured and golden letters. A stream of water fell from each side into a deep tank, out of which some poor Turkish women were filling their little earthen water-jars. Further on, under the shade of some magnificent plane-trees, sat the women of a higher class, on cushions which their slaves had brought from the caïques.

Nothing, in point of colouring and grouping, could be more strikingly beautiful than these clusters of women by the trees and fountain. Imagine five or six in a row; their jet-black eyes shining through their white veils, under which you can see the gleam of jewels which confine their hair (often dressed, by the bye, very much *à la Eugénie*). Your first impression is that they look just like a bed of splendid flowers. The lady at the top of the row of cushions, and evidently the chief wife, is dressed in a feridjee of the palest pink, edged with black velvet or silver; her face and neck all snow-white gauze, under which gleams a silver wreath or sprigs of jewels: for the *yashmak* in these days is so transparent as rather to add to the beauty of the wearer than to hide it.[1] She generally carries a large fan of peacocks' feathers, with both sides alike. The next is arrayed in the palest straw-colour shot with white; then perhaps follows an emerald-green, edged with gold, and by her side a lovely violet. The white yashmak contrasts prettily with all these colours. The feridjees of the slaves are often of a bright yellow or scarlet, edged with black, which, with the few dressed in darkest brown and green, harmonize perfectly with the light and delicate colours.

The Turkish women have certainly wonderful art in blending colours. In fact, I hardly know how my eyes will bear a return to England. Here the water, the sky, the houses, the dresses, the boats are so gay and beautiful, – the cypress-trees and the valleys so rich and green.

The Valley of the Sweet Waters takes its name from a small stream which winds through it and falls into the Bosphorus just above the fountain I mentioned. The water of this stream is highly prized for its purity, but, owing to the heavy rains of a day

[1] During the war the Turkish ladies wore particularly gay-coloured and beautiful feridjees; since that time, – first from motives of national economy, and afterwards from the present Sultan being a more strict Mussulman than Abdul Medjid, – an imperial order has been issued forbidding the use of any but plain and dark ones.

or two before, it was now rather muddy. So I braved the anger of the nymph of the spring by refusing to taste of its tiny waves, but invoked of her health and beauty for the poor Turkish women, – for it is their only possession, – and gave up my place to a veiled lady who was trying to drink without showing her face, which seemed to be a difficult process. We then walked through the valley, and watched the beautiful effect of light and shade upon the surrounding hills, crowned with cypress and other trees, and with here and there a pretty kiosk and garden. There are no roads here; so by a lane that would shame the roughest in Ireland, came the Sultan's married daughter, – married to Aali Ghalib Pasha, the son of Reschid Pasha. Edmund helped Lady Robinson *into some brambles* on the steep bank; I was already safely wedged in the roots of an old fig-tree; and thus we quietly awaited the passing of the Asiatic beauties. . . . We could not see much of the lady (who is said to be very lovely), the Negroes keeping close to the windows, as they splashed up the mud all over their uniforms; besides which, her yashmak was thickly folded. I could only see plainly her beautiful fan of snow-white feathers, the handle glittering with emeralds.

The lady on the opposite seat (there were three in the carriage) was more thinly veiled, very young, and very pretty. I saw her face plainly, and her feridjee being a *little* off her shoulders, I threw an envious glance on a violet-coloured velvet jacket embroidered with gold, and fastened at the throat with a large jewelled clasp, which gleamed through the gauzy veil. As to beauty of mere dress and ease of attitude, nothing that I have seen in life or in pictures can give the slightest idea of the wonderful grace, the extreme delicacy, and bird-of-paradise-like uselessness of the Turkish belle. Women of rank look like hothouse flowers, and are really *cultivated* to the highest perfection of physical beauty, having no other employment but to make their skins as snow-white and their eyebrows as jet-black as possible. When young, their skin is literally as white as their veils, with the faintest tinge of pink on the cheek, like that in the side of a shell, which blends exquisitely with the tender apple-leaf green, and soft violet colours, of which they are so fond.

The reverse of the picture is, that after the first bloom of youth is past, the skin becomes yellow and sickly-looking, and you long to give the yashmak a pull and admit a fresh breeze to brighten up the fine features.

A fountain at the Sweet Waters of Asia, on the Bosphorus; drawing by William H. Bartlett in Julia Pardoe's *The Beauties of the Bosphorus*, 1861

[91] The Sweet Waters of Asia (Kiat Haneh) in the 1920s; from *Constantinople, Settings and Traits* by H.G. Dwight.

On this hilltop stood in old times the castle of Cosmidion, where Godfrey of Bouillon and Bohemund stopped with their men on the way to the first crusade. The castle took its name from the adjoining church of SS. Cosmas and Damian, built by Theodosius the Younger and rebuilt with magnificence by Justinian. . . . Two small streams come together here, the Cydaris and the Barbyses as they once were called, and they played a particular part in the mythology of Byzantium. Io, fleeing from the jealousy of Hera, gave birth to her daughter Keroessa at the foot of the hill where the two streams meet. The child was nursed by Semistra, who gave her name to the hill in question, and in whose honour an altar anciently stood at the meeting-place of the rivers. Keroessa became in turn the mother of Byzas, founder of

Byzantium. The father of Byzas was no less a personage than Poseidon, god of the sea, and the son married Phidalia, daughter of the river Barbyses. How it happened that Byzas also came from so far away as Megara I do not pretend to know; but in the name Keroessa, which seems to be connected with the metamorphosis of Io, we have the mythic origin of the name of the Golden Horn.

The two rivers are now called Ali Bey Souyou and Kiat Haneh Souyou, and a power-house has taken the place of the altar of Semistra. The upper branches of both valleys are bridged by a number of aqueducts, of all periods from Justinian to Süleïman, and emperors and sultans alike loved to take refuge in this pleasant wilderness. . . . It is with the name of Ahmed III, however, that the two valleys are chiefly associated. . . . He delighted above all things in flowers, water, and illuminations – though I cannot conceal that he also cherished an extreme admiration for breathing beauty. He was one of the greatest builders who have reigned in Constantinople, and he had the good fortune to discover a grand vizier of like tastes with himself. It happened that an intelligent young envoy of theirs, known by the curious name of Twenty-eight Mehmed, from the number of his years when he signed the Peace of Passarowitz went, in 1720, on a special embassy to Paris. He brought back such accounts of the court of Louis XV, such pictures and presents also, as to change the whole course of Ottoman architecture. So vivid a description in particular did the ambassador give the new palace of Versailles and of its older rival at Marly-le-Roi, that Ahmed III resolved to imitate them. He had already built a seat on the banks of the Ali Bey Souyou, whose magnificent planes and cypresses may still be admired there. He then turned his attention to the Kiat Haneh valley, where he played strange tricks with the river, laid out gardens, built a palace, and commanded his courtiers to follow his example – *à la* Louis XIV and the Signs of the Zodiac. There grew up as by magic a continuous line of villas and gardens from the village of Kiat Haneh to that of Sütlüjeh, opposite Eyoub. And the fête which the sultan gave when he inaugurated this new pleasure-ground was the most splendid of the many that marked his long reign. . . .

For a few weeks in spring, beginning with the open-air festival of Hîdîr Eless, the lower part of the valley is a favourite place of resort. Sunday and Friday are the popular days. Then arbours of saplings thatched with dried boughs follow the curve of the river; then picnic parties spread rugs or matting on the grass, partaking of strange meats while masters of pipe and drum enchant their ears; then groups of Turkish ladies, in gay silks, dot the sward like tulips; then itinerant venders of fruit, of sweets, of nuts, of ice-cream, do hawk about their wares; then fortune-tellers, mountebanks, bear tamers, dancers, Punch and Judy shows may be seen; and boats pass and repass on the river like motors on the Corso. Most of them are *sandals* of the smarter kind. . . . I remember noticing one day on the river a gaudy little skiff rowed by two young and gaily costumed boatmen. In the stern sat an extremely fat Turkish lady, steering. She was dressed decorously in black, and the black veil thrown back from her face allowed every one to remark that she was neither in her first youth nor particularly handsome. Yet boatmen snickered as she passed, and rowdies called after her in slang which it seemed to me should not be used to a lady. I said as much to my *kaïkhi*, who told me that the lady was a famous *demi-mondaine*, named Madam Falcon, and that for the rest I must never expect such good manners at Kiat Haneh as at Gyök Sou. I must confess that I looked at Madam Falcon with some interest the next time we passed; for the Turkish half-world is of all half-worlds the most invisible, and so far as I knew I had never seen a member of it before. Madam Falcon paid no attention to the curiosity she aroused. Sitting there impassively in her black dress, with her smooth yellow skin, she made one think of a graven image, of some Indian Bouddha in old ivory. So venerable a person she seemed, so benevolent, so decorous and dead to the world, that she only made her half-world more remote and invisible than ever. But she was a sign – in spite of the smart brougham driving slowly along the shore with a Palace eunuch sitting on the box – that the great days of Kiat Haneh are gone.

[92] The building of the castle of Rumeli Hisari on the Bosphorus; from *Narrative of Travels in Europe, Asia, and Africa* . . . by Evliya Efendi, translated by Ritter J. von Hammer-Purgstall.

It was formerly an old convent of the Infidels on the top of the hill inhabited by a monk, who was secretly a Mussulman, and was at

The Castle of Rumeli Hisari; from *Descrizione Topografica,* 1784 by C. Comidas de Carbognano

the head of three hundred Dervíshes. As soon as he heard of Mahommed II having ascended the throne at Adrianople, he sent him a message to let him know the good news, that for him had been reserved the conquest of Constantinople, suggesting at the same time that he should build a castle here and two at the Dardanelles to intercept all provisions for Constantinople; and that meanwhile the army should move from Adrianople. Mohammed overjoyed with this news made all possible exertions. He went first, with the leave of the Greek Emperor Constantine, on a hunting party to Terkos on the shore of the Black Sea; where, exchanging presents with the commanding officer, he pursued his hunting without the smallest resistance, and sent presents of what he killed to Constantinople. He begged leave to build on the spot where the castle now stands a hunting house, and consulted with the monk, who in secret was a Mussulman, and enjoyed his intimacy. Envoys came from Constantinople with the answer, that the Emperor would allow as much ground as a bull's hide would cover, but no more. Sultan Mohammed now traced out in the Envoy's presence the foundation of a tower no larger than a bull's hide. At the same time he commanded from Constantinople many thousand workmen and miners, who brought from the harbour of Borghaz on the Black Sea in one night from forty to fifty guns, placed them along the seashore and covered them with bushes. He then began to build the castle, concealing in the same way the foundations by bushes; after which he cut the hide by the monk's advice into small strips, by which he marked out the circumference of the castle on the lime rocks. The monk said, 'Gracious Emperor, your name being Mohammed, the same as the prophet, let this castle be built in the shape of the characters that form the name. It is now forty-one years since I received the destination to superintend this building, being a perfect architect, but I kept it secret from the world.' Thus saying, he called his workmen together, and built the castle of Rumeli in the form of the word Mohammed, as written in Cufic characters, which is to be read perfectly from the mountains of Anatoli. The tower on the top of the hill, seven stories high, represents the *mim* (m), the gate of the Dizdar the letter *ha* (h), the great tower on the sea-shore, the second *mim*, and the square on the side of the convent of Durmish Dedeh the *dal* (d). The letters which form the name of Mohammed, if taken in their arithmetic value give the number 92, which is also that of the bulwarks of this fortress. The arithmetic value of the letters, which compose the word khan being 651, there is the same number of battlements. The castle being built in six months, they burned the bushes, which hid it from the sight; the troops entered it rejoicing, with the necessary artillery and ammunition, and the architect throwing away the mask of a monk, declared himself publicly to be a faithful Moslim. He begged to be made Dizdar, or commanding officer of the castle, which was granted him. The Greek Emperor receiving this news sent an ambassador to complain, that a castle had been built contrary to the peace. Sultan Mohammed in answer sent the hide of the bull cut into small pieces, and said that he would plead guilty of the breach of the peace, if the castle exceeded in the least this granted measure. The Infidels now wished to make a new treaty of peace, but Mahommed would not grant it, and built two other castles at the Dardanelles, by which means he intercepted from both seas the conveyance of provisions, so that he nearly reduced Constantinople by famine. Such is the castle of Rumeli resting on the west side on towering rocks, and therefore without a fosse.

[93] The aqueducts of the Forest of Belgrade; from *Sinan* by Arthur Stratton.

In the last year of his life, the Sultan [Süleyman], with his Royal Chief Architect, who had twenty-two years of life ahead of him, saw the water of the aqueducts pour in from the Belgrade Forest to the Forty Fountains in abundance, clear, fresh, pure water, sparkling in the sunlight. It has never since ceased to flow (except today in the hours of the night when the supply now has to be rationed in the expanding city). . . .

On one of his good days, probably before 1564, Süleyman rode out to get away, to take a breath of air, and to savor his only remaining pleasure - watching his Royal Chief Architect at work. Sinan, seventy-five that spring, was five years older than the Sultan, but he was flexible and quick in all his muscles and joints. The Sultan rode along, ambling, following the line of the aqueducts that Sinan had surveyed and drawn on the maps. The water from the springs and reservoirs in the Belgrade Forest flows by gravity seeking its own level, a matter of fifteen or twenty miles to the fountains in the city. The forest watershed took its name from Süleyman's and Sinan's first victory, the one as a young Sultan in the first year of his reign, the other as the Janissary engineering cadet out in 1521 on campaign, in action for the first time. As the phrase goes, Belgrade was the baptism of fire for both men; and it had taken place forty-two or forty-three years earlier in their lives.

Süleyman searched the piers and arches of the masonry aqueduct, some of them complete, others rising from the centering and scaffoldings, with the stone-cutters and masons at work on the ground and on the platforms in the air, shouting down for mortar. Süleyman reined in to look for Sinan, and, not finding him, to watch the men pulling at the end of the system of ropes and pulleys to haul up the required load.

He looked at the arches and the piers striding across the rolling landscape of hills and valleys, green and sunlit on that good day, the skies blue and high above the white clouds scudding from the north and casting moving shadows on the fields of wheat and the groves and orchards of apples and peaches with Lombardy poplars standing guard. Here and there the finger of a minaret pointed above a village dome to call attention to God and to man in his nature.

From the imperial walled city on its seven hills to the Belgrade Forest on the Black Sea, the landscape is old and gentle. There at the end of winter first wild cyclamen and snowdrops bloom, and later in spring pink tree peonies. Above the Bosphorus there is no violence to be seen in the fertile countryside. But at the mouth of the strait craggy little mountains pile up, one topped by the frowning ramparts of a Genoese castle above rock cliffs along the wild shore. The upended strata there bear witness to the cataclysm that raised the Alps and the Himalayas, sunk the basin of the Mediterranean, and split open the channel that lets the waters of the Danube and the Russian rivers flow out of the Black sea past Byzantium-Constantinople-Istanbul into the deep Sea of Marmara. Turkey is a country of earthquakes.

In 1564, before the mortar of the finished aqueducts had had the time to harden, an earthquake threw down the greatest of the spans, the largest of them built up in two and three tiers of arches to carry the water across ravines, the longest 170 meters (560 feet) and 265 meters (875 feet) in length. In those days before geologists charted the faults and the rifts in the earth's unfinished surfaces, earthquakes were accepted as mysterious acts of God.

[94] The Sultan's Palace at Beylerbey on the Bosphorus; from *The City of the Sultan and the Domestic Manners of the Turks in 1836* by Miss Pardoe.

The first glance of the interior is not imposing. The double staircase, sweeping crescentwise through the centre of the entrance, contracts its extent so much as to give it the appearance of being insignificant in its proportions; an effect which is, moreover, considerably heightened by the elaborated ornaments of the carved and gilded balustrades and pillars. But such is far from being the case in reality; as, from this outer apartment, with its flooring of inlaid woods, arabesqued ceiling, and numerous casements, open no less than eight spacious saloons, appropriated to the Imperial Household.

Above this suite are situated the State Apartments; gorgeous with gilding, and richly furnished with every luxury peculiar alike to the East and to the West. The Turkish divans of brocade and embroidered velvet are relieved by sofas and lounges of European fashion – bijouterie from Geneva – porcelain from Sèvres – marbles from Italy – gems from Pompeii – Persian carpets – English hangings – and, in the principal saloons, six of the most magnificent, if not actually *the* six *most* magnificent, pier glasses in the world; a present to the Sultan from the Emperor of Russia, after the treaty of Unkiar Skelessi.

Upwards of twelve feet in height, and about six feet in width, of one single plate, and enclosed in a deep frame of silver gilt, bearing the united arms of the two empires; these costly glasses reflect in every direction the ornaments of the apartment; and produce an effect almost magical. While the highly elaborated ceiling, richly ornamented with delicate wreaths of flowers; and the bright-patterned carpet covering the floor, combine to fling over the vast saloon an atmosphere of light and gladness, which is increased by the dazzling glories of the parterre spread out beneath the windows; with its flashing fountain, golden orangery, and long line of gleaming lattices. . . .

The Banquetting Hall is entirely lined with inlaid woods of rare and beautiful kinds finely mosaiced; the ceiling and the floor being alike enriched with a deep garland of grapes and vine-leaves, flung over groups of pine-apples of exquisite workmanship.

Hence, a long gallery conducted us to the private apartments of the Sultan; and on every side were graceful fountains of white marble, whose flashing waters fell with a musical sound into their sculptured basins. In one, the stream trickled from a plume of feathers wrought in alabaster; and so delicately worked that they almost appeared to bend beneath the weight of the sparkling drops – in another, the stream gushed forth, overflowing a lotus-flower, upon whose lip sported a group of Cupids. The private apartments, which separated the harem from the state wing of the Palace, were the very embodiment of luxurious comfort; two of them were lined with wicker-work painted cream colour; the prettiest possible idea, executed in the best possible style. . . .

The Bath was beautiful. As we passed the crimson door with its crescent-shaped cornice, we entered a small hall in which two swans, the size of life, and wrought in pure white marble, were pouring forth the water that supplies the cold stream necessary to the bathers. The cooling-room was richly hung with embroidered draperies; and the mirror was surmounted by the Ottoman arms wrought in gold and enamel. The Bath itself realized a vision of the Arabian Nights, with its soft, dreamy twilight, its pure and glittering whiteness, and its exquisitely imagined fountains – and the subdued effect of our voices, dying away in indistinct murmurs in the distance, served to heighten the illusion.

Altogether, the Summer Palace of Sultan Mahmoud is as fair within, as without; and I have already said that it is the most elegant edifice on the Bosphorus.

[95] The Empress Eugénie of France is insulted (by mistake) by the Sultana Validé, mother of Sultan Abdul Aziz, in 1869 at the Beylerbey Palace; from an unpublished memoir of Isabel Vesey, written *c.*1922.

[The Empress Eugénie] had been to Constantinople shortly before the fall of the Empire, as the official representative of France, in 1869, after [*sic. In fact before*] opening the Suez Canal. She was received with great pomp, although unaccompanied by Napoleon III. She represented France, the powerful and dreaded France of that period, and must have been fully conscious of this. On the day we arrived [*a later visit in 1910*], she contemplated the Bosphorus from the deck and told many anecdotes of the 1869 visit. Sultan Abdul Aziz in 1869 put the Begler Bey at her disposal, so of course she re-visited it in 1910. Arrangements were made for us to see the Palace, and we spent one afternoon there wandering through the large rooms and gardens, finishing up with Turkish coffee in the pavilion. She had some trying moments in 1869 which caused her much amusement to look back upon . . . On one occasion the mother of the Sultan, who takes precedence of all the other ladies, even of the Sultana, was to receive the Empress in her Palace. All went well till she saw her arrive, on the arm of the Sultan, who was to present her. The sight was too much for the outraged feelings of the Queen Mother. The Sultan, I believe, appeared to be enjoying himself. Stepping forward, she slapped the Empress on the cheek! 'This reception', said H.M., 'naturally alarmed me; and when I was offered coffee later on, the affair having settled down, I suspected it of being poisoned and left it. However, it was pointed out to me that this would be considered an insult, so to avoid giving rise to international complications, I was obliged to swallow it!' . . .

As we were leaving Begler Bey Palace, she stopped on the threshold and turned to take a last look. She said to one of us, 'Do you know, the windows of my room pleased me so much that I had the measurements and designs of the frames taken, and a similar frame made to fit the window of my bedroom at the Tuileries. The carpenter finished his work and fitted it to the window early in September 1870, and the last thing I did in the Tuileries on the morning of my last day there, was to inspect the new window to make sure that the copy was well carried out.' Begler Bey Palace is on the banks of the Bosphorus, with marble steps leading to the water's edge. The Empress descended them in silence, but when we had all entered the launch and put out from shore, she told us that in 1869, as she was going from Begler Bey to the official dinner given in her honour by the Sultan, the Imperial caique nearly ran into another boat. Seeing danger, the Empress motioned to the rowers to stop, and was barely in time to avoid a collision.

Life, Customs and Morals in Istanbul

The Empress Theodora; from a sixth-century mosaic at Ravenna

[96] The morals of Theodora before the Byzantine Emperor Justinian fell in love with her and married her, in the sixth century; from *The Secret History* by Procopius, translated by G.A. Williamson.

In Byzantium there was man called Acacius, a keeper of the circus animals, belonging to the Green faction and entitled the Bearward. This man died of sickness while Anastasius occupied the imperial throne, leaving three daughters, Comito, Theodora, and Anastasia, of whom the eldest had not yet completed her seventh year. The widow married again. . . . When the children were old enough, they were at once put on the stage there by their mother, as their appearance was very attractive; not all at the same time, however, but as each one seemed to her to be mature enough for this profession. The eldest one, Comito, was already one of the most popular harlots of the day. Theodora, who came next, clad in a little tunic with long sleeves, the usual dress of a slave girl, used to assist her in various ways, following her about and invariably carrying on her shoulders the bench on which her sister habitually sat at public meetings. For the time being Theodora was still too undeveloped to be capable of sharing a man's bed or having intercourse like a woman; but she acted as a sort of male prostitute to satisfy customers of the lowest type, and slaves at that, who when accompanying their owners to the theatre seized their opportunity to divert themselves in this revolting manner; and for some considerable time she remained in a brothel, given up to this unnatural bodily commerce. But as soon as she was old enough and fully developed, she joined the women on the stage and promptly became a courtesan, of the type our ancestors called 'the dregs of the army'. For she was not flautist or harpist; she was not even qualified to join the corps of dancers; but she merely sold her attractions to anyone who came along, putting her whole body at his disposal.

Later she joined the actors in all the business of the theatre and played a regular part in their stage performances, making herself the butt of their ribald buffoonery. She was extremely clever and had a biting wit, and quickly became popular as a result. There was not a particle of modesty in the little hussy, and no one ever saw her taken aback: she complied with the most outrageous demands without the slightest hesitation, and she was the sort of girl who if somebody walloped her or boxed her ears would make a jest of it and roar with laughter; and she would throw off her clothes and exhibit naked to all and sundry those regions, both in front and behind, which the rules of decency require to be kept veiled and hidden from masculine eyes.

She used to tease her lovers by keeping them waiting, and by constantly playing about with novel methods of intercourse she could always bring the lascivious to her feet; so far from waiting to be invited by anyone she encountered, she herself by cracking dirty jokes and wiggling her hips suggestively would invite all who came her way, especially if they were still in their teens. Never was anyone so completely given up to unlimited self-indulgence. Often she would go to a bring-your-own-food dinner-party with ten young men or more, all at the peak of their physical powers and with fornication as their chief object in life, and would lie with all her fellow-diners in turn the whole night long: when she had reduced them all to a state of exhaustion she would go to their menials, as many as thirty on occasions, and copulate with every one of them; but not even so could she satisfy her lust.

One night she went into the house of a distinguished citizen during the drinking, and, it is said, before the eyes of all the guests she stood up on the end of the couch near their feet, pulled up her dress in the most disgusting manner as she stood there, and brazenly displayed her lasciviousness. And though she brought three openings into service, she often found fault with Nature, grumbling because Nature had not made the openings in her nipples wider than is normal, so that she could devise another variety of intercourse in that region. Naturally she was frequently pregnant, but by using pretty well all the tricks of the trade she was able to induce immediate abortion.

Often in the theatre, too, in full view of all the people she would throw off her clothes and stand naked in their midst, having only a girdle about her private parts and her groins – not, however, because she was ashamed to expose these also to the public, but because no one is allowed to appear there absolutely naked: a girdle round the groins is compulsory. With this minimum covering she would spread herself out and lie face upwards on the floor. Servants on whom this task had been imposed would sprinkle barley grains over her private parts, and geese trained for the purpose used to pick them off one by one with their bills and swallow them. Theodora, so far from blushing when she stood up again, actually seemed to be proud of this performance. For she was not only shameless herself, but did more than anyone else to encourage shamelessness.

Many times she threw off her clothes and stood in the middle of the actors on the stage, leaning over backwards or pushing out her behind to invite both those who had already enjoyed her and those who had not been intimate as yet, parading her own special brand of gymnastics. With such lasciviousness did she misuse her own body that she appeared to have her private parts not like other women in the place intended by nature, but in her face! And again, those who were intimate with her showed by so doing that they were not having intercourse in accordance with the laws of nature; and every person of any decency who happened to meet her in the forum would swing round and beat a hasty retreat, for fear he might come in contact with any of the hussy's garments and so appear tainted with this pollution. For to those who saw her, especially in the early hours of the day, she was a bird of ill omen. As for her fellow-actresses, she habitually and constantly stormed at them like a fury; for she was malicious in the extreme.

[97] The dress and conversation of the Sultana Fatima in the early eighteenth century; from *Letters of the Right Honourable Lady Mary Wortley Montagu.*

(Lady Mary Wortley Montagu (1689–1762) was the daughter of the Marquess of Dorchester and wife of Edward Wortley Montagu, MP for Huntingdon, who was appointed Ambassador to Sultan Ahmed III in 1716. The Sultan was at war with the Holy Roman Empire, and Montagu was expected to act as mediator and peace-maker. They spent two years in Constantinople. While there, Lady Mary set out to learn Turkish. Later in life she separated from her husband and settled in Italy. An accomplished poet, satirist and blue-stocking, she had a famous row with Pope who lampooned her mercilessly.)

Her dress was something so surprizingly rich, that I cannot forbear describing it to you. She wore a vest, called Dualma, which differs from a Caftan by longer sleeves, and folding over at the bottom. It was of purple cloth, strait to her shape, and thick set, on each side down to her feet and round the sleeves, with pearls of the best water, of the same size as their buttons commonly are. You must not suppose that I mean as large as those of my Lord – , but about the bigness of a pea; and to these buttons, large loops of diamonds, in the form of those gold loops, so common on birth-day coats. This habit was tied at the waist, with two large tassels of smaller pearls, and round the arms embroidered with large diamonds. Her shift was fastened at the bottom, with a great diamond, shaped like a lozenge; her girdle as broad as the broadest English ribband, entirely covered with diamonds. Round her neck she wore three chains, which reached to her knees; one of large pearl, at the bottom of which hung a fine coloured emerald, as big as a turkey-egg; another, consisting of two hundred emeralds, close joined together, of the more lively green, perfectly matched, every one as large as a half-crown piece, and as thick as three crown pieces, and another of small emeralds, perfectly round. But her ear-rings eclipsed all the rest. They were two diamonds shaped exactly like pears, as large as a big hazle nut. Round her Talpoche she had four strings of pearl – the whitest and most perfect in the world, at least enough to make four necklaces, every one as large as the Duchess of Marlborough's, and of the same shape, fastened with two roses, consisting of a large ruby for the middle stone, and round them twenty drops of clean diamonds to each. Besides this, her head-dress was covered with bodkins of emeralds and diamonds. She wore large diamond bracelets, and had five rings on her fingers (except Mr. Pitt's) the largest I ever saw in my life. 'Tis for jewellers to compute the value of these things; but, according to the common estimation of jewels in our part of the world, her whole dress must be worth a hundred thousand pounds sterling. This I am sure of, that no European Queen has half the quantity, and the Empress's jewels, though very fine, would look very mean near hers. She gave me a dinner of fifty dishes of meat, which (after their fashion) were placed on the table but one at a time, and was extremely tedious. But the magnificence of her table answered very well to that of her dress. The knives were of gold, and the hafts set with diamonds. But the piece of luxury which grieved my eyes, was the table cloth and napkins, which were all tiffany embroidered with silk and gold, in the finest

Turkish woman's jewelled head-dress; from *A Voyage to the Levant* by N. Corneille de Bruyn, 1702

manner, in natural flowers. It was with the utmost regret that I made use of these costly napkins, which were as finely wrought as the finest handkerchiefs that ever came out of this country. You may be sure, that they were entirely spoiled before dinner was over. The sherbet (which is the liquor they drink at meals) was served in china bowls; but the covers and salvers massy gold. After dinner, water was brought in gold basons, and towels of the same kind with the napkins, which I very unwillingly wiped my hands upon, and coffee was served in china with gold Soucoups [*saucers*].

The Sultana seemed in a very good humour, and talked to me with the utmost civility. I did not omit this opportunity of learning all that I possibly could of the Seraglio, which is so entirely unknown amongst us. She assured me that the story of the Sultan's throwing a handkerchief [*see page 229*] is altogether fabulous; and the manner, upon that occasion, no other than this: He sends the Kyslir Aga, to signify to the lady the honour he intends her. She is immediately complimented upon it by the others, and led to the bath, where she is perfumed and dressed in the most magnificent and becoming manner. The Emperor precedes his visit by a royal present, and then comes into her apartment: neither is there any such thing as her creeping in at the bed's foot. She said, that the first he made choice of, was always after the first in rank, and not the mother of the eldest son, as other writers would make us believe. Sometimes the Sultan diverts himself in the company of all his ladies who stand in a circle round him. And she confessed, they were ready to die with envy and jealousy of the happy she, that he distinguished by any appearance of preference. But this seemed to me neither better nor worse than the circles in most courts, where the glance of the monarch is watched, and every smile is waited for with impatience, and envied by those who cannot obtain it.

[98] A seventeenth-century account of the 'filthy and unnaturall lust of the Bassa' and of the men and the ladies at Court; from *The History of the Serrail and of the Court of the Grand Seigneur, Emperour of the Turks* by Seigneur Michael Baudier of Languedoc.

The great fortunes which are found in the Courts of great Monarches, produce great riches: and these furnish Courtiers with delights, in the which they glut their sensuall and brutish appetites. The *Bassa's* of the Court, great in dignities and abounding in riches, plunge themselves in all sorts of voluptuousnesse, and their spirits mollified in the myre of filthy pleasures, they seeke them by a contrary course, and demand that of nature which she hath not: Being many times tired with the love of women, they abandon their affections to young Boyes, and desperatly follow the allurements of their beauties: They imbrace them, and use them in the place of women. This abhominable vice is so ordinary in the *Turks* Court, as yee shall hardly find one *Bassa* that is not miserably inclined unto it: It serves for an ordinary subject of entertainment among the greatest when they are together; they speake not but of the perfections of their *Ganimedes*: One sayes, they have brought mee from *Hungarie* the most beautifull and accomplished Minion, that ever was borne among men: he is the height of my felicitie, and the only object that my thoughts adore. Another saith, I have lately bought a young Infant of *Russia*, who hath not his like in all the East, and I dare assure you his countenance is not humane, but that of an Angell: Some Sot of the company intreats him earnestly to have a sight, and that hee may bee satisfied by his eyes. These are the discourses of those lustfull Goats. The care they have to keepe neatly, and to attire richly these poore creatures, designated to so damnable an use is not small: the Eunuches which have them in guard are alwayes neere them, to beautifie them outwardly, they plaite their haire with Gold, and sometimes with Pearles, they perfume them, they attire them in Robes of Cloth of Gold, and adde to their naturall beauty whatsoever Arte can invent: what vertue, what wisdome, what pietie can be found in a Court composed of such men? He that is the Head and commands them, doth furnish this pernicious example; for the *Sultans Serrail* is full of such Boyes, chosen out of the most beautifull of the East, and vowed to his unnaturall pleasures. . . .

The provocations of a hot Climate, the servitude of women restrained, and the bad example of loose and luxurious husbands, are the principall Motives of the loves, wherunto the Turkish Ladies abandon themselves. Some to have free exercise, take occasion to see their Lovers, when as they are allowed to goe to the Bath, to receive the Purifications which their Law doth enjoyne them: others better qualified, from whom the commoditie of Waters and Stones which are in their houses, hath taken away this pretext, make use of other men. Sometimes they borrow the habit of their slaves, and thus disguised goe to find them they love: When this course is difficult, by the encounter of some great obstacle, they imploy men and women (whom they reward) to find them subjects which may please their eyes, and content their passions; but this last meanes is more apparent and better knowne in *Constantinople*: for such Messengers of love discovering themselves to some that refuse them, they divulge their secret. They addresse themselves usually to Christian strangers of the West, and if they can finde Frenchmen, the service they doe unto their Mistresses is the more pleasing: The disposition of their humours, the grace of their bodies (say they) and the ordinary courtesie of their Nation, makes them more desired: But it is dangerous to serve the passions of such Lovers, where the recompence and the reward of a painfull love, is a Dagger or a Glasse of poyson: For these cruell women, when they have kept some young stranger three or foure dayes hidden in their Chambers, and have made use of him untill he be so tired and weary with their lasciviousnesse, as hee is no longer profitable, they stab him or poyson him, and cast his bodie into some Privie: Whether it be that they feare their affections should be discovered, or that their light and inconstant humours, doth alwayes demand new subjects, or that it is the nature of their lascivious love, to change into Rage and Fury tragically cruell.

[99] Byzantine eunuchs; from *Byzantine Civilisation* by Steven Runciman

Offices about the persons of the Emperor and Empress and about the Palaces were reserved for eunuchs: a custom that had begun in Diocletian's day and had developed since. Each Palace was under its Papias, the Papias of the Great Palace being assisted by a Deuteras who saw to the ceremonial robes and furniture of the Court. We are never actually told the numbers and duties of lesser members of the Household. The Emperor and Empress each had their Controllers of the Table and of the Wardrobe. But the chief of the eunuchs was the High Chamberlain, the Paracoemomenus, who in the late Ninth and the Tenth Centuries was the chief minister of the Empire. Samonas under Leo VI, Theophanes under Romanus I and Basil for almost all the latter half of the Tenth Century, were practically Grand Viziers. The office was not always filled, and once it had been held not by a eunuch but by Basil the Macedonian, under Michael III. The advantage of having eunuchs in high confidential positions was obvious. They had no descendants for whom to intrigue: and an unwritten but unbreakable law debarred them from the Imperial throne. The employment of eunuchs, characteristic in particular of the Empire at its zenith in the Tenth Century, was one of its most useful weapons against feudal devolution. . . .

For a boy to be really successful, it might be wise to castrate him; for Byzantium was the eunuch's paradise. Even the noblest parents were not above mutilating their sons to help their advancement, nor was there any disgrace in it. A eunuch could not wear the Imperial crown nor could he, from his nature, transfer hereditary rights; and therein lay his power. A boy born too close to the throne could thus be side-tracked and then be safely allowed to go forward as he pleased. Thus Nicetas, the young son of Michael I, was castrated when his father fell, and later, despite his dangerous birth, rose to be the Patriarch Ignatius. Thus Romanus I castrated not only his bastard Basil, who as Paracœmomenus, the Great Chamberlain, ruled the Empire for several decades, but also his youngest legitimate son, Theophylact, whom he intended to be Patriarch. A large proportion of the Patriarchs of Constantinople were eunuchs; and eunuchs were particularly encouraged in the Civil Service, where the castrated bearer of a title took precedence of his unmutilated compeer and where many high ranks were reserved for eunuchs alone. Even over the army and navy a eunuch was often in command. Narses in the Sixth Century and Nicephorus Uranus in the Tenth were perhaps the most brilliant examples. Alexius I had a eunuch admiral, Eustathius Cymineanus: while after the disasters of the Manzikert campaign it was a eunuch, Nicephorus the Logothete, who managed to reform the army. A few posts such as the Prefecture of the City were traditionally closed to them.

[100] Eunuchs in the Ottoman Empire; from *Constantinople* by Edmondo de Amicis.

But there are other beings at Constantinople who excite more compassion than the dogs, and they are the eunuchs, who, as they were introduced among the Turks, despite the formal precepts of the Koran, that condemns the infamous degradation of nature, still subsist, notwithstanding the recent laws which prohibit the traffic, since avidity for gold, and selfishness are stronger than the law. These unfortunates are to be met at every step in the streets, as they are found on every page of history. In the background of every event in the history of Turkey stands one of these sinister figures, with a list of conspirators in his hand; covered with gold, and stained with blood, victim, favorite or executioner, openly or secretly formidable, upright like a spectre in the shadow of the throne, or dimly seen in the opening of a mysterious door. So now in Constantinople, in the midst of the busy crowd, in the bazaars, among the merry multitude at the Sweet Waters, under the arches of the mosques, beside carriages, in the steamers and caiques, at all feasts, in all crowds, is seen this semblance of a man, this doleful figure, whose presence makes a dark, lugubrious stain upon the smiling aspect of Oriental life. Their political importance has diminished with the omnipotence of the court, and as Oriental jealousy relaxes, their consequence in private houses has also much declined; it is difficult for them now to find in riches and domination, a compensation for their misfortune; no Ghaznefer Agà could now be found to consent to mutilation in order to be made chief of the white eunuchs; they are all in these days most certainly victims, and victims without hope of redress; bought or stolen as children in Abyssinia or in Syria, about one in three survives the infamous knife, and he is sold in defiance of the law, with a hypocrisy of secrecy more odious than an open market. They do not need to be pointed out, they are easily recognized. Almost all are tall, fat and flabby, with beardless, withered faces, short bodied, and long in the legs and arms. They wear the scarlet fez, a long dark frock coat and European trousers, and they carry a whip of hippopotamus hide, which is their insignia of office. They walk with long soft steps like big children. They accompany the ladies on foot or on horseback, either before or behind the carriage, sometimes one, sometimes two together, and keep a vigilant eye about them, which at the least irreverent look or action in the passer by, assumes an expression of ferocious anger. Except in such a case, their faces are absolutely void of expression, or else it is one of infinite weariness and depression. I do not remember ever to have seen one smile. There are some very young ones that look fifty years old, and some old ones that seem youths fallen into decrepitude in a day.

There are many so round, soft, fat, and shining, that they look like fattened swine; all are dressed in fine cloth, and perfumed like vain young dandies. There are heartless men who can pass these unfortunate beings with a laugh. Perhaps they think that having been such from childhood they do not comprehend their own wretchedness. On the contrary, it is known that they do understand and feel it . . .

And this infamy is still allowed; these unhappy wretches walk about the streets of a European city, live in the midst of men, and do not howl, or bite, or kill, or spit in the faces of that coward humanity that can look upon them without blushing or weeping, and that forms associations for the protection of dogs and cats! Their lives are one continual torture. When their mistresses do not find them helpful in their intrigues they hate them as spies and jailors, and torment them with cruel coquetries that drive them mad with fury, like the poor eunuch in the *Lettres Persanes*. Everything is sarcasm for them; they bear the names of flowers and perfumes, in allusion to the ladies whose custodians they are: they are *possessors of the hyacinths, guardians of the lilies, custodians of the roses and violets*, and sometimes, the miserable wretches fall in love! because in them the passions are not eradicated; and they are jealous and weep tears of blood; and often lose their reason altogether and strike. In the time of the Crimean war, a eunuch struck a French officer across the face with his whip, and the latter cut him down with his sabre. Who can say what sufferings are theirs at the sight of smiles, and beauty, or how often their hands grasp the hilt of the dagger. It is no wonder that in the immense void of their hearts there is room for the cold passions of hatred, revenge, and ambition; that they grow up acrid, biting, envious, cowardly, ferocious; that they are either stupidly faithful, or astutely treacherous, and that when they are powerful they seek to avenge upon men the wrong that has been done to them.

[101] The sale of slaves in Constantinople in the early nineteenth century; from Byron's *Don Juan*.

CXIV

Some went off dearly; fifteen hundred dollars
For one Circassian, a sweet girl, were given,
Warranted virgin; beauty's brightest colours
Had deck'd her out in all the hues of heaven:
Her sale sent home some disappointed bawlers
Who bade on till the hundreds reach'd eleven[1];
But when the offer went beyond, they knew
'Twas for the Sultan, and at once withdrew.

CVX

Twelve negresses from Nubia brought a price
Which the West Indian market scarce could bring,
Though Wilberforce, at last, has made it twice
What't was ere Aboliton; and the thing
Need not seem very wonderful, for vice
Is always much more splendid than a king:
The virtues, even the most exalted, Charity,
Are saving – vice spares nothing for a rarity.

[1] The manner of purchasing slaves is thus described in the plain and unaffected narrative of a German merchant, 'which,' says Mr. Thornton, 'as I have been able to ascertain its general authenticity, may be relied upon as correct.' The girls were introduced to me one after another. A Circassian maiden, eighteen years old, was the first who presented herself: she was well dressed, and her face was covered with a veil. She advanced towards me, bowed down and kissed my hand: by order of her master she walked backwards and forwards, to show her shape and the easiness of her gait and carriage. When she took off her veil, she displayed a bust of the most attractive beauty: she rubbed her cheeks with a wet napkin to prove that she had not used art to heighten her complexion; and she opened her inviting lips, to show a regular set of teeth of pearly whiteness. I was permitted to feel her pulse, that I might be convinced of the good state of her health and constitution. She was then ordered to retire while we deliberated upon the bargain. The price of this beautiful girl was four thousand piastres.

[102] Slaves under Ottoman rule in the late nineteenth century; from *Three Centuries: family chronicles of Turkey and Egypt* by Emine Foat Tugay.

(Emine Foat Tugay was born in 1897 to very distinguished parents and grandparents on both sides of her family. Her father was General Mahmud Muhtar Pasha, and her grandfather the famous Field-Marshal, Gazi Ahmed Muhtar Pasha. On her mother's side she descended from the Viceroys of Egypt (Mohammed Ali the Great), and Ismail Pasha. Her mother was the Princess Nimetullah. Nobody has better recorded and explained the sweet ways of aristocratic life in Ottoman Turkey before it was swept away by the Young Turks, Atatürk himself, and finally today's cost of living.)

During Ottoman rule, slaves were so much a part of family life that I am giving the subject full treatment, since any description of this period would be incomplete without it. So many false reports and inaccurate statements have been published regarding slaves and harem life that a brief description of the actual facts may not be out of place here. The word harem, of Arab origin, means privacy and seclusion. In so far as men and women led separate lives, it defined the building or the part of it where the family lived. This was inhabited mainly by women and the only men entitled to live in it, or even to enter it, were members of the family or, exceptionally, in cases of illness, a physician.

Just as the harem was the women's sphere so the selamlik was the room, wing, or separate building reserved for men. No woman was allowed to enter it, and service here was done by men. The selamlik was an indispensable adjunct of every house, konak, or palace. It should be understood that the Sultan's ceremonial procession to prayer in a mosque on Fridays, also called the Selamlik because it was attended only by men, had no connexion whatever with that part of a building similarly named. . . .

Possibly the most humane form of slavery was practised in the Ottoman Empire, where slaves were protected by laws and employed only in the house. Laws also safeguarded the child which a woman slave bore to her master. There was no difference between such a child and the children by the legal wife, as to either status or inheritance, after the father's death. The mother could not inherit from her master unless she was legally married, but, should she survive them, she was one of her children's rightful heirs entitled to a mother's legal share. Even the master's favourites, called *odalik* (whence the European term odalisque), were treated with consideration, his favour raising them above their companions. Although it had its humane aspects, this system was a source of much misery to legitimate wives. Custom obliged them to address their rivals as 'sister' and treat their children kindly, but it mitigated neither secret jealousy nor heartache. This situation was strictly limited to slaves and did not apply, under any circumstances, to unmarried women who were free, or to their children, who were illegitimate.

Slaves were divided into two categories, the white-skinned and the black. For whites the legal term of servitude was nine years, but for the others, because of their more delicate constitutions and the colder climate they were employed in, it was limited to seven. At the end of their term they would be given a certificate of liberation valid in a Court of Justice. Should slaves be unhappy with their masters they could ask to be resold, and if this was refused escape was considered legal. But they could neither demand freedom nor obtain it by flight before the appointed term of servitude was fulfilled. In such cases they then applied, according to their sex, to male or female slave-dealers, who undertook to inform their masters and to re-install them in other homes.

With the exception of eunuchs, the custom of employing male slaves in households disappeared so long before my time that I know nothing about them. So far as girls and women were concerned, a fugitive slave never pilfered the house from which she was fleeing. She would leave equipped with only a bundle of underclothing, abandoning her bedroom slippers either at the front door, or, if she had to climb over this, at the foot of the garden wall.

Slaves in great houses were called kalfas to distinguish them from the maid-servants, on whom they looked down, as the position of the slave in the household was considered superior to that of the ordinary servant. In the majority of cases they shared fully in the family life, and were well-dressed, given the same food, and cared for in illness. Once freed, the slave could either choose to remain with her former masters, or could request to be married. Besides the jewels which she had already received, she was provided, if she wished to marry, with a husband, a trousseau, further jewels, and the necessary furniture for her new home. Frequently part of her dowry would consist of a house of her own. Gifts varied with the position and wealth of the master, but every married slave invariably received a pension for life. After liberation and marriage old ties of gratitude and affection continued to bind freed slaves to the families of their former masters. To these they would turn in time of trouble, certain to find help and sympathy. The children of the family also treated them with consideration, calling them baci, an old Turkish word applied to women and expressing regard.

As a rule slaves trained in great houses would marry men of high position. These girls were sought for their good manners, rich dowry, and the life pension they would receive as a parting gift. Nöber Baci, the nurse of my aunt Princess Emina Aziza, is an example. Her first husband was a pasha who became Governor of the Sudan. The salute of twenty-one guns fired on her husband's arrival, and the glories of her position as the Governor's lady were a never-tiring source of conversation in her later life. When the pasha died she again married a government official, who incidentally, because of his less exalted rank, found little room in the lady's reminiscences. . . .

Some slaves could not bear to be separated from their masters and insisted on remaining with them for life. With the passing of the years they attained much authority in the household and enjoyed many privileges. As for the legal nine years of servitude, my grandmothers and other members of the family liberated and married off their slaves after only five or six years.

In the nineteenth century the majority of the white slaves were Circassian and the rest Georgian, both of these Caucasian races then being the only people who trafficked in the sale of children. Circassians and Georgians were grouped in clans ruled by chieftains, who kept slaves for breeding, as their offspring provided a profitable source of income. Circassian and Georgian slave-dealers bought and brought these human wares to Istanbul. There they were put in charge of female slave-traders, who acted as agents between purveyor and customer. These unscrupulous women had access to all the konaks, where by flattering the mistress or an influential kalfa, they disposed of the slaves as profitably as possible.

Slaves varied in price according to their age, qualities, or defects. Scanty hair, bad teeth, a dwarfish figure considerably reduced their value. Flat feet were believed to bring ill luck and those who suffered from this defect were difficult to dispose of. Girls who were no longer virgins would be sold at half price, whereas a mother with a suckling child was much appreciated as a *taya*, or wet nurse. Mother and child were bought together, and the child placed in care of a wet-nurse in town, till it was old enough to come home. Henceforth it became 'milk-brother' or sister of the master's child, and held a privileged position for the rest of his or her life. In Islam, this fraternal bond is considered to be so strong that marriage between a milk-brother and sister is prohibited. This rule does not apply to children born before the acquisition of the taya, the saying being that milk flows downwards not upwards.

[103] The important ceremony of circumcision; from *A Late Voyage to Constantinople (1680)* by G.J. Grelot, translated by J. Philips.

This same act of *Circumcision*, which the *Turks* call *Shoonet*, is only a mark of their obedience to the verbal commands of *Mahomet*, there being no such injunction in his *Alcoran*; only it was a thing by him afterwards appointed, finding that he had many followers, to distinguish his party from the Christians who never Circumcis'd, and the Jews who Circumcis'd after another fashion. Now in regard it is a mark of disobedience to their Law to be uncircumcis'd, therefore they never admit any to their publick prayers that are not distinguish'd so; that is to say, neither Christians, nor children of five or six years of age. However I never heard of any Inspectors that ever stood to search at the Entrance of the Temple; besides that, I knew my self two Christian travellers that perfectly understood the *Arabic* and *Turkish* Languages, who pass'd for as good Musselmen as any were in *Turkie*, and were well receiv'd where ever they went, as being in the habit of *Derviches*, and because they knew how to mumble over the *Turkish* Prayers in the Mosquees, when they could not avoid going thither. But had it been known that those persons were not Circumciz'd, they had not only been refus'd admittance, but burnt alive, or else empal'd upon a stake.

Now they never Circumcise any till they come to six or seven years of age: Elder than these are often Circumciz'd, but never younger, sometimes at twelve, fifteen years or more, according to the pleasure of the Parents: Especially if they be poor people, for then not being able to defray the charges of a private, they must stay till the Rich make a publick Circumcision of their own. The day for the Ceremony being appointed, the Master of the house prepares a great Feast, and makes his Son as fine as his quality will reach; then the boy being mounted upon a Horse or Camel, is led in triumph through the Village, or only that quarter of the City where his Parents live, if it be large. His School-fellows and friends wait upon him on foot, hollowing and hooping for joy that he is going to be admitted into the number of true *Musselmen*. The *Cavalcade* being thus finish'd, and the guests return'd back to the house, the *Iman* makes a pithie Harangue upon the operation that is to ensue; at the end of which comes a Chirurgion, who having plac'd the lad upon a *Sopha* or *Turkish* Table, two Servants holding a linnen napkin before him, draws out the Preputium in length as far as he can pull it, and so keeping it from running back, by clapping a pair of little Pincers at the end of the nut, takes off the surplusage with a sharp Razor, and then holds it up in his fingers to be seen by all the Company, who cry out at the same time, *Alla Hecher in Alla Alla*. Which done he dresses the Wound, not a little to the torment of the party Circumciz'd, who by his roaring convinces the standers-by what pain he endures by the wounding so sensible and tender part of his body. But his friends are so far from compassionating his lamentations, that they presently come all to congratulate his admission into the number of the Faithful, and then take their places at the *Sopha*, or *Turkish* Table, where they are entertain'd according to the quality of the Parents.

And often the liberality of Rich men at their Child's Circumcision amounts to large sums. For besides the Almes which they give to a great number of poor Children which are Circumciz'd, frequently at their charges, at the same time, they also distribute considerable Almes to the poor of the Neighbourhood, to the end they may obtain the blessing of God upon the new Circumciz'd Lad, and all the rest of their Family.

[104] A wedding-feast in honour of Sultan Mahmoud's daughter, Saliheh, in 1834; from *Turkey, Greece and Malta* by Adolphus Slade.

I saw two or three of the Turkish line-of-battle ships to great advantage on my arrival, for they were in all the vanity of new paint, moored in line off the quays of Salybazar, Dolmabakcheh and Beshik-tash, for the purpose of firing a series of salutes in honour of the marriage of Sultana Saliheh with Halil Pasha, in which display they were also assisted by a squadron of miniature frigates which sailed about amongst the leviathans, and occasionally indulged in a sham fight with two gaily decorated and illuminated castles, moored for the occasion off the palace.

Constantinople undergoes a transformation at such ceremonies which generally last ten days, and which we saw when repeated at the nuptials of the Sultana Mihirmah. Freedom of speech and action is allowed, police restrictions are withdrawn by day and by night, and everybody is required to rejoice. While the fêtes last you need not expect a tradesman to work, or your servants to be scrupulous in their attendance. . . .

Next morning the princess left her father's roof, and threaded the same crowds whom we might have supposed to have slept on the ground. More adapted, more eloquent, seemed the stillness, the subdued gaze of the spectators, than the vociferous shouts of western Europe on such occasions. Music and troops preceded: then rode the pashas two and two: afterwards came the bride and her mother, shrouded in a superb coach, a present from the Czar, followed by the female household in carriages: then appeared the Kislar Aga and his creatures mounted on the royal horses: and the pashas' ladies, in carriages and four, closed the procession. It passed on over more distant hills, the trumpets sounded fainter and fainter. At the gate of her palace the bridegroom waited. He knelt before her car: he offered flowers of hope: he combated with assumed ardour the coyness of etiquette. At length she yielded. He assisted her to descend; he lifted her over the threshold, the auspicious moment for which a dervish pointed out, and the instant roar of artillery announced it far and wide. He led her upstairs, and there for the first time saw his bride unveiled. But three days of form, devoted to receiving compliments, elapsed ere he might call her his wife.

Each night, at such times, the Bosphorus may realize one's

imaginings of Bagdad under Haroun al Raschid and Zobeide. The noble stream flows along for ten miles between palaces of fire. Every house on either bank is illuminated fancifully. There are Gothic temples, and Grecian colonnades with scrolled frontispieces, and gardens – but all of living flame. The Seraglio Point, one of Europe's extremities, is a blaze of light, and reflects itself on Asia's cliffs. Nothing of the sort in Christendom can give the slightest idea of Constantinople and the Bosphorus when thus lighted up. The effect is most striking on the water. As no object is visible except the creations of fire, the ships, which are traced out by lamps, appear to float in mid-air at indefinite distances, while the refulgent kiosks on the hilltops of either continent may give the idea of magicians' abodes, for they also seem unconnected with earth or water . . . From time to time, however, fireworks disclose the scene in detail. Huge wooden whales are moored for that purpose, and from their mouths thousands of rockets fly up over the gilded stream, to mingle first their evanescent brightness with the stars, then fall again in Danae's showers on its bosom. Numerous caiques then, previously hidden by the glare, emerge into form, and where you fancied yourself to be solitary, your rowers have scarcely room to move. You also see large fish, with shining tails and flaming eyes, paddled about by invisible hands; and carriages and horses, ingeniously built on boats, seem to be driving over the water as securely as on dry land. All is liquid radiance for a few minutes, save where a cypress-grove on either bank throws its shadow forth – as if, like the masked skeleton at an ancient Egyptian feast, to be a silent monitor. As the temporary brightness dies away, illusion obtains complete mastery of the soul: you see a splash, and you look for a sea-god to rise; you hear a voice, and you listen for a Nereid's song. . . .

In the joy of his heart, Sultan Mahmoud declared that the offspring of the union which called forth such festivity and splendour in the summer of 1834, should be permitted to live.[1] A

[1] Revolting and inexcusable as the practice is of destroying the male offspring of royalty, it might nevertheless be said to have proved humanity in the end. The inevitable consequence, under oriental despotism, of a large family, has ever been, either the death of the princes in cold blood during the sovereign's life, or civil war afterwards; in the latter case, mutilation awaits the vanquished. Look at the result of the civil war for the Persian throne, in 1835,

boy gladdened the young mother's heart for a few months, then died.

Sultana Saliheh was seventeen or eighteen years old; not pretty, but ladylike, according to the reports of some Frank ladies. She was reported to be haughty and passionate. She affronted the lady pashas, it was said, when they paid their duties to her after the marriage: her foot they were bound to kiss, but instead of smiling on her worshippers, she turned away her head. More secluded than Mussulman women in general, no man (except the doctor) ever setting eyes even on her garments, a princess of the house of Othman hails her marriage-day as the day of escape from bondage. She is at once free, excepting in the usual checks of Mohammedanism. Her husband is slave by law and custom. Chosen by the sultan, he must obey; discard his wife if he have one; break off old connexions; then, perhaps, surrounded by his royal mistress's spies, live tormented by the fiend jealousy. The present sultan's sister (a widow) used to watch her husband so narrowly, that, on visiting the isles of the Archipelago, as capitan pasha, he deemed it prudent not to land without sending previously to make the Greeks veil.

[105] The wedding night; from *Memoirs of Halidé Edib*.

Hava Hanum used to tell a vivid story about the first night of her marriage which I can never forget. She would forget that her audience consisted of two little girls and a foolish Circassian slave, and would get into a dramatic mood.

'We used to have our hair plaited and left hanging down our backs in my young days,' she would begin. 'I had forty plaits; they were like a fringed shawl reaching from one shoulder to the other.' (In fact, old as she was, she still had two thick plaits, henna-coloured, wound over her soft head-dress.) 'I had such

among the numerous sons of Feth Ali Schah: the eyes of some of the conqueror's uncles extinguished, others strangled, others fugitives. Amurath III, on his accession, killed five brothers and two odalisques left *encientes*. Mahomet III. also put all his brothers to death, amounting to nineteen; on which occasion two of the bereaved mothers heightened the tragedy by poniarding themselves in despair on the bodies of their sons. Maternal feelings were consulted in the practice of royal infanticide; the task was assigned to the midwife.

beautiful teeth!' (Her mouth was like an empty black hole, but she ate wonderfully, managing the hardest morsels.) 'My cheeks were like two bright peaches.' (They were loose wrinkled leather now.) 'My husband when led to my bridal chamber saw everything through my veil. He asked me three times to lift my veil,[1] but of course he opened it himself, offering me the face-seeing present.[2] But he had hardly looked at me before he called in the woman attendant.

'"Undo one of these plaits," he ordered her.

'"O Effendi, her hair has been plaited by the professional bath hair-dressers. She only goes once a fortnight because it is such a tremendous business each time. How can I undo it?"

'"Undo it quickly. It cannot be real hair. It is n't possible she should have such a quantity. I must be sure that it is not false."

'Two professional hair-dressers from the bath she used to go to were accordingly called in, and they undid my plaits while he wetted his handkerchief in his mouth and rubbed my cheeks.'

'Why did he do that, Hava Hanum?' I would ask.

And my sister nudged me angrily for interrupting the story. 'To see if the paint would come off of course, you stupid!'

Well, finally the gentleman made sure that none of the beauteous attributes of his wife were false, and he shook his head over the possibility of such hair and such colouring.

For years and years the first night ceremonial of marriages meant for me a repetition of this particular scene. As I had not acquired a femininistic turn of mind, I did not in the least object to any gentleman who tested the physical virtues of his wife as if he were examining any other property such as slaves or cows. I made a moral out of this story, after I had heard other versions of first night ceremonies from other ladies, which were more or less alike; and I concluded sadly that a bride could never cheat a Turkish husband by paint or false hair if her hair was thin and her cheeks pale. The evenings in Hava Hanum's sitting-room were in their way as instructive as a French salon before the Revolution.

[1] This is the ceremonial performance of old Turkish marriages.

[2] A bracelet, necklace, etc., according to the wealth of the bridegroom.

[106] The Turks' sense of drama – the Marquis de Bonneval's account of a penitential procession; from *Un Parisien à Constantinople* by Vicomte René Vigier. Translated by Laurence Kelly.

The love of the Turks for theatricality outstrips the imagination; here every event becomes an occasion for processions, or public signs of joy and grief. The number of mummers' troupes that I have met since being in Constantinople is incalculable. Especially after wars, each victory or defeat becomes the justification for a cheerful or lugubrious cavalcade. Here is an example of the procession that marched through the principal streets of Stamboul after the defeat of Panzora. First there was paraded a coffin full of the bones of janissaries and spahis killed, of broken swords, flattened cuirasses, snapped bows and unusable arrows. This coffin was carried by six bareheaded and barefooted bearers clothed in haircloth. Second, three hundred Muslims, covered in squalid clothes dyed in blood and smeared in ashes, followed the coffin, striking themselves and howling fearfully. Third, six thousand men, naked to the belt, were flogging each other with thorns so piercing that their blood flowed to the ground. Fourth, a model of Mahomet's tomb was carried by thirty turbanless spahis, escorted by four hundred Pashas, sword in hand, ready to massacre any who would stare at the holy tomb. All had to prostrate themselves face down to earth as it passed them. Fifth, at each quarter-mile a donkey was sacrificed and left swimming in its own sea of blood. One hundred and forty were killed during this ceremony. Sixth, thirty Pashas marched with their heads covered in turbans drenched in donkey's blood, one hand tied behind their backs without a sword. In their left hands they dragged horse-tails to cause the dust to swirl up. Seventh, four thousand janissaries armed only with sticks shouted fanatically, 'Let God my protector forgive me.' Eighth, the Grand Muphti riding a donkey, in a bloodied blue turban, kept striking his head crying, 'Lord, forgive me my ingratitude.' In ninth position, there came a chest full of money for the poor, but no beggar could pick this up during the ceremony under threat of being impaled alive. Finally, this pretentious masquerade was terminated by a huge concourse of people amidst whom there were a hundred Turks dressed as penitents, flaying each other and making deep cuts. From time to time they raised their right hand, crying, 'I call upon God that he should strengthen me against my enemies!'

[107] The burial of the Byzantine emperors; from *Constantin VII Porphyrogénète: Le Livre des Cérémonies* by Albert Vogt. Translated by Laurence Kelly.

The protocol [describing the burial of the Emperors] is exactly that used to describe the burial of Constantine VII. The 'Caballarios' was the 'covered' Hippodrome. One has to pass through it to arrive at the Hall of the Nineteen Couches. The court also gathered in it to receive and greet the mortal remains resting there whilst the funeral bier was being prepared in the Nineteen Couches. The body was then transported thither, and the Court officers, civil servants and Demes (who were not usually admitted to the Aolic Court) could file past and see the dead Emperor's face in the vast and ancient triclinos. It was also probably there that the first liturgical prayers were recited. The Patriarch and clergy of St Sophia and the Senate met there with ... possibly the Confraternities, mourning or otherwise, whose hoods gave them the appearance of spectres.

After lying in state in the Caballarios, and then in the Hall of the Nineteen Couches, the body was transported to the Chalce by officers of the Household Guards who there 'did the usual things'. As today, they must have stood guard around the coffin whilst the people of the whole city passed before the bier, as much for motives of curiosity as of respect. It is not specifically said that burial took place in the Church of the Holy Apostles, since there are exceptions to this rule.

[108] The burial of a Sultan in the seventeenth century; from *The History of the Serrail and of the Court of the Grand Seigneur, Emperour of the Turks* by Seigneur Michael Baudier of Languedoc.

The Emperours Body is carried in a Coffin covered with Linnen very rich, or of Velvet: His Turbant is set before it, with a Plume of Herons Feathers: The *Talismans*, *Santons*, *Alphaquis*, *Dernis*, and the like rabble of the Alcoran, carry in their hands Tapers lighted, to shew that their Prophet is the Ape of Christianity; goe before singing in their Language such Verses, *Alla rahumani arhamubula Alla, illa Alla, Alla humana Alla*, that is to say, *Mercifull God have pittie on him, there is no God but God, God is God* . . . Before the Corps doth march the *Mutaferaga*, who carries the Emperours Turbant upon a Lance, with the tayle of a Horse tied neere unto it: The *Ianizaries*, the *Solachi*, and the rest of the Imperiall Guard follow the Hearse: After these the Officers of the *Sultans* house march in order under the conduct of *Gasnegirbassi*, or Master of the Household: The *Malundarb hedith mandura*, carrieth the deceased *Grand Seigneurs* Armes, and the Royall Standard dragging upon the ground: The *Bassa's* and all the great Men of the Port, yielding their last duty unto their Master, assist at their Funerall pleasantly attired in mourning: They have a piece of Grey-cloth hangs before and behind from the head to the foot, like unto the Frock which the Brethren of the Hospitall, of the Charity, in the Suburbes of Saint *Germain* at *Paris* do weare: some of them for that they will not seeme too sorrowfull, tie only a long piece of Linnen cloth, to the end of their Turbants, which hangs downe unto their heeles. In this great Mourning the most eminent in the *Othoman* Court, hold their Rancks in this Funerall Pompe, whereas the Men make but a part of the Convoy, Beasts supply the rest, with lesse griefe and more teares: For all the *Sultans* great Horses are at his Interment; they carry their Saddles turned upward, and better covered than the *Bassa's* in their Grey Frockes, they have blacke Velvet hanging unto the ground: They weepe and sigh without heavinesse: They put *Assagoth* or Tobacco into their nostrils, to make them sneeze, and into their eyes to draw forth teares: Such is the vaine pompe of the Turkish *Sultans*, who being unable to binde men to weepe for their losse, constraine beasts to shed teares: In this manner they conduct the body (the head first after the Turkish manner) to the Tombe where they wil inclose him. It is usually joyning to the Mosquee, which the deceased *Sultan* hath caused to be built, in a Chappell apart: the Sepulchre is covered with black Velvet. If the Prince died in the Warre, they lay his Semiter upon it; if not, his Turbant is advanced, and set against the wall neere unto the Tombe, with rich Plumes of Herons feathers for an Ornament; two Candlestickes which carry great Tapers gilt, are at the foot of the Sepulchre: Some Turkish Priests which are instituted to that end, repeate continually the *Azoares* of the Alcoran in their turnes, and one after another sayes the Turkes Chapelet; whereof we have spoken in the History of their Religion, and pray continually for the soule of the deceased. On Fridayes these Imperiall Tombes, are adorned with new Coverings, and strewed with flowres: They which come in such dayes pray for the dead, or powre forth their teares, and take a Nosegay when they returne. Sometimes they doe also set much meat, to give Almes unto the poore, and they call to the Funerall Feasts, not only poore Beggers, but also Beasts, as Dogges, Cats, and Birds, the which are honourably received, and feasted with as much liberty and safety as the Men . . . Thus they shut him up in sixe foot of ground whom all the World could not containe, and whose unrestrained ambition aspired to more Empire than the Earth containes: And after that he had bin a terrour to Men, and the cruell scourge of many Nations, he is made the subject of Wormes, and their ordinary food. In this manner passeth, and ends the glory of the World.

[109] The burial of an ordinary Muslim; from *Un Parisien à Constantinople* by Vicomte René Vigier. Translated by Laurence Kelly.

When a Turk feels that his last hour is approaching, he places his receipts under the bed in case of claims from beyond the tomb, and sends for the '*Emmaüs*', who offers him consolation. After his death, his family will hasten to wash his body with water, to wrap the body in a seamless shroud, (so that he can kneel down on Judgement Day), and to carry him at top speed to his place of burial, where his soul already awaits him impatiently. A thin layer of earth covers the coffin planks that are hardly joined, for the skeleton of a Moslem must be able to shake off effortlessly such a burden at the Resurrection. And so the cemeteries are littered with bones, skulls, and one is almost tempted to repeat Hamlet's famous 'To be or not to be'! Often at night, famished dogs scratch away at the freshly dug sand, and the corpses of the faithful become the food of unclean animals and wheeling vultures.

[110] A Turkish bath in 1540; from 'I Costumi e i Modi Particolari de la Vita de Turchi' by Bassano da Zara, in N.M. Penzer's *The Harem.*

The design of these baths seems to me, especially as far as the domes are concerned, to be copied from the Thermæ of Diocletian in Rome, although very much smaller. At the entrance is a room shaped like a church, but round and domed with lead, large and commodious, almost like the Rotunda at Rome.... In the middle of this there is usually a beautiful basin of fine marble, with a fountain of four jets, around which are seats made of brick three cubits long and so high from the ground that a man sitting there could not touch the floor with his feet. All the vaulting of this first room is of marble slabs. The abovementioned seats are all partitioned by a small wall a cubit in height, or by a wooden shutter of a considerable size so that they are divided up and allow one to lean on one's elbow. Each of the seats is about four cubits wide, and those who wish to bathe can undress there. The seat is covered first with a mat, on which is placed a rug or tapestry. On wishing to enter and take a bath one must first speak to the custodians of the bath, who are stationed around the walls of this room, and then to the cashier, who sits in a corner on a stool just as our lawyers do. When this is done you may undress on one of those seats ... you must be careful not to show any immodest parts, for shameless ones are beaten and thrown out of the baths. When undressed you make your clothes into a bundle and place it on the seat with your hat, cap, or turban which you wear, on top. Your clothes will not be safe unless you have a servant to guard them, because the custodians of the baths themselves will steal your purse and other belongings. Before you take your shirt off they will give you a long ample towel to cover yourself – that is to say, if you haven't got one of your own – and others to dry yourself with. ... Having then covered your privities with the towel, all the rest of you being bare, you enter the first room of the bath, where there are always about fifteen servants varying with the size of the bath, some shaving, some kneading the bones, some washing, so that all are busy at their task set them by their master. From this you pass through several rooms of all different kinds, each hotter than the last, adorned with fine marble and porphyry all round, like the vaulting; and in each are two water-pipes, one hot and the other cold, which flow into marble basins, and the water which overflows on to the ground escapes through holes in the floor. From here you enter the main part of the bath, which is usually spacious and covered with marble so smooth that it is hard to stand upright. This place, like the other rooms, is domed and has several glass windows tightly shut, the whole being covered above with lead. The dome in the middle is very high. In winter the baths are heated at midnight (in summer every one washes in cold water), thereby consuming vast quantities of wood. They use pine-trees four or five cubits long, thicker than a man's thigh, and also a small amount of oak. In the centre of this room, which we have called the heart of the baths, there is a square stone of marble, porphyry, and very fine serpentine, a palm thick, longer than the height of a man, and two palms from the ground. It is set on four beautiful marble balls. As soon as anybody arrives they are invited to stretch themselves on this stone body downward, and one of the servants mounts with his feet on your back and pulls out your arms in a certain manner peculiar to them. But it never pleased me, and I would never lie down there, although they often begged me to do so. . . . After this you lie on the ground close to the basin and one of the servants throws water over you from a bowl, while another washes you, covering the opening of the little room with a towel. . . . To rub you down they use a kind of bag made of a thick dark cloth; no soap is supplied if you don't bring your own. If you want your head, beard, or other hairs shaved a man who specializes in that business will attend to you. So also if you want to get rid of your hair in any part without shaving they give you a paste, in a different room from the others. The Turks use this paste a great deal, for they consider it a sin to have hairs on their private parts, and you never find any of them, either man or woman, who have any. And in this matter the women are more superstitious than the men, and as soon as they feel the hairs coming they hurry off to the baths. When you have finished washing you change the towel you have been wearing, which they call *futà*, in the bath, and on coming out a servant approaches from behind with a basin to wash your feet again.

[111] Julia Pardoe takes a Turkish bath in the 1830s; from *The City of the Sultan and the Domestic Manners of the Turks in 1836* by Miss Pardoe.

As I have previously resolved to visit every part of the establishment, I followed the example of my companion, who had already undergone the fatigue of an Oriental bath, and exchanged my morning dress for a linen wrapper, and loosened my hair: and then, conducted by the Greek waiting-maid who had accompanied me, I walked barefooted across the cold marble floor to a door at the opposite extremity of the hall, and, on crossing the threshold, found myself in the cooling-room, where groups of ladies were sitting, or lying listlessly on their sofas, enveloped in their white linen wrappers, or preparing for their return to the colder region whence I had just made my escape.

This second room was filled with hot air, to me, indeed, most oppressively so; but I soon discovered that it was, nevertheless, a *cooling-room*; when, after having traversed it, and dipped my feet some half dozen times in the little channels of warm water that intersected the floor, I entered the great bathing-place of the establishment – the extensive octagon hall in which all those who do not chuse, or who cannot afford, to pay for a separate apartment, avail themselves, as they find opportunities, of the eight fountains which it contains.

For the first few moments, I was bewildered; the heavy, dense, sulphureous vapour that filled the place, and almost suffocated me – the wild, shrill cries of the slaves pealing through the reverberating domes of the bathing-halls, enough to awaken the very marble with which they were lined – the subdued laughter, and whispered conversation of their mistresses murmuring along in an under-current of sound – the sight of nearly three hundred women only partially dressed, and that in fine linen so perfectly saturated with vapour, that it revealed the whole outline of the figure – the busy slaves, passing and repassing, naked from the waist upwards, and with their arms folded upon their bosoms, balancing on their heads piles of fringed or embroidered napkins – groups of lovely girls, laughing, chatting, and refreshing themselves with sweetmeats, sherbet and lemonade – parties of playful children, apparently quite indifferent to the dense atmosphere which made me struggle for breath – and, to crown all, the sudden bursting forth of a chorus of voices into one of the wildest and shrillest of Turkish melodies, that was caught up and flung back by the echoes of the vast hall, making a din worthy of a saturnalia of demons – all combined to form a picture, like the illusory semblance of a phantasmagoria, almost leaving me in doubt whether that on which I looked were indeed reality, or the mere creation of a distempered brain.

Beside every fountain knelt, or sat, several ladies, attended by their slaves, in all the various stages of the operation; each intent upon her own arrangements, and regardless of the passers-by; nor did half a dozen of them turn their heads even to look at the English stranger, as we passed on to the small inner cabinet that had been retained for us.

The process of Turkish bathing is tedious, exhausting, and troublesome; I believe that the pretty Greek who attended me spent an hour and a half over my hair alone. The supply of water is immense, and can be heated at the pleasure of the bather, as it falls into the marble basin from two pipes, the one pouring forth a hot, and the other a cold, stream. The marble on which you stand and sit is heated to a degree that you could not support, were the atmosphere less dense and oppressive; and, as the water is poured over you from an embossed silver basin, the feeling of exhaustion becomes almost agreeable. Every lady carries with her all the appliances of the bath, as well as providing her own servant; the inferior ranks alone availing themselves of the services of the bathing women, who, in such cases, supply their employers with every thing requisite. . . .

Having remained in the bath about two hours and a half, I began to sicken for pure air and rest; and, accordingly, winding a napkin with fringed ends about my head, and folding myself in my wrapper, I hastily and imprudently traversed the cooling-room, now crowded with company, looking like a congregation of resuscitated corses clad in their grave-clothes, and fevered into life; and gained the outer hall, where the napkin was removed from my head, my hair carefully plaited without drying, and enveloped in a painted muslin handkerchief; and myself buried among the soft cushions of the divan. . . .

I should be unjust did I not declare that I witnessed none of that unnecessary and wanton exposure described by Lady M.W. Montague. Either the fair Ambassadress was present at a peculiar ceremony, or the Turkish ladies have become more delicate and fastidious in their ideas of propriety.

The excessive exhaustion which it induces, and the great quantity of time which it consumes, are the only objections that can reasonably be advanced against the use of the Turkish bath.

[112] The police ordinance of Mehmet IV (1680) relating to bath-houses; from *La Vie Quotidienne à Constantinople* . . . by R. Mantran. Translated by Laurence Kelly.

No. 53: Let the bath keepers see that their baths are clean; that the water be temperate and the bath hot; that the bath house boys be attentive and quick; that the razors be cutting; that the boys be skilful in shaving heads; that leeches be applied where a man has a right to them. Let the services be properly rendered; washings should be by soap, and scrubbing firmly done with the serge hand-sachet. Razors and sachets must be clean. The head of a Muslim must not be shaved with a razor that was used to shave an Infidel or a scabby fellow. The towels of the bath house must be clean and squared off, one per customer; no towel should be with holes or too short. Infidels should have their own towels; separately marked. The linen used to dry off the face of an Infidel should not be used for a Muslim's face. In short, everything used for Muslims must be separate.

Let those that contravene this be corrected and punished.

[113] The execution of a Christian caught in adultery in 1599, and of the Turk's wife similarly caught; from *Adventures of Baron Wenceslas Wratislaw* . . . translated by A.H. Wratislaw.

[A young Christian woman, betrothed to a Christian man who is temporarily out of the country, is wooed by an elderly Turk, who imprisons her parents and forces her into a splendid marriage with him. On his return, her distraught lover visits her secretly in the gardens by night. Their liaison is discovered and both are condemned to death.]

As soon as it became generally known that two such handsome people were to be led to death a countless multitude assembled, and the execution took place in the following order. First rode the sub-pasha, or imperial judge, after him other councillors, judges, and officials, with a guard of janissaries, and with heralds and other officers of justice. Upon this the young man was led out of prison with his hands bound behind his back, and an iron ring on his neck, through which a chain was passed, while two executioners, well-made fellows, in handsome clothes, (for such people are in no odium with the Turks,) held him by the chain on each side; the guard of janissaries went in front and rear, and a countless number of people on horses and in carriages looked on. When the young Greek was led out of prison a great cry arose from both men and women, that it would be a great shame to destroy such a youth; and all compassionated and advised him to become a Turk, promising that they would petition the Emperor himself to grant him his life. He, however, briefly refused to agree to their proposal, and become a Turk. The chiaous pasha, as he was led past his palace, seeing how handsome he was, sent a message to him, saying that, if he would become a Mahometan, he would contrive that he should save his life, and that the beautiful lady should become his wife; but the young man did not allow himself to be moved, but answered that he was sprung from Christian parents, had been baptized and brought up as a Christian, and would also die as a Christian.

They therefore led out the lady, also, from another prison, and placed her on a mule, round which walked a great number of veiled women; she herself was not veiled, but had her beautiful hair plaited in long plaits on both sides, in the Turkish fashion, with one plait hanging on her back behind. She wore a red carmine dress, and had very beautiful pearls round her neck and in her ears, and was certainly a very lovely woman. She wept so piteously that all had great compassion upon her. When the executioners brought her in front of the serail of the chiaous pasha, and related the offer which the pasha had made, she begged the executioners to lead her nearer the Greek, her former lover, on seeing whom she for a long time could not speak for weeping. When, after long wailing, she was able to call him by name, she begged him in Greek, with all her heart, for God's sake, to take pity upon the youth of both of them, and to become a Mohametan, saying that they could then live together many years in joy and happiness. . . . In answer to these words he briefly answered her that she should rather entrust her soul to the Lord God, and not speak in vain.

The Turks, on hearing this, gnashed their teeth at him with great anger, crying out, – '*Hai, hai! pregaar gidy Tuipek, gidy anaseny, sigligum iste mes sentu kazdyny?*' – 'Ah! utterly accused traitor, dog, why refusest thou that beautiful lady?' And thus, with great clamour and tumult, they led him to execution, she, also, riding after him on the mule, weeping from her heart, while the Turks, and Turkish women, comforted and encouraged her. When they had conducted him beyond the *Unkapy*, (*i.e.* beyond the sand-gate,) under the wooden gallows itself, to which were suspended six large hooks, two executioners with their sleeves tucked up fixed the pulleys by which they intended to hoist him up. They then stripped him of his coat and all his clothes, leaving him only his linen trousers, tied his hands and feet, and drew him up towards the gallows upon these pulleys higher than a man's height.

Just at this moment the lady rode out from the gate, which is not far off, and on seeing him swooned away. When they brought her to again she begged to be allowed to speak with him once more, and give him counsel. Being, therefore, brought under the gallows, she clasped her hands together, and, raising them up, made him a long speech with tears, recounting all their love which they had had towards each other from their youth upwards, and begged him only to say one word, that he would become a Mahometan. Amongst other things, she said to him as follows: – 'But thou hast always had a compassionate heart towards me; how, then, has it turned to stone against me, seeing death before thine eyes? Alas! what, then, thinkest thou? Why art thou not in thy right mind, that thou wilt not speak to me? Alas! cursed be that love which I had for thee!' And, being enraged at him, because he would neither speak to her nor turn Mahometan, she immediately changed her love into hatred, and said to him: – 'Never wert thou worthy that I should love thee so with my whole heart. Dog! traitor! pagan! Jew! die, since thou desirest thus to die; only, O that I could be freed from this terrible death, which I shall suffer guiltless on thy account! Alas! comfort me some of you, dear people!' Having said this she swooned away.

The Turks, seeing that the young man would not be converted, angrily gnashed their teeth at him, and cried out that he should be thrown on a hook. Two executioners then standing on the gallows raised him about half an ell above a hook, and

Turkish punishments – throwing on the hook (top); impaling (centre); and the bastinado (below); drawing by Peter Mundy in his *Travels in Europe and Asia*, 1608–67

threw him on to it. This having been done, all the women and men also surrounded the lady, and, had there not been so strong a guard, they would not have allowed her to be drowned, and, had the chiaous met them, he would have been torn to pieces, like the celebrated Orpheus, by the infuriated women, or stoned by the Turks, who vehemently reviled him. When the lady had ended her prayers, the women took leave of her with great shrieking and weeping, although she was already quite unconscious, and as pale as a white sheet. An executioner took her down from the mule, tied her hands with one cloth, passed another round her waist, and fastened a third round her feet. He then placed her with her mouth downwards in a small boat, and rowing about two fathoms from the shore, for the gallows was close to the sea-shore, fixed a long staff in the cloth round her waist, pushed her lightly out of the boat into the sea, and held her under water till she was drowned. Then bringing a bier, and wrapping the corpse in a winding-sheet, they accompanied her to the tomb with Turkish honours. The poor young man lived hanging on the hook till the third day, and complained of great thirst, begging them to give him water, but nobody ventured to do so. On the third night some one, moved with compassion towards him, shot him through the head; but it was impossible to ascertain who it was that did it.

[114] The execution of a Pasha in the seventeenth century; from *A New Relation of the Inner-Part of the Grand Seignor's Seraglio* by J.B. Tavernier.

When the death of a *Bassa* is resolv'd upon, the Grand Seignor delivers the Commission to him, whom he has design'd to be kind to; and he finds it much more advantageous, to bring him the Sentence of his death, than to bring him a Present from the Prince.

If the Execution is to be done in *Constantinople*, the ordinary Executioner is the *Bostangi-bachi*, who is alwaies about the Grand Seignor's Person, and he himself does the Work. But if there be a necessity of going into some remote Province, 'tis commonly either a *Kapigi-bachi*, or one of the principal *Bostangis*, whom the Prince has a mind to shew his kindness to, who is sent to perform the Execution.

... the *Capigi-bachi* enters, attended by his people and presents the *Bassa* with the *Grand Seignor*'s Letter. He receives it with great respect, and having put it three several times to his forehead, he opens it, reads it, and finds that the Prince demands his head. He makes no other answer to that Order, then what he does in these few words; *Let the Will*, says he, *of my Emperour be done: only give me leave to say my Prayers*; which is granted him. His Prayers being ended, the *Capigis* seize him by the Arms, and the chief of them presently takes off his Girdle or Sasche, and casts it about his Neck. That Girdle consists of several small strings of Silk, with knots at both ends, which two of the company immediately catch hold of, and one drawing one way, and the other, t'other-way, they dispatch him in an instant.

If they are unwilling to make use of their Girdle, they take a handkerchief, and with the Ring which they use, in the bending of their Bowes, and which they ordinarily wear on the right-hand Thumb, they thrust the hand between the handkerchief, which is ty'd very close, and the Throat, and so break the very Throat-Bone. Thus they make a shift to strangle a man in an instant, suffering him not to languish in pain, that he may dye a faithful *Mahumetan*, and not have the time to enter into despair; the *Turks* thinking our way of hanging Criminals, who are so long in torment upon the Gibbet, a strange kind of Execution.

Though I have often us'd this expression, That the *Grand Seignor* sends to demand the Head of any person, whom he would rid out of the way; yet they never cut it off, but when he expresly declares his desire to see it, and then it is brought to him. If it be from some place at a great distance, they take out the Brains, and fill the empty place with Hay; and it was my fortune to see two Heads so order'd, at the same time, which they carried in a Bag. They were the Heads of the *Baffa's* of *Kars*, and *Erzeram*. . . .

When there is no order given for the bringing of the Head, they bury the Body about Mid-night, without any ceremony, and the memory of the *Bassa*, who had made so much noise before, is soon extinguish'd and laid in the dust. But it is moreover to be noted, That it is the Custome in *Turkey*, not to cut off the Head of any one, till after they have strangled him, and that the blood is quite cold; it being against their Law, That the blood of a *Mussulman* (that is, one of the Faithful) should be spilt, upon any occasion, but in Warr.

The execution being over, he who brought the Order for it, makes an immediate Seizure of all that belong'd to the deceas'd

Bassa; and after he has set aside what he liked best for his own use, whether in Gold or Jewels, he brings the same persons, who had been at the precedent Council, to proceed to the Inventory of his Goods, which are afterwards, as I have said elsewhere, transmitted to the Chambers of the Treasury.

[115] The Evil Eye; from *The City of the Sultan and the Domestic Manners of the Turks in 1836* by Miss Pardoe.

The Turk decorates the roof of his house, the prow of his caïque, the cap of his child, the neck of his horse, and the cage of his bird, with charms against the Evil Eye; one of the most powerful of these antidotes being garlic: and it must be conceded that, here at least, the workers of woe have shown their taste. Every hovel has its head of garlic suspended by a string; and bouquets of flowers formed of spices, amid which this noxious root is nestled, are sent as presents to the mother of a new-born infant, as a safeguard both to herself and her little one.

A blue eye is supereminently suspicious, for they have an idea that such is the legitimate colour of the evil orb; and you seldom see a horse, or a draught ox, or even a donkey, which has not about its neck a string of blue beads, to preserve it from the dark deeds of witchcraft. I was considerably amused on one occasion, when, being about to meet the carriage of a friend, the horse that drew it, either from idleness or caprice, suddenly stood still, and the arabajhe exclaimed with vehemence to his mistress, 'You see, madam, you see that the horse is struck – the new Hanoum has blue eyes!' turning his own on me as he spoke, with a most unloving expression. I am perfectly convinced that, had the animal met with any misfortune, or been guilty of any misdemeanour during the remainder of the day, the whole blame would have inevitably been visited on my unlucky eyes, which had counteracted the effect of a row of glass beads, and a crescent of bone!

To protect the reigning Sultan from the power of the Evil Eye during his state progresses through the streets of the capital, a peculiar headdress was invented for the Imperial body-pages, whose ornamented plumes were of such large dimensions as, collectively, to form a screen about his sacred person. Even Sultan Mahmoud, who is superior to many of the popular prejudices, has just caused a Firman to be published, prohibiting the women from looking earnestly at him as he passes them, on pain of – what think you, reader? – of subjecting their husbands or brothers to the bastinado! The Turkish laws are too gallant to condemn females to suffer this punishment in their own persons, and Mahmoud is consequently to be protected from the possibly fatal effects of the ladies' eyes by their fears for their male relations.

[116] The importance attached by Muslims to paper; from *Travels Into Turkey . . .* by A.G. Busbequius.

The *Turks* gave a great deal of Difference to Paper, because the Name of God may be written in it: And, therefore, they will not suffer the least Bit of Paper to lie upon the Ground, but presently they take it up, and thrust it into some Chink or Hole or other, that so it may not be trampled under Foot; and hitherto, perhaps, their Superstition may be tollerable, but mark what follows.

In the Day of Judgment, say they, when *Mahomet* shall call up his Followers from their *Purgatory*, (to which they were condemned for their Sins) to Heaven, to be there made Partakers of Eternal Blessedness; there will no Way be left for them to come to their Prophet, but over an huge red-hot Iron Grate, which they must run over bare-foot, (how painfully, you may guess, when you imagine a Cock to skip thro' hot-burning Coals.) But at that Instant, (believe it if you can!) all those Bundles of Papers, which they have preserved from being trod upon, will immediately appear, and put themselves under their Feet; by which Means they will pass the red-hot Iron-Gate with less Damage; so necessary do they count the Work of saving a little Paper. And, to add to the Story, I remember that my *Turkish* Guides were once very angry with my Servants, for making use of Paper to cleanse their *Posteriors*, and thereupon made a grievous Complaint to me of their horrid Offence therein: I had no Way to put them off, but by telling them, 'twas no Wonder my Servants did such strange Things, seeing they also used to eat Swines Flesh, which the *Turks* abhor. Thus I have given you a Taste of the *Turkish* Superstition; I shall add, That they account it a damnable Sin, if any of their own People chance (though unwillingly) to sit upon the *Alcoran*, (which is a Book containing the Rites of their Religion) and, if a *Christian* do it, 'tis Death by their Law. Moreover, they will not suffer *Rose-Leaves* to lie upon the Ground, because, as the Ancients did fable, the Roses spring out of the Blood of *Venus*; so the *Turks* hold, That it had its Rise from the Sweat of *Mahomet*.

[117] Karagöz: Turkish puppet theatre; from *Turkish Shadow Theatre* by Metin And.

Whether it was through the Byzantines, the Italians, the Spanish or the Jews that Turkey got Karagöz, all might have bequeathed a slight influence in their way. However, in essence, Karagöz is a rich cross-section of Turkish culture; namely of poetry, miniature painting, music, folk customs and the oral tradition. And in this deep rooted indigenous tradition, influence from and contribution by the West is very negligible. . . .

We are confronted with three clearly defined groups [of characters]: (1) The pillars or the basic figures, those who generally headed the list of the characters and form the backbone of the plot and appear with the greatest frequency like: Karagöz and Hacivat; (2) Feminine roles, children, young girls, servants, old women, witches and dancing girls. These characters, though frequently present, occasionally had minor parts to play . . . (3) *Taklits*, roles rich in comic value, were characters such as professionals, provincials, colonials and foreigners. There were also teratological characters such as dwarfs, stammerers, hunchbacks or mentally defectives like opium addicts and the neighbourhood idiot . . .

(a) Karagöz and Hacivat. It is always doubtful whether Karagöz and Hacivat ever really existed and, as we have already seen, there are many legends about this. Karagöz was supposed by some to be a gypsy and there are many allusions and much evidence in the plays to support this theory. Karagöz has a round face, his eye is boldly designed with a large black pupil, hence his name 'Black Eye'. He has a pug nose and a round thick curly black beard. His head, completely bald, sports an enormous turban which, when knocked off, suddenly exposes his bald head which always provokes laughter. In all dialogue between Karagöz and Hacivat, we find Hacivat always uses flowing language full of prose rimée while Karagöz uses the language of the common people. His promptness with repartee procured for him his fame and reputation. This contrasts artificiality with simplicity and is the first satire to attain these differences. This contrasting language is also noticeable in Hacivat's erudition. He can recite famous poems, has a vast knowledge of music, is conversant with the names of various rare spices, the terminology of gardening, many varied encyclopaedic extracts, and with the etiquette of the aristocracy. This however is superficial and gives him only a scholastic type of importance. Karagöz on the other hand only thinks of making a living for himself and his family. Because he has no trade, he is usually unemployed and fails to provide for his family, and has enough sense to realize that to rectify this, he does not need Hacivat's superficial knowledge. Though he is stupid and easily taken in, he is constantly able to deceive Hacivat and others.

Hacivat is a reflective character with a pointed turned-up beard.Each movement is well calculated and worked out before hand. Karagöz, on the contrary is impulsive and his character is shown by his speech and behaviour. Hacivat's reasoning limits his actions. Even though while on the screen, he makes few gestures with hands, Karagöz is the more dynamic and energetic. Where Hacivat is always ready to accept the situation and maintain the status quo and the establishment, Karagöz is always eager to try out new ideas and constantly misbehaves himself. . . .

Hacivat is always bound by the moral principles of the upper class and can easily adapt himself to these principles. He sometimes becomes instrumental in providing pleasure for the upper classes and is always worried that Karagöz's tactlessness will spoil these pleasures. Karagöz, the traditional symbol of the 'little man', on the other hand, finds that his tactless behaviour generally upsets most intrigues. Hacivat also serves as a foil to each character, underlining their helplessness and distress. Most of these lesser characters depend upon the machination of Hacivat to provide either the needed money, job or house. He is loquacious, credulous and good natured. Usually Hacivat offers useful advice to others, aiding them in their schemes. Because of his knowledge of etiquette and language and his opportunism, he is a most desirable, likeable character in the neighbourhood. He is not only the local headman but is looked upon as counsellor especially by the neighbourhood spendthrift. When he partners Karagöz in various undertakings, he prefers merely to find the clients and share the profit. Conversely Karagöz is not respected. He is always insulted by the dandies, is a target for the anger of the opium addict, a victim of the village idiot's practical jokes and the threats of the neighbourhood drunkards.

(b) Women in Karagöz plays are young, middle-aged and old, flighty, quarrelsome, only just faithful and always prone to gossip. The main type is always flighty and given to intrigue. In nearly every play, this type causes a scandal in the neighbourhood. Karagöz's wife often abuses him for not feeding her and not clothing her. . . .

We have a very important witness in a Frenchman, whose father was in Turkey between the years 1820–1870. This gentleman was conversant with all Turkish political affairs and political figures. In a book on his father's experiences, he devoted one long chapter to Karagöz. In this he claims the basis of the Karagöz play was political, employed for the purpose of social and political satire directed at events and persons current at that time. He gives several illustrations from the several performances he himself attended. According to him, even the Grand Vizier or the Sultan himself was not spared from Karagöz' malicious invective and caustic wit. In one play, the political ideas of the vizier, Georgian Mehmet Rasit Pasa, and his deeds as military man were shown in a humorous tone. In another performance, Karagöz poked fun at the Sultan's son-in-law, who was the chief admiral and a thoroughly worthless man. Commenting on this, Karagöz advised a young man, who seeks to begin his career, by saying, 'As you do not know anything, I advise you to become a chief admiral.' . . . As a result political satire was banned strictly and forever. The author goes on to say that since that time, Karagöz has fallen into childish vacuity and meaningless farce. As a matter of fact, Karagöz was never able to restore this pungent side of his character again. Yet this tradition of the political spirit of Karagöz survived in the newspapers, many of them bearing titles taken from Karagöz and *Ortaoyunu*. *Karagöz*, the last of these sheets, was published until recently as a popular political weekly.

Another freedom enjoyed by Karagöz, as well as by other forms of Turkish popular theatre, is its obscenity and extreme licentiousness. This is a very natural thing for popular theatres in the manner of *commedia dell'arte*. An English observer, whose account of a Karagöz performance we have already referred to, pointed out that:

> 'Then followed a scene with the "fair ladies" which I may not describe – not even in Latin.'

Many foreign observers' accounts confirm this. Some observers were shocked at seeing women and children at these obscene performances of Karagöz. Another observer having the same experience, asked an elderly Turk sitting next to him, who had brought two very young girls to the show, how he could allow children to see such scenes of obscenity. The answer was: 'They should learn; sooner or later they should know; it is better for them learn these facts than to be ignorant in these matters'. Even in the year of 1861, in Pera, a fashionable quarter of Istanbul, a permanent Karagöz theatre built in a popular amusement spot, Petit Jardin des Fleurs, was opened to public and attracted large crowds even though the entertainment offered was very obscene.

[118] Nineteenth-century manners and customs of the Turks; from *The Handbook for Travellers in Turkey in Asia including Constantinople*, published by John Murray in 1878.

The customs of Orientals have ever been in striking contrast to those of the people of the West, and though Turkey is rapidly undergoing many changes in this respect, owing to the inroads of European civilization, yet these differences still meet the stranger at every step. With Orientals, the shaving of the head is generally adopted as an old and useful custom, for it conduces to cleanliness. We uncover our heads before a superior, and walk into his presence with our boots or shoes upon our feet, while they take off their shoes, cover their hands; and draw their turbans or caps lower down upon their foreheads: the same is true of the act of worship. Our women appear in public in gay colours, and our men in sombre hues; while with them, it is the men who walk the streets decked in all the colours of the rainbow, embroidered with silver and gold cord, and the women carefully veil themselves from head to foot. In fine, the East presents ever renewed contrasts to the west. Nor is it any easy task to decide which of the two is right. Each has a good reason to act as it does; and the customs of either are so well fitted to its circumstances, that a change would probably, in many cases, do more harm than good, and would, moreover, require innumerable other changes to follow suit. The real improvement to be sought for each lies in a better education of the masses.

In the larger cities of Turkey the style of domestic architecture is rapidly changing. European salons and furniture are taking the place of the Oriental. Turkish houses of the better class, and old style, consist of at least two open courts – an outer and an inner, into each of which chambers open. The outer court contains the apartments of the head of the house, where alone he receives his guests and transacts his business. The inner court is the *Hareem*, and is reserved exclusively for the women. It is entered from the outer court by a narrow, winding passage, and is usually guarded by eunuchs.

Each chamber is divided into two sections – a lower section near the door, usually flagged with marble, and occasionally ornamented with a little fountain; and an upper section surrounded on three sides by a low divan, or dais, and having the floor covered with mats or small carpets. The over-shoes are taken off on the lower section before stepping on the dais.

The Osmanli guest rides into the court, and dismounts on the stone for that purpose, close to the landing-place. He has been preceded and announced by an attendant. A servant of the house gives notice to his master in the selamlik, not by proclaiming his name aloud, but by whispering the visitor's name. The host, according to his rank, proceeds to meet him at the foot of the stairs, at the top of the stairs, at the door of the room, or he meets him in the middle of the room, or he only steps down from the sofa, or stands up on the sofa, or merely makes a motion to do so. It belongs to the guest to salute first. As he pronounces the words '*Selam aleikum,*' he bends down as if to touch the dust, or the host's robe, with his right hand, and then carries it to his lips and forehead. The master of the house immediately returns, '*Aleikum selam,*' with the same action, so that they appear to bend down together. This salutation is given to Moslems alone. This greeting quickly dispatched, without pause or interval, the master immediately precedes his guests into the room, and then, if they are equals or the guest be the superior, turning round, makes way for his passage to the corner, which if he refuses to take, he may for a moment insist upon, and each may take the other's arm, as leading him to that part. With the exception of this single point the whole ceremonial is performed with a smoothness and regularity, as if executed by machinery. The guest being seated, it is now the turn of the master of the house, and of the other guests, if any, to salute the new comer, if a stranger from a distance, by the words, '*Hosh geldin, sefa geldin*;' and if a neighbour, by the words, '*Sabahiniz haïrolah*,' '*aksham sherifler haïrolah*,' &c., according to the time of day, repeating the same action already described. The guest returns each salute separately. There is no question of introduction or presentation. It would be an insult to the master of the house not to salute his guest. The master then orders the pipes and coffee, by the words '*Caïvé smarla*;' or, if for people of low degree, '*Caïvé getir*;' of if the guest is considered the host – that is, if he is of superior rank to the host – he orders, or the master asks from him permission to do so. The pipes having been cleared away on the entrance of the guest of distinction, the attendants now reappear with pipes, as many servants as guests, and, after collecting in the lower part of the room, they step up together, or nearly so, on the floor, in the centre of the triclinium, and then radiate off to the different guests, measuring their steps so as to arrive at once, or with a graduated interval. The pipe, which is from 5 to 7 feet in length, is carried in the right hand, poised upon the middle finger, with the bowl forward, and the mouthpiece towards the servant's breast, or over his shoulder. He measures with his eye a distance from the mouth of the guest to a spot on the floor, corresponding with the length of the pipe he carries. As he approaches, he halts, places the bowl of the pipe upon the spot, then, whirling the stick gracefully round, while he makes a stride forward with one foot, presents the amber and perhaps jewelled mouthpiece within an inch or two of the guest's mouth. He then drops on his knee, and raising the bowl of the pipe from the ground, places under it a brass platter (*tepsi*) which he carried in his left hand. This servant is called a chibookji.

Next comes coffee. If the word has been, '*Caïvé smarla*,' the *kaïvehji* presents himself at the bottom of the room, on the edge of the raised floor, supporting on the palms of both hands, at the height of his breast, a small tray containing the little coffee-pots and cups, entirely concealed with rich brocade. The attendants immediately cluster round him, the brocade covering is raised from the tray, and thrown over the *kaïvehji's* shoulders. When each attendant has got his cup ready, they turn round at once and proceed in the direction of the different guests, measuring their steps as before. . . . After finishing his cup of coffee, each guest makes his acknowledgment to the master of the house, by the salutation called *temena*, which is in like manner returned; and the master of the house, or he who is in his place, may make the same acknowledgment to any guest whom he is inclined particularly to honour. This practice of the *temena* after refreshment has given way of late years in the best circles. When the guest retires, it is always after asking leave to go. To this question the master of the house replies, '*Devlet ikbalileh,*' or '*saadet ileh,*' or '*saghlig ileh,*' according to the rank of his guest, which expressions mean, 'with the fortune of a prince', 'with prosperity', 'with health.'

[119] Inside a Turkish house; from *Turkish Life in Town and Country* by Lucy M.J. Garnett.

The *haremlik* has besides, of course, its separate entrance through a courtyard, and its garden. Like the generality of Eastern houses, the front door opens into a large hall, which gives access to rooms on each side, and has several windows at the opposite end. One of these rooms is the *kahvé ojak*, or 'coffee-hearth', where a shrivelled old woman may always be found presiding over a charcoal brazier, ready to boil coffee at a moment's notice; the others are storerooms and sleeping apartments for the inferior slaves. The kitchen, which is very spacious, is generally an outbuilding. One side of it is occupied by the great arched cooking-stove with its numerous little grates, on which the contents of brightly burnished copper pans or earthenware vessels simmer over charcoal fires, fanned by the negress cook with a turkey's wing. A wide staircase leads from the entrance hall to the upper floor, the centre of which is generally occupied by a spacious ante-room, on which the other apartments open. In some of the older mansions the *divan-khané*, or reception-room, contains a large alcove, the floor of which is raised about a foot above the level of the rest of the apartment. A low divan furnishes its three sides, and in the most comfortable corner, which is the *hanum's* habitual seat, is a pile of flat rectangular and somewhat hard cushions, and here may also be found her hand-mirror and *chekmejé*, or jewel-box. If the *divankhané* has not such a recess, one end and half the two adjoining sides of the room are usually occupied by a continuous sofa, and the fourth wall is furnished with a marble-topped console table, surmounted by a mirror and candelabra, and flanked on either side by shelves in niches containing rosewater sprinklers, sherbet goblets, and other objects at the same time useful and ornamental. A few common European chairs stand stiffly against the wall in every space left vacant, and one or two walnut tray-stools, or coffee-tables, inlaid with mother of pearl, are placed near the divan to hold ashtrays, matches, and other trifles.

Bedsteads are not used by the Turks. Each room contains a large cupboard, built into the wall, in which the bedding is piled during the day, and at night the slaves come in when summoned to make up the beds on the floor. Other bedroom requisites, in the shape of washstands, dressing-tables, and wardrobes, are dispensed with as superfluous. For everyday ablution there is a small washing-room with a hole in the floor for the water to escape through, and if the *hanum* would wash her hands and face only, a slave brings the ewer and basin, and pours the water over her hands. For special ablutions, she will go either to her own private *hammam*, or to the public baths. She 'does her hair', or has it done for her, seated cross-legged in her corner of the divan; and the old walnut-wood chests and coffers in her treasure-room suffice to store her gauzes and brocades, her silks and embroideries. Here also may often be found priceless treasures in metal, porcelain, glass and gems, which, were they displayed in the reception-rooms, would add greatly to the cheerfulness of their appearance. But such is not the practice of the Osmanlis, who retain in many of their habits the characteristics of their nomadic ancestors.

All Turkish houses are, however, constructed with a view to the summer, and winter, though in the north of Turkey especially often severe, seems to be hardly at all provided against. The walls seem to be all windows, and the arrangements for heating are most inadequate. Very often there is but a brazier, in the form of a shallow brass or copper pan containing charcoal half buried in wood ashes, and placed either on an elegantly shaped receptacle of wrought metal, or on a heavy stand of polished wood, from two to three feet square, and about eight inches high, which occupies the centre of the room. A somewhat curious warming apparatus is the *tandur*, which, though fallen into disuse in the capital and in the European provinces, may still be seen in Asia Minor, even in the houses of Europeans. It consists of a kind of four-legged square table made of deal, having a shelf, covered with tin, a few inches from the foot, in the centre of which is placed a pan of charcoal guarded by a metal screen. Over all is thrown a large thickly wadded quilt, which the ladies – for this is an eminently feminine luxury – seated on two sides of the *tandur* in the angle of the divan, drawn over their knees. The use of American stoves, is however, increasing every year, and the picturesqueness of many of the old *konaks* is destroyed by the hideous black stove-pipes which emerge from the windows or walls and climb up to the roofs.

[120] The importance attached to water by the Turks: from *Pavilions of the Heart* by Lesley Blanch.

Curiously, although Constantinople is not a city of great heat and is surrounded by water and green forests where springs abound, the element is apotheosized in the number and beauty of its street-fountains. Some are set exquisitely under gilded eaves, some behind lace-like marble grilles; some gush from porphyry basins in the courtyards of mosques, or beside the entrance to a hammam. Everywhere such hammams, known loosely as Turkish baths, have an element of the temple about them, where the rituals and worship of water prevails. The image of water is found translated into many terms: in the Anatolian cemetery rugs of tradition, which were taken to the cemetery upon which to pray beside the tomb, and to picnic, too, for grave-side feasts with the departed's favourite foods were *de rigueur*. Such rugs are all woven with a blue ribbon of water, a stream, traced round the flowers and cypress trees representing the Gardens of Paradise. Nor do the mourners forget the birds, for Turkish graves often have a little scooped-out hollow where dew collects, and where the birds may drink their fill. . . . Water everywhere, life-giving water, treasured and symbolized in many ways, in mosques or palaces, sacred or profane. . . . Those fabulous diamond sprays that tremble on fine gold wires, a typically Turkish type of jewellery – surely these too were inspired by showers of raindrops, dewdrops, or the jet of a fountain?

[121] Fountains and chronograms; from *Constantinople, Settings and Traits* by H.G. Dwight.

A number [of fountains], however, are to be seen in the old palace of Top Kapou. Perfectly simple but characteristic and charming of their kind are the tiny wall fountains of a room in the 'Cage', at each end of the window-seat in front of each of the four windows. The same principle is used for more ornamental purposes by putting one basin below another in such a way that the second will catch the overflow of the first. There is a big wall fountain of this sort in the splendid hall of Süleïman the Magnificent. In a private house of much later date I have seen three graduated basins projecting from their niche, rounded and scalloped like shells. There is also a pretty *selsebil* of a new kind in one of the baths of the Seraglio, where the surface of the mirror stone is notched into a series of overlapping scales so as to multiply the ripple of the water. But the prettiest dripping fountain I know is in an old house in Bebek, on the European shore of the Bosphorus. It stands in the entrance hall, at an odd little angle where it will best catch the light, and it combines the miniature basins of an ordinary *selsebil* with a lower surface of marble scales. What is least ordinary about it, however, are the spaces of marble lace work bordering the shallow arched niche where the water trickles. There is a free space behind them in order to give the proper relief to the design. And there is an irregularity about the intertwined whorls which a Western artist would have thought beneath him, but which only adds interest to the work.

This original *selsebil* partakes also of the nature of a *fîskieh*, as the Turks onomatopoetically call a spurting fountain. In the stalactites bordering the two shallow basins at the bottom are jets which used to add to the complicated tinkle of the fountain. Spurting fountains seem to be rarer indoors than out, though I have already mentioned the beautiful one in the Kyöprülü kiosk. They are not uncommon in the outer hall of public baths. One that contravenes the canons of orthodox Mohammedan art is to be admired in the handsome bath of St Sophia – a work of Sinan – where three dolphins, their tails in the air, spout water into a fluted basin. I have wondered if these unorthodox creatures, like the lions of so many gardens, may not perpetuate a Byzantine tradition if not actual Byzantine workmanship. . . .

The commonest of all inscriptions [on fountains] is a verse from the Koran: 'By water all things have life.' Other verses, mentioning the four fountains of Paradise and the pool Kevser into which they flow, are also frequent, together with references to the sacred well Zemzem, which Gabriel opened for Hagar in Mecca, to Hîzîr and the Spring of Life, and to the battle of Kerbela, in which Hüsseïn and his companions were cut off from water. Or the central tenet of Islam, 'There is no God but God and Mohammed is the Prophet of God', may be carved above the niche – sometimes without any indication of the name or epoch of the founder. The majority, however, are not so modest. They are more likely to give ampler information than he who runs may read. And after the time of Süleïman the Magnificent it became increasingly the fashion for celebrated poets to compose the verses which celebrated calligraphs designed. Thus the historian Chelibi-zadeh records the end of the inscription on a reservoir of Ahmed III: 'Seïd Vehbi Effendi, the most distinguished among the word-wizards of the time, strung these pearls on the thread of his verse and joined together the two lines of the following chronographic distich, like two sweet almonds breast to breast: "With what a wall has Ahmed dammed the waters! For of astonishment stops the flood in the midst of its course."'

Chronograms are as common on fountains as they are on other monuments. . . . The ideal chronogram should contain the name of the builder of the fountain and that of the writer of the verse – though I must confess I never found one that attained that height of ingenuity. . . . Various ingenious devices are resorted to, of which a handsome Renaissance fountain in Kassîm Pasha is an excellent example: 'The famous Vizier, the victorious warrior Hassan Pasha, made this fountain as a trophy for Mohammedans. His aims were always philanthropic and he provided this fountain with water like Zemzem. This fountain is so well situated and built in so pleasant a place that one would take it as the site where flows the water of eternal life. Those who look upon it drive away all sorrow from their hearts.' The numerical value of the last sentence is 2080, a date even farther from the Mohammedan calendar than from ours. But the value of the single word 'sorrow' is 1040. Drive it away, or in other words subtract 1040 from 2080, and you get 1040 again, which is evidently the date of the construction (1631) . . .

The taste for chronograms has continued to this day, but in

time the arithmetic of the reader was helped out by an incidental date. The earliest numerals I have found are of the time of Süleïman the Magnificent, on a fountain built by a Jew in the suburb of Hass-kyöi (931/1525). The same fountain is also decorated with the earliest reliefs I have noted, consisting merely of a little tracery on the mirror stone. Altogether this period was an important one for fountains as it was for all Turkish architecture. But while a few of them are admirably proportioned, like the little fountain in Avret Bazaar at the gate of the soup-kitchen of the *Hasseki* – she was Hourrem, the Joyous One, who bore to Süleïman his ill-fated son Moustafa – many of them are disappointingly heavy. It may be that the great Sinan did not consider such small monuments worth his while, or that they have suffered by restoration. At all events, the lesser sultans who followed Süleïman left fountains generally more graceful. Ahmed I is said to have built not less than a hundred of them.

[122] Coffee-houses; from *Constantinople, Setting and Traits* by H.G. Dwight.

The coffee-houses indeed are an essential part of Stamboul, and in them the outsider comes nearest, perhaps, to intimacy with that reticent city. The number of these institutions in Constantinople is quite fabulous. They have the happiest tact for locality, seeking movement, strategic corners, open prospects, the company of water and trees. No quarter is so miserable or so remote as to be without one. Certain thoroughfares carry on almost no other form of business. A sketch of a coffee-shop may often be seen on the street, in a scrap of sun or shade, according to the season, where a stool or two invite the passer-by to a moment of contemplation. And no *ban* or public building is without its facilities for dispensing the indispensable. . . .

The etiquette of the coffee-house, of those coffee-houses which have not been too much infected by Europe, is one of their most characteristic features. I have seen a newcomer salute one after another each person in a crowded coffee-room, once on entering the door, and again on taking his seat, and be so saluted in return – either by putting the right hand on the heart and uttering the greeting *merhaba*, or by making the *temenna*, that triple sweep of the hand which is the most graceful of salutes. [But it is not in favour with the republic.] I have also seen the entire company rise on the entrace of an old man, and yield him the corner of honour. As for the essential function of the coffee-house, it has its own traditions. A glass of water comes with the coffee, and a foreigner can usually be detected by the order in which he takes them. A Turk sips his water first. He lifts his coffee-cup, whether it possess a handle or no, by the saucer, managing the two in a dexterous way of his own. And custom favours a rather noisy enjoyment of the cup that cheers, as expressing appreciation and general well-being. The current price for a coffee, in the heart of Stamboul, is, or was, something like a penny – for which the waiter will say: 'May God give you blessing'. Mark, too, that you do not tip him. I have often been surprised to be charged no more than the tariff, although I gave a larger piece to be changed, and it was perfectly evident that I was a foreigner. That is an experience which rarely befalls a traveller even in his own land. It has further happened to me to be charged nothing at all, nay, to be steadfastly refused when I persisted in attempting to pay, simply because I was a traveller, and therefore a 'guest'.

Altogether the habit of the coffee-house is one that requires a certain leisure. Being a passion less violent and less shameful than others, I suppose, it is indulged in with more of the humanities. You do not bolt coffee as you bolt the fire-waters of the West, without ceremony, in retreats withdrawn from the public eye. Neither, having taken coffee, do you leave the coffee-house. On the contrary, there are reasons why you should stay – and not only to take another coffee. There are benches to curl up on, if you would do as the Romans do, having first neatly put off your shoes from off your feet. There are texts and patriotic pictures to look at, to say nothing of the wonderful brass arrangements wherein the *kahveji* concocts his mysteries. There is, of course, the view. To enjoy it you sit on a low rush-bottomed stool in front of the coffee-shop, under a grape-vine, perhaps, or a scented wistaria, or a bough of a neighbourly plane-tree; and if you like you may have an aromatic pot of basil beside you to keep away the flies.

Coffee-house in Istanbul; painting by an unknown artist, late sixteenth century

[123] Food; from *Three Centuries: family chronicles of Turkey and Egypt* by Emine Foat Tugay.

Our 'frugal' meals of six courses, which had so shocked my mother's family, always began with either fish, eggs, or *börek*, a dish comprising various kinds of pastry stuffed with cheese and herbs, or spiced minced meat. Then came meat or fowl with potatoes and salad, two vegetable courses, the first eaten cold and cooked in oil, the second in butter and served hot, pilav, each day a different kind, and either a milk pudding or pastry soaked in syrup. Fruit always finished off the meal. Coffee was served in the drawing-room or in summer in the entrance hall, which was delightfully cool. . . .

Turkish cooking of the past ranked among the great cuisines of the world. Much of it has disappeared together with the excellent chefs, who had learnt their trade as apprentices in konaks and palaces, where they had to satisfy the exigent palates of their masters.

Hünkar Beyendi, or *Sultan's Pleasure*, is a purée of egg-plant, with small pieces of meat cooked in butter and tomato juice placed in the centre. As in the salad, the egg-plant is cooked on a hot baking tin, peeled, and mashed. A little melted butter is poured over it just before serving. The dish derives its name from a legend. Once upon a time a sultan went out hunting. Whilst pursuing his quarry, he penetrated into a large forest, and soon lost sight of both the game and his attendants. He wandered about till nightfall, getting farther and farther into unknown country until, hungry and exhausted, he at last saw a light in the distance. Filled with hope, the sultan urged his weary horse towards it till he came to the house whence the light had proceeded. Here he was hospitably received, and his host immediately sent word to the cook to prepare a meal. It was late, dinner was over long since, and all that remained in the kitchen were some scraps of meat and a few egg-plants. The cook, being a resourceful man, cut up the meat and put it in a pot, the vegetables he threw on the hot cooking range, and mashed them. The result was a steaming dish, of which the sultan ate every morsel. Replete and rested he sent a purse filled with gold to the cook and asked the name of the dish, never having eaten it before. He was told that the cook had invented it on the spot, whereupon the sultan declared that henceforth it should be called Sultan's Pleasure.

There was less variety then in the ways of cooking meat. It was either grilled or cooked in a pot. Formerly roasted meat or fowl was unknown in the Turkish cuisine. The pilav, which we had adopted from Iran, was prepared in many different ways, but ours never attained the complicated forms of the thirty varieties devised by the Persians. On the other hand we excelled in pastry, which we called *börek*. Served at the beginning of a meal, as in my mother's family and at home, or at the end of a meal, as in some other houses, it was always stuffed either with cheese and herbs, or with spiced minced meat. The difference lay in the dough and the manner of its cooking. Börek was not among my own favourite dishes, and I do not remember all the varieties which were made with a dough which resembled the French *mille feuille*. I preferred such as were made of a paste rather like noodles, and which were boiled. Both the Tartar börek and the *piruhi* were made of thinly rolled-out dough. The former was cut into squares, stuffed with cream cheese and herbs and folded into triangles, boiled and eaten with yoghurt; with piruhi, the little squares were left open and minced meat was sprinkled between them. Browned butter was poured over it. The best börek of this kind is the *su börek*, or water börek, so named because it too is boiled. Afterwards the dough is spread in layers in a round flat börek dish made of silver, with a high edge, half of it being filled with cream cheese and the other half with minced meat or chicken. Browned in the oven it is a dish for kings.

The undeniable king of all böreks is called, when rolled to look like a cigarette, *sigara börek*, and when rolled into a ball the size of a walnut, *ceviz börek*. Very few cooks nowadays are able to make it as it should be and once was produced. . . . Wrapped many times round minced meat in the sigara börek, or round grated kashar cheese in the ceviz börek, and cooked in deep fat, it is one of the superlative achievements of Turkish cooking.

Of the sweets, some, like the *talish tatlisi*, a brittle hollow roll which melted in the mouth and was garnished with *kaymak*, the Turkish cream, have now disappeared entirely. The *hurma tatlisi* (date sweet), so-called because it had the shape of a ripe date, and both crisp and melting, is also hardly ever seen nowadays. The sweets which are easier to make still survive. Among the desserts made with milk, the most deceptive under its bland appearance is the *tavuk gögsü*, or breast of chicken. The white flesh of chicken wings was beaten to an absolutely smooth pulp. Not one little solid piece was allowed to remain. The pulp was then cooked with milk, sugar, and a little powdered *sahleb* root, till it became a thick mass. Poured into a dessert dish, its surface was garnished with powdered cinnamon. Tavuk gögsü had a delicious flavour and when it was properly made the presence of meat was quite imperceptible. My parents sometimes had it served when they had foreign guests. They always liked it and could hardly believe that they had been eating camouflaged chicken. This dish is also dying out for lack of chefs who can make it. There are of course several simpler milk puddings, which would take too long to describe in detail. My favourite dessert boasted the name of *keshkül-ü-fukara*, or bowl of the pauper. Long ago dervishes and holy men, who called themselves 'the paupers of God', went begging food from house to house. Everyone gave a little piece of what they had, until finally the bowl was filled with many different kinds of food. The name was applied to the dessert, which is made from the juice and flesh of coconuts and milk of almonds, because its surface was covered with little mounds of different kinds of very finely chopped nuts. Walnuts, hazel-nuts, almonds, green pistachios, and the snow-white flesh of the coconut formed a pleasing pattern, satisfying both to the eye and to the palate.

With the exception of sweets, every kind of food was cooked in broth. Besides the meat used for consumption, meat for broth was provided in every palace and konak. At our house about ten pounds of beef and mutton were used every day for that purpose and then discarded.

[124] Lady Mary describes the Turkish dress she has adopted, and the liberty of Turkish women; from *The Complete Letters of Lady Mary Wortley Montagu, 1708–1720.*

The first peice of my dresse is a pair of drawers, very full, that reach to my shoes and conceal the legs more modestly than your Petticoats. They are of a thin rose colour damask brocaded with silver flowers, my shoes of white kid Leather embrodier'd with Gold. Over this hangs my Smock of a fine white silk Gause edg'd with Embrodiery. This smock has wide sleeves hanging halfe way down the Arm and is clos'd at the Neck with a diamond button, but the shape and colour of the bosom very well to be distinguish'd through it. The Antery is a wastcoat made close to the shape, of white and Gold Damask, with very long sleeves falling back and fring'd with deep Gold fringe, and should have Diamond or pearl Buttons. My Caftan of the same stuff with my Drawers is a robe exactly fited to my shape and reaching to my feet, with very long strait falling sleeves. Over this is the Girdle of about 4 fingers broad, which all that can afford have entirely of Diamonds or other precious stones. Those that will not be at that expence have it of exquisite Embrodiery on Satin, but it must be fasten'd before with a clasp of Di'monds. The Curdée is a loose Robe they throw off or put on according to the Weather, being of a rich Brocade (mine is green and Gold) either lin'd with Ermine or Sables; the sleeves reach very little below the Shoulders. The Headress is compos'd of a Cap call'd Talpock, which is in winter of fine velvet embroidier'd with pearls or Di'monds and in summer of a light shineing silver stuff. This is fix'd on one side of the Head, hanging a little way down with a Gold Tassel and bound on either with a circle of Di'monds (as I have seen several) or a rich embrodier'd Handkercheif. On the other side of the Head the Hair is laid flat, and here the Ladys are at Liberty to shew their fancys, some putting Flowers, others a plume of Heron's feathers, and, in short, what they please, but the most general fashion is a large Bouquet of Jewels made like natural flowers, that is, the buds of Pearl, the roses of different colour'd Rubys, the Jess'mines of Di'monds, Jonquils of Topazes, etc., so well set and enammell'd tis hard to imagine any thing of that kind so beautifull. The Hair hangs at its full length behind, divided into tresses braided with pearl or riband, which is allways in great Quantity. . . .

I am a little acquainted with their ways, I cannot forbear admiring either the exemplary discretion or extreme Stupidity of all the writers that have given accounts of 'em. Tis very easy to see they have more Liberty than we have, no Woman of what rank so ever being permitted to go in the street without 2 muslins, one that covers her face all but her Eyes and another that hides the whole dress of her head and hangs halfe way down her back; and their Shapes are wholly conceal'd by a thing they call a Ferigée, which no Woman of any sort appears without. This has strait sleeves that reaches to their fingers ends and it laps all round 'em, not unlike a rideing hood. In Winter 'tis of Cloth, and in Summer, plain stuff or silk. You may guess how effectually this disguises them, that there is no distinguishing the great Lady from her Slave, and 'tis impossible for the most jealous Husband to know his Wife when he meets her, and no Man dare either touch or follow a Woman in the Street.

This perpetual Masquerade gives them entire liberty of following their Inclinations without danger of Discovery. The most usual method of Intrigue is to send an Appointment to the Lover to meet the Lady at a Jew's shop, which are as notoriously convenient as our Indian Houses, and yet even those that don't make that use of 'em do not scrupule to go to buy Pennorths and tumble over rich Goods, which are cheiffly to be found amongst that sort of people. The Great Ladys seldom let their Gallants know who they are, and 'tis so difficult to find it out that they can very seldom guess at her name they have corresponded with above halfe a year together. You may easily imagine the number of faithfull Wives very small in a country where they have nothing to fear from their Lovers' Indiscretion, since we see so many that have the courrage to expose them selves to that in this World and all the threaten'd Punishment of the next, which is never preach'd to the Turkish Damsels. Neither have they much to apprehend from the resentment of their Husbands, those Ladys that are rich having all their money in their own hands, which they take with 'em upon a divorce with an addition which he is oblig'd to give 'em. Upon the Whole, I look upon the Turkish Women as the only free people in the Empire.

Bibliography

ABBOTT, G.F. *Under the Turk in Constantinople: a record of John Finch's Embassy 1674–1681*, London, 1920.

AND, METIN, *Turkish Shadow Theatre*, Istanbul, 1979.

AMICIS, EDMONDO DE, *Constantinople*, transl. from the Italian by Caroline Tilton, London, 1878.

AS'AD, MUHAMMAD SAFVAT, *Précis Historique de la Destruction du Corps des Janissaires par le Sultan Mahmoud en 1826*, traduit du turc par A.P. Caussin de Perceval, Paris, 1833. (Transl. by Laurence Kelly).

BABINGER, FRANZ, *Mehmed the Conqueror and his Time*, transl. from the German by Ralph Manheim, ed. William E. Hickman, Princeton, 1978.

BAUDIER, SEIGNEUR MICHAEL, OF LANGUEDOC, *The History of the Serrail and of the Court of the Grand Seigneur, Emperour of the Turks*, transl. out of French by Edward Grimeston, London, 1635.

BLANCH, LESLEY, *Pavilions of the Heart*, London, 1974.

BOPPÉ, A., *Les Peintres du Bosphore*, Paris, 1911. (Transl. by Marie Noële Kelly).

BUSBEQUIUS, A.G., *Travels into Turkey, Containing the most Accurate Account of the Turks and Neighbouring Nations*, translated from the Latin, London, 1744.

BYRON, GEORGE GORDON, LORD, *Don Juan*, London, 1863.

CLARI, ROBERT DE, *The Conquest of Constantinople*, transl. from the French by E.H. McNeal, New York, 1936.

COLUM, PADRAIC, *The Golden Fleece*, New York, 1965.

COMNENA, ANNA, *The Alexiad of Anna Comnena*, transl. from the Greek by E.R.A. Sewter, London, 1969.

DEUIL, ODE DE, *De Profectione Ludovici VII in orientem*, transl. by V.G. Berry, New York, 1948.

DIEHL, CHARLES, *Byzantine Empresses*, transl. from the French by Harold Bell and Theresa de Kerpely, London, 1964.

DORYS, GEORGES, *Abdul-Hamid Intime*, Paris, 1903. (Transl. by Laurence Kelly).

DUCAS, MICHAEL, *The History of the Emperors John Manuel, John and Constantine Paleologus*, Bucharest, 1948.

DWIGHT, H.G., *Constantinople, Settings and Traits*, London, 1927.

EDIB, HALIDÉ, *Memoirs of Halidé Edib*, London, *c.*1940.

ELIOT, SIR CHARLES, KCMG, *Turkey in Europe*, London, 1908.

ELLIOT, FRANCES, *Diary of an Idle Woman in Constantinople*, London, 1893.

Encyclopaedia of Islam, Leiden-London, 1960.

EVLIYA CELEBI EFENDI, *Narrative of Travels in Europe, Asia, and Africa in the Seventeenth Century*, transl. from the Turkish by Ritter J. von Hammer-Purgstall, London, 1834.

FRESNE-CANAYE, PHILIPPE DU, *Le Voyage du Levant*, Paris, 1897. (Transl. by Marina Berry).

GARNETT, LUCY M.J., *Turkish Life in Town and Country*, London, 1904.

GIBB, E.J.W., *History of Ottoman Poetry*, 6 Vols, London, 1900–1909.

GIBBON, EDWARD, *The History of the Decline and Fall of the Roman Empire*, ed. J.B. Bury, London, 1897.

GILLES, PETER (PETRUS GYLLIUS), *The Antiquities of Constantinople, with a description of its Situation, the Conveniences of its Port, its Publick Buildings, the Statuary, Sculpture, Architecture and other Curiosities of that City*, transl. by John Ball, London, 1729.

GRAVES, ROBERT, *Count Belisarius*, London, 1955.

GRELOT, G.J., *A Late Voyage to Constantinople (1680)* transl. by J. Philips, London, 1683.

GYLLIUS, *see* GILLES.

HASLUCK, F.W., *Christianity and Islam under the Sultans*, ed. Margaret M. Hasluck, Oxford, 1929.

HEARSEY, JOHN, *The City of Constantine 324–1453*, London, 1963.

HOBHOUSE, J.C., *A Journey through Albania . . . to Constantinople during the years 1809 and 1810*, London, 1813.

HORNBY, LADY, *Constantinople during the Crimean War*, London, 1863.

HUBBARD, G.E., *The Day of the Crescent: glimpses of old Turkey*, Cambridge, 1920.

JANIN, R., *Constantinople Byzantine*, Paris, 1950.

JOINVILLE AND VILLEHARDOUIN, *Chronicles of the Crusades*, transl. and intro. by M.R.B. Shaw, London, 1963.

KINROSS, LORD, *The Ottoman Centuries: the rise and fall of the Turkish Empire*, London, 1977.

KRITOVOULOS, M., *The History of Mehmet the Conqueror*, transl. by Charles T. Riggs, Princeton, 1954.

LAMARTINE, A. DE, *Voyage en Orient*, Paris, 1819.

LETHABY, W.R., and SWAINSON, HAROLD, *Sancta Sophia Constantinople: a study of Byzantine Building*, London, 1894.

LOTI, PIERRE, *Constantinople (Aziyadé)*, transl. by Marjorie Lawrie, London, 1927.

— *Les Désenchantées*, Paris, 1906. (Transl. by Marina Berry).

LIUTPRAND, BISHOP, *The works of Liutprand of Cremona*, transl. and intro. by F.A. Wright, London, 1930.

MANTRAN, R., *La Vie Quotidienne à Constantinople au temps de Suleiman le Magnifique*, Paris, 1965. (Transl. by Laurence Kelly.)

MCCULLAGH, FRANCES, *The Fall of Abd-ul-Hamid*, London, 1910.

MOORE, THOMAS, *Letters and Journals of Lord Byron*, Paris, 1833.

MURRAY, JOHN, *The Handbook for Travellers in Turkey in Asia, including Constantinople*, London, 1878.

ORGA, IRFAN and MARGARETE, *Atatürk*, London, 1962.

PALLIS, ALEXANDER, *In the Days of the Janissaries*, London, 1951.

PARDOE, MISS JULIA, *The City of the Sultan and the Domestic Manners of the Turks in 1836*, London, 1837.

PENZER, N.M., *The Harem: an account of the institution as it existed in the Palace of the Turkish Sultans with a history of the Grand Seraglio from its foundation to the modern times*, London, 1936.

PERTUSIER, CHARLES, *Promenade Pittoresques dans Constantinople et sur les rives du Bosphore*, Paris, 1815. (Transl. by Marina Berry.)

PSELLUS, MICHAEL, *Fourteen Byzantine Rulers, the Chronographia*, transl. and intro. by E.R.A. Sewter, London, 1966.

PROCOPIUS, *The Secret History*, transl. and intro. by G.A. Williamson, London, 1966.

Purchas, his Pilgrimes, in five bookes, London, 1625.

RUNCIMAN, STEVEN, *Byzantine Civilisation*, London, 1933.

SLADE, CAPTAIN ADOLPHUS, RN, FRAS, *Records of Travels in Turkey, Greece, etc, and of a Cruise in the Black Sea with the Capitan Pasha*, London, 1854.

— *Turkey, Greece and Malta*, London, 1837.

STRATTON, ARTHUR, *Sinan*, London, 1972.

SUMNER-BOYD, H., 'The Seven Hills of Istanbul', unpublished MS in the Bodleian.

SUMNER-BOYD, H., and FREELY, J., *Strolling through Istanbul*, Istanbul, 1983.

TAVERNIER, J.B., *A New Relation of the Inner-Part of the Grand Seignor's Seraglio*, London, 1677.

TCHIHATCHEF, P. DE, *Le Bosphore et Constantinople*, Paris, 1866.

TUGAY, EMINE FOAT, *Three Centuries: family chronicles of Turkey and Egypt*, Oxford, 1963.

URE, P.N., *Justinian and his Age*, London, 1951.

VAN DER VIN, J.P.A., *Travellers to Greece and Constantinople: Ancient Monuments and Old Traditions in Medieval Travellers' Tales*, Vol. II, Istanbul, 1980.

VAN MILLINGEN, ALEXANDER, *Byzantine Churches in Constantinople, their history and architecture*, London, 1912.

— *Byzantine Constantinople: the Walls of the City and adjoining historical sites*, London, 1899.

VESEY, ISABEL, unpublished memoir written *c.*1920, copyright Mrs Veronica Burnett.

VIGIER, VICOMTE RENÉ, *Un Parisien à Constantinople*, Paris, 1886. (Transl. by Marina Berry and Laurence Kelly.)

VOGT, ALBERT, *Constantin VII Porphyrogénète: Le Livre des Cérémonies*, Tome II, Paris, 1935–40. (Transl. by Laurence Kelly)

VON HAMMER-PURGSTALL, RITTER JOSEPH, *Histoire de l'Empire Ottoman*, traduit de l'Allemand par J.-J. Hellert, Paris, 1835. (Transl. by Marie Noële Kelly and Laurence Kelly.)

WITHERS, ROBERT, 'The Description of the Grand Signior's Serraglio, or Turkish Emperor's Court', in *Purchas, his Pilgrimes.*

WORTLEY MONTAGU, LADY MARY, *Letters of the Right Honourable Lady Mary Wortley Montagu, Written during her Travels in Europe, Asia and Africa, to Persons of distinction, Men of Letters, etc, in different parts of Europe*, London, 1789.

— *The complete letters of Lady Mary Wortley Montagu*, Vol. I 1708–1820, ed. Robert Halsband, Oxford, 1965.

WRATISLAW, A.H., *Adventures of Baron Wenceslas Wratislaw, what he saw in the Turkish metropolis, Constantinople, experienced in his captivity, and after his happy return to his country, committed to writing in the year of Our Lord 1599*, London, 1862.

YEATS, W.B., *Collected Poems*, London, 1933.

YOUNG, GEORGE, *Constantinople*, London, 1926.

ZARA, BASSANO DA, 'I costumi e i Modi Particolari de la Vita de Turchi', in N.M. Penzer's *The Harem.*

Index

Numbers in *italics* refer to illustrations

INDEX OF PLACES

GENERAL INDEX